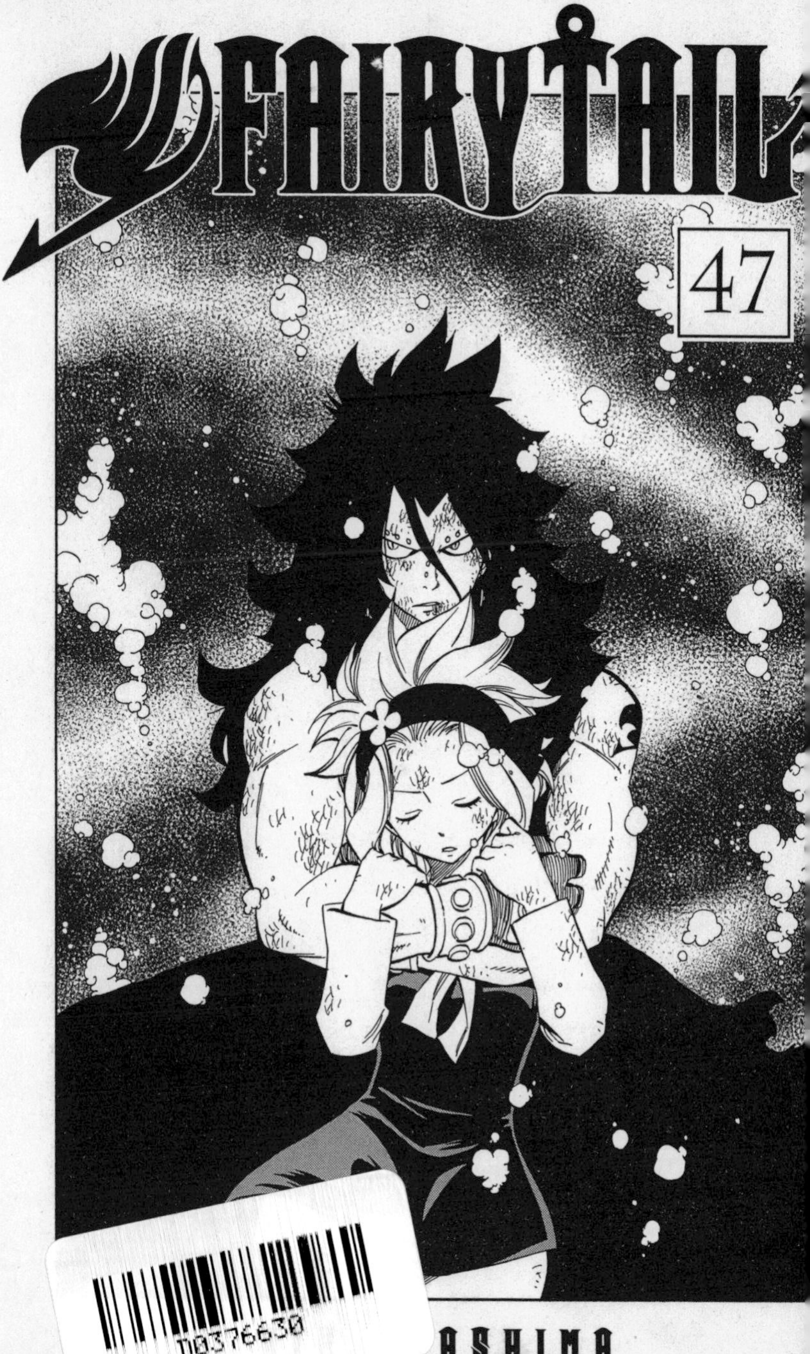
FAIRY TAIL
47

FAIRY TAIL 47 CONTENTS

FAIRY TAIL
フェアリーテイル

Chapter 395: Tartaros Arc, Part Five: Ultimate Pain

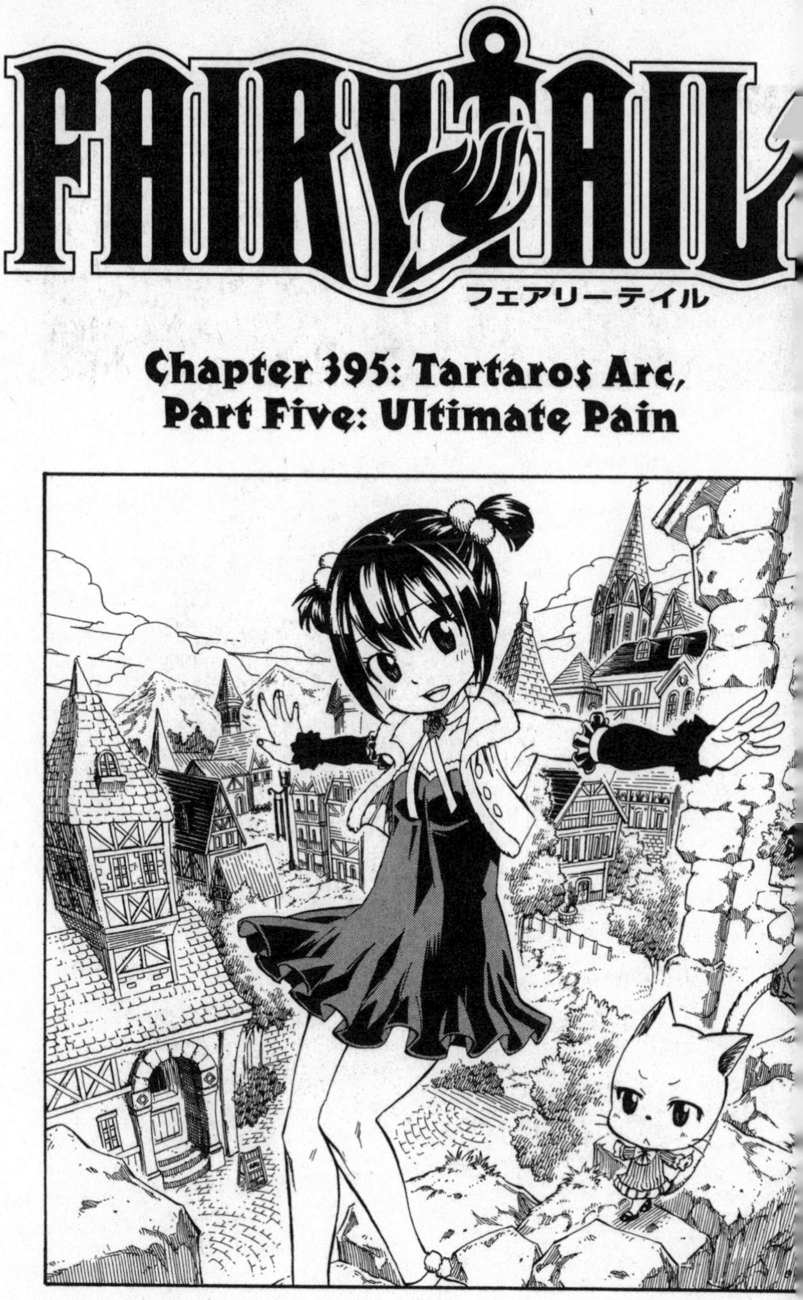

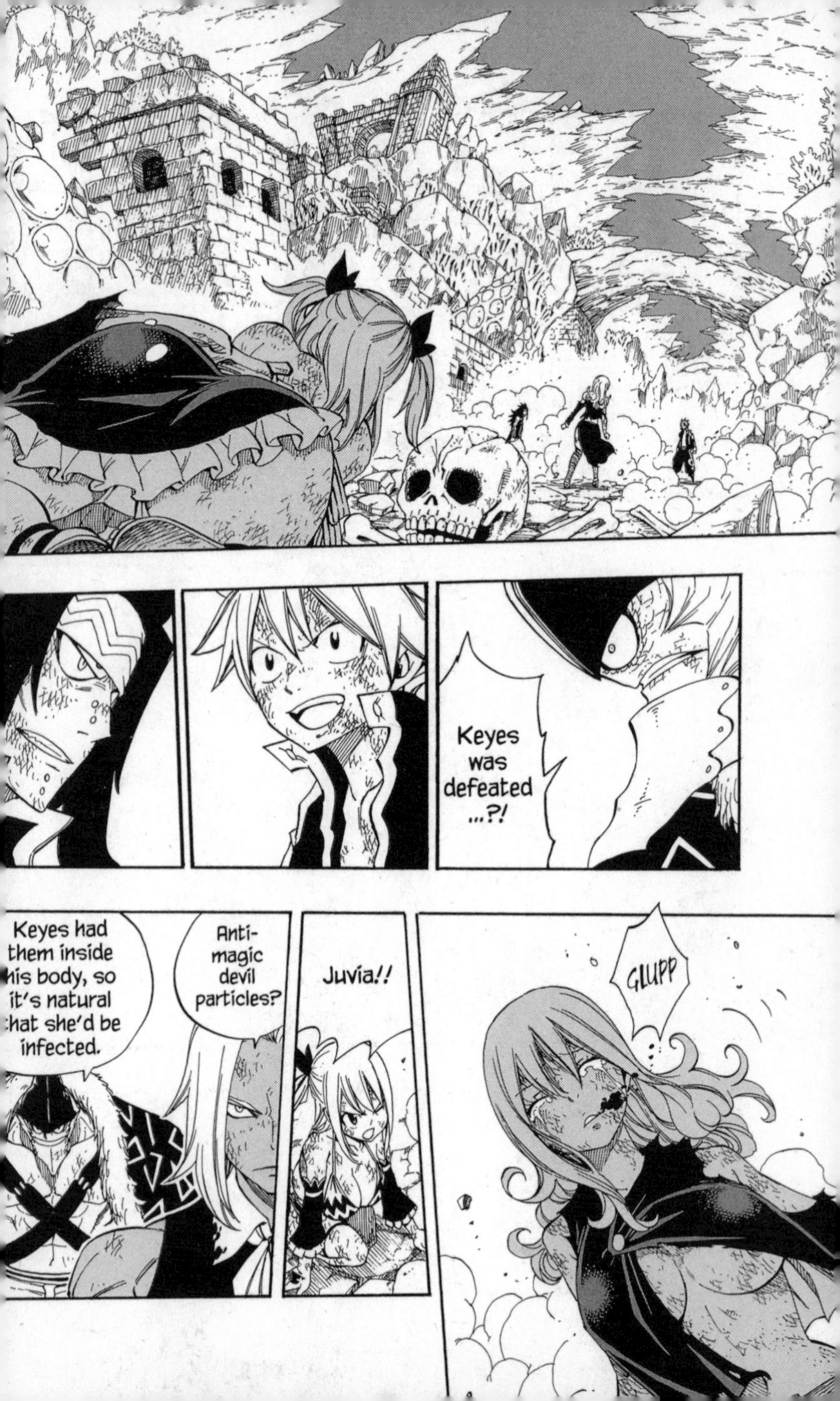
Keyes was defeated ...?!
GLUPP
Juvia!!
Anti-magic devil particles?
Keyes had them inside his body, so it's natural that she'd be infected.

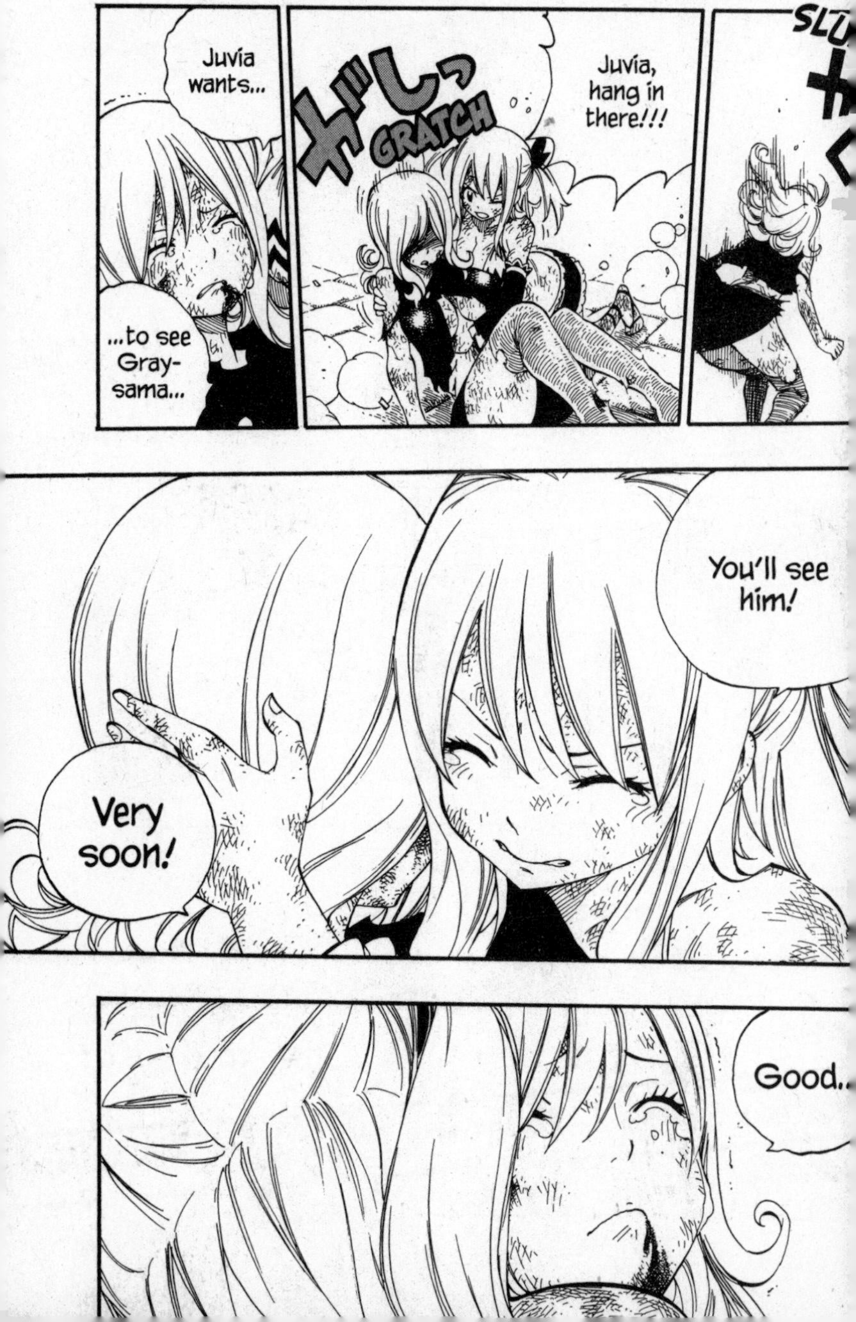
GRATCH
Juvia, hang in there!!!
Juvia wants...
...to see Gray-sama...
You'll see him!
Very soon!
Good..

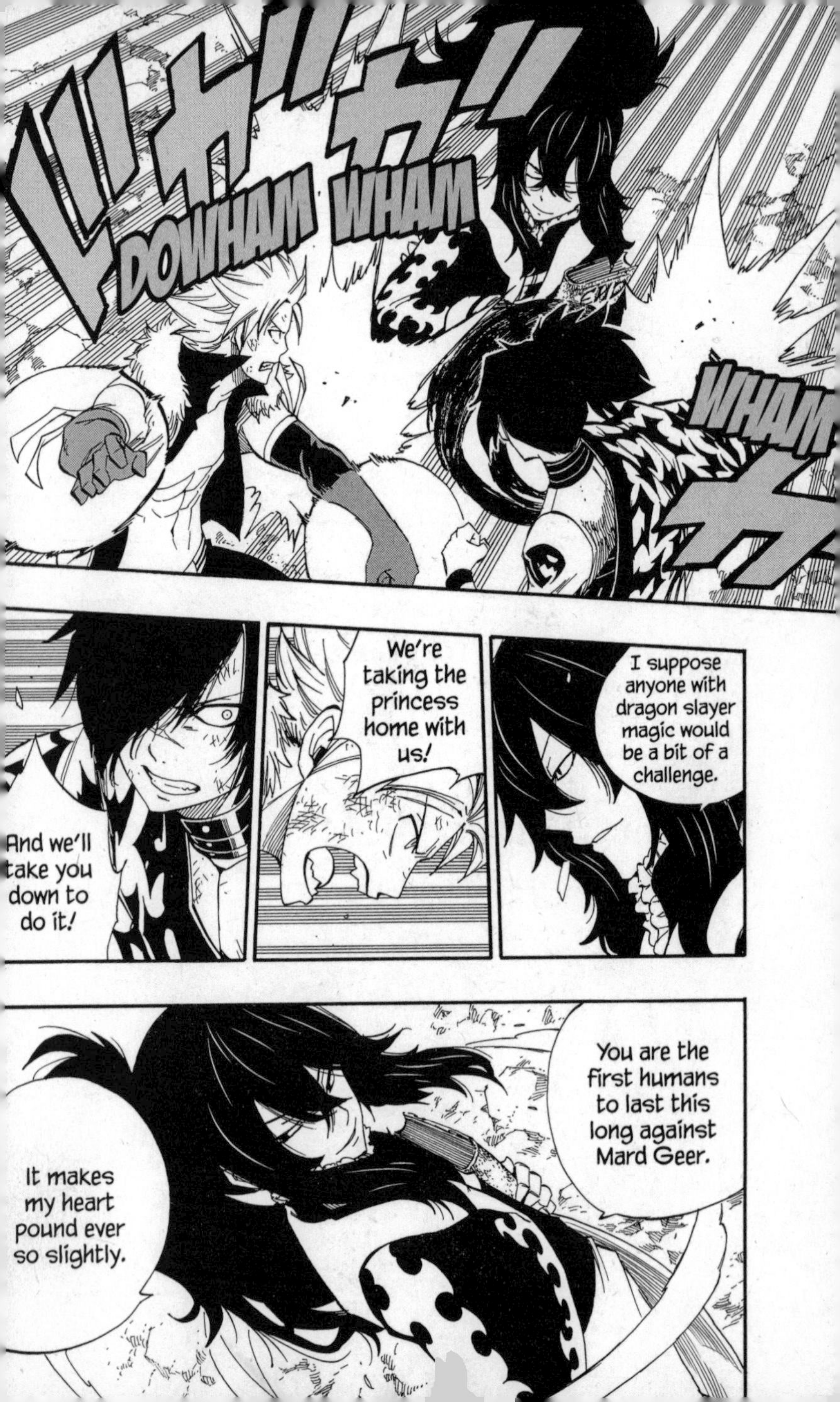
DOWHAM WHAM
WHAM
I suppose anyone with dragon slayer magic would be a bit of a challenge.
We're taking the princess home with us!
And we'll take you down to do it!
You are the first humans to last this long against Mard Geer.
It makes my heart pound ever so slightly.

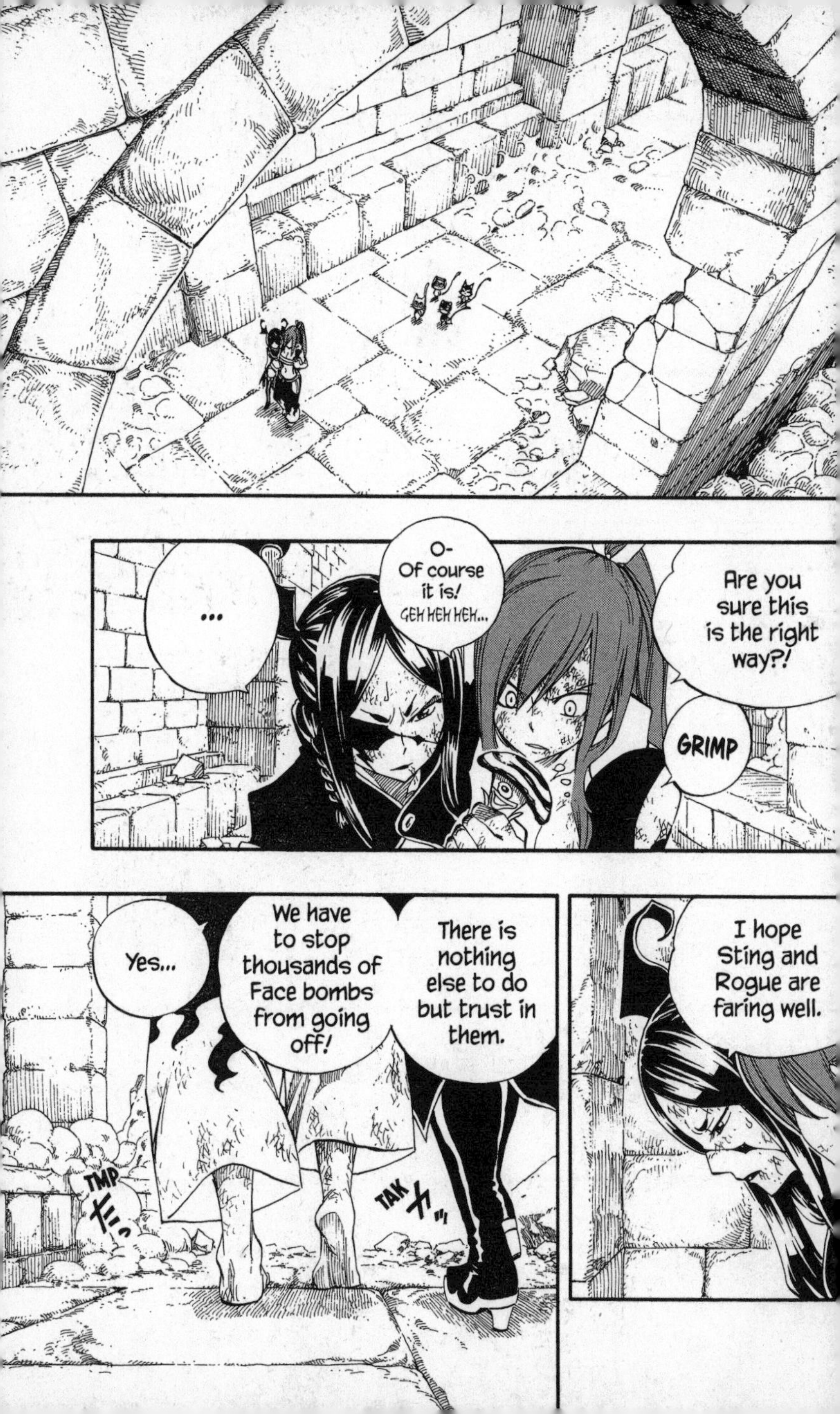
Are you sure this is the right way?!
GRIMP
O- Of course it is!
GEH HEH HEH...
...
I hope Sting and Rogue are faring well.
There is nothing else to do but trust in them.
We have to stop thousands of Face bombs from going off!
Yes...
TAK
TMP

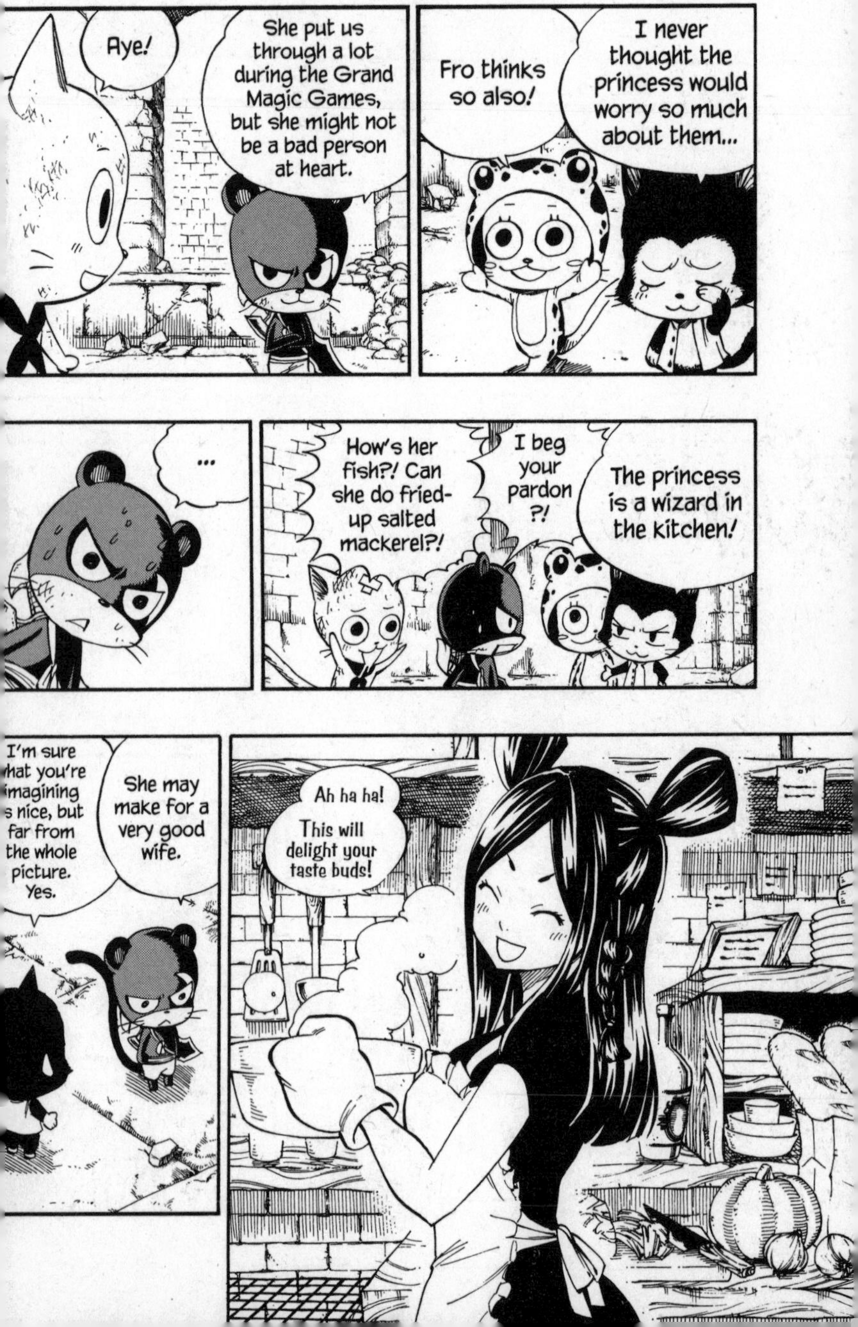
I never thought the princess would worry so much about them...
Fro thinks so also!
She put us through a lot during the Grand Magic Games, but she might not be a bad person at heart.
Aye!
The princess is a wizard in the kitchen!
I beg your pardon?!
How's her fish?! Can she do fried-up salted mackerel?!
...
Ah ha ha!
This will delight your taste buds!
She may make for a very good wife.
I'm sure hat you're imagining s nice, but far from the whole picture. Yes.

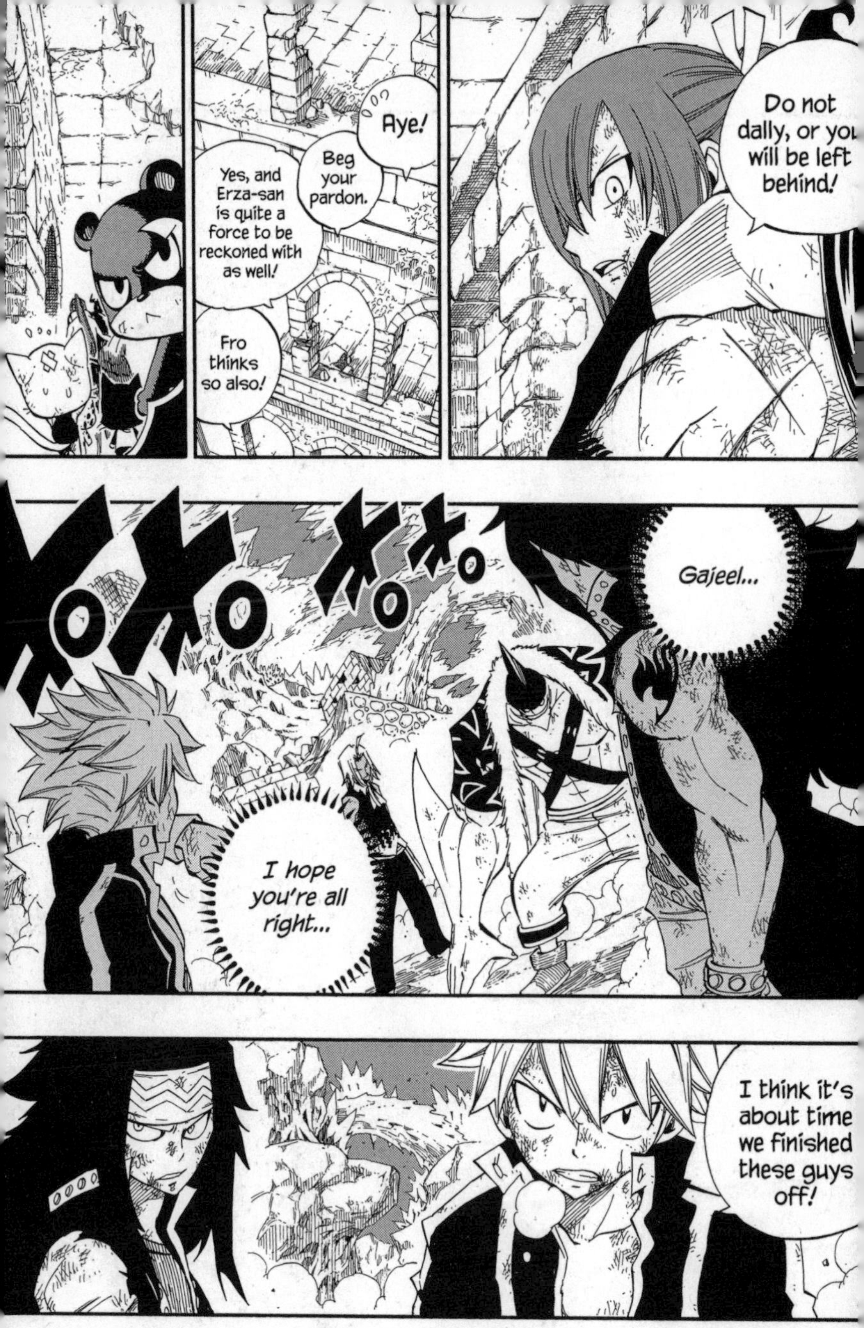
Do not dally, or you will be left behind!
Aye!
Beg your pardon.
Yes, and Erza-san is quite a force to be reckoned with as well!
Fro thinks so also!
Gajeel...
I hope you're all right...
I think it's about time we finished these guys off!

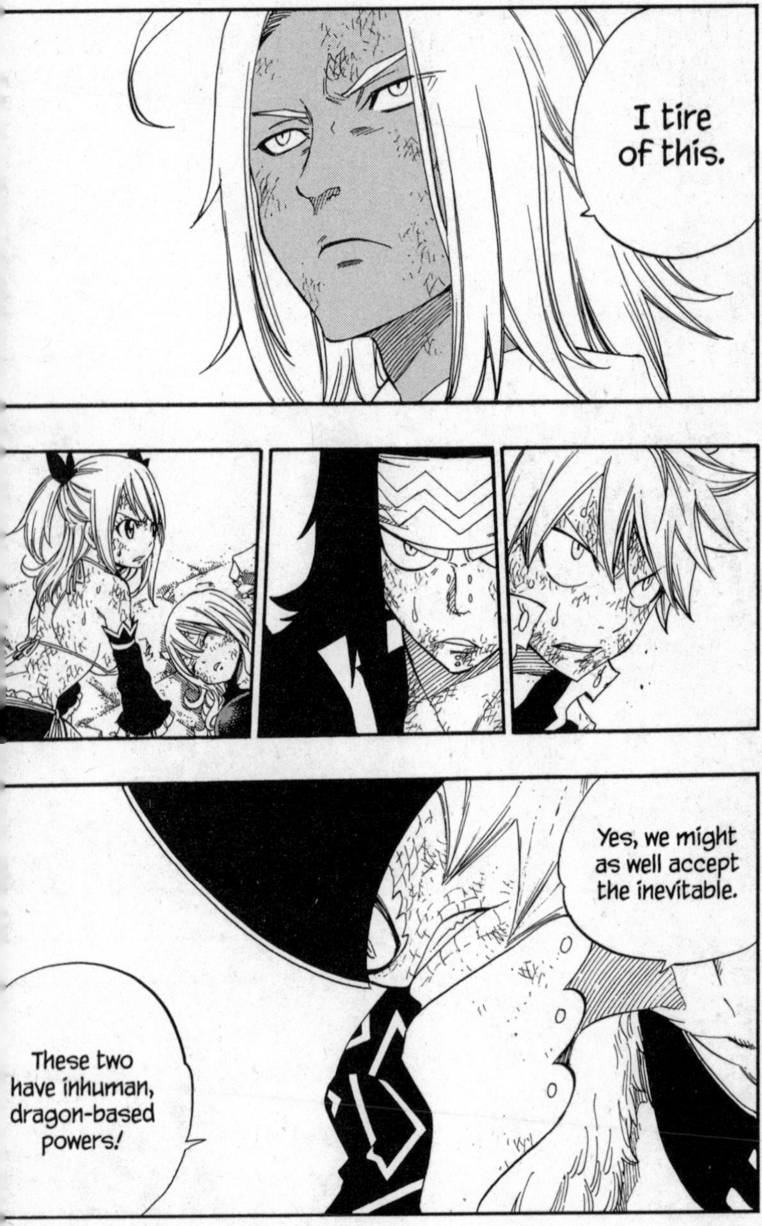
I tire of this.
Yes, we might as well accept the inevitable.
These two have inhuman, dragon-based powers!

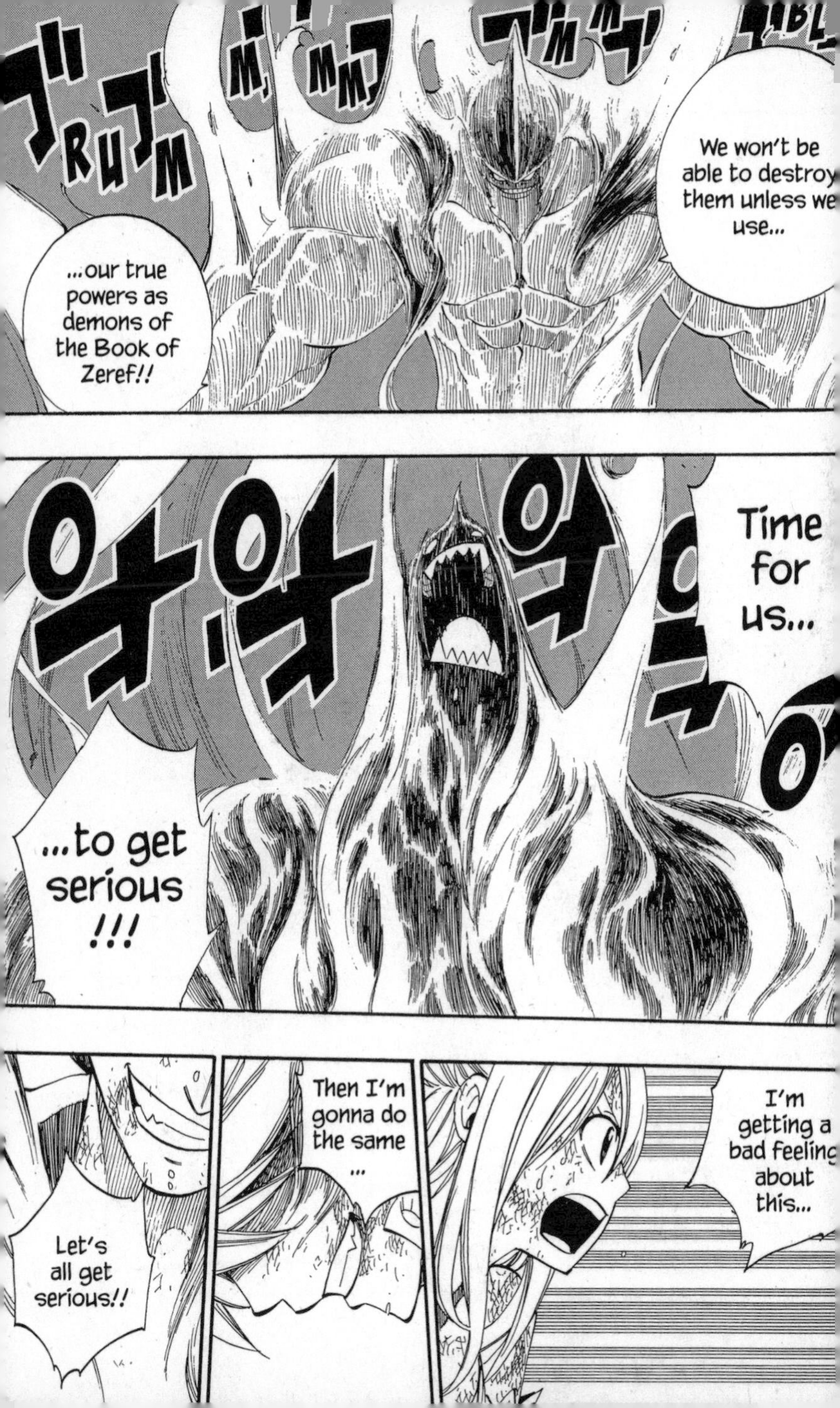
We won't be able to destroy them unless we use...
...our true powers as demons of the Book of Zeref!!
Time for us...
...to get serious!!!
I'm getting a bad feeling about this...
Then I'm gonna do the same...
Let's all get serious!!

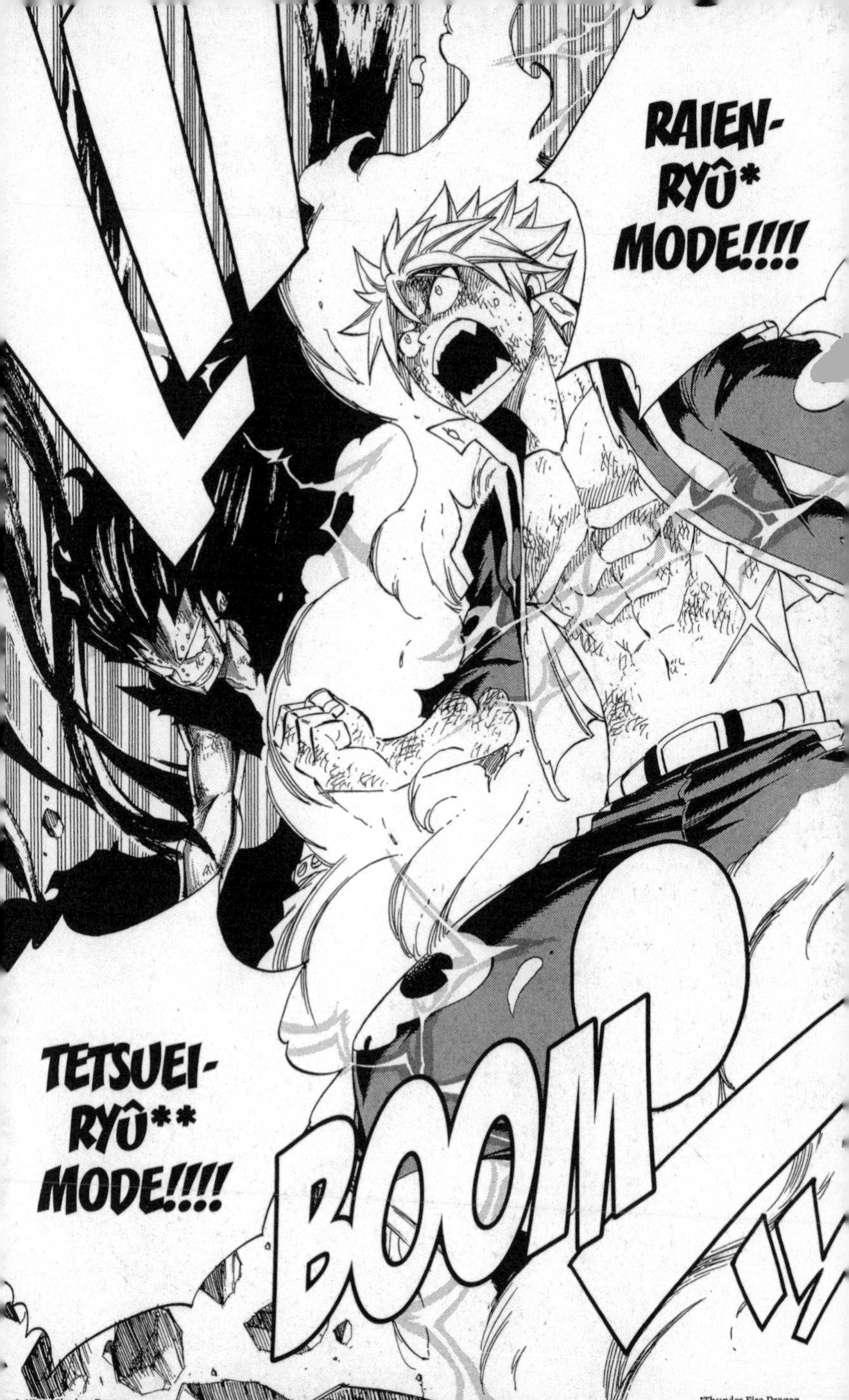
RAIEN-RYÛ* MODE!!!!
TETSUEI-RYÛ** MODE!!!!
BOOM

*Thunder Fire Dragon

**Iron Shadow Dragon

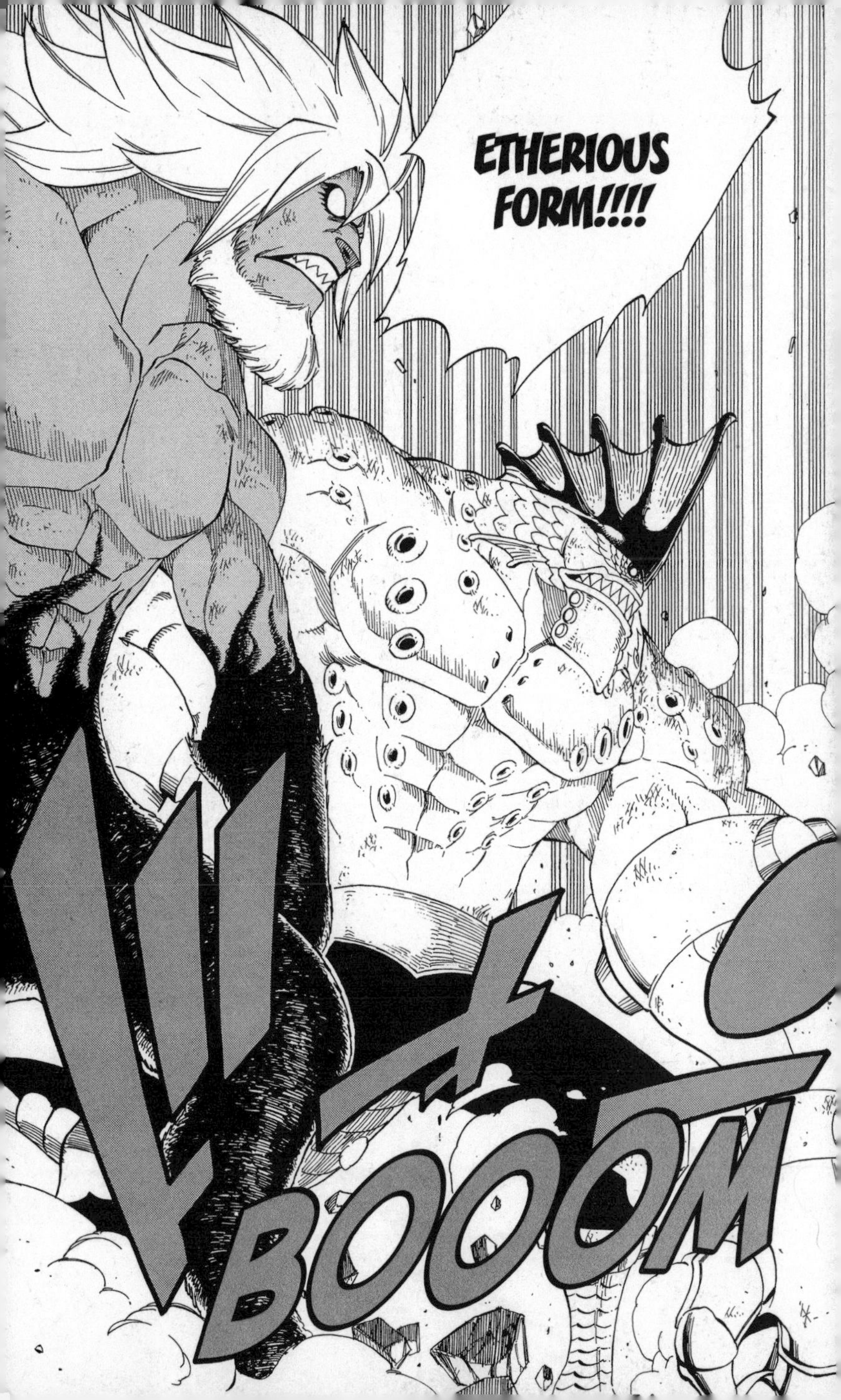
ETHERIOUS FORM!!!!
BOOOOM

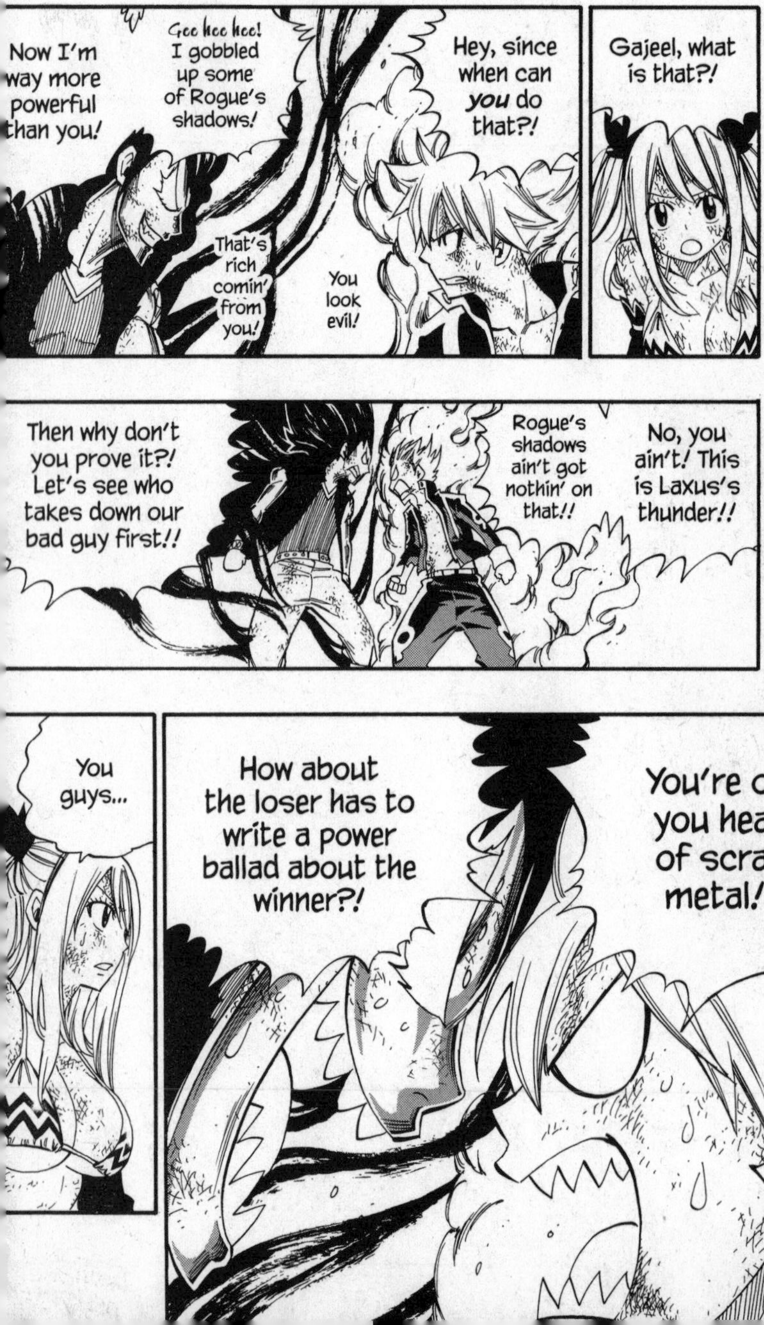
Gajeel, what is that?!
Hey, since when can *you* do that?!
Gee hee hee! I gobbled up some of Rogue's shadows!
Now I'm way more powerful than you!
You look evil!
That's rich comin' from you!
No, you ain't! This is Laxus's thunder!!
Rogue's shadows ain't got nothin' on that!!
Then why don't you prove it?! Let's see who takes down our bad guy first!!
You're on, you heap of scrap metal!!
How about the loser has to write a power ballad about the winner?!
You guys...

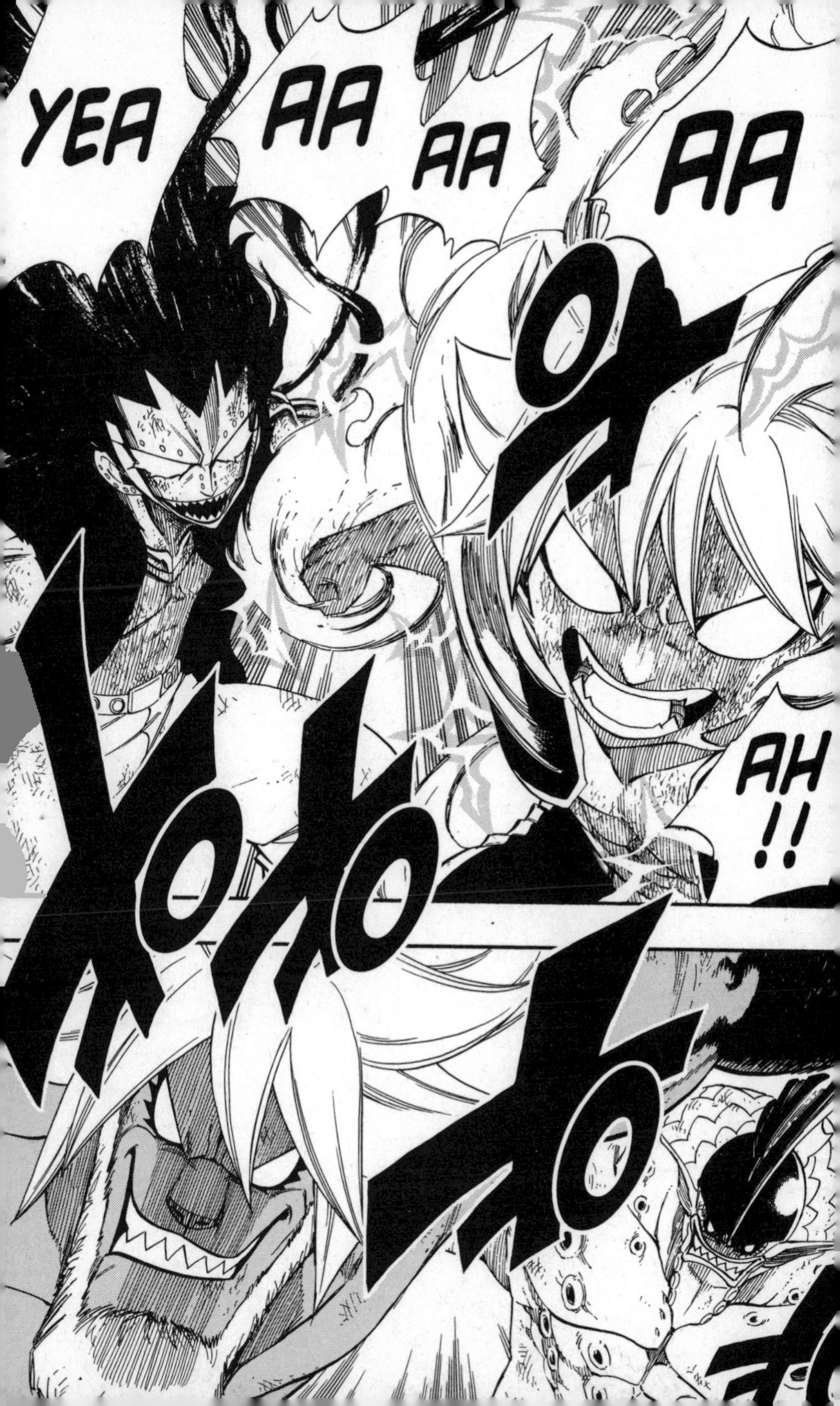
YEA AA AA AA
AH!!

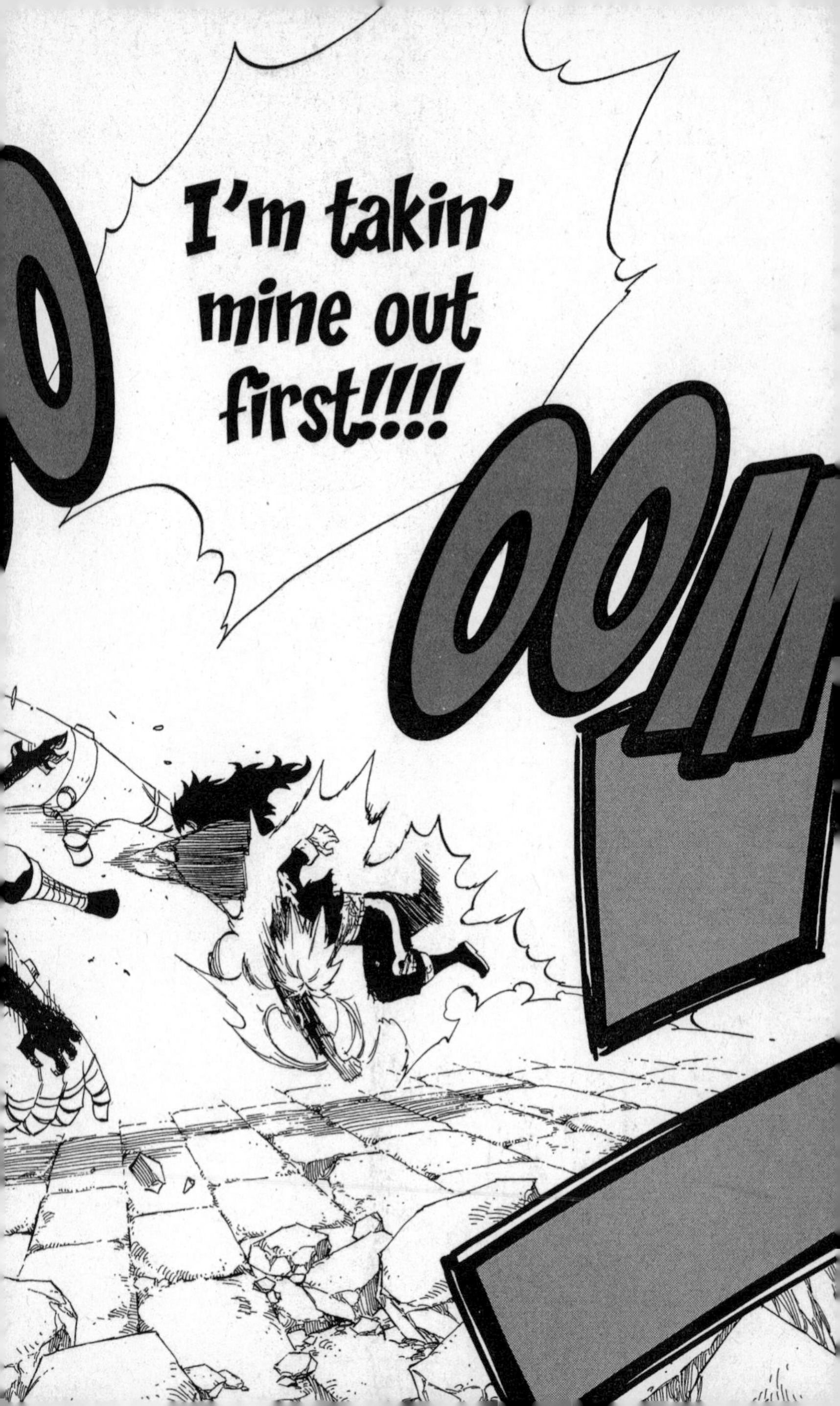
I'm takin' mine out first!!!!

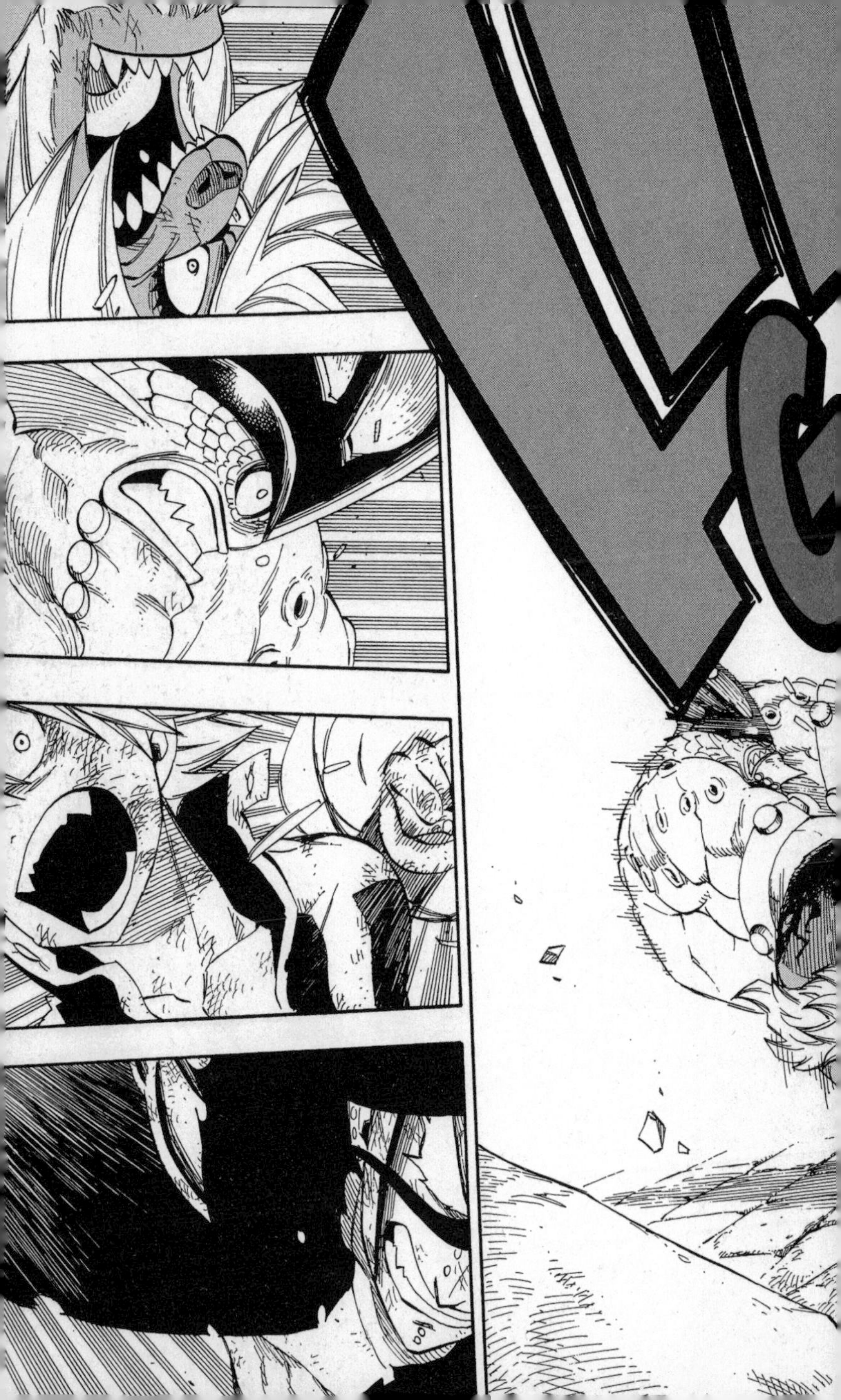

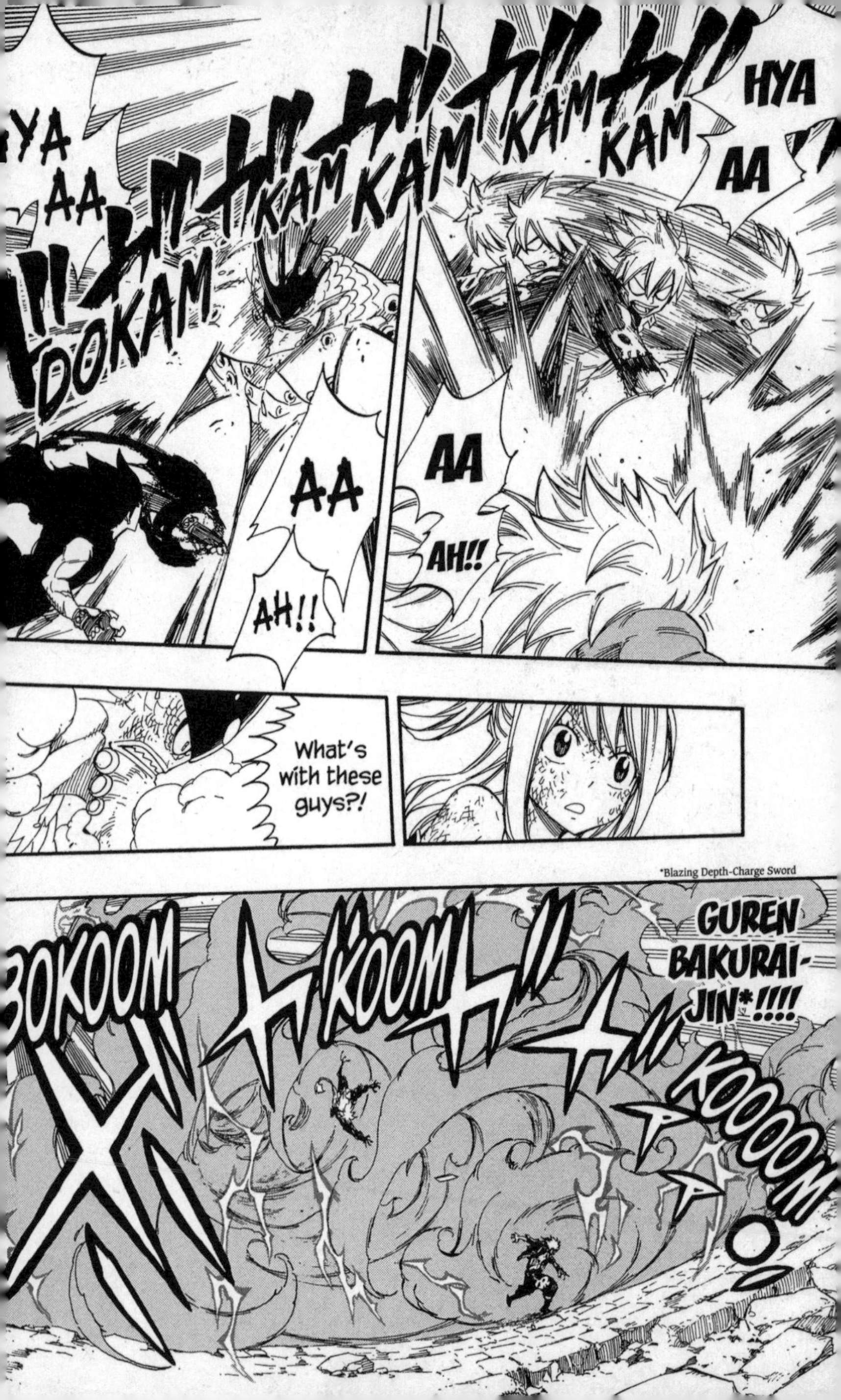
HYA
AA
KAM
KAM
KAM
KAM
KAM
DOKAM!!
HYA
AA
AA
AH!!
AA
AH!!
What's with these guys?!
GUREN BAKURAI-JIN*!!!!
BOKOOM
KOOM
KOOOOM

*Blazing Depth-Charge Sword

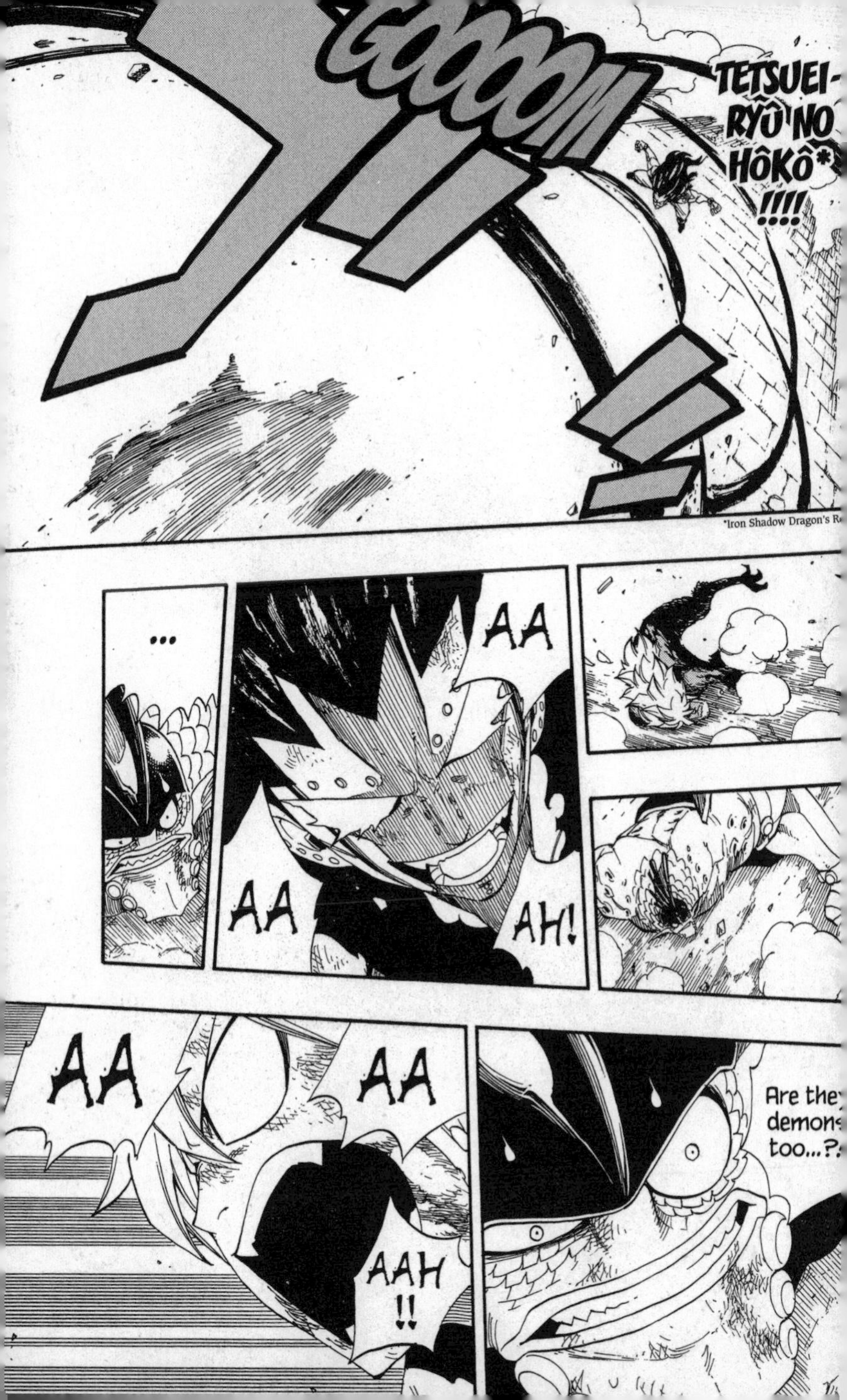
TETSUEI-RYÛ NO HÔKÔ*!!!!
GOOOM
*Iron Shadow Dragon's R
AA
AA
AH!
...
Are they demons too...?!
AA
AA
AAH!!

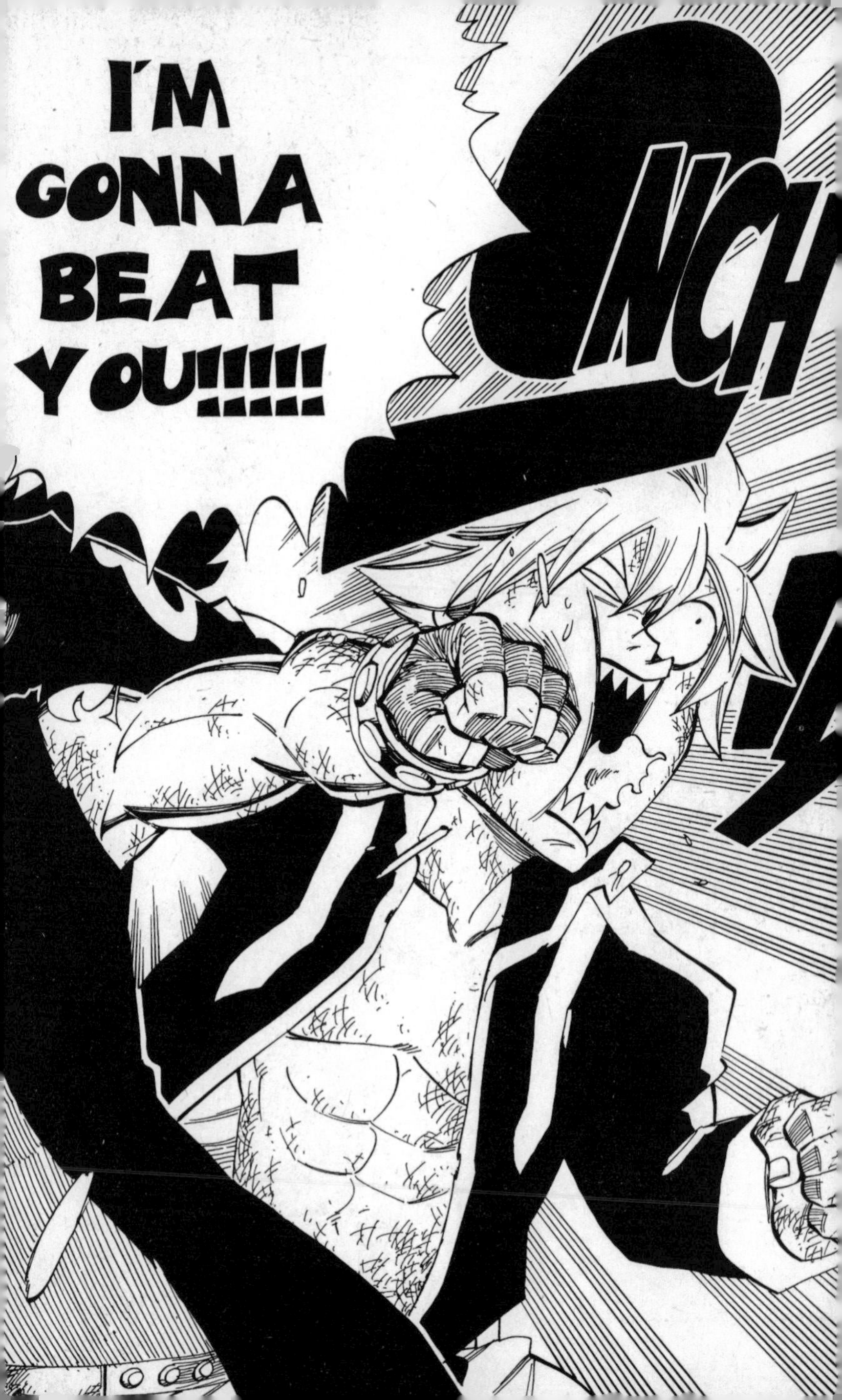
I'M GONNA BEAT YOU!!!!!
NCH

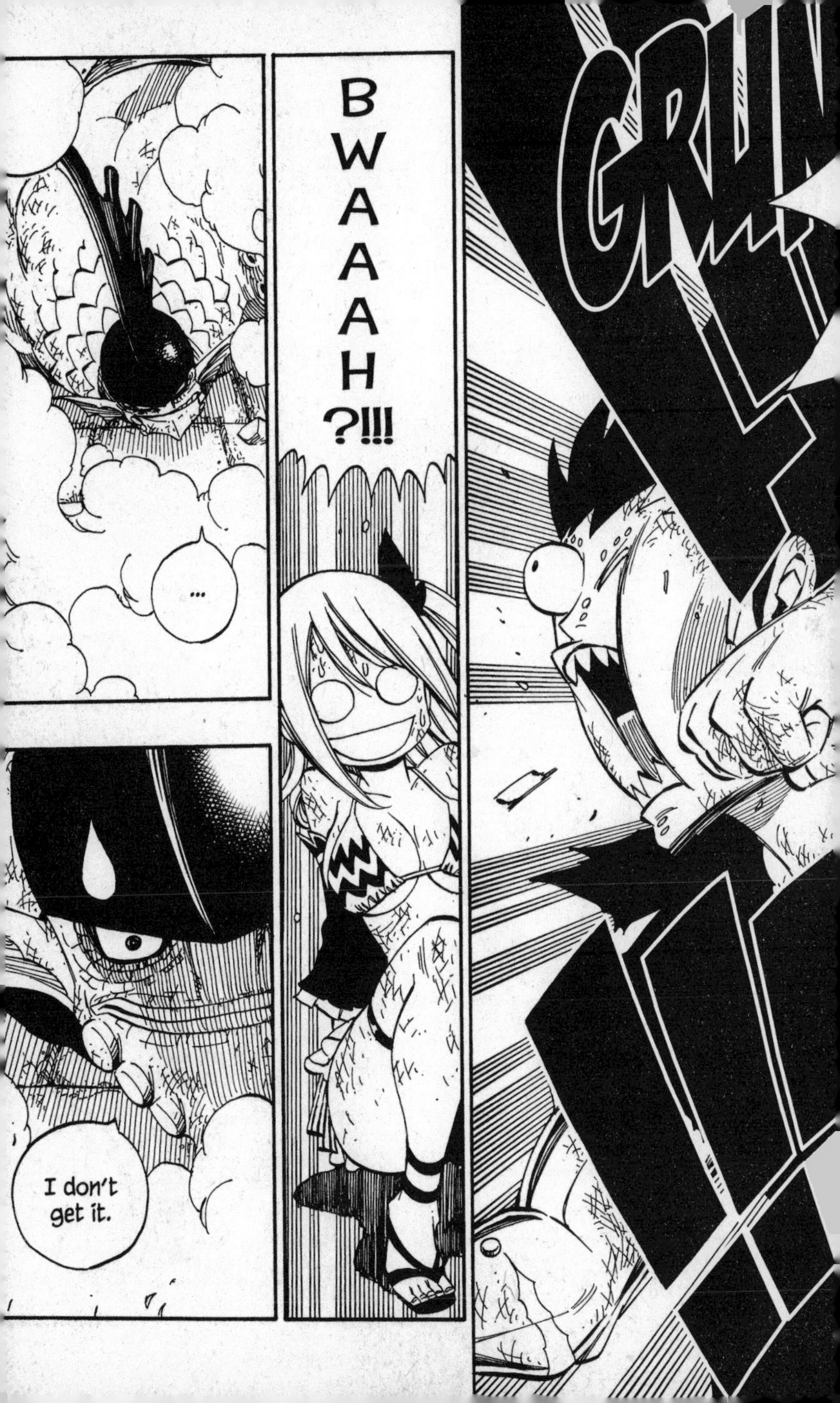
GRU
BWAAAH?!!!
...
I don't get it.

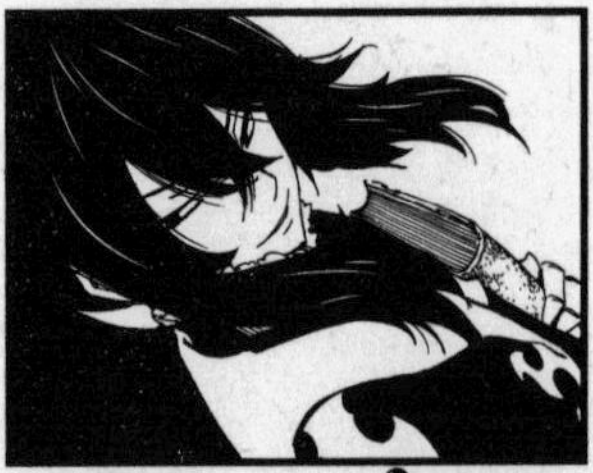

FAIRY TAIL

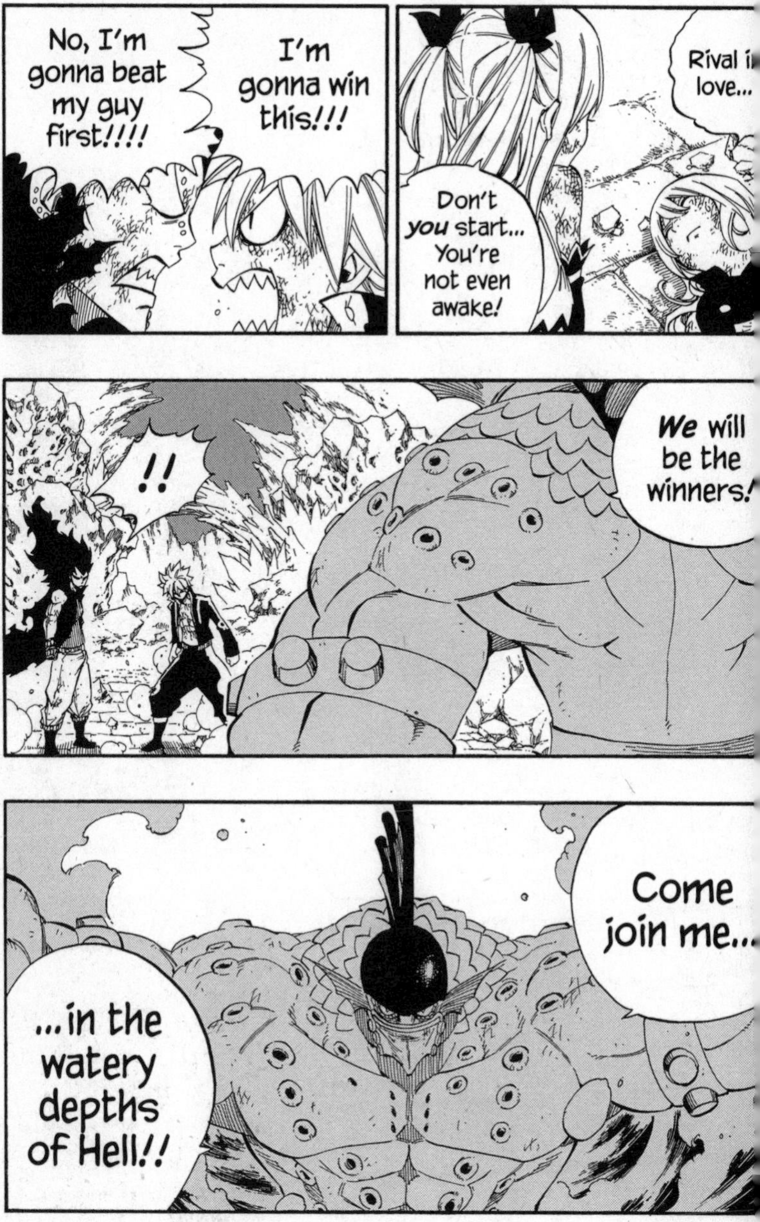
Rival i love...
Don't *you* start... You're not even awake!
I'm gonna win this!!!
No, I'm gonna beat my guy first!!!!
We will be the winners!
!!
Come join me...
...in the watery depths of Hell!!

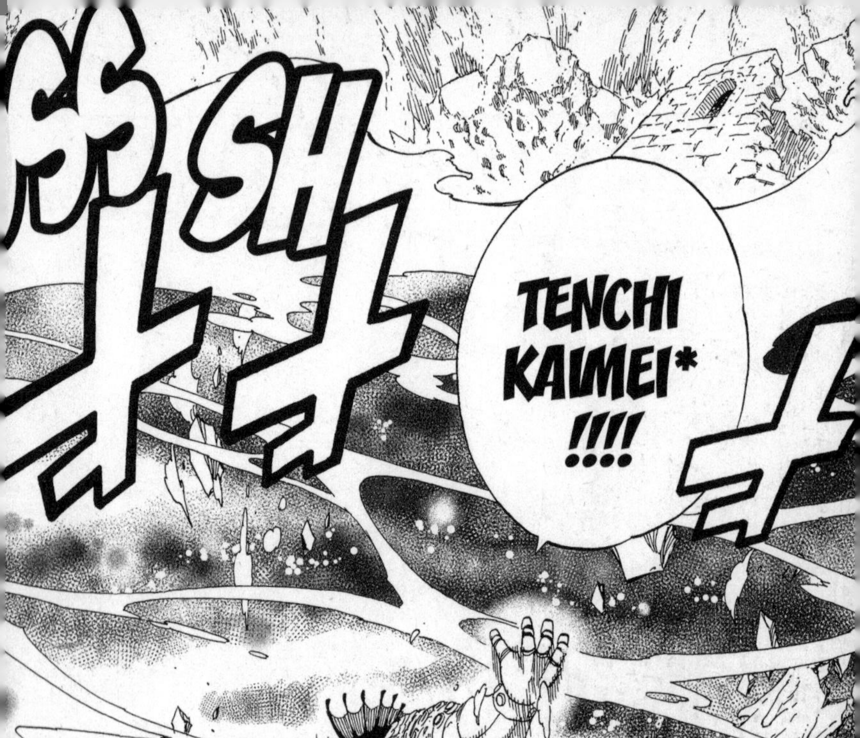
TENCHI KAIMEI* !!!!

*Depths of Hell's Darkness

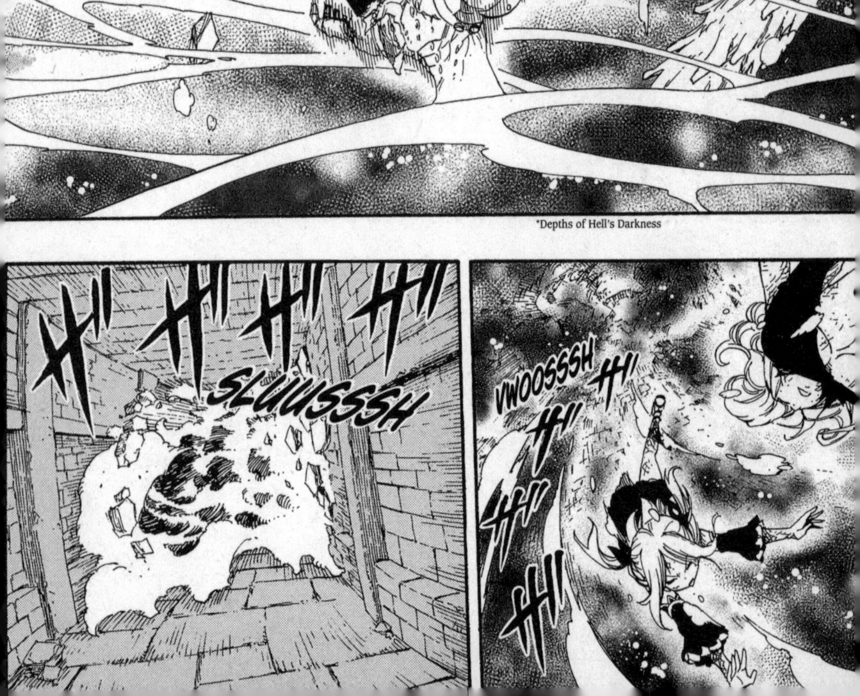
VWOOSSSH
SLUUSSSH

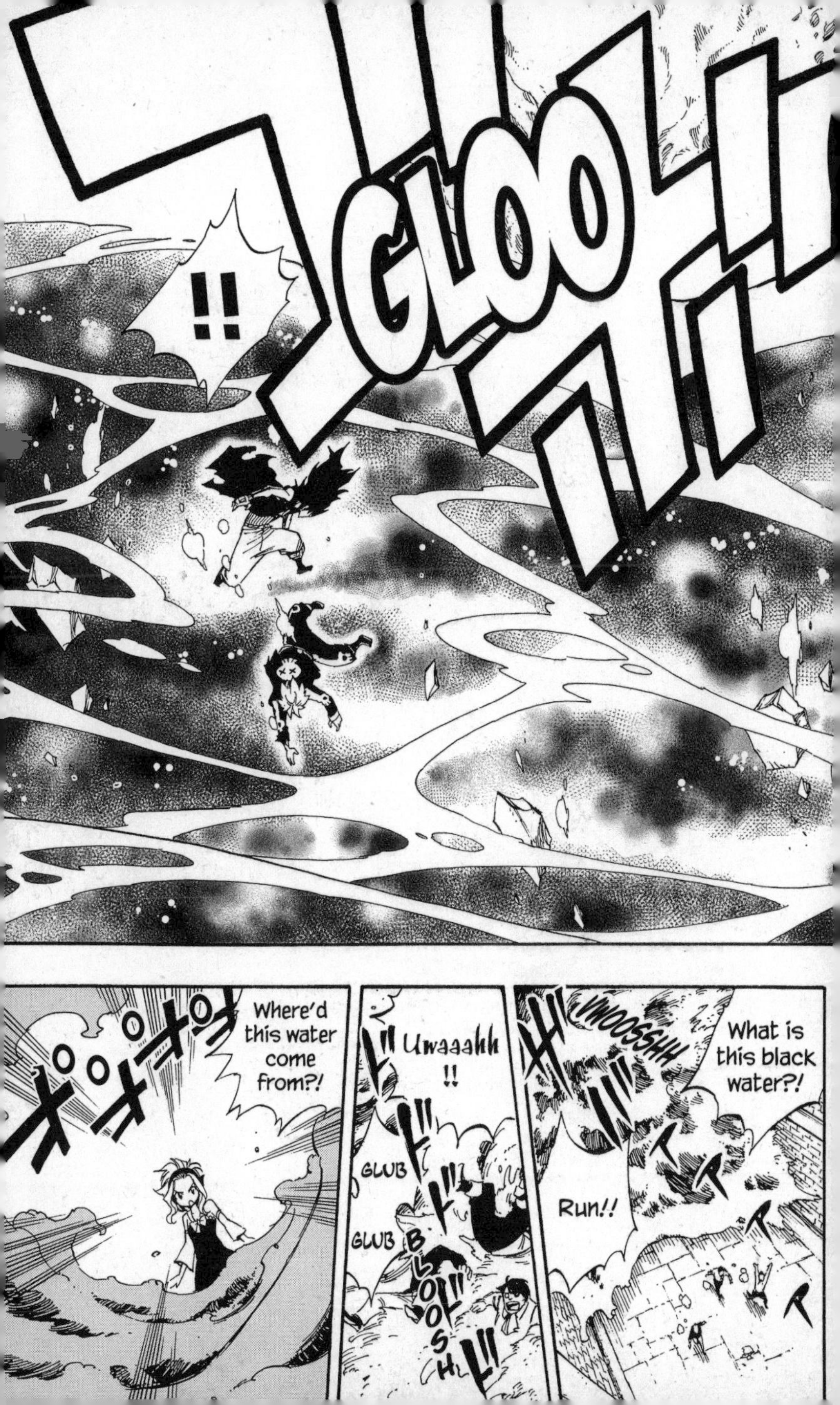

!!
What is this black water?!
WHOOSSHH!!
Run!!
Uwaaahh !!
GLUB
GLUB
BLOOOSH!!
Where'd this water come from?!

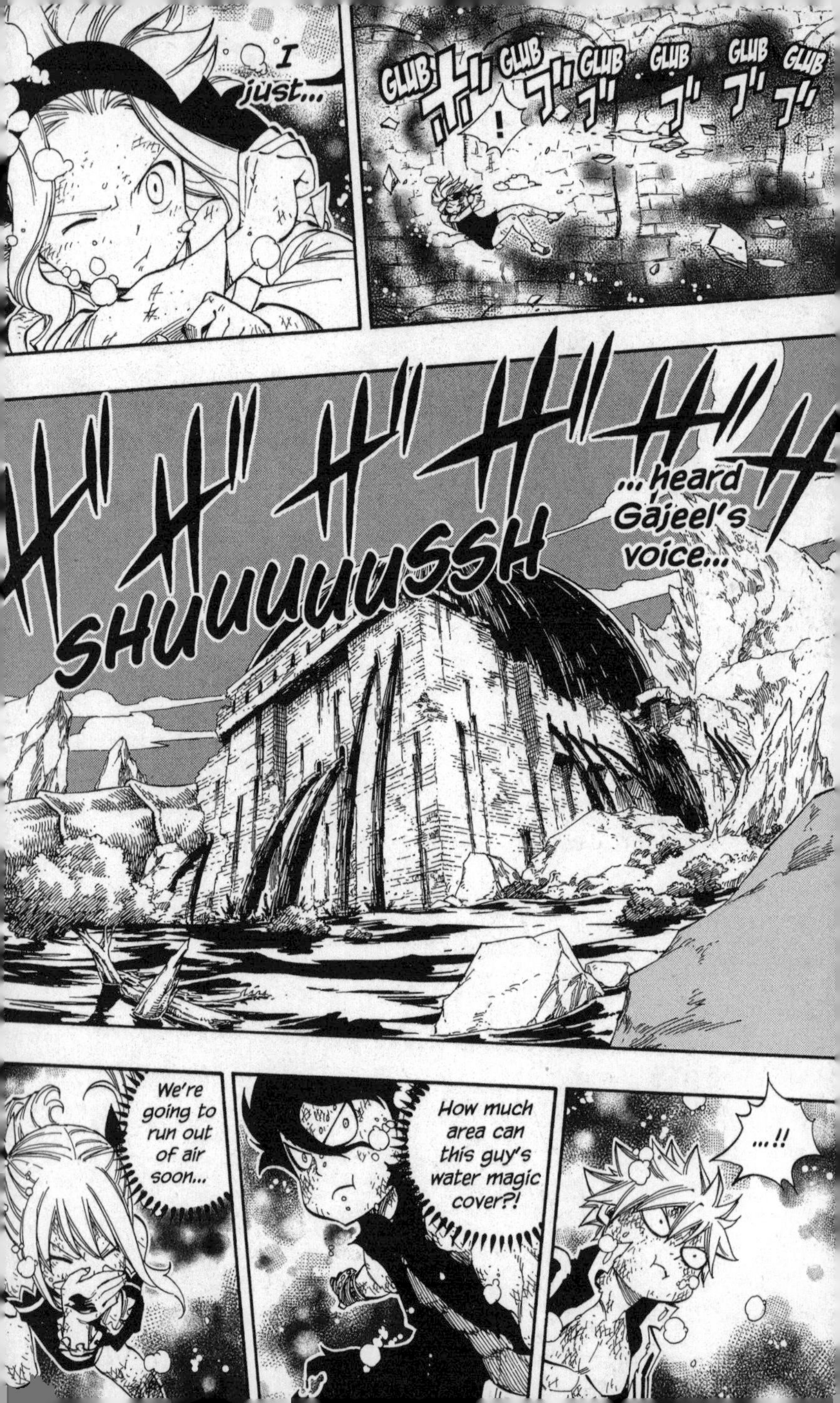
GLUB GLUB GLUB GLUB GLUB GLUB
I just...
SHUUUUUSSH
...heard Gajeel's voice...
...!!
How much area can this guy's water magic cover?!
We're going to run out of air soon...

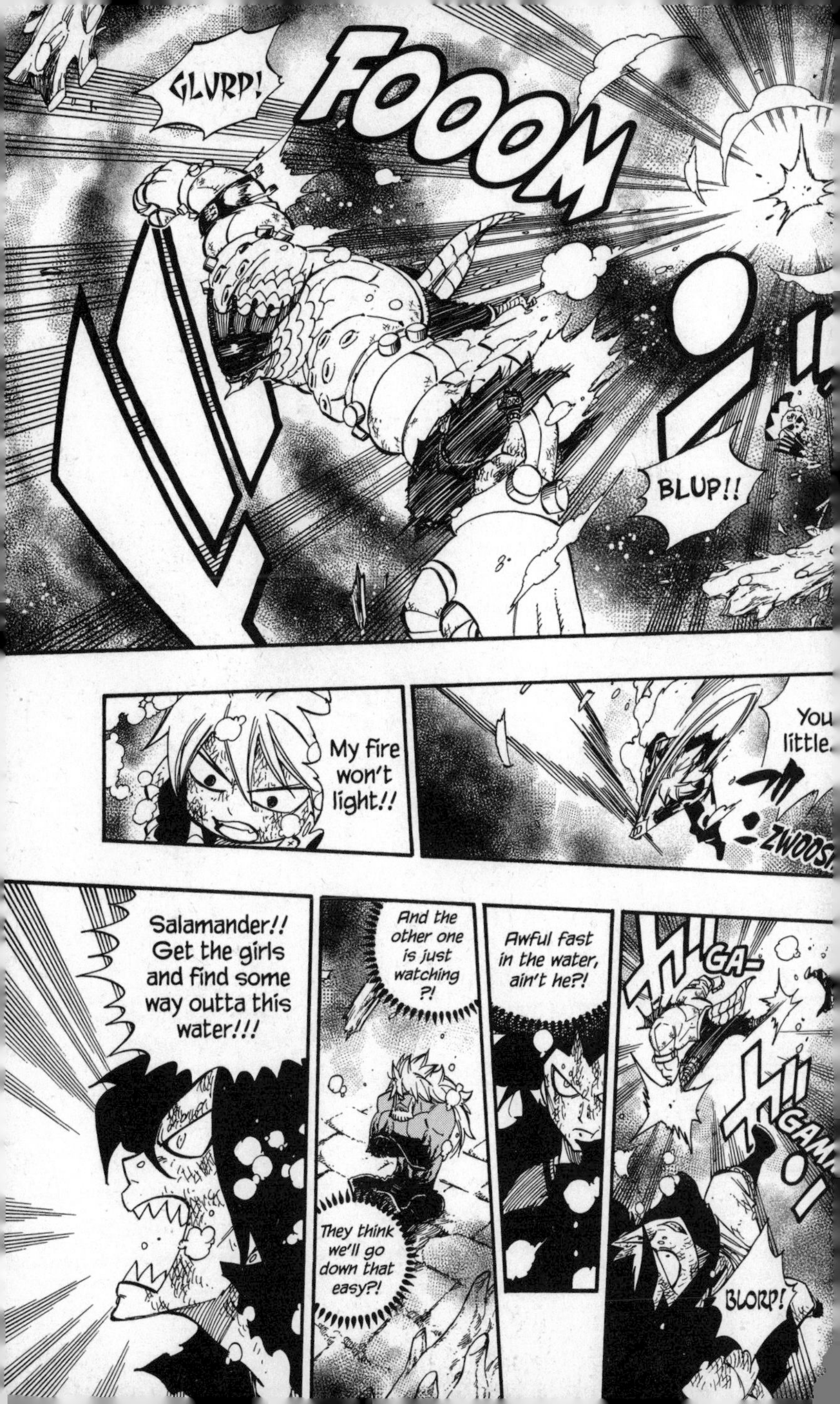
FOOOM
GLURP!
BLUP!!
You little.
ZWOOS
My fire won't light!!
GA-
GAM
BLORP!
Awful fast in the water, ain't he?!
And the other one is just watching?!
They think we'll go down that easy?!
Salamander!! Get the girls and find some way outta this water!!!

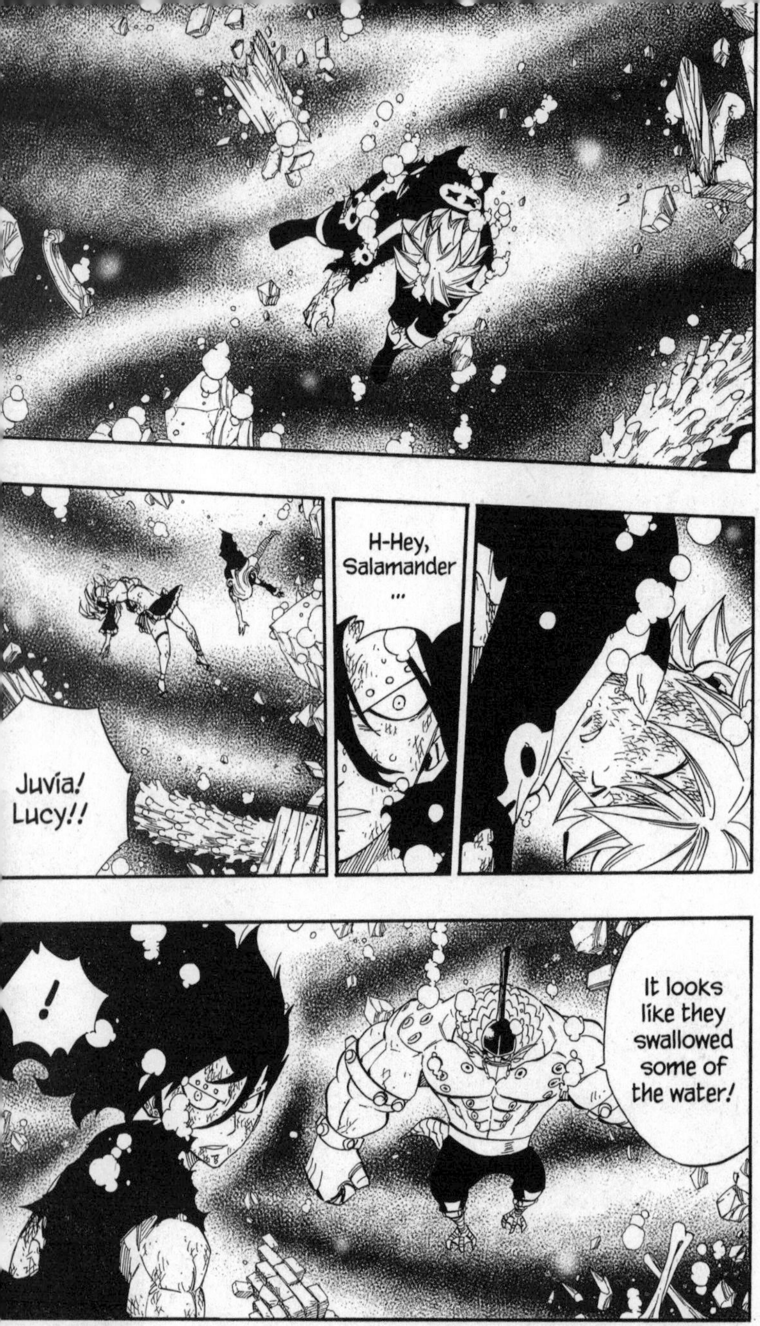
H-Hey, Salamander ...
Juvia! Lucy!!
It looks like they swallowed some of the water!
!

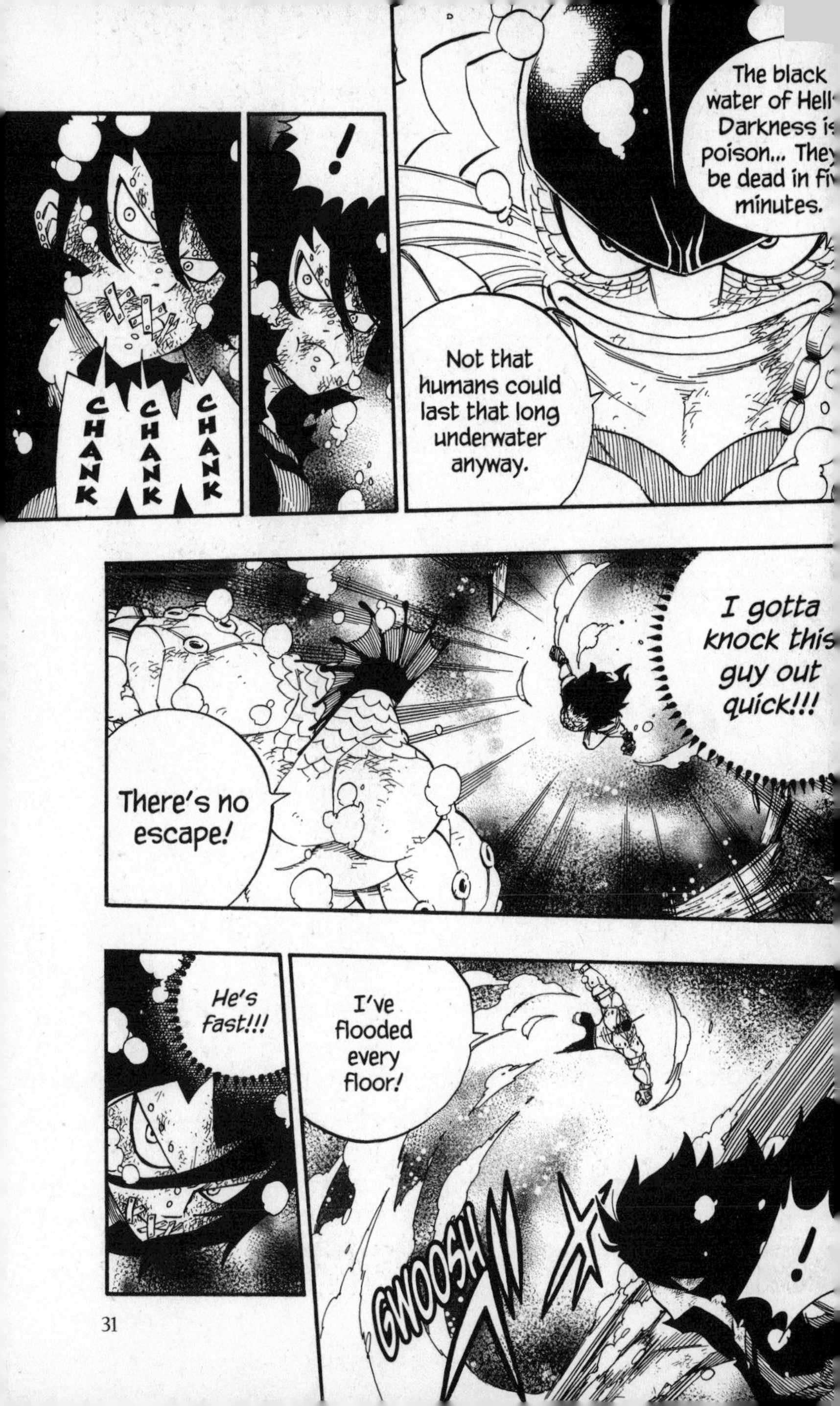
The black water of Hell Darkness is poison... They be dead in fi minutes.
Not that humans could last that long underwater anyway.
!
CHANK CHANK CHANK
I gotta knock this guy out quick!!!
There's no escape!
I've flooded every floor!
GWOOSH
!
He's fast!!!

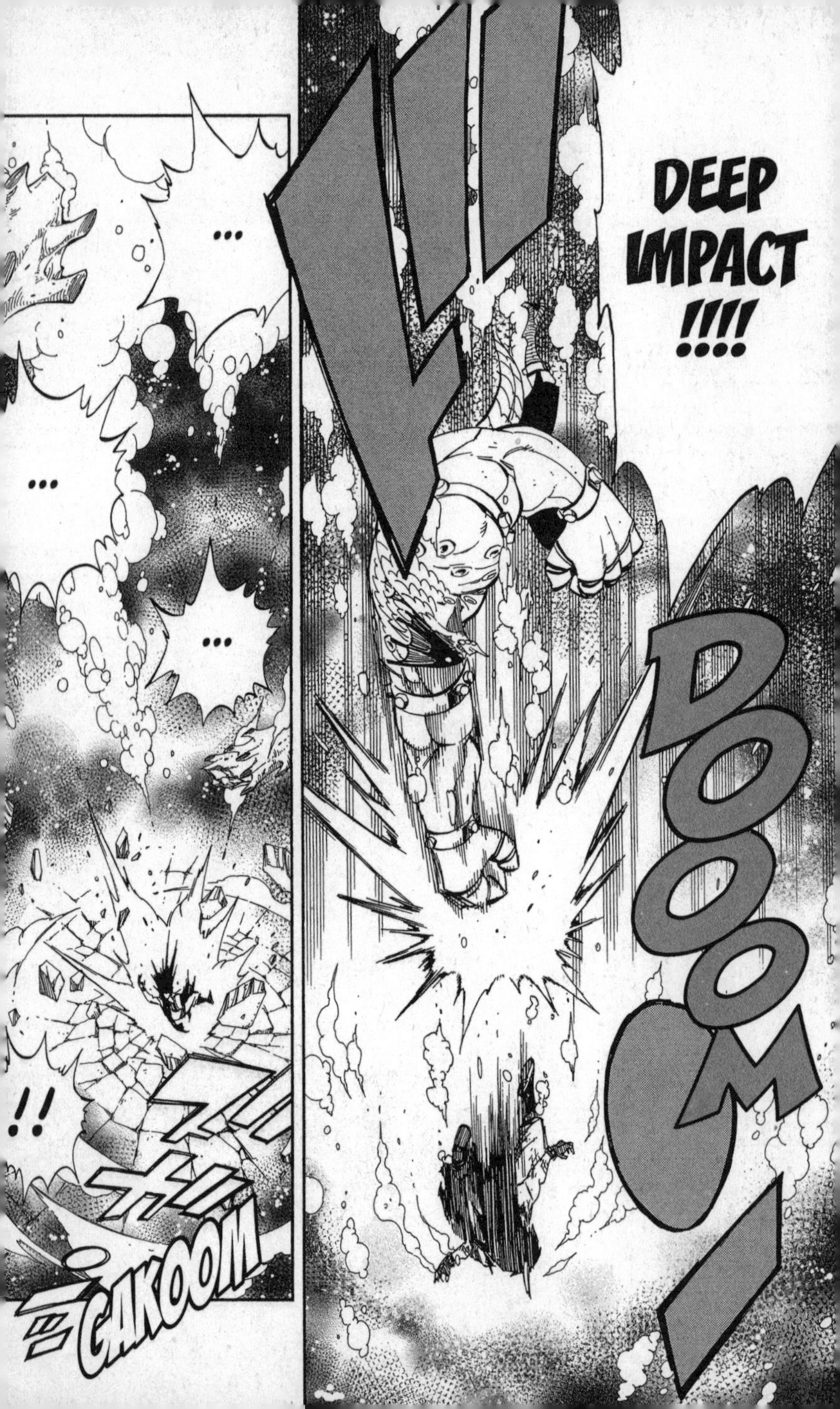
DEEP IMPACT !!!!
DOOOM
...
...
...
!!
GAKOOM

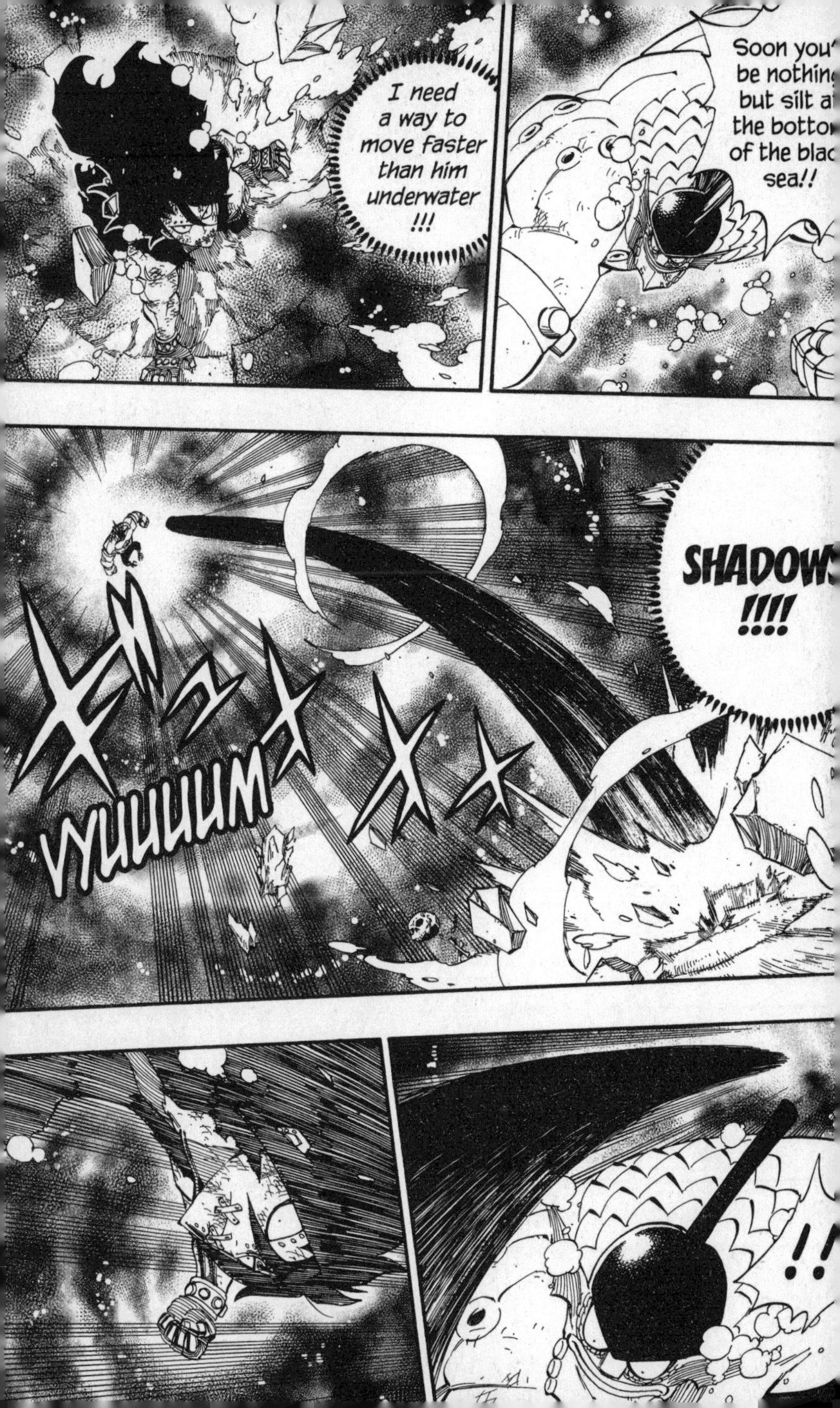
Soon you'
be nothin
but silt a
the bottor
of the blac
sea!!
I need a way to move faster than him underwater !!!
SHADOWS !!!!
VYUUUUM
!!

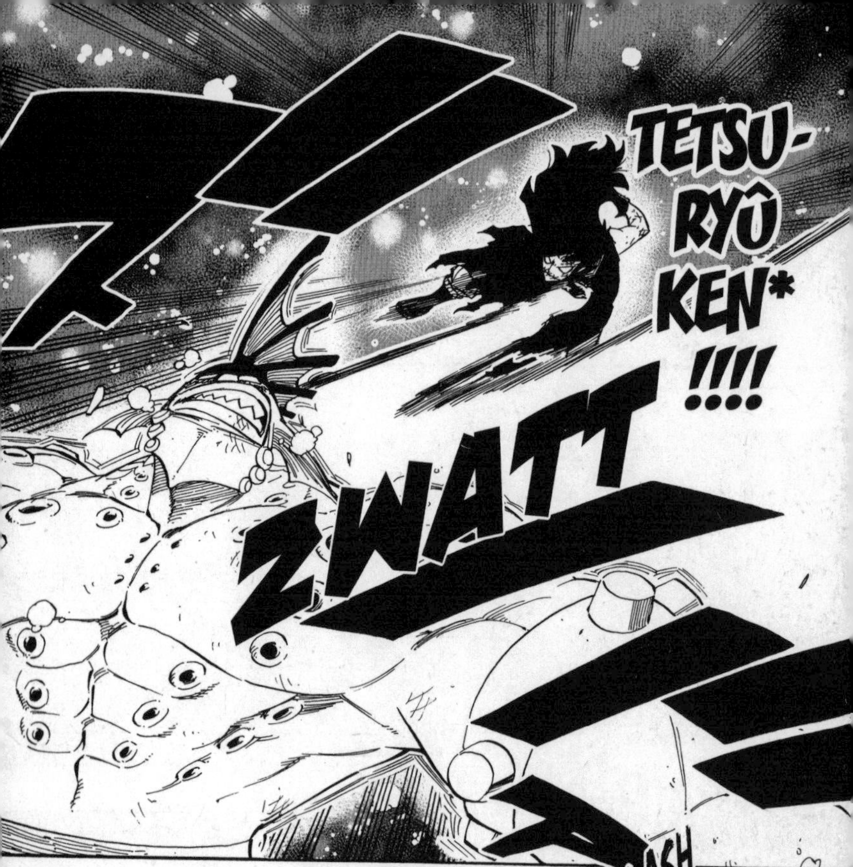
TETSU-RYÛ KEN*!!!!
ZWATT

*Iron Dragon Sword

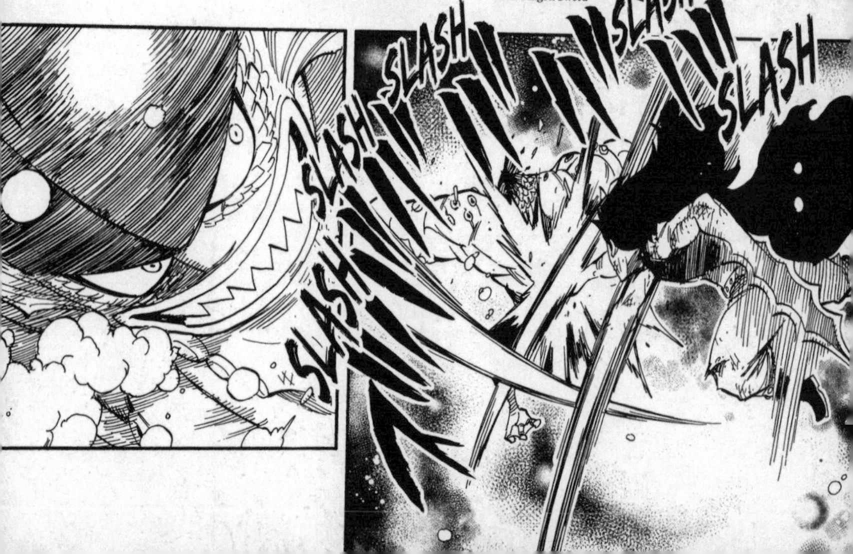
SLASH
SLASH
SLASH
SLASH
SLASH

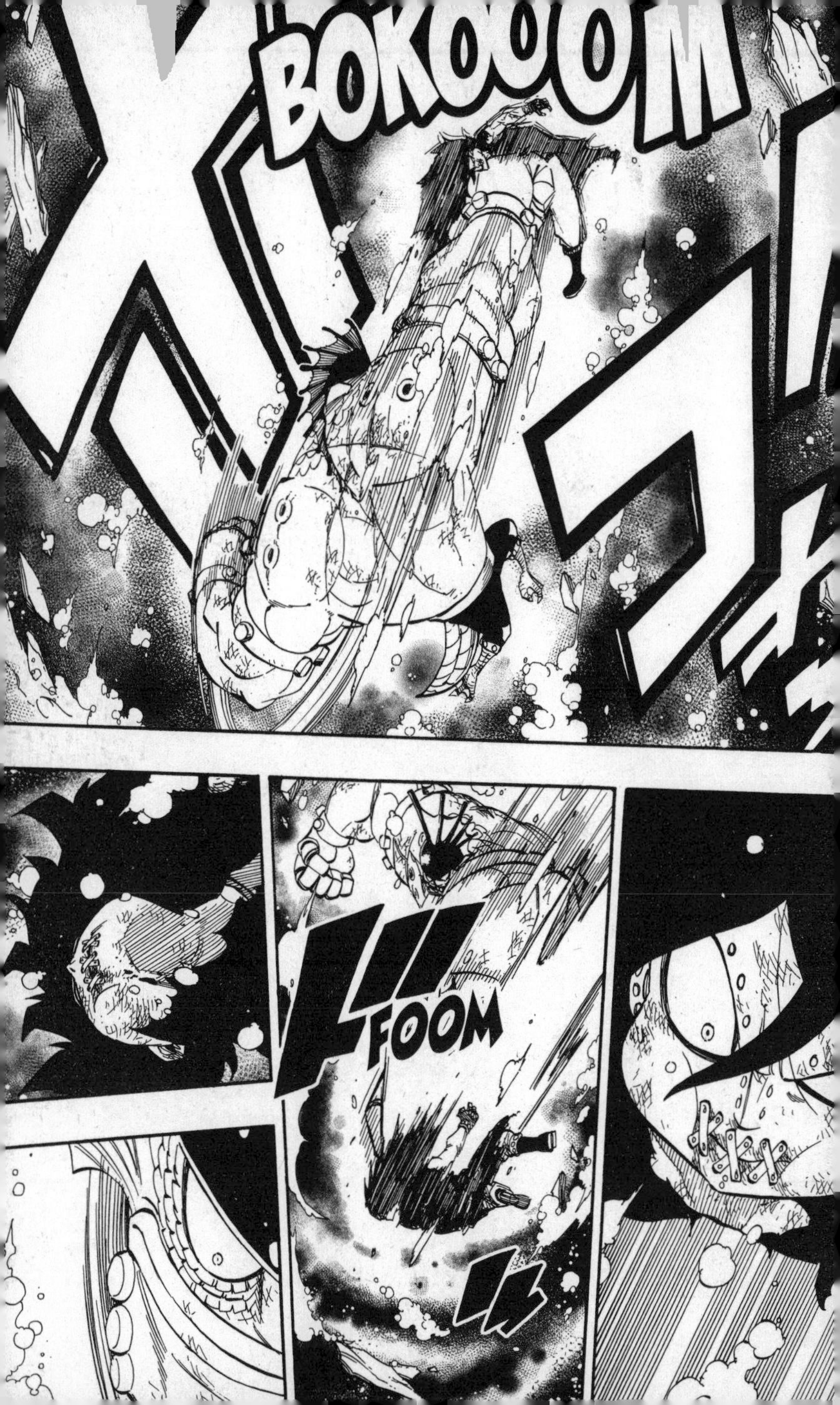
BOKOOOM
FOOM

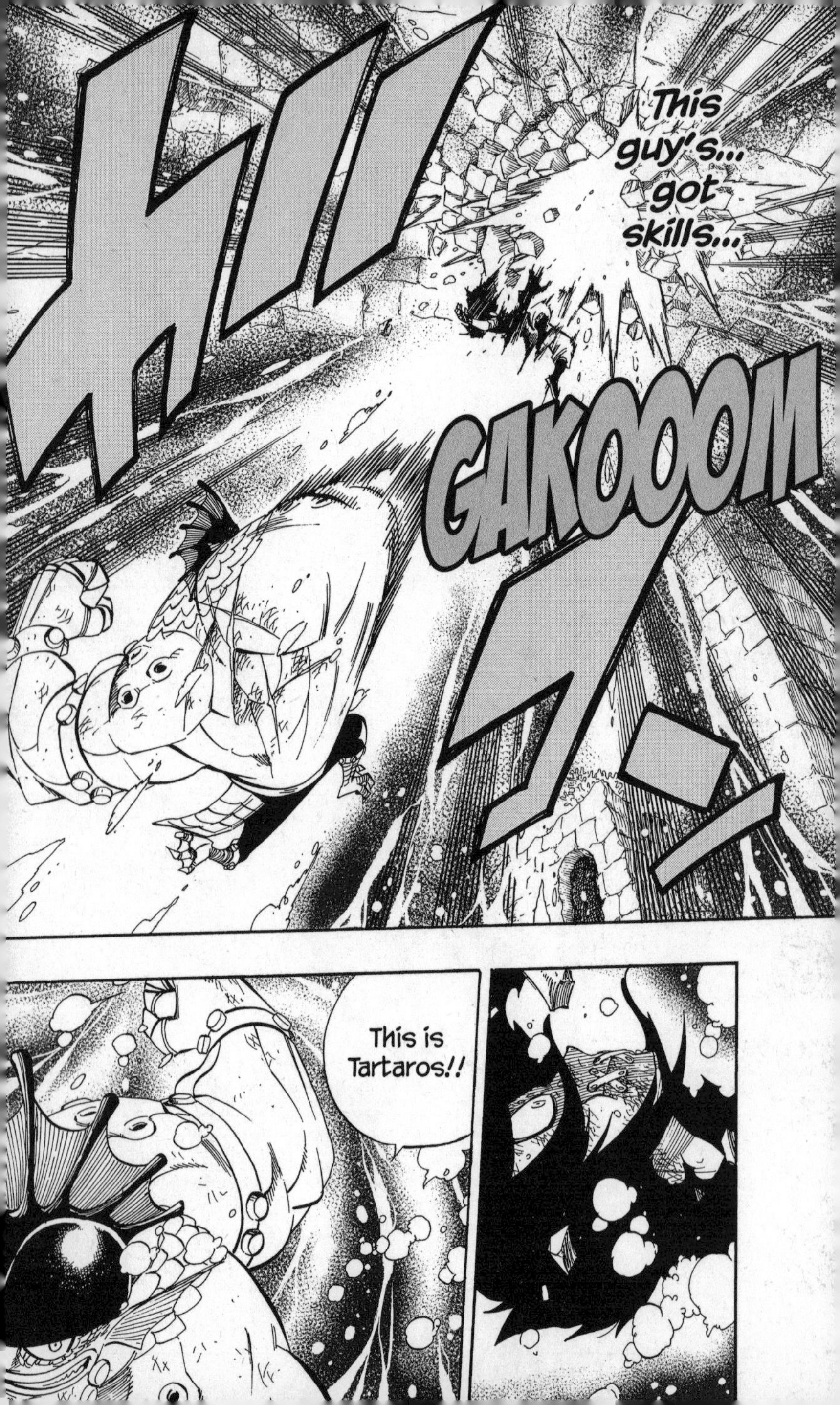
This guy's... got skills...
GAKOOOM
This is Tartaros!!

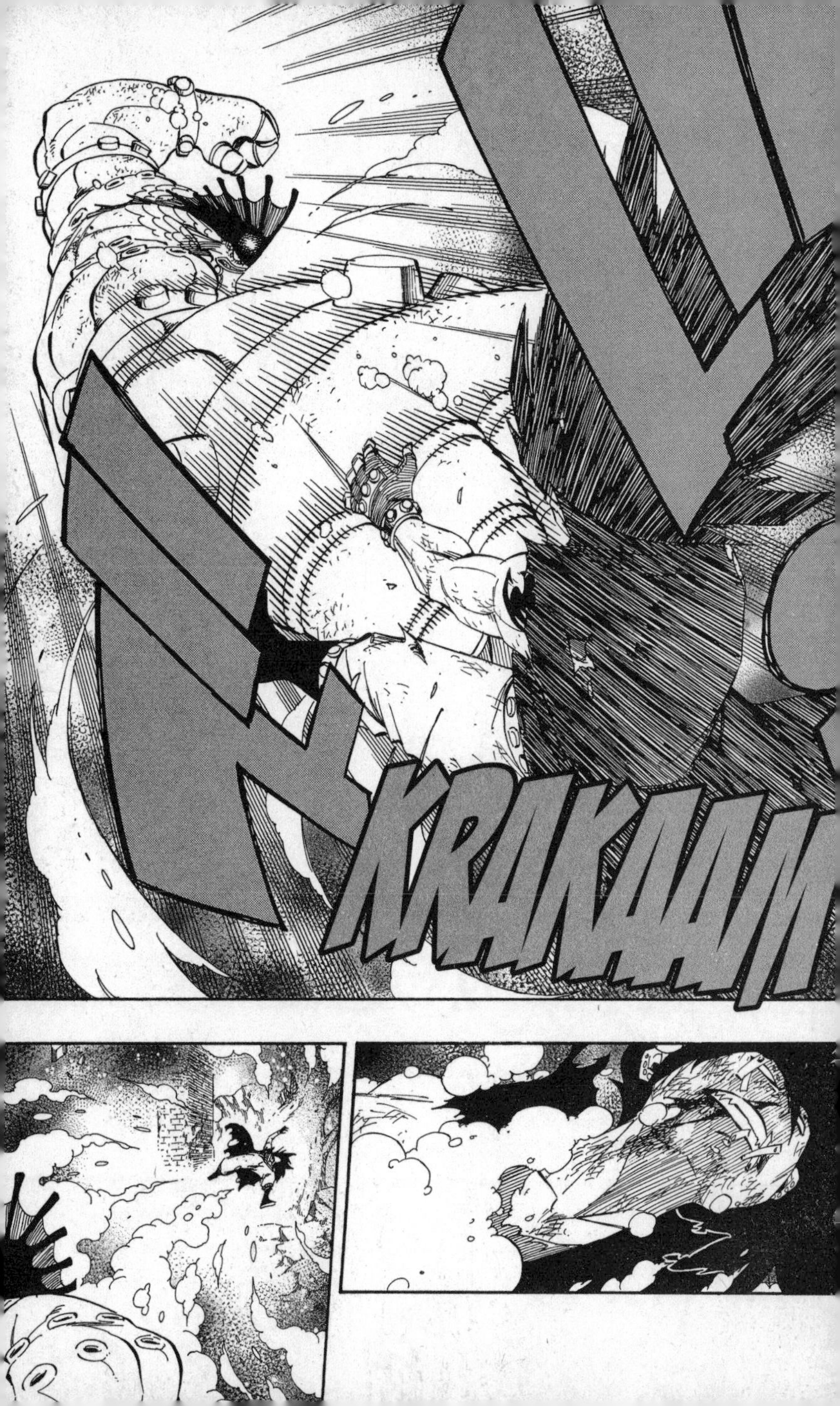
KRAKAAM

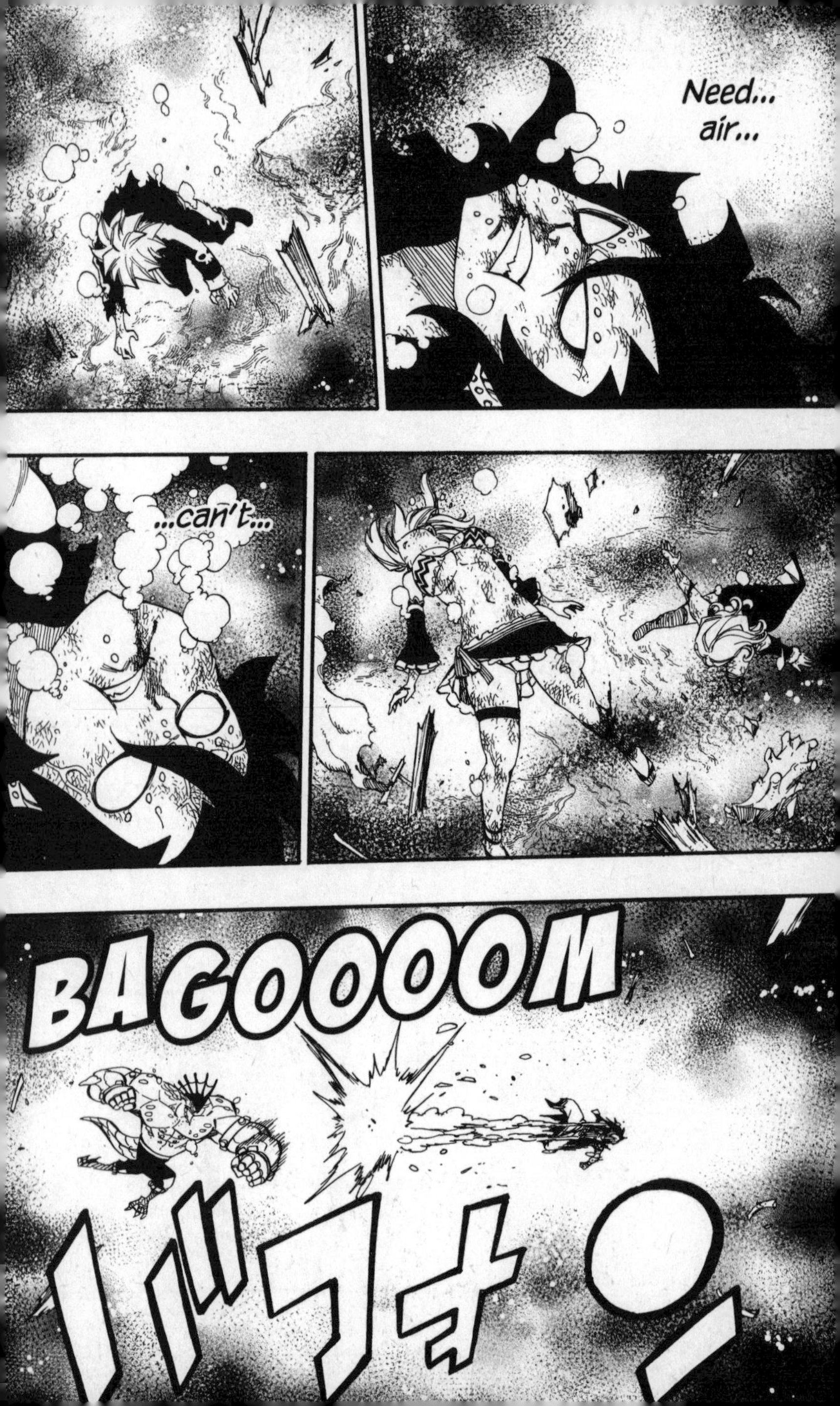
Need... air...
...can't...
BAGOOOOM

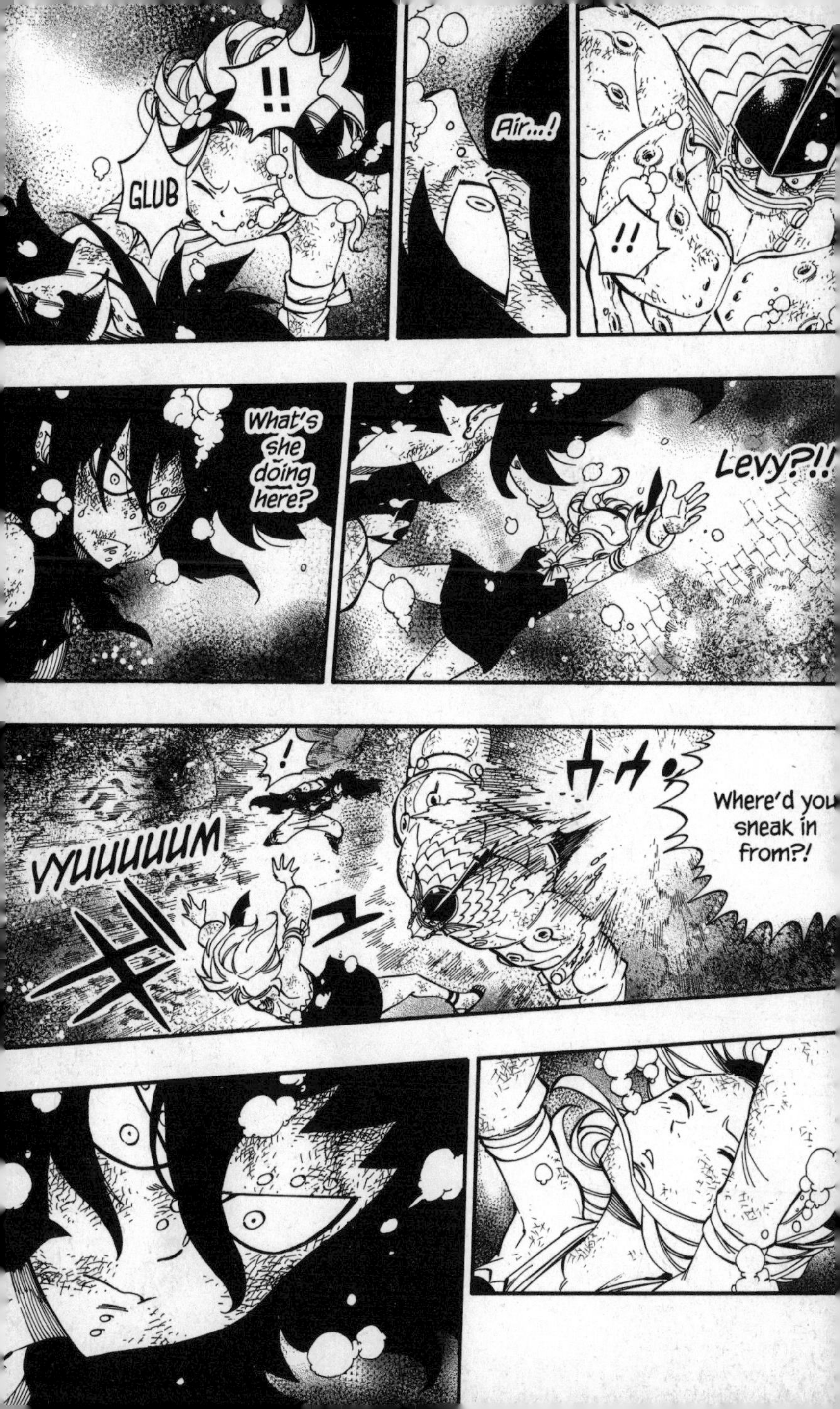

!!
Air...!
!!
GLUB
Levy?!!
What's she doing here?
Where'd you sneak in from?!
!
VYUUUUUUM

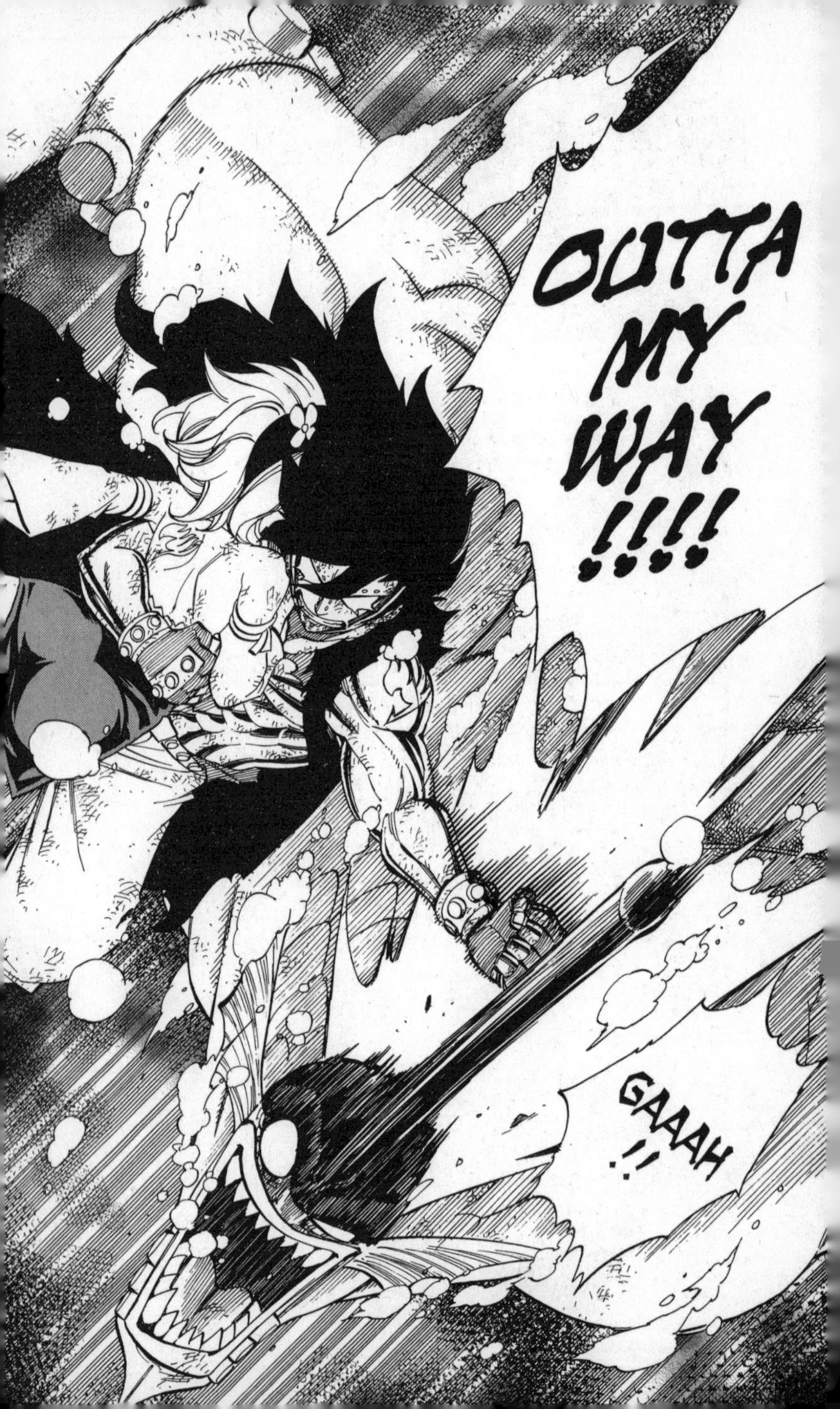
OUTTA MY WAY!!!!
GAAAH!!

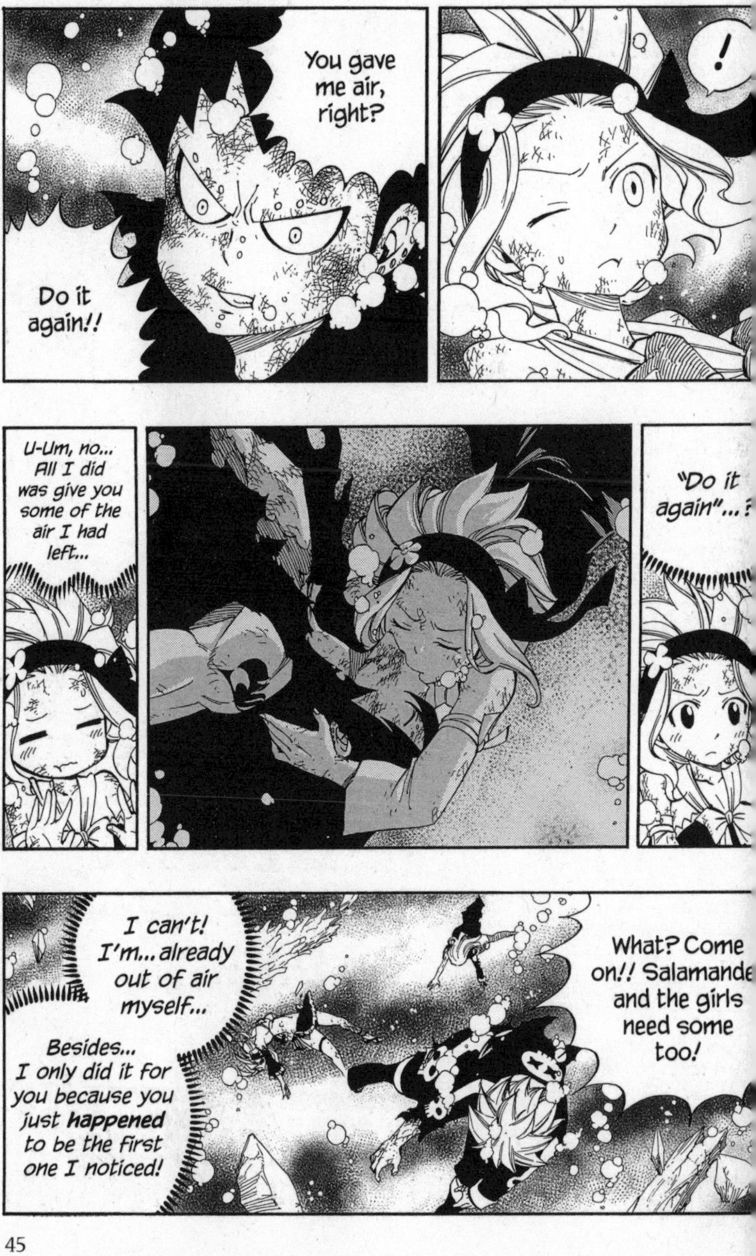
!
You gave me air, right?
Do it again!!
"Do it again"...?
U-Um, no... All I did was give you some of the air I had left...
What? Come on!! Salamande and the girls need some too!
I can't! I'm...already out of air myself...
Besides... I only did it for you because you just **happened** to be the first one I noticed!

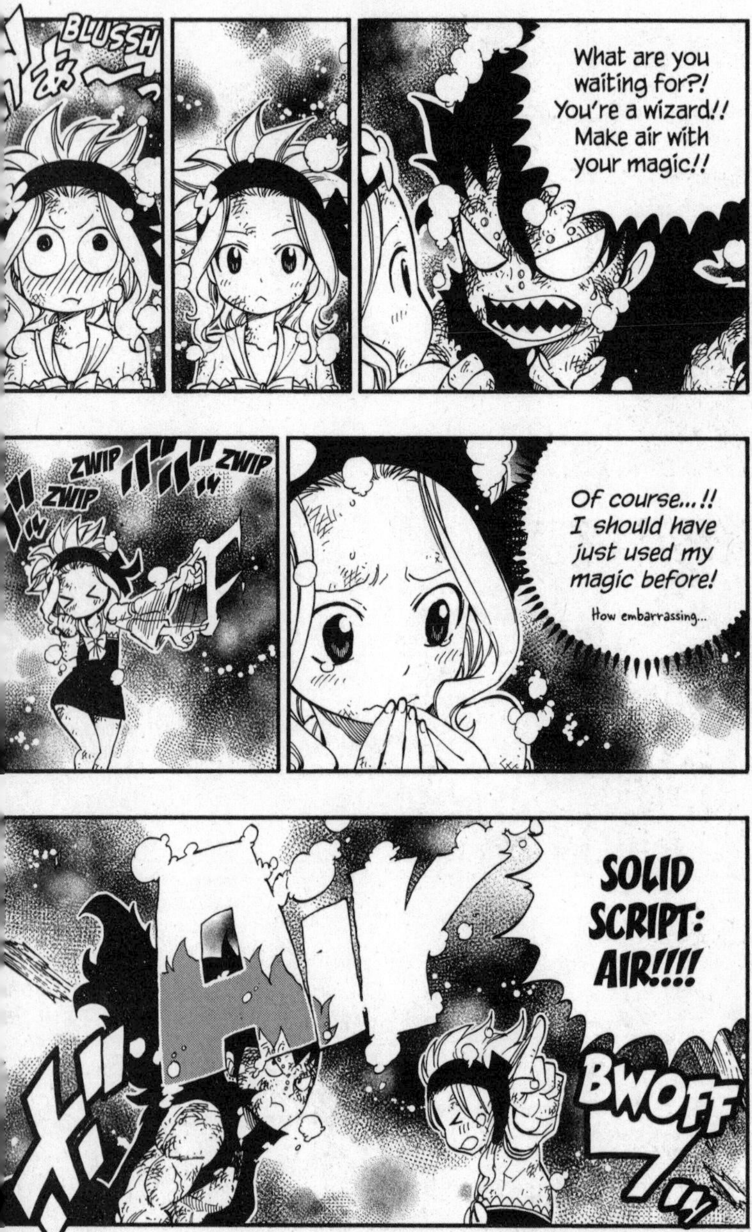
What are you waiting for?! You're a wizard!! Make air with your magic!!
BLUSSH
Of course...!! I should have just used my magic before!
How embarrassing...
ZWIP
ZWIP
ZWIP
SOLID SCRIPT: AIR!!!!
BWOFF

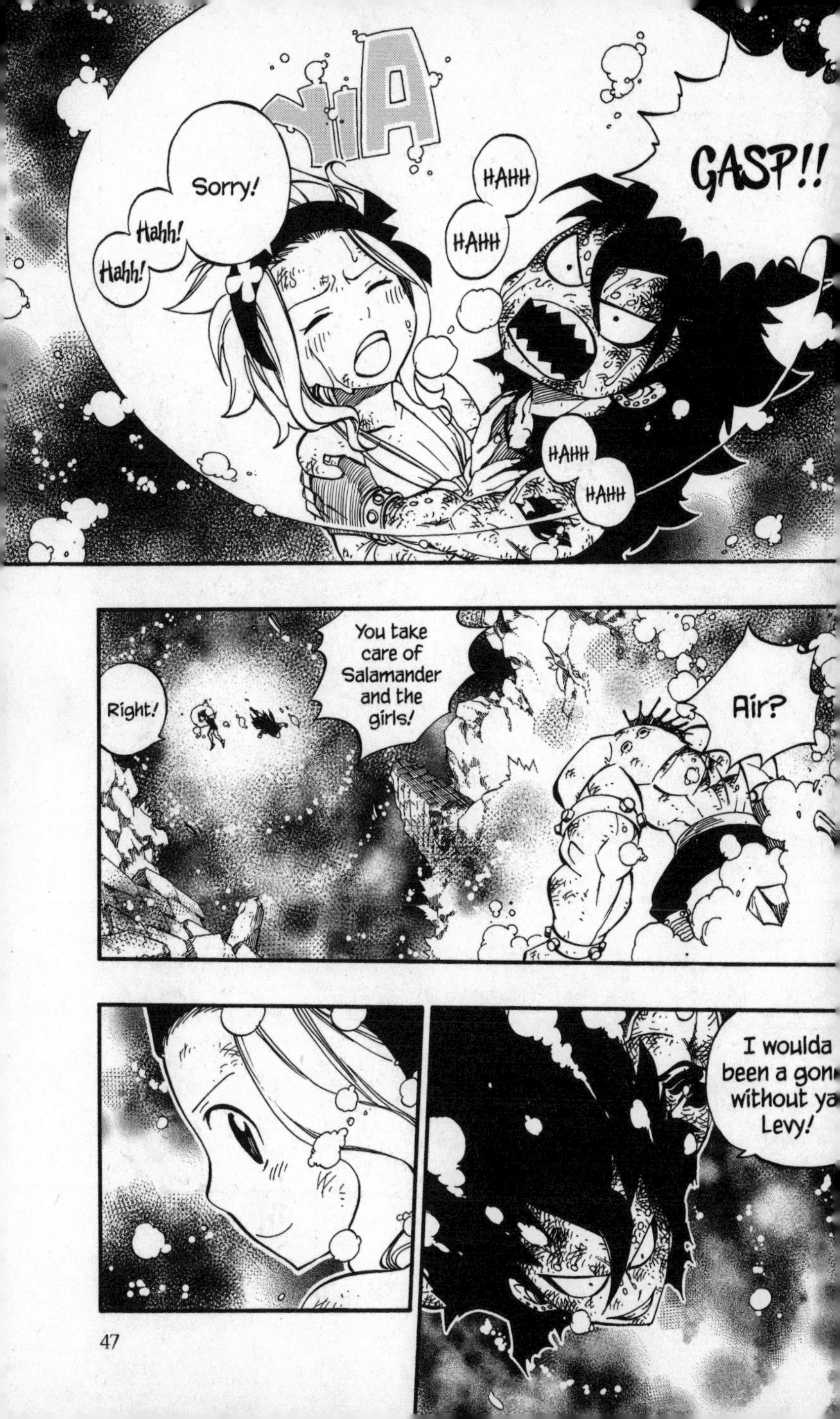
GASP!!
HAHH
HAHH
HAHH
HAHH
YIIA
Sorry!
Hahh!
Hahh!
Air?
You take care of Salamander and the girls!
Right!
I woulda been a gon without ya Levy!

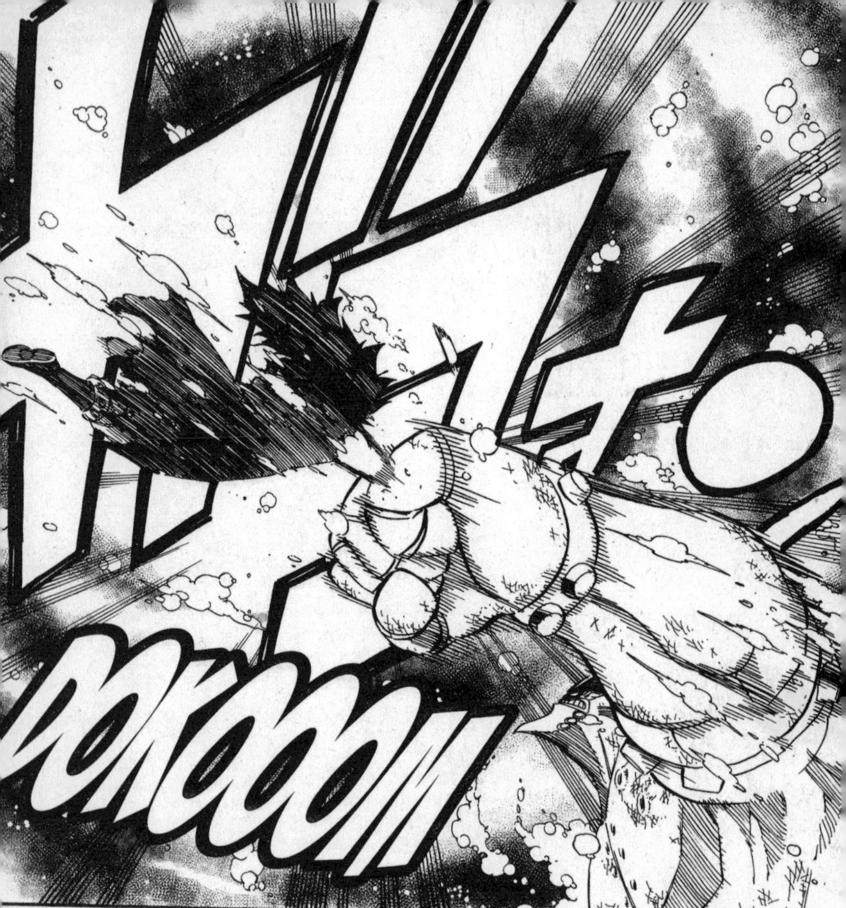

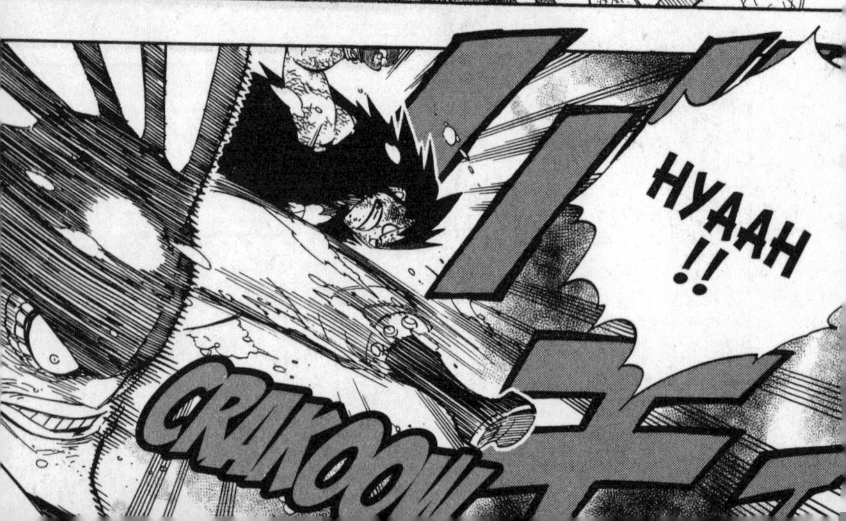
HYAAH!!

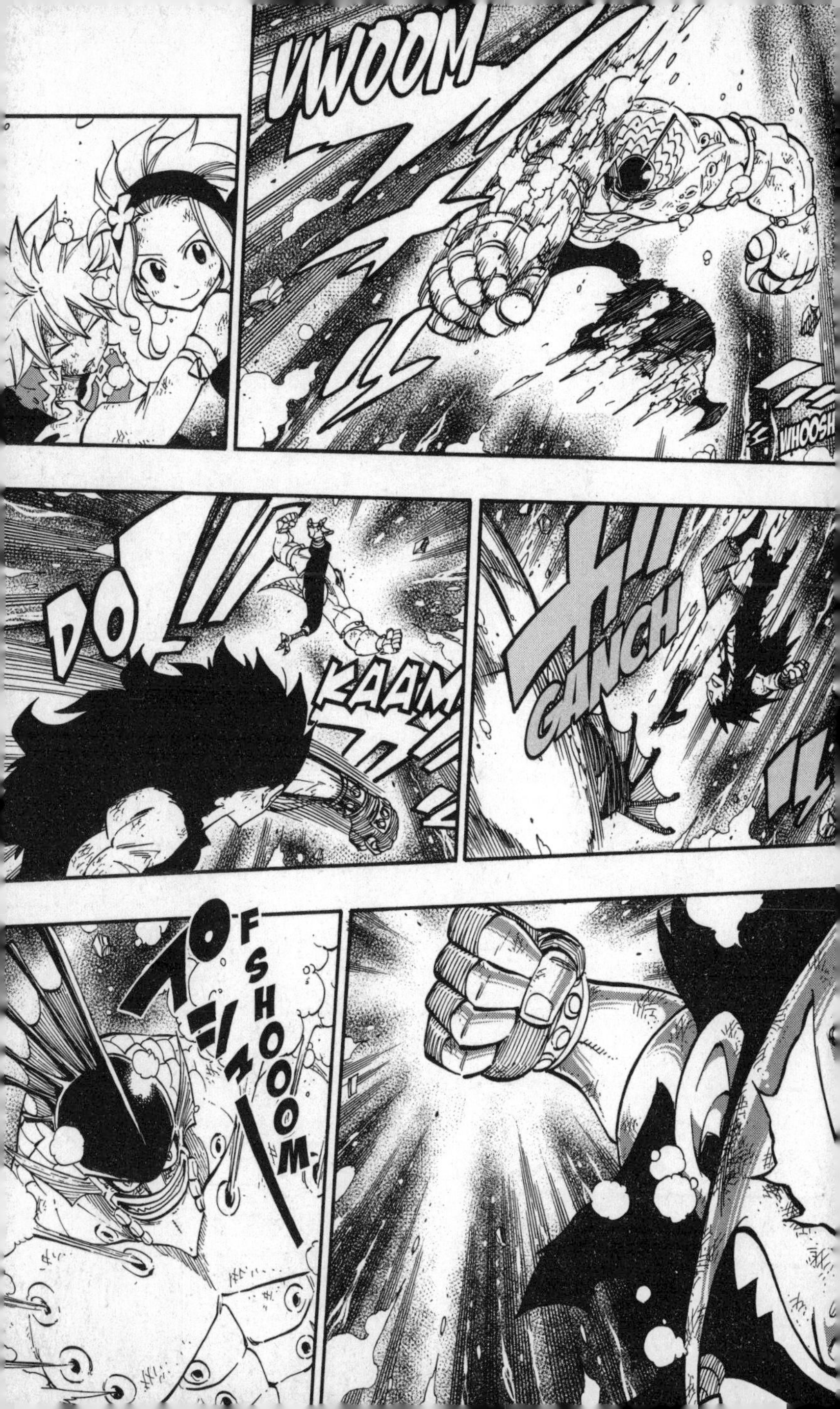
VWOOM
WHOOSH
GANCH
KAAM
DO
FSHOOOOM

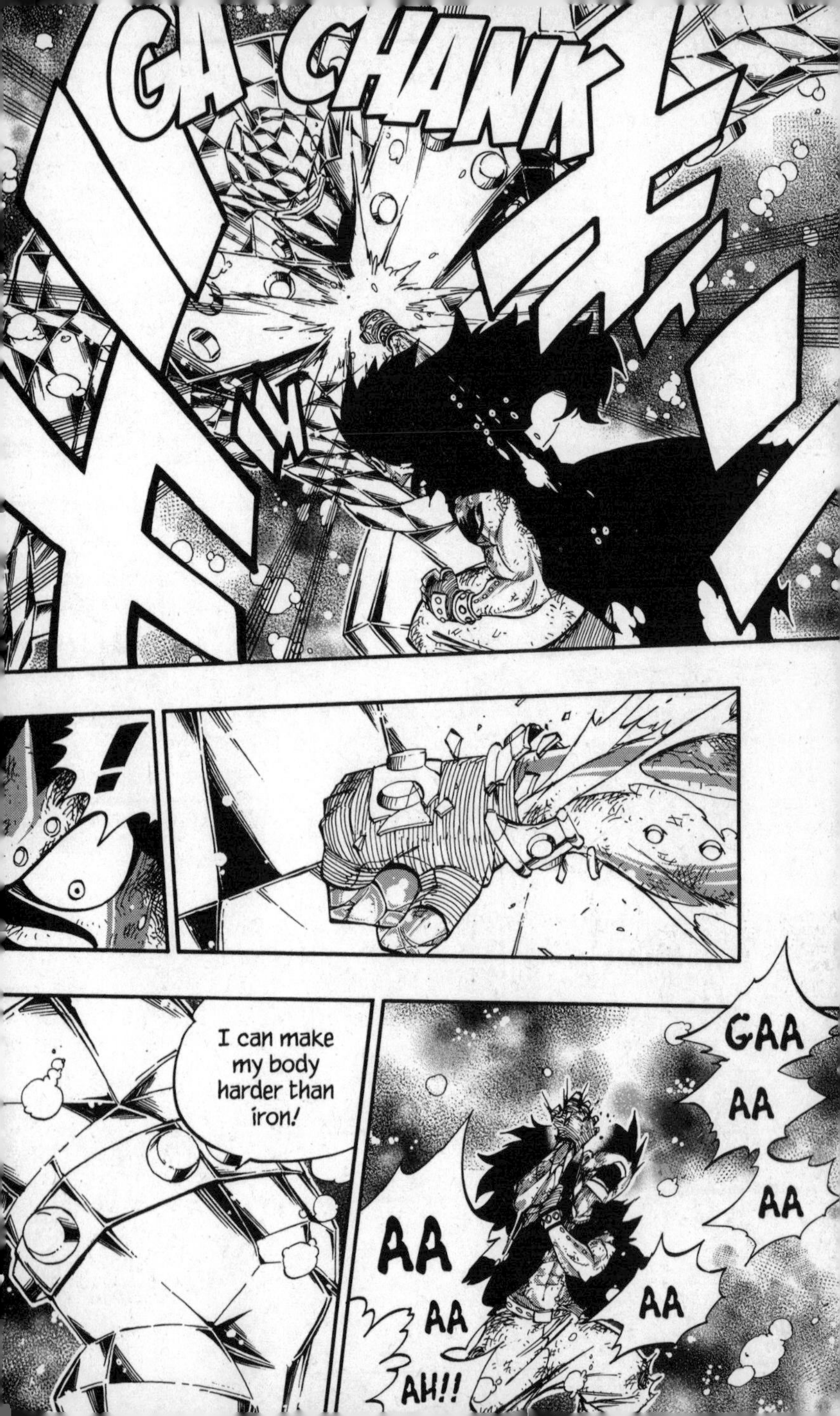
GA CHANK
GAA
AA
AA
AA
AA
AA
AH!!
I can make my body harder than iron!

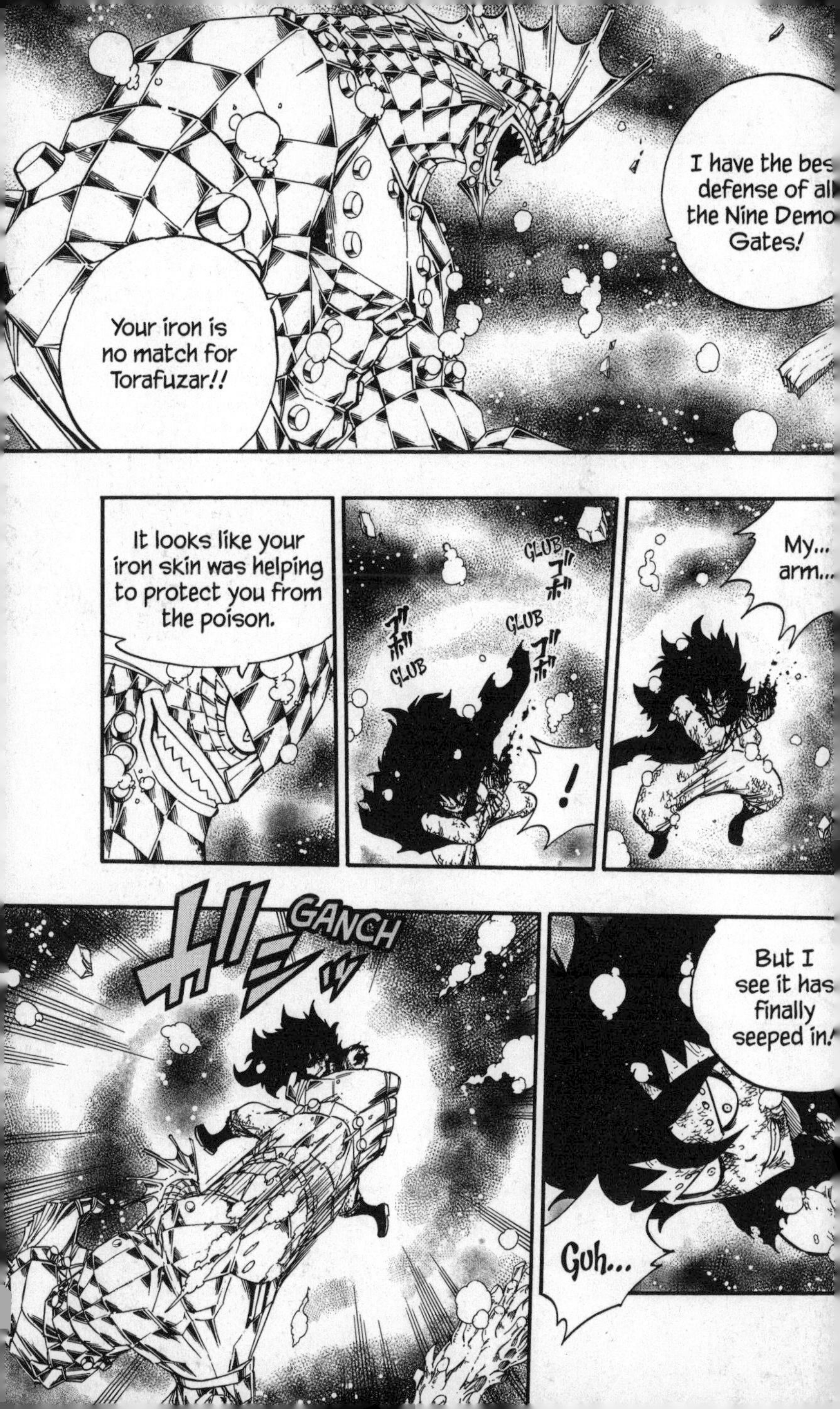
I have the bes defense of all the Nine Demo Gates!
Your iron is no match for Torafuzar!!
My... arm...
GLUB
GLUB
GLUB
!
It looks like your iron skin was helping to protect you from the poison.
But I see it has finally seeped in!
Guh...
GANCH

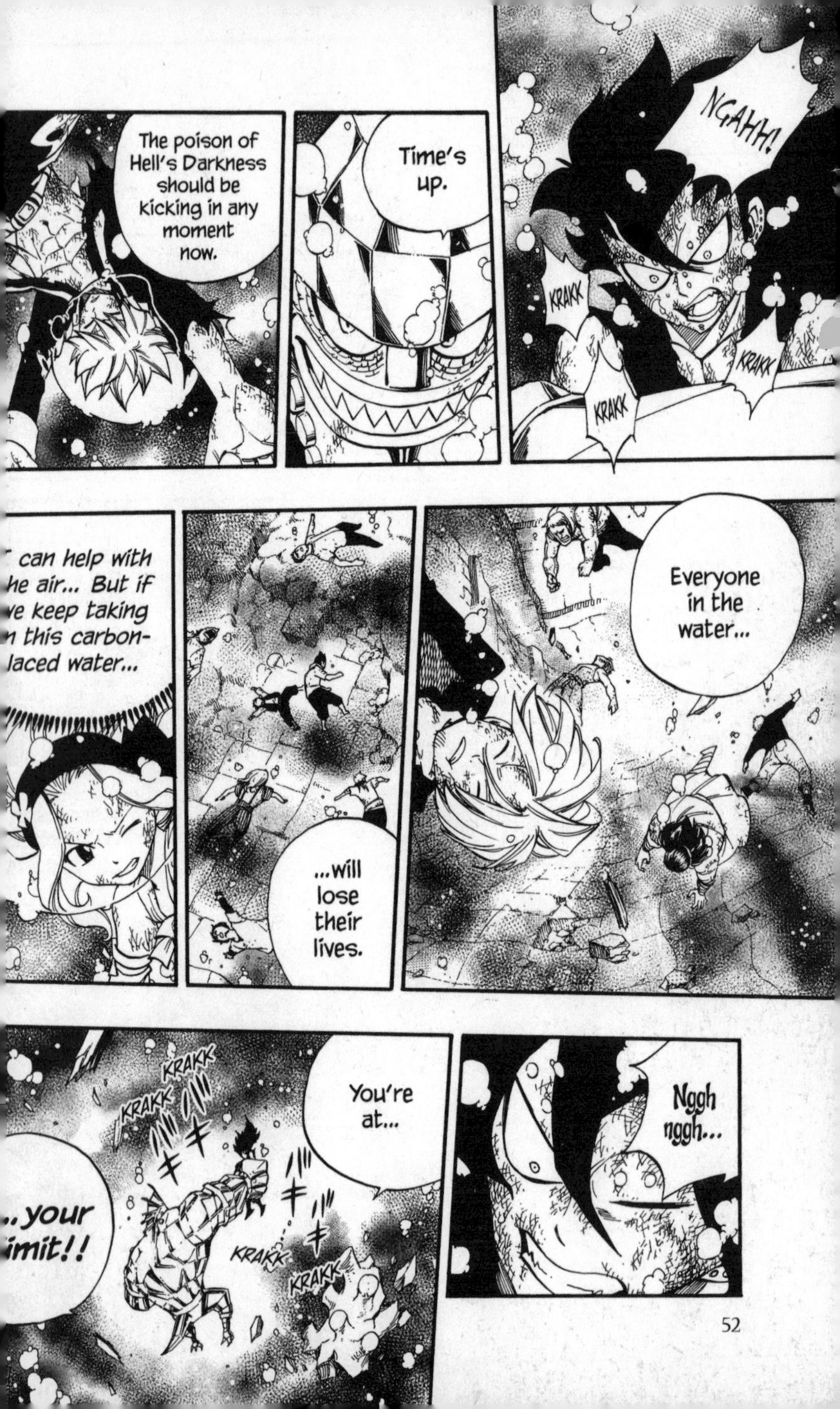
NGAHH!
KRAKK
KRAKK
KRAKK
Time's up.
The poison of Hell's Darkness should be kicking in any moment now.
Everyone in the water...
...will lose their lives.
can help with he air... But if ve keep taking n this carbon-laced water...
Nggh nggh...
You're at...
KRAKK
KRAKK
KRAKK
KRAKK
..your imit!!

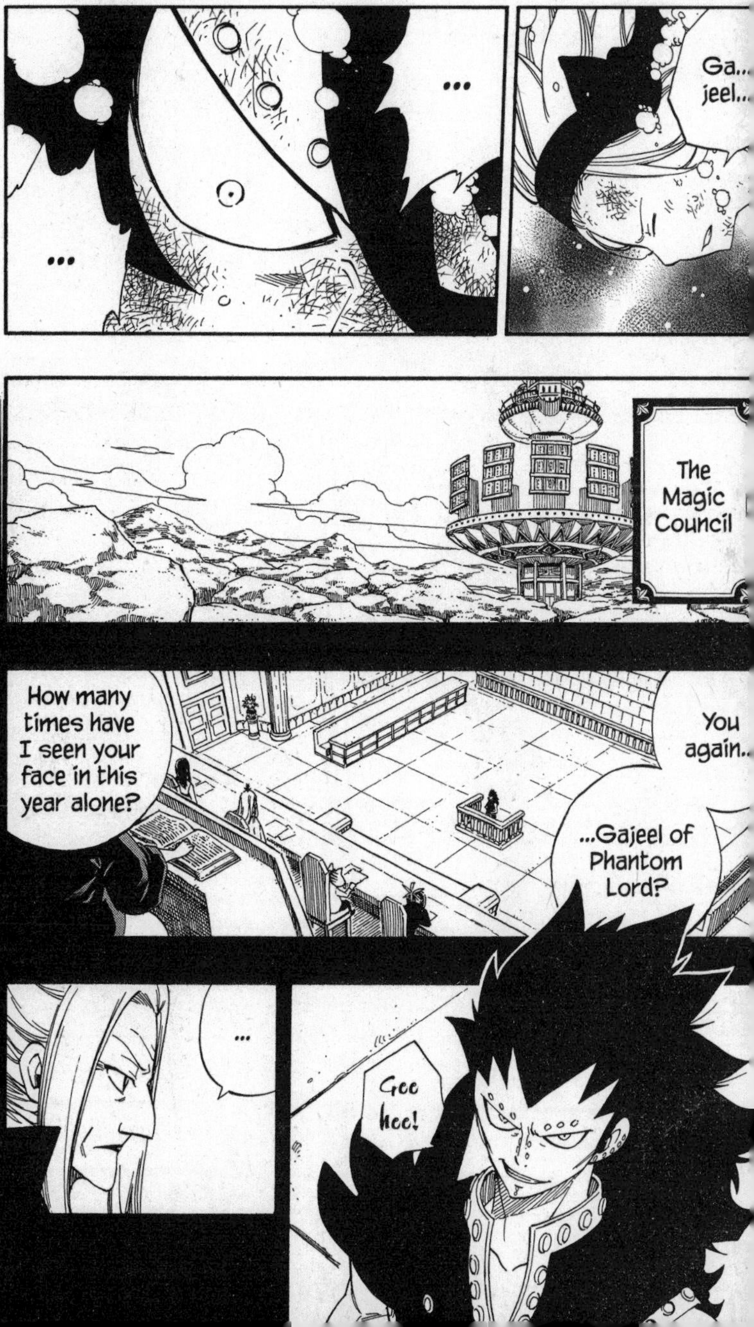

Ga... jeel...
...
...
The Magic Council
You again...
...Gajeel of Phantom Lord?
How many times have I seen your face in this year alone?
Gee hee!
...

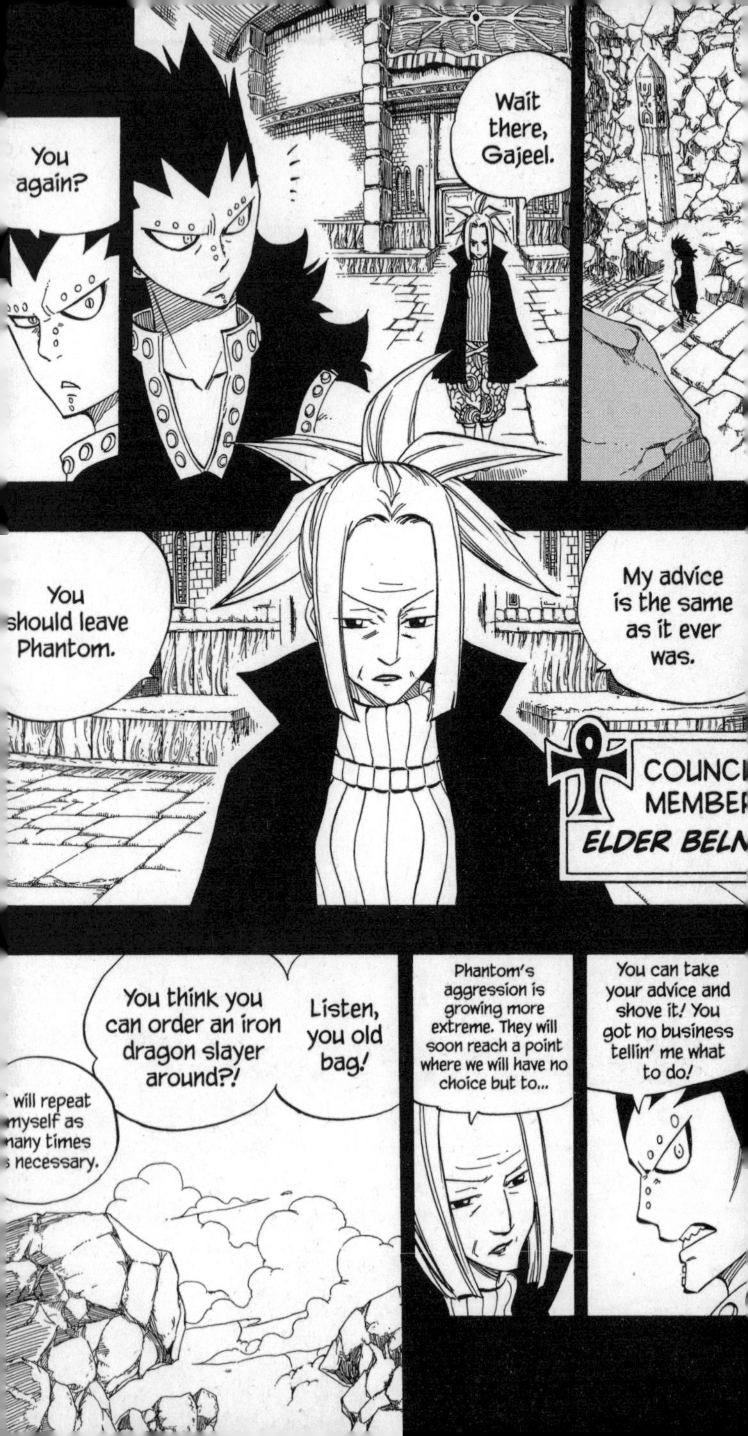

Wait there, Gajeel.
You again?
My advice is the same as it ever was.
You should leave Phantom.
COUNC
MEMBE
ELDER BEL
You can take your advice and shove it! You got no business tellin' me what to do!
Phantom's aggression is growing more extreme. They will soon reach a point where we will have no choice but to...
Listen, you old bag!
You think you can order an iron dragon slayer around?!
will repeat myself as many times necessary.

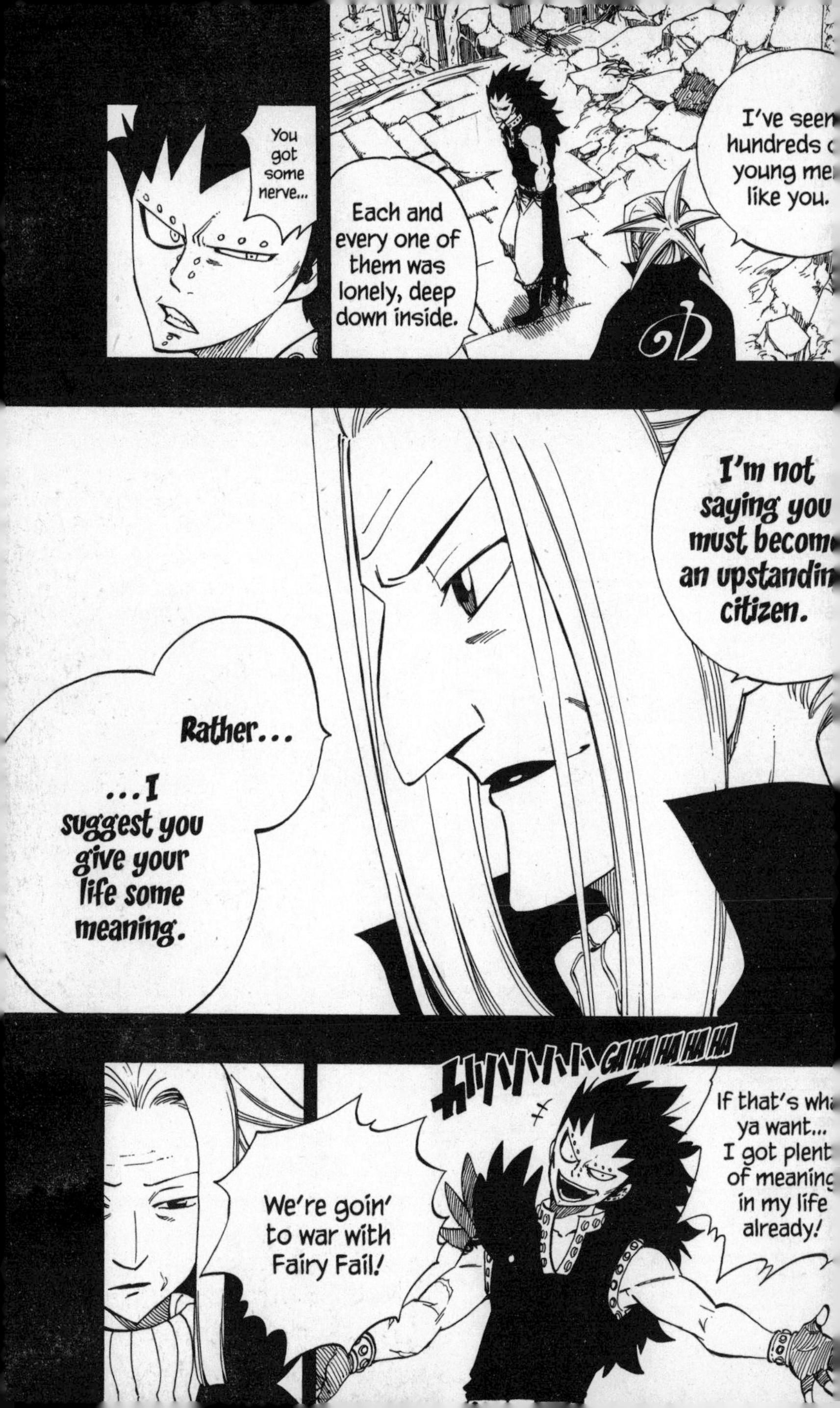

I've seen hundreds o young me like you.
Each and every one of them was lonely, deep down inside.
You got some nerve...
I'm not saying you must becom an upstandin citizen.
Rather...
...I suggest you give your life some meaning.
GA HA HA HA HA
If that's wha ya want... I got plent of meaning in my life already!
We're goin' to war with Fairy Fail!

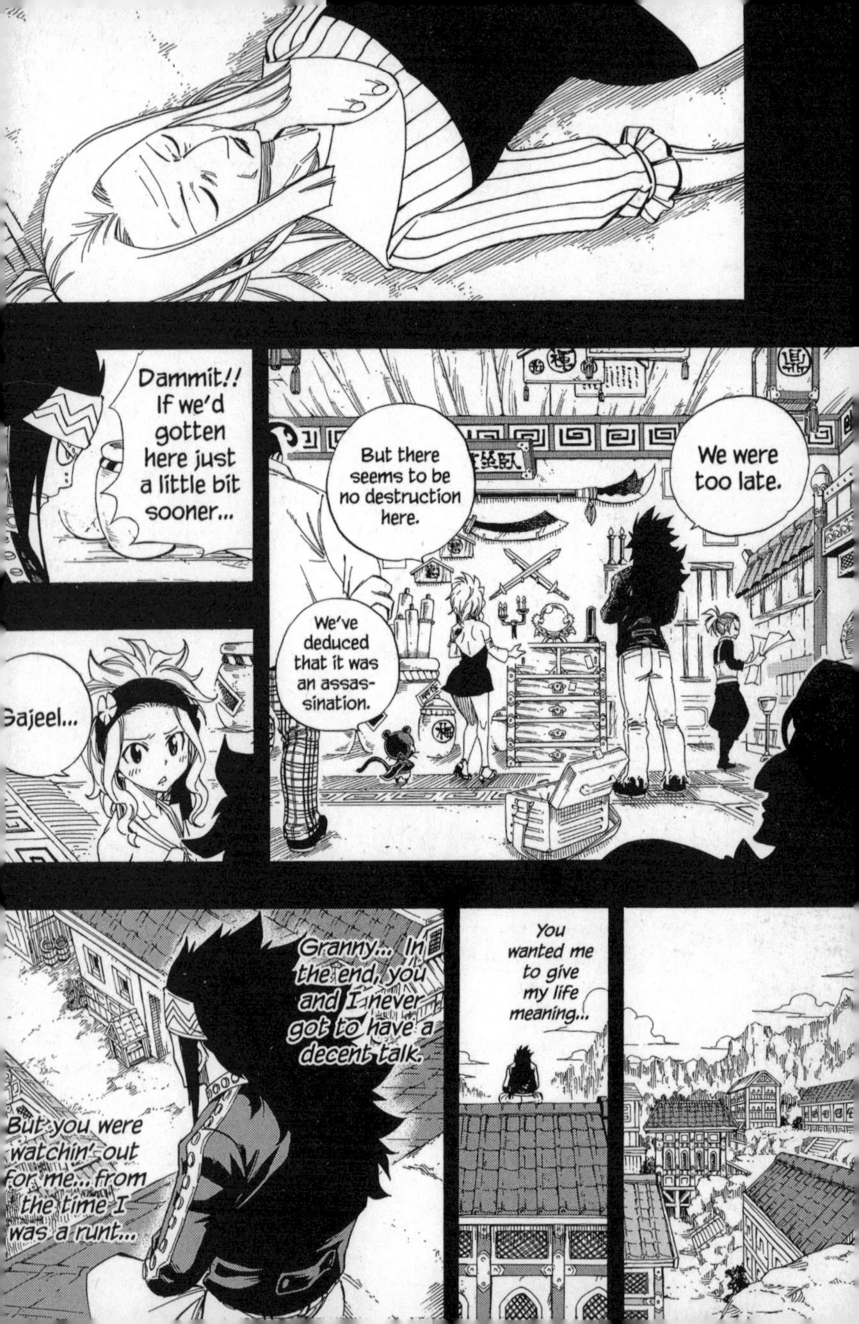
We were too late.
But there seems to be no destruction here.
We've deduced that it was an assas-sination.
Dammit!! If we'd gotten here just a little bit sooner...
Gajeel...
You wanted me to give my life meaning...
Granny... In the end, you and I never got to have a decent talk.
But you were watchin' out for me... from the time I was a runt...

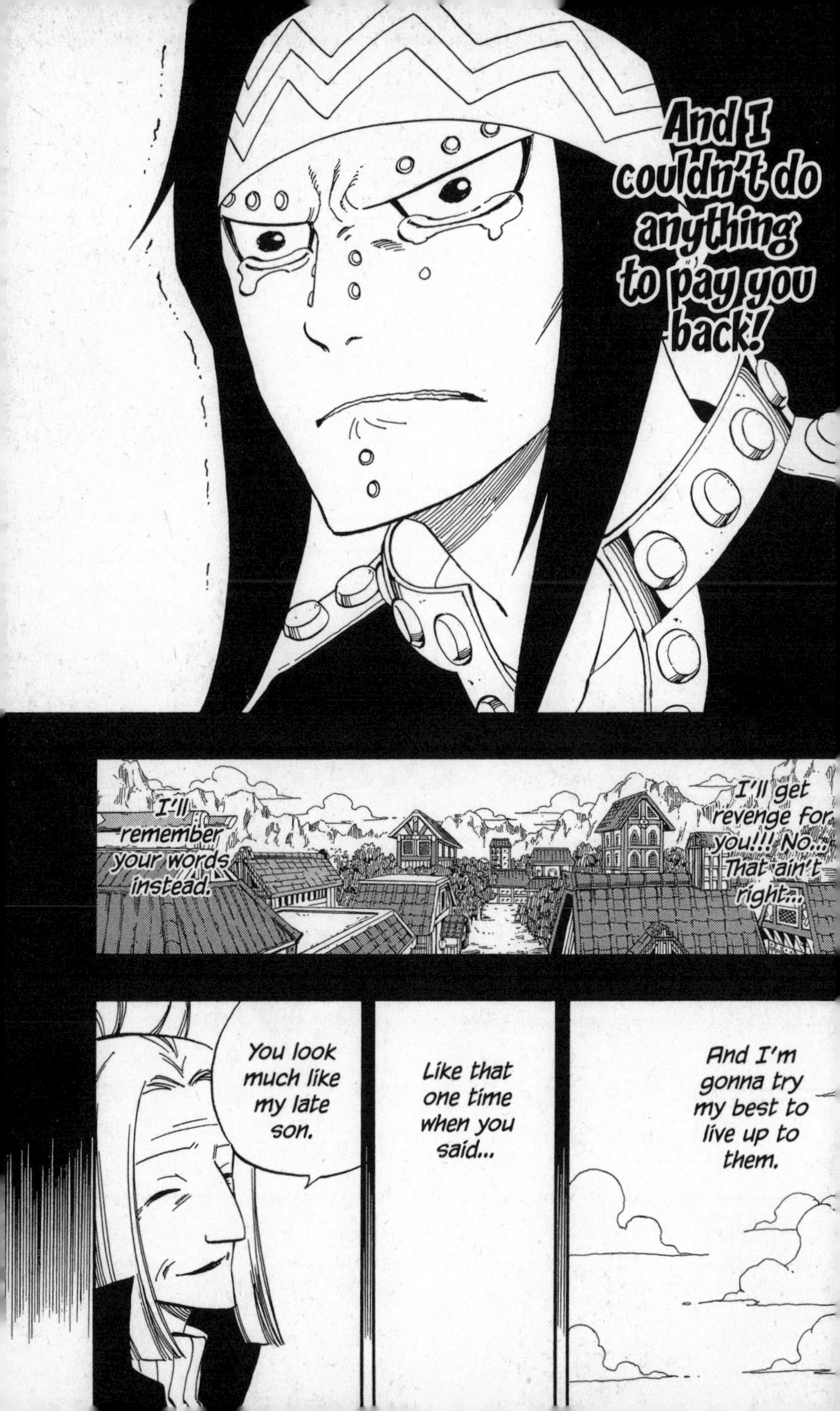
And I couldn't do anything to pay you back!
I'll get revenge for you!!! No... That ain't right...
I'll remember your words instead.
And I'm gonna try my best to live up to them.
Like that one time when you said...
You look much like my late son.

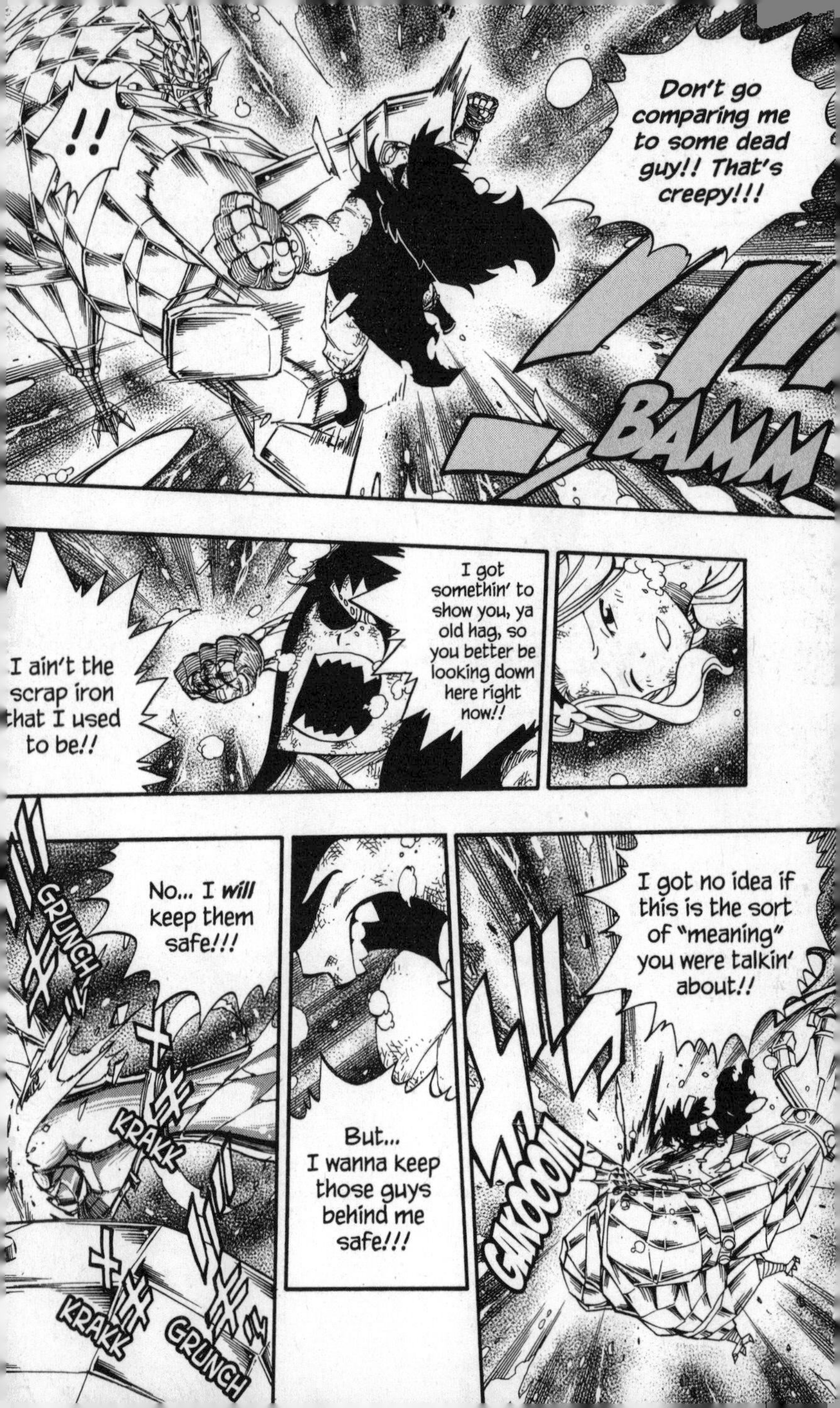
Don't go comparing me to some dead guy!! That's creepy!!!
!!
BAMM
I got somethin' to show you, ya old hag, so you better be looking down here right now!!
I ain't the scrap iron that I used to be!!
I got no idea if this is the sort of "meaning" you were talkin' about!!
GAKOOOM
But... I wanna keep those guys behind me safe!!!
No... I *will* keep them safe!!!
GRUNCH
KRAKK
KRAKK
GRUNCH

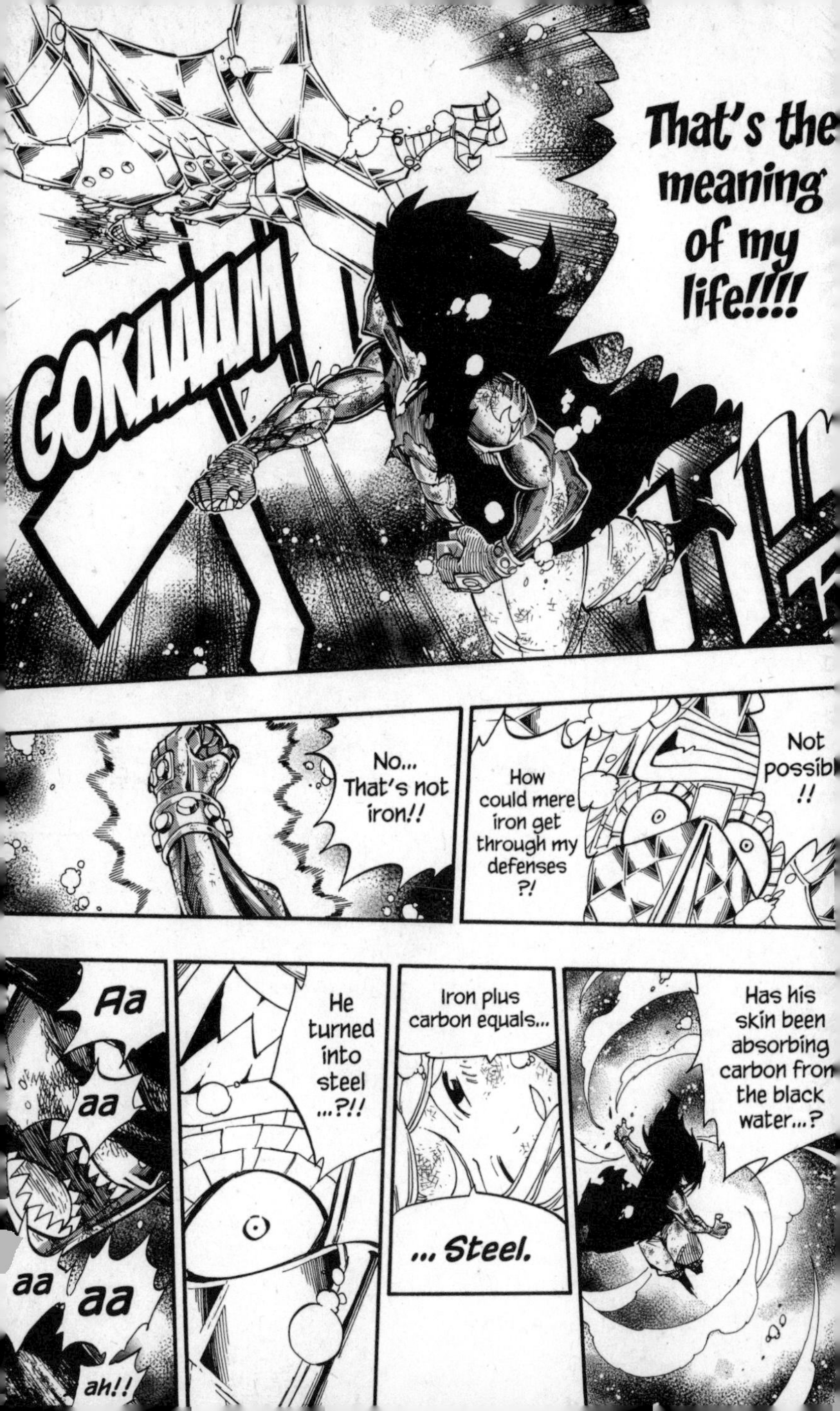
That's the meaning of my life!!!!
GOKAAAM
Not possib !!
How could mere iron get through my defenses ?!
No... That's not iron!!
Has his skin been absorbing carbon from the black water...?
Iron plus carbon equals...
... Steel.
He turned into steel ...?!!
Aa
aa
aa
aa
ah!!

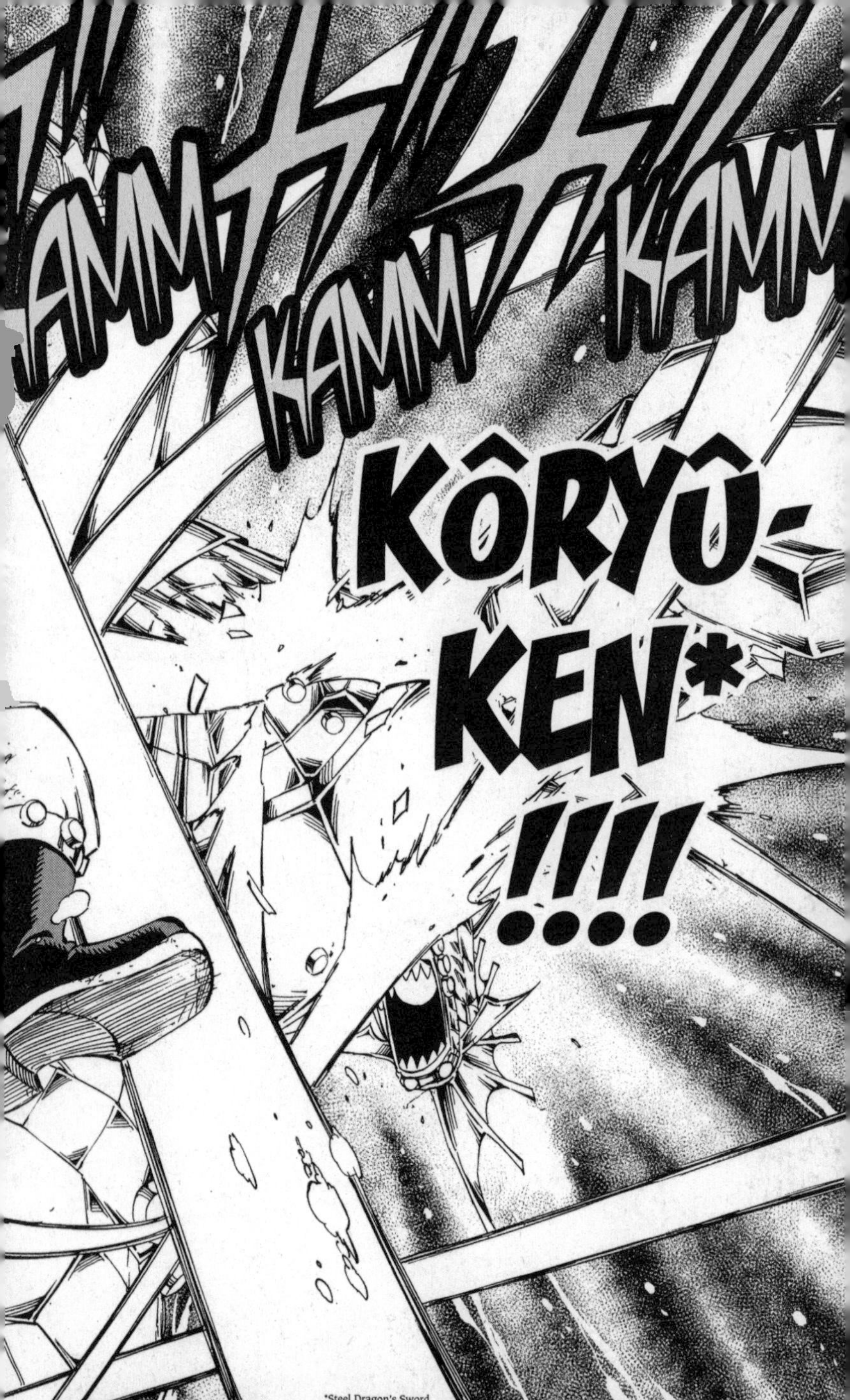
KAMM
KAMM
KÔRYÛ-KEN*!!!!

*Steel Dragon's Sword

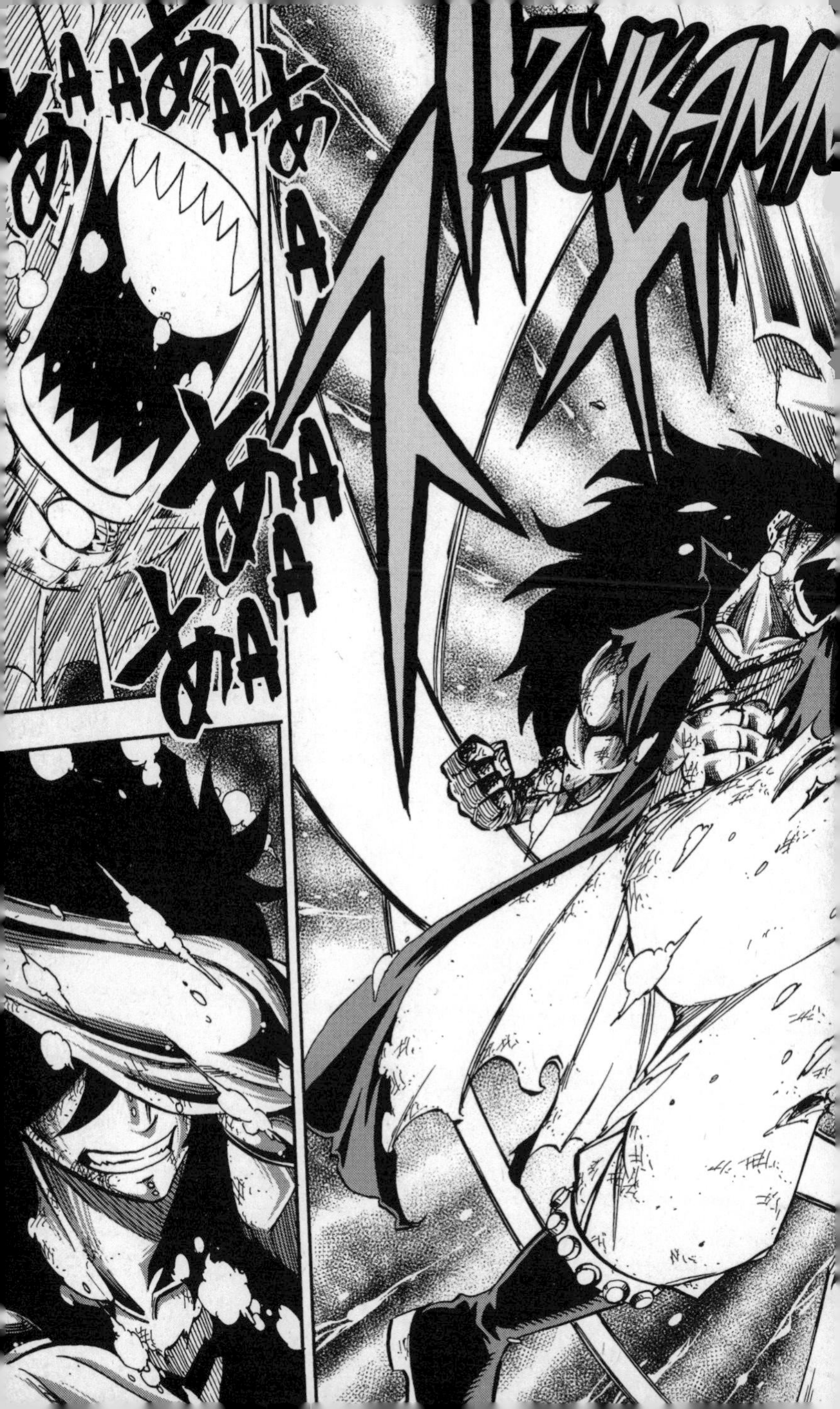
ZUKAM
あAあAあAあAA
あAあAあAA

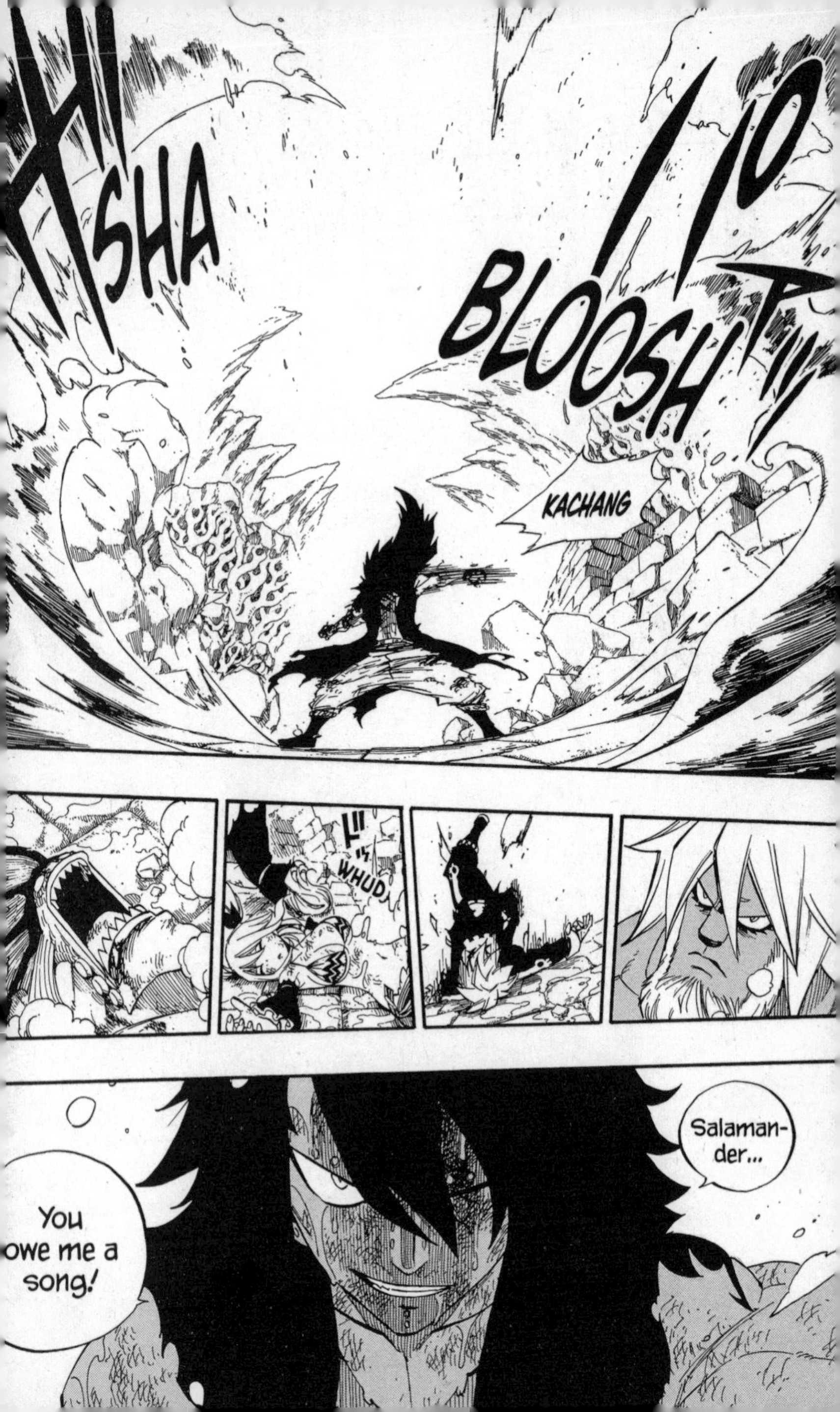
BLOOSH
KACHANG
SHA
WHUD
Salaman-der...
You owe me a song!

FAIRY TAIL

フェアリーテイル

Chapter 398: The Final Duels

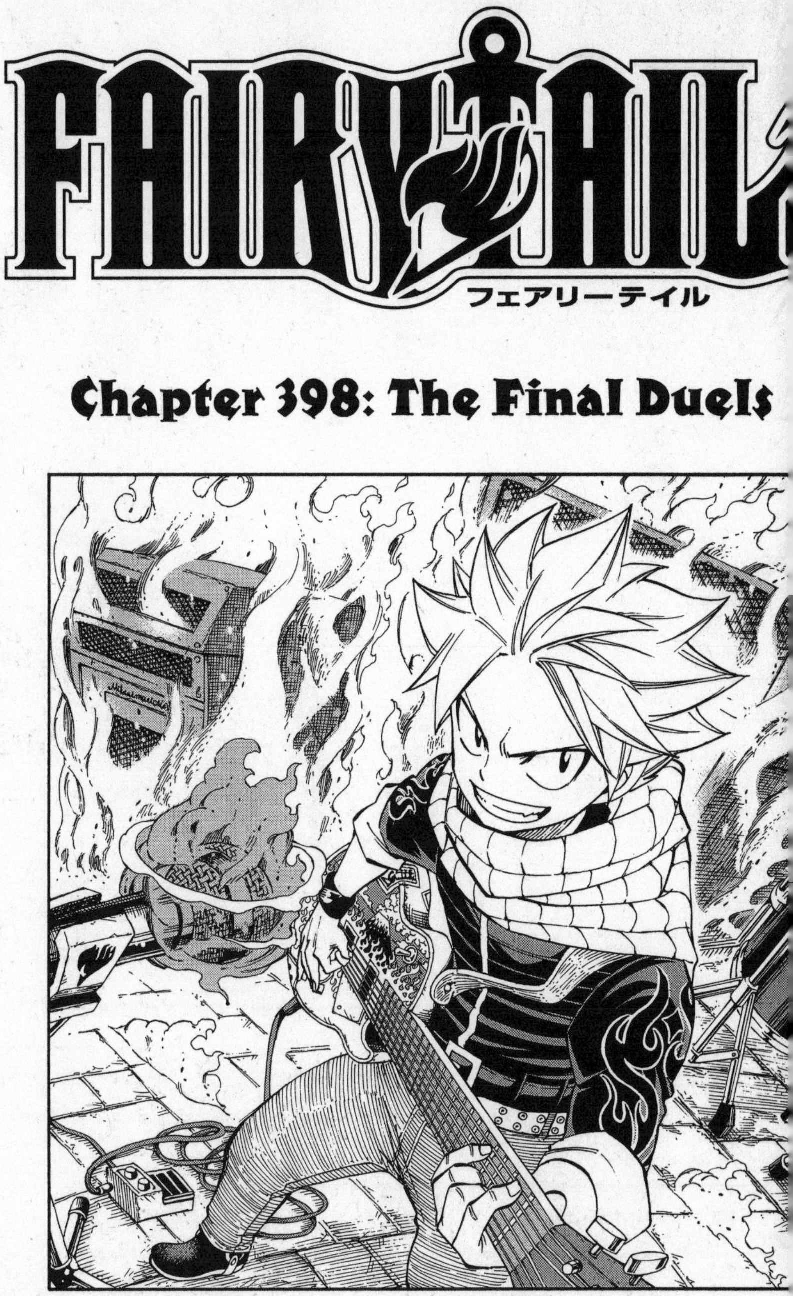

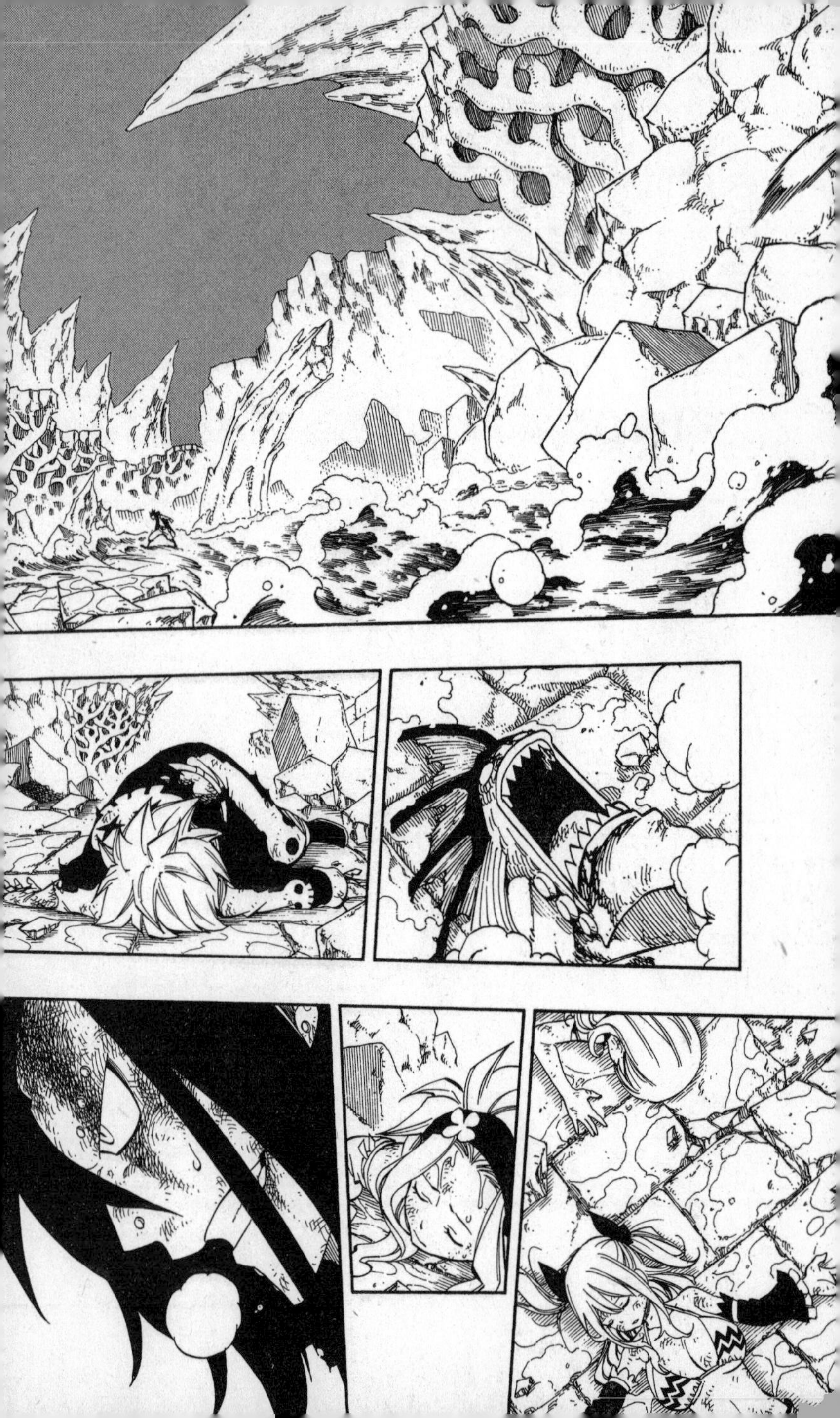

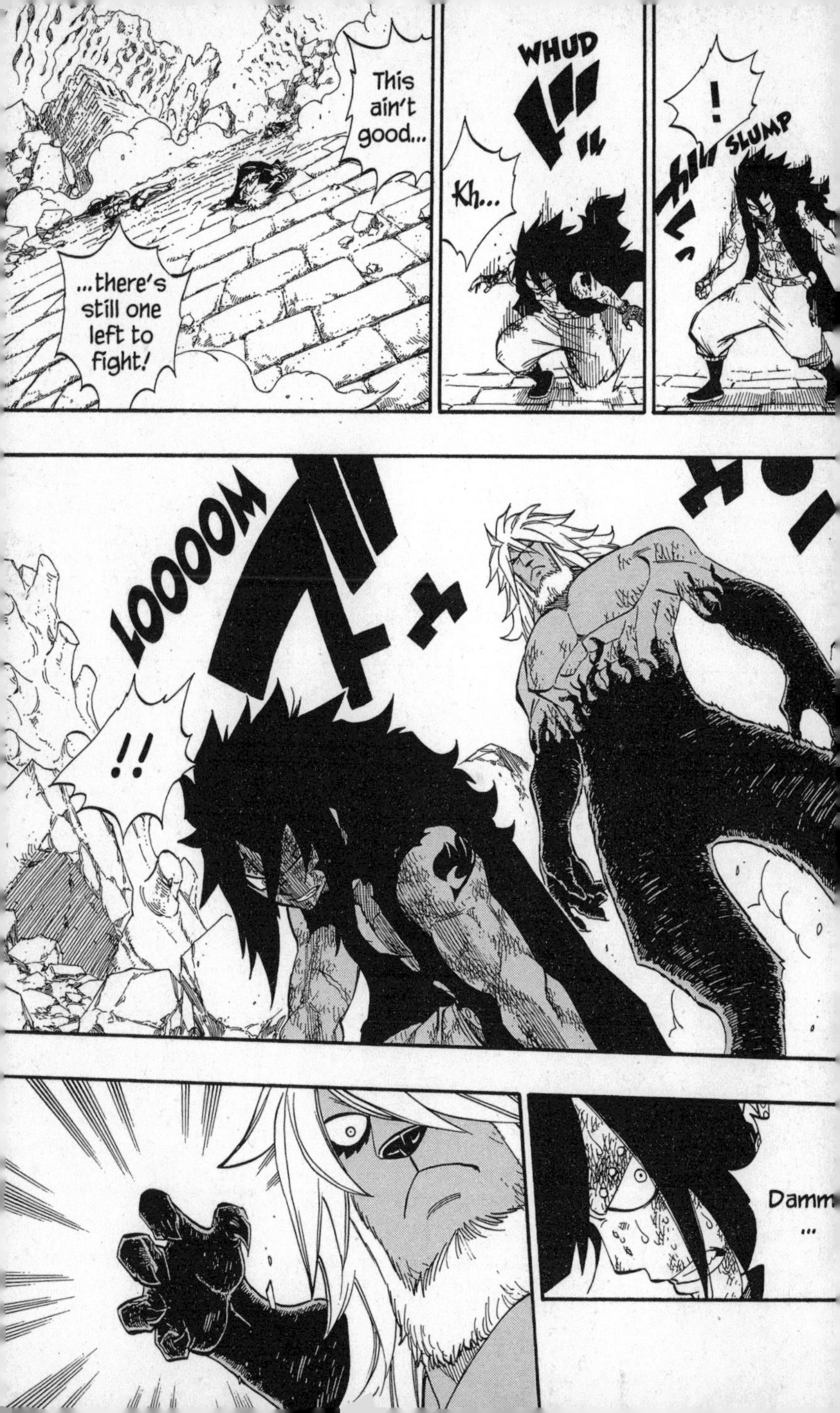
!
SLUMP
WHUD
Kh...
This ain't good...
...there's still one left to fight!
!!
LOOOOM
Damm
...

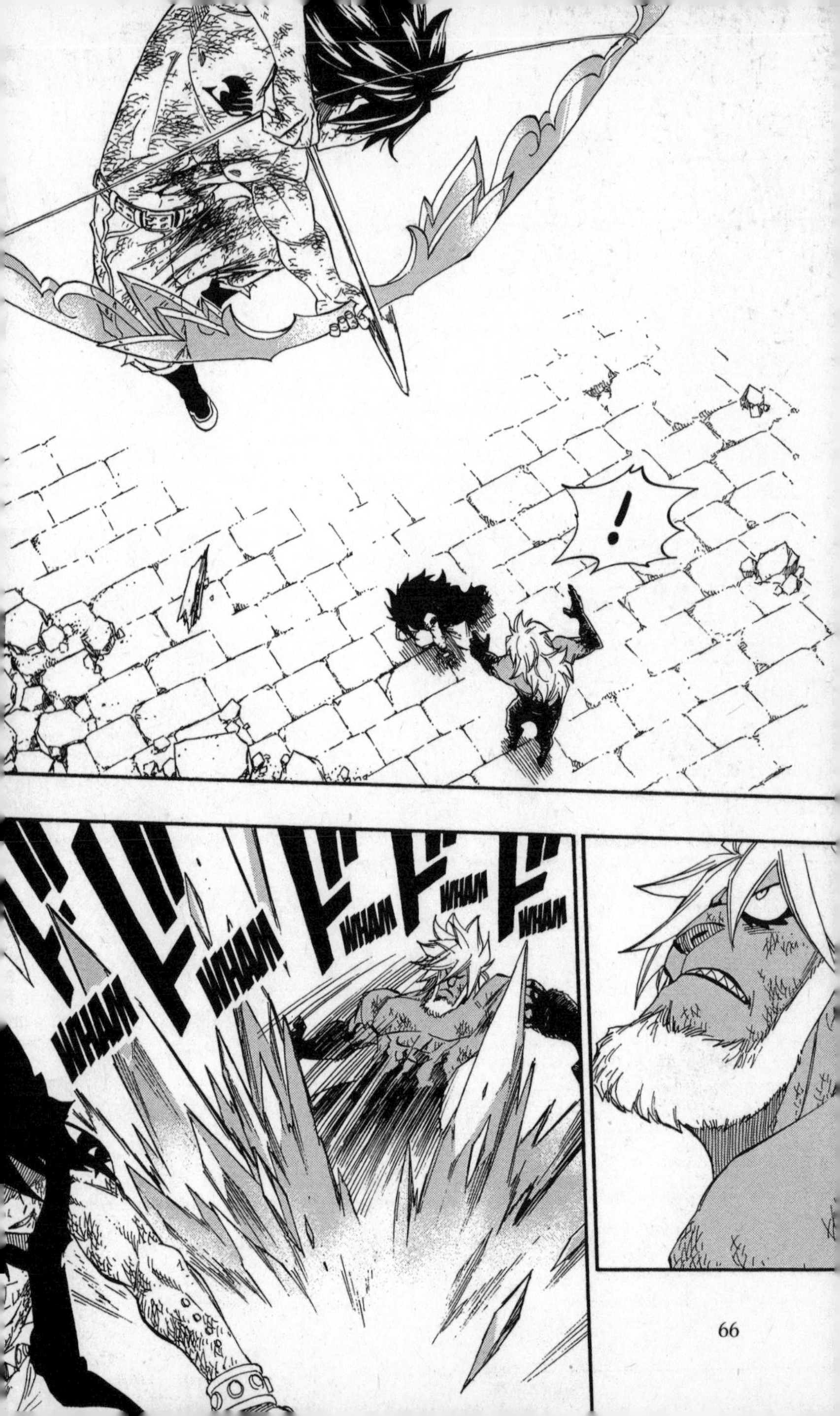
!
WHAM
WHAM
WHAM
WHAM
WHAM

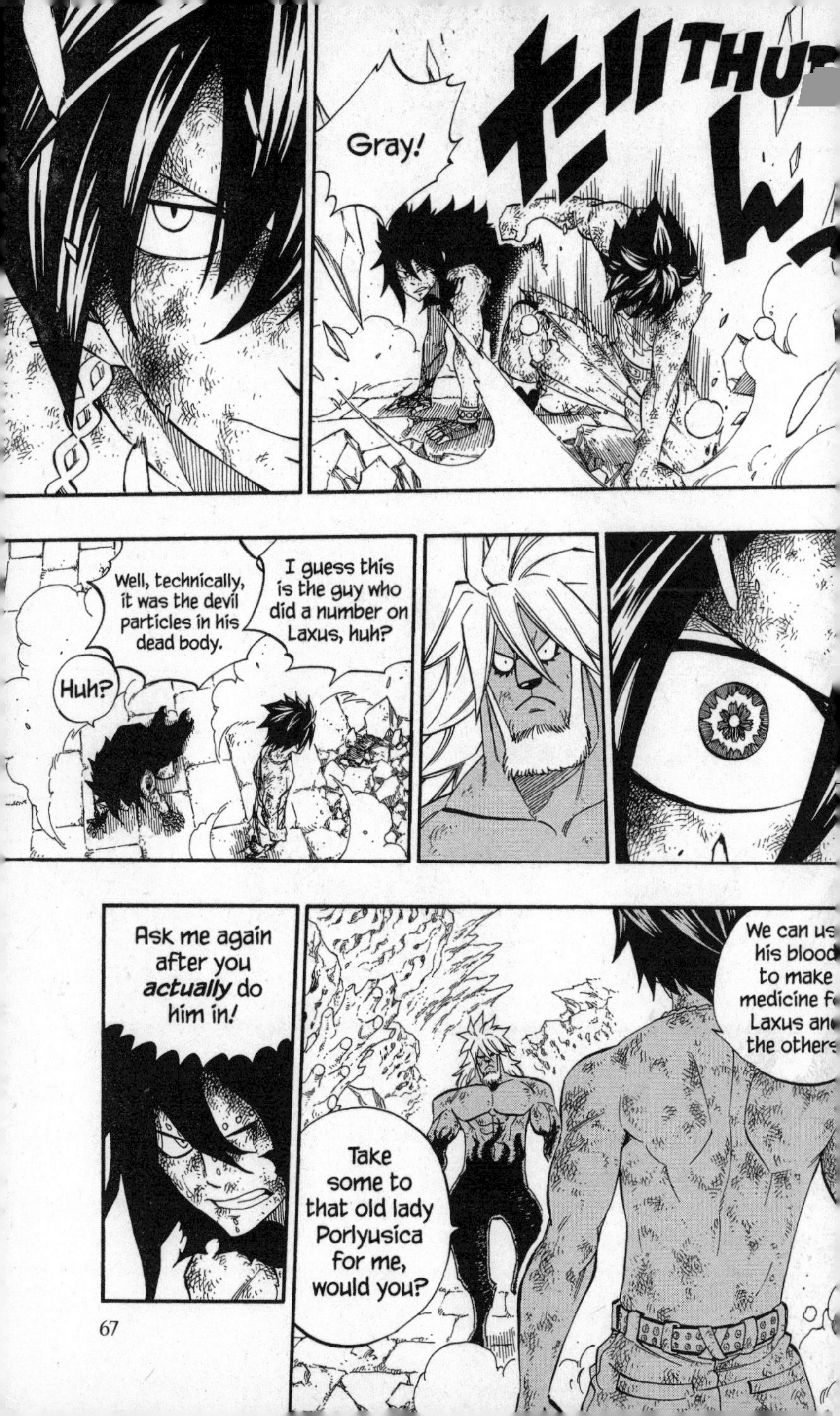

THU
Gray!
I guess this is the guy who did a number on Laxus, huh?
Well, technically, it was the devil particles in his dead body.
Huh?
We can us his blood to make medicine f Laxus an the others
Take some to that old lady Porlyusica for me, would you?
Ask me again after you *actually* do him in!

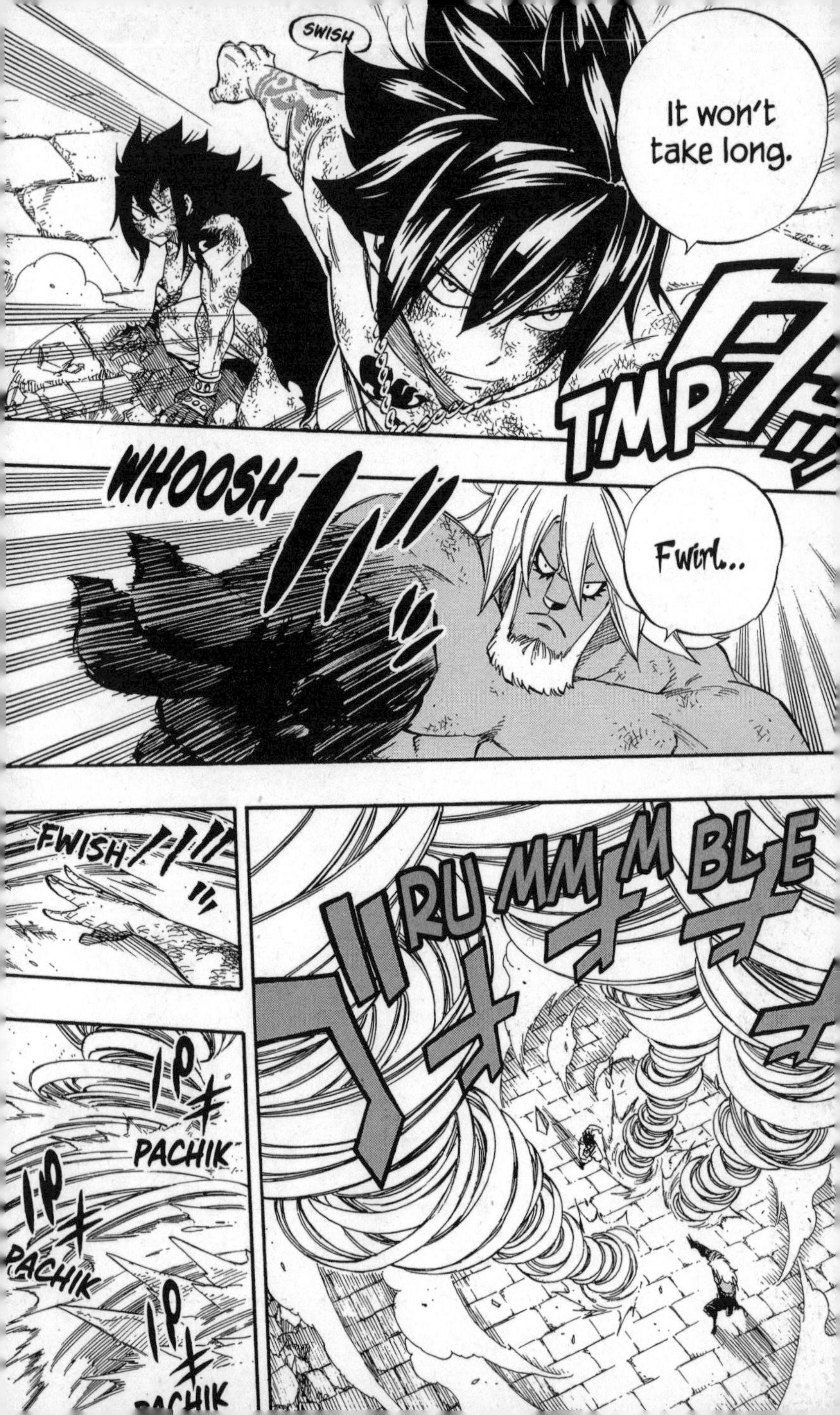
It won't take long.
SWISH
TMP
Fwirl...
WHOOSH
RUMMMBLE
FWISH
PACHIK
PACHIK
PACHIK

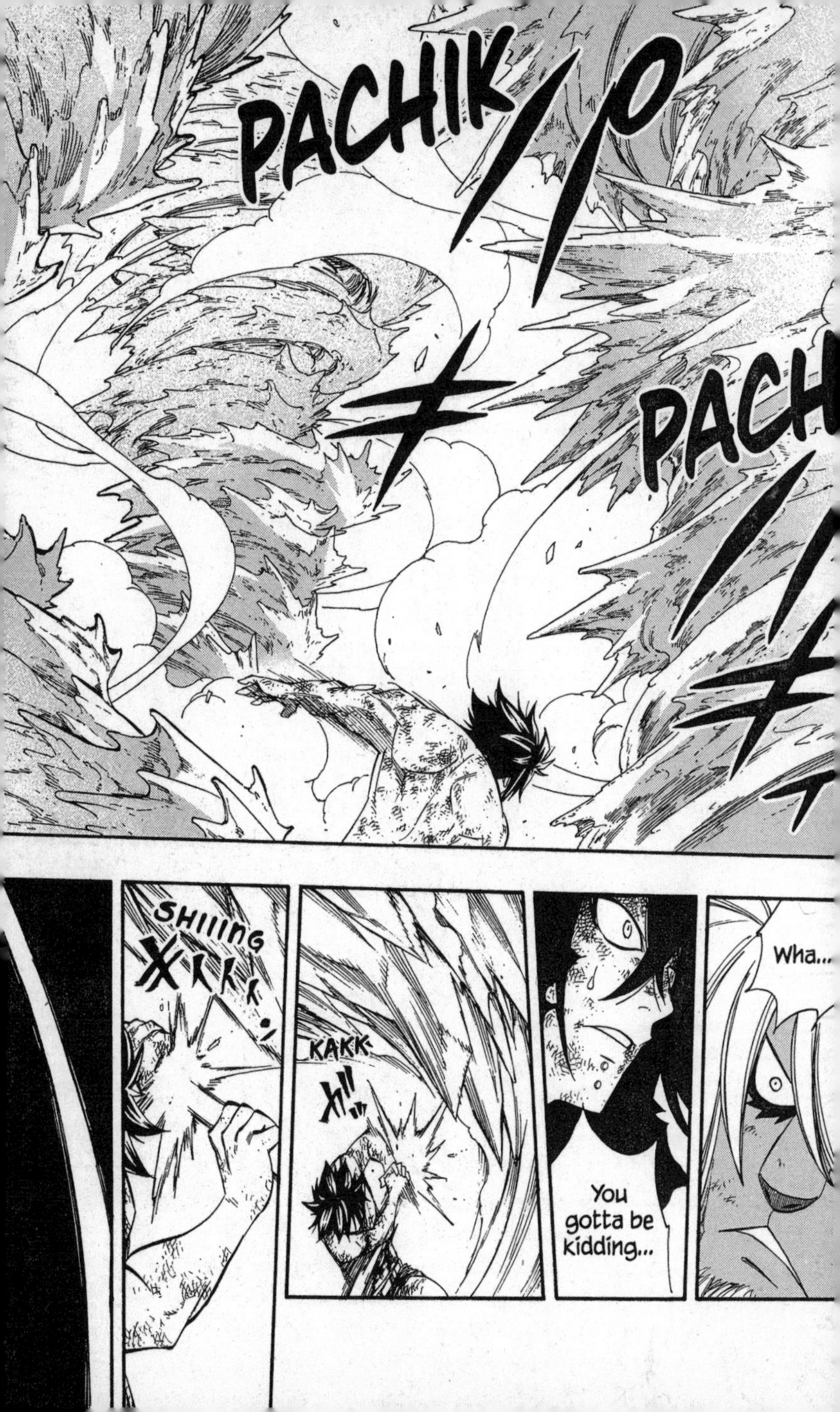
PACHIK
PACH
Wha...
You gotta be kidding...
KAKK
SHIIING

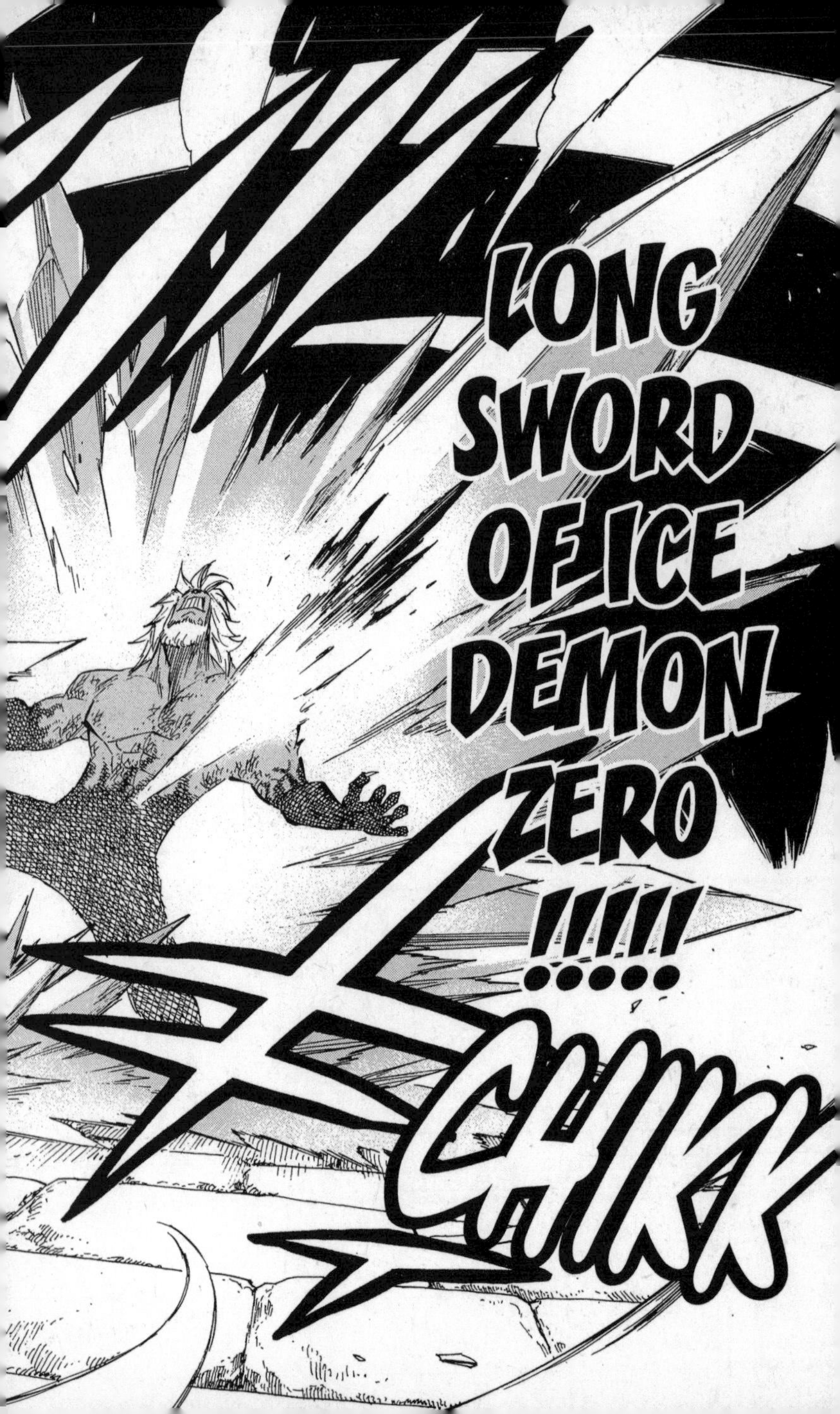
LONG SWORD OF ICE DEMON ZERO!!!!!
CHKK

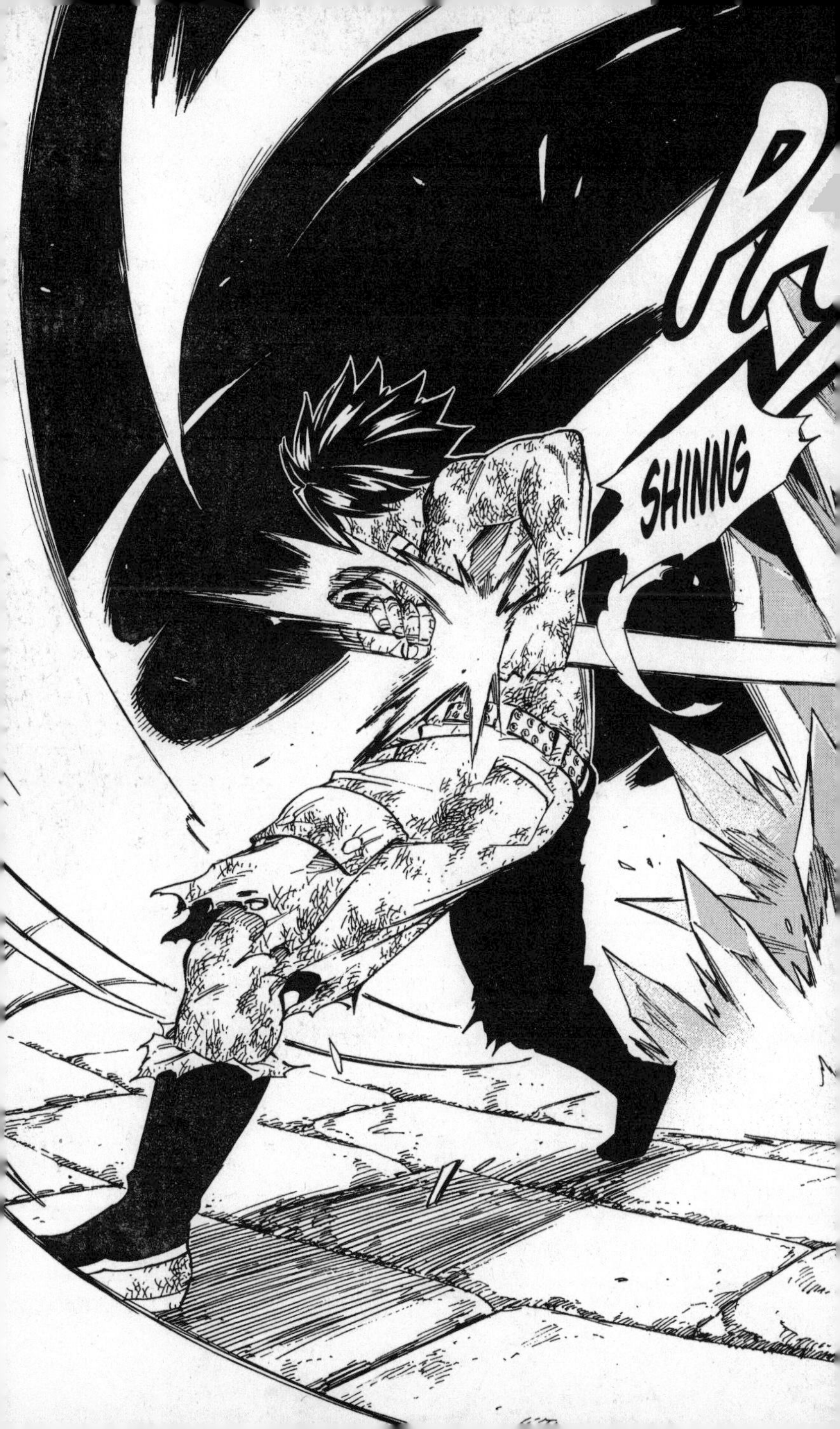
SHINNG

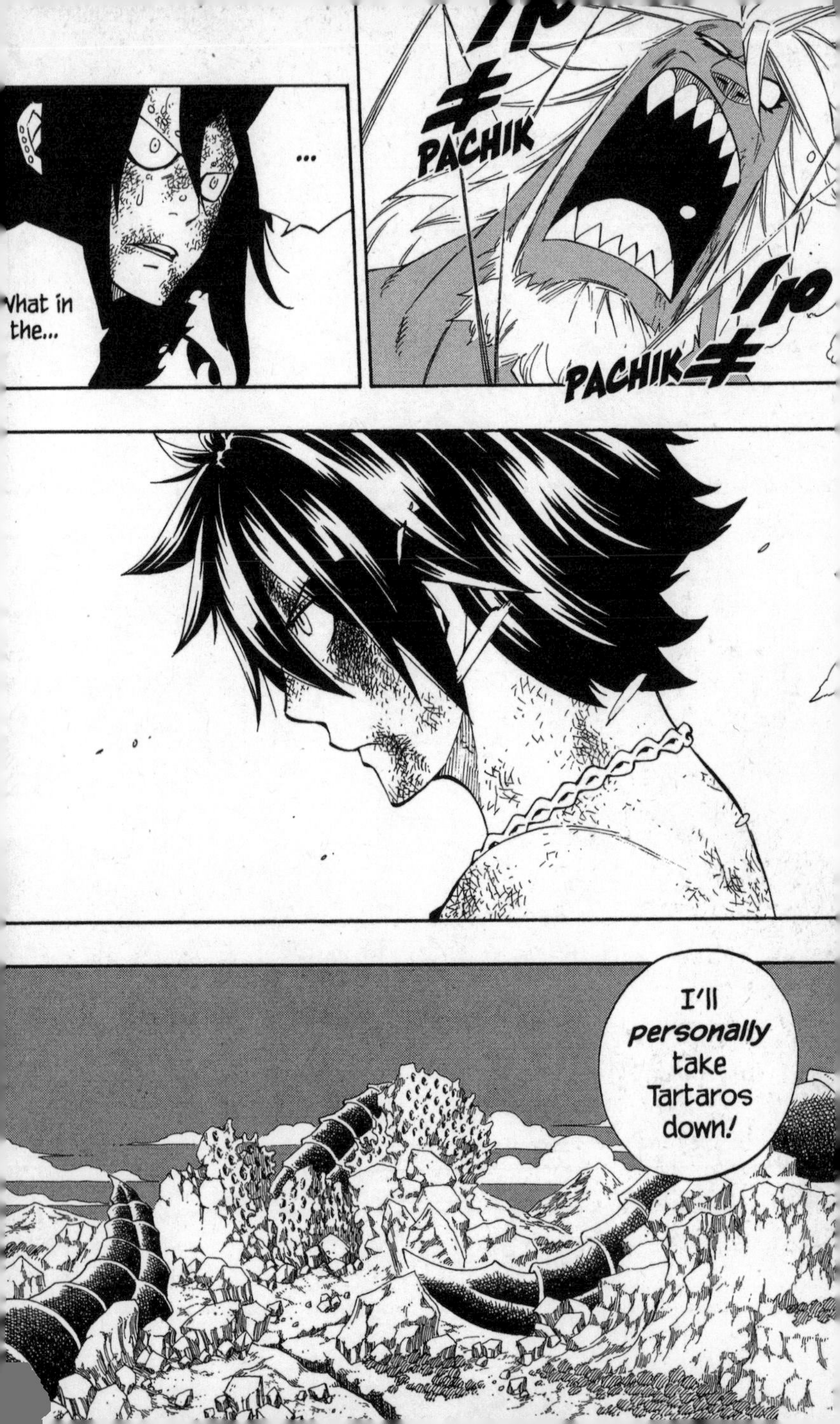
PACHIK
PACHIK
...
What in the...
I'll *personally* take Tartaros down!

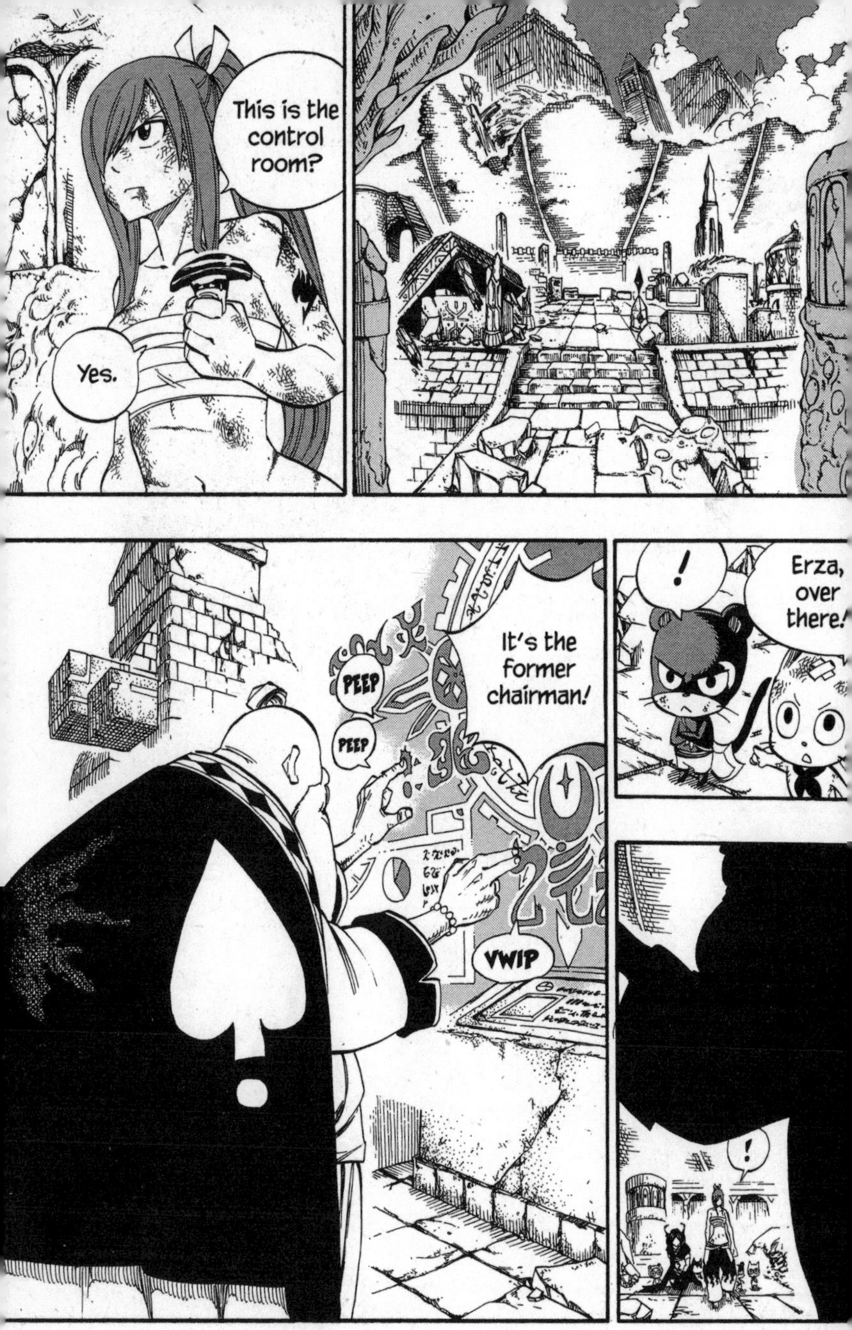
This is the control room?
Yes.
Erza, over there!
!
!
It's the former chairman!
PEEP
PEEP
VWIP

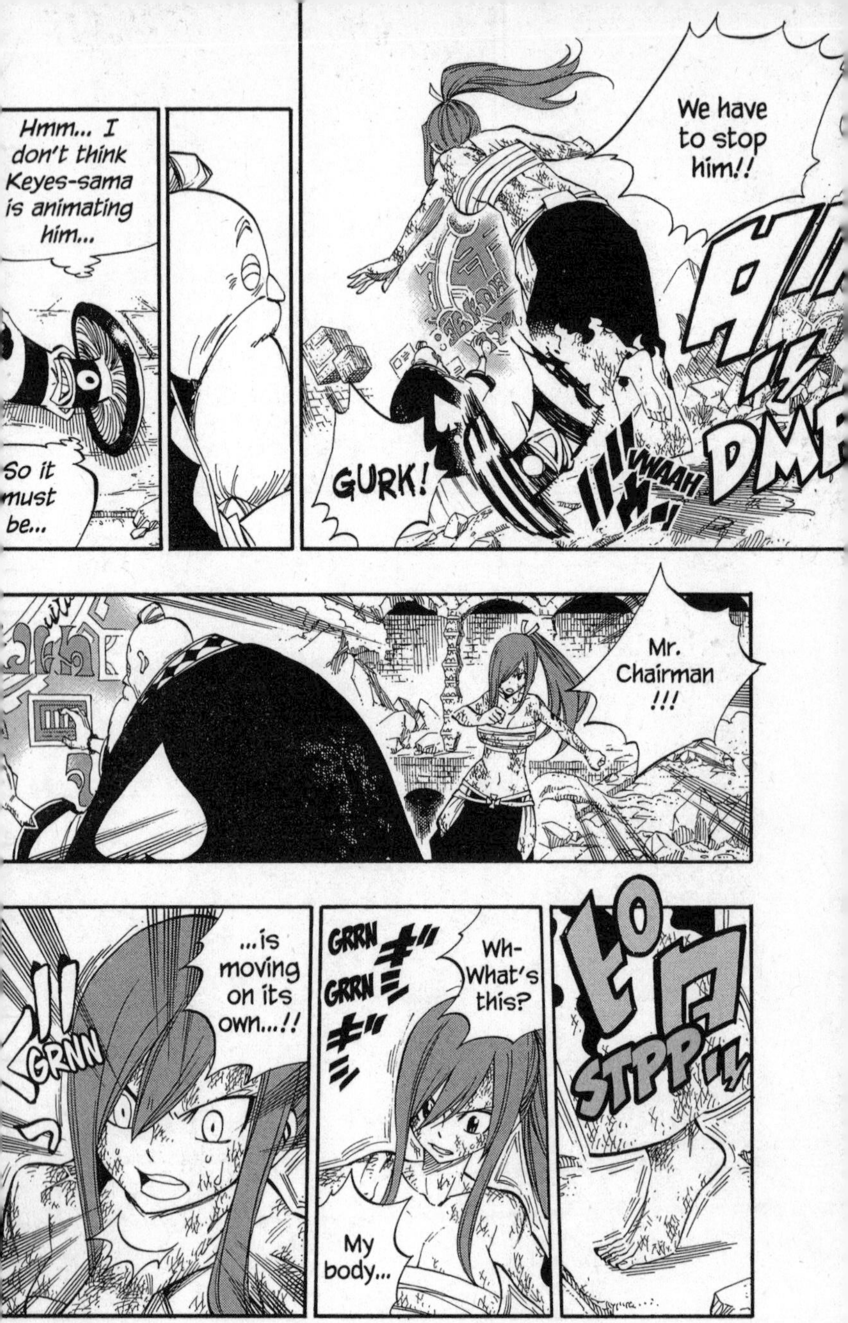
We have to stop him!!
DMP
WAAH
GURK!
Hmm... I don't think Keyes-sama is animating him...
So it must be...
Mr. Chairman!!!
STPP
Wh-What's this?
GRRN
GRRN
My body...
...is moving on its own...!!
GRNN

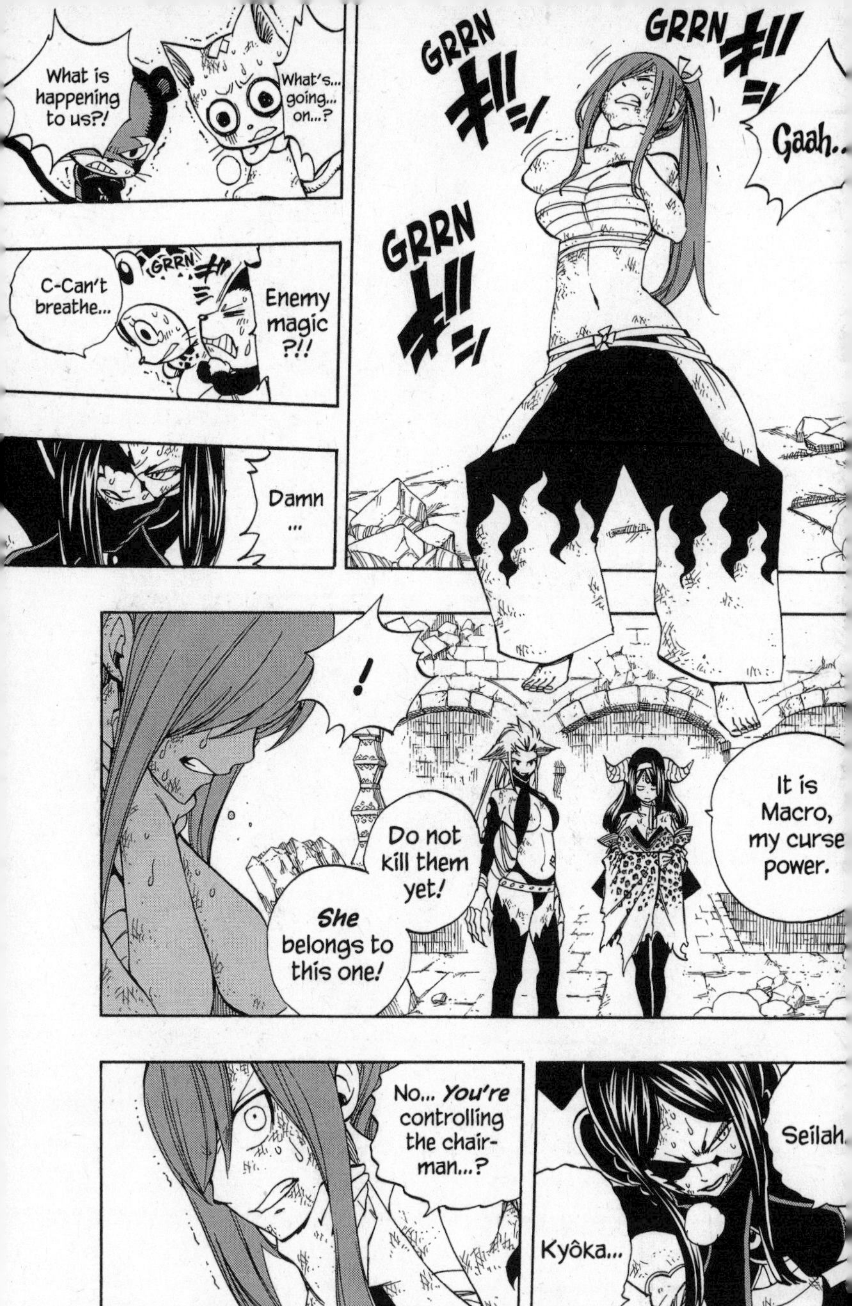
GRRN
GRRN
GRRN
Gaah...
What's... going... on...?
What is happening to us?!
Enemy magic ?!!
GRRN
C-Can't breathe...
Damn ...
!
It is Macro, my curse power.
Do not kill them yet!
She belongs to this one!
Seilah.
Kyôka...
No... *You're* controlling the chair-man...?

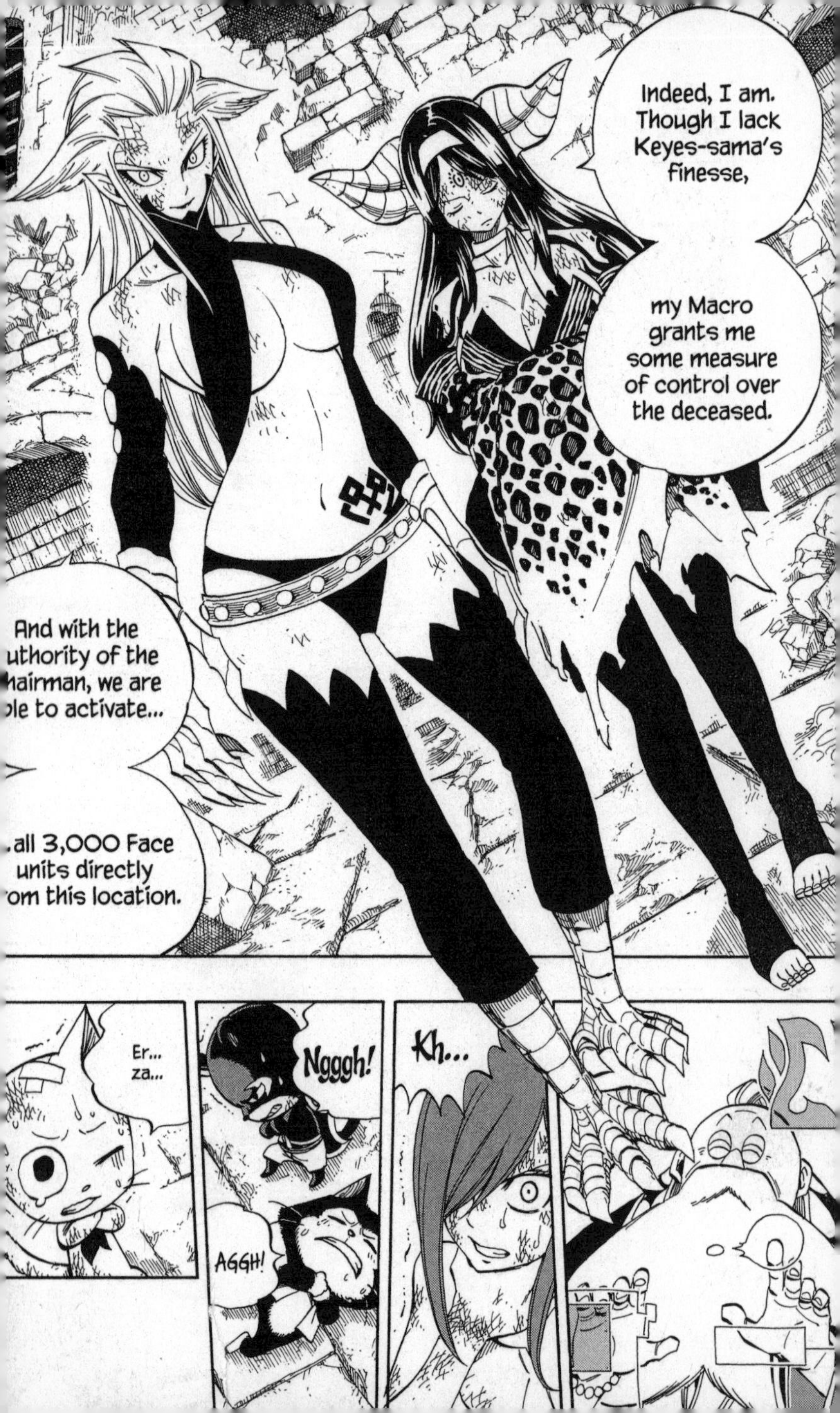

Indeed, I am. Though I lack Keyes-sama's finesse,
my Macro grants me some measure of control over the deceased.
And with the uthority of the hairman, we are ble to activate...
.all 3,000 Face units directly rom this location.
Kh...
Ngggh!
AGGH!
Er... za...

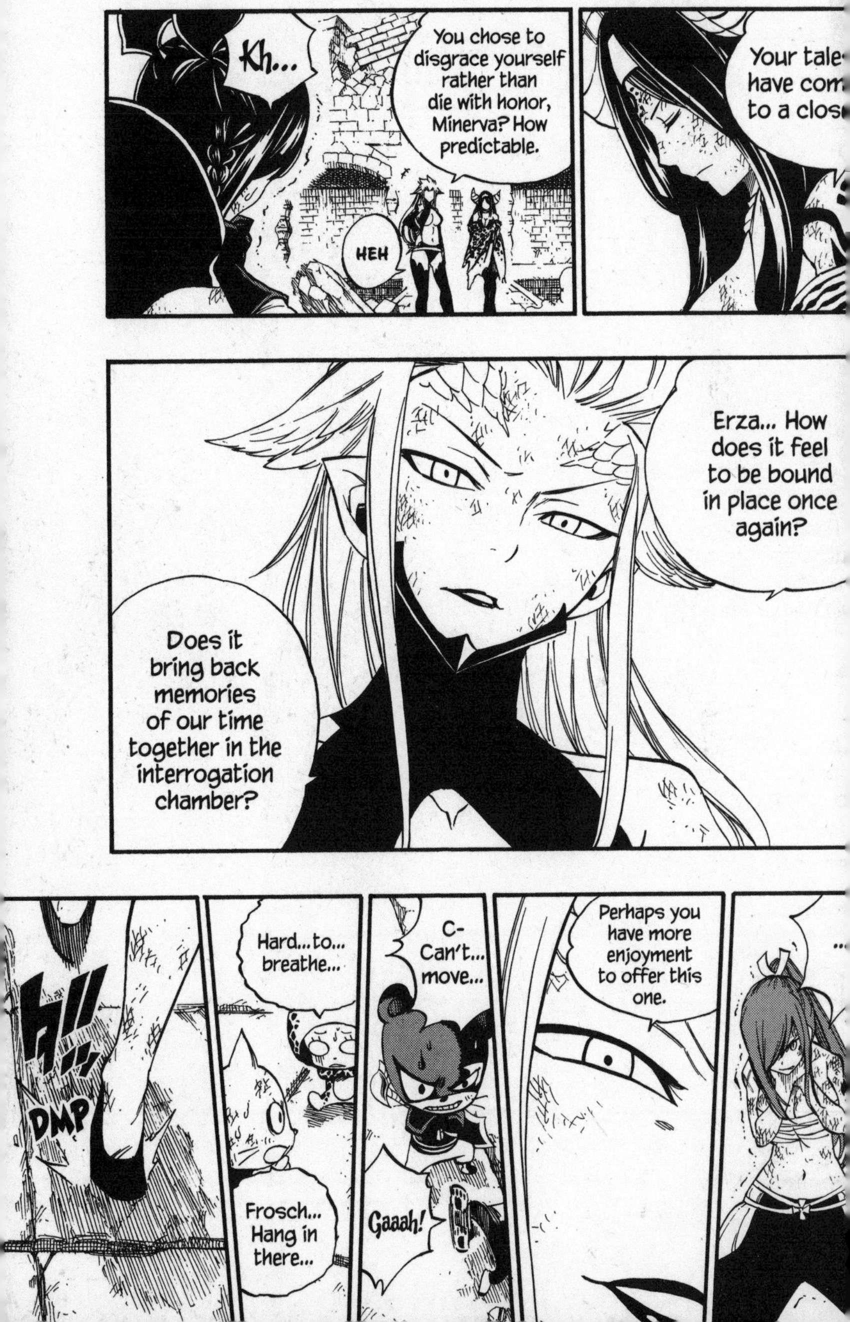

Your tale- have com to a clos
You chose to disgrace yourself rather than die with honor, Minerva? How predictable.
Kh...
HEH
Erza... How does it feel to be bound in place once again?
Does it bring back memories of our time together in the interrogation chamber?
...
Perhaps you have more enjoyment to offer this one.
C- Can't... move...
Gaaah!
Hard...to... breathe...
Frosch... Hang in there...
DMP

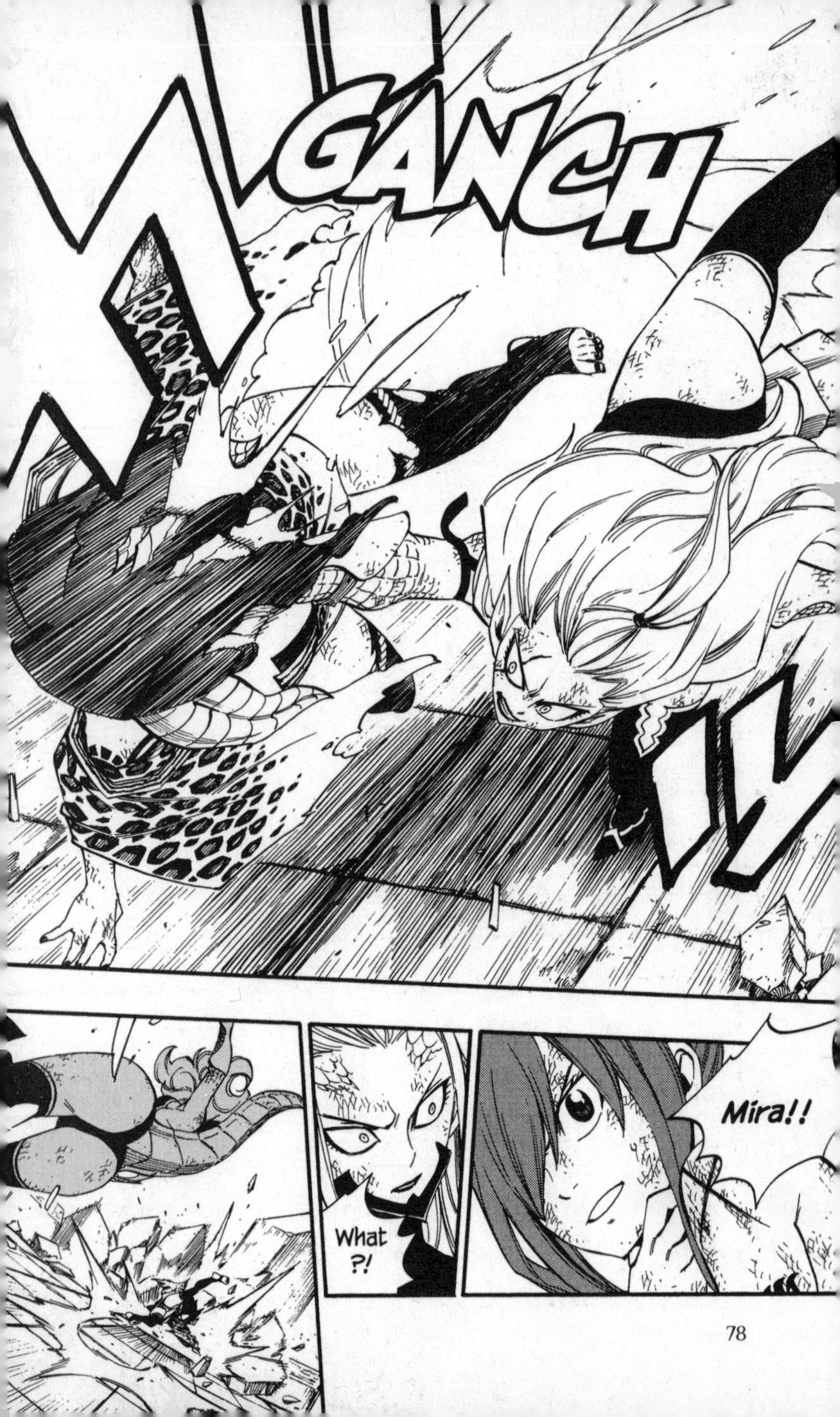
GANCH
Mira!!
What ?!

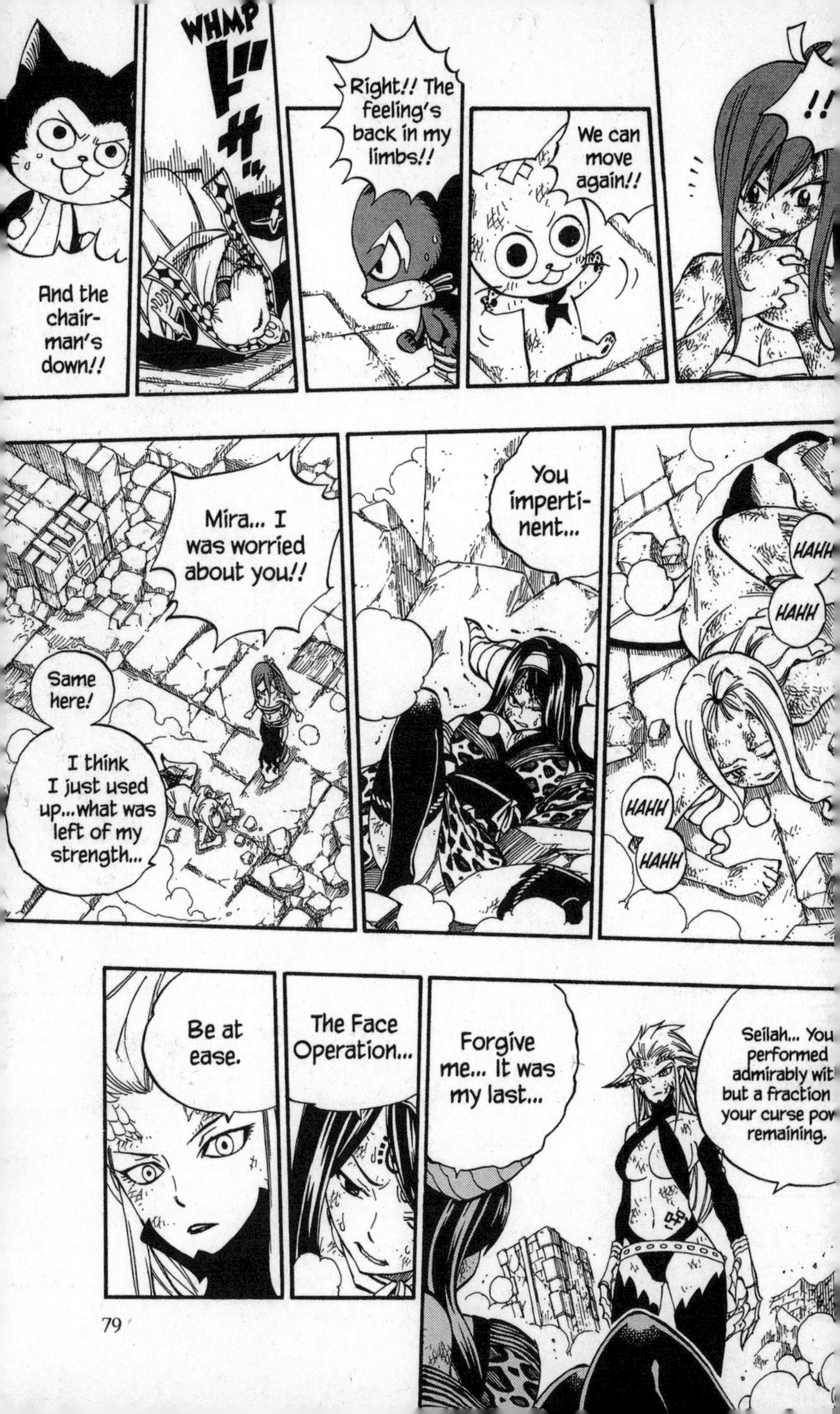
!!
We can move again!!
Right!! The feeling's back in my limbs!!
WHMP
And the chair-man's down!!
HAHH
HAHH
HAHH
HAHH
You imperti-nent...
Mira... I was worried about you!!
Same here!
I think I just used up...what was left of my strength...
Seilah... You performed admirably wit but a fraction your curse pow remaining.
Forgive me... It was my last...
The Face Operation...
Be at ease.

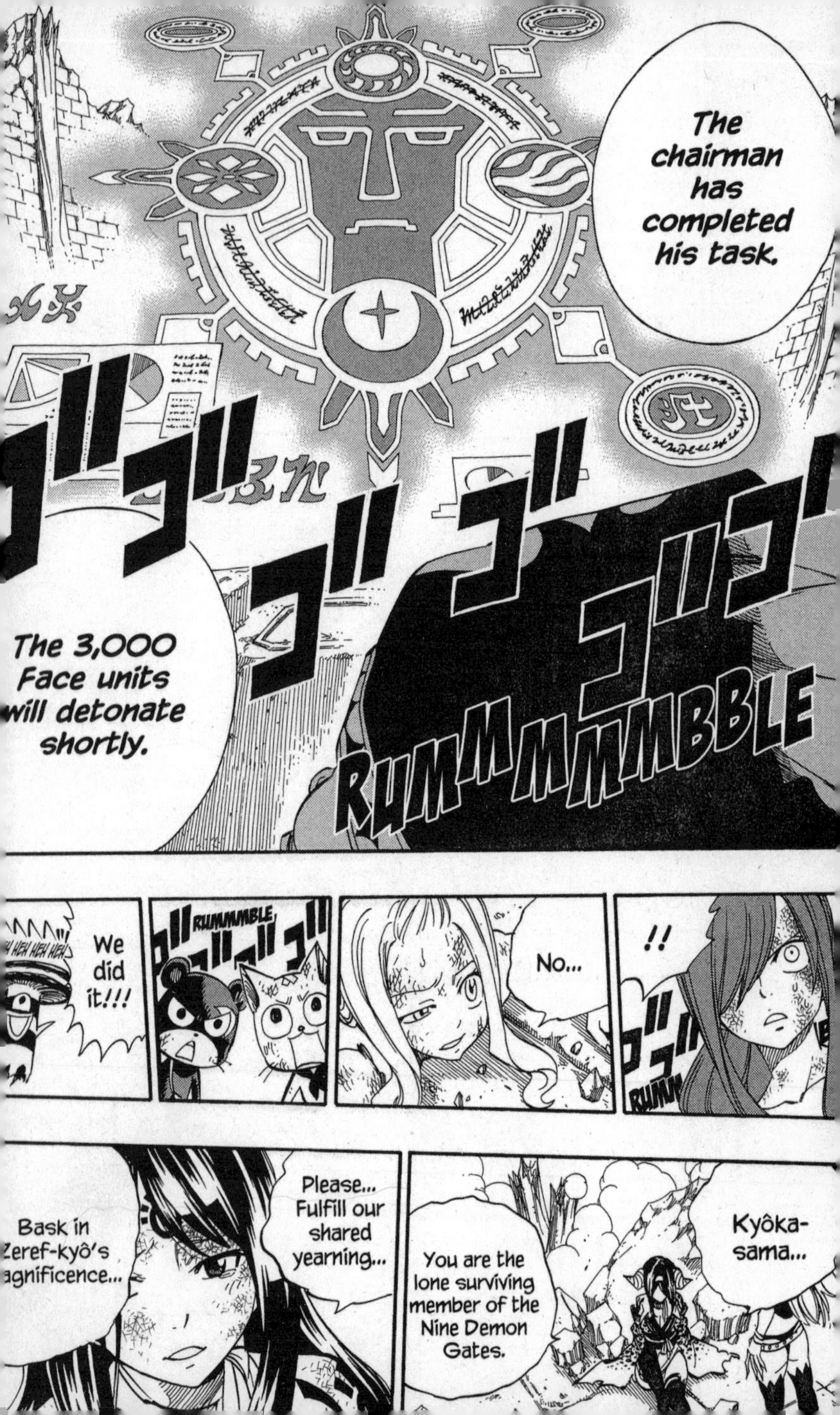

The chairman has completed his task.
The 3,000 Face units will detonate shortly.
RUMMMMMMMBBLE
!!
No...
RUMMMBLE
HEH HEH HEH HEH
We did it!!!
Kyôka-sama...
You are the lone surviving member of the Nine Demon Gates.
Please... Fulfill our shared yearning...
Bask in Zeref-kyô's agnificence...

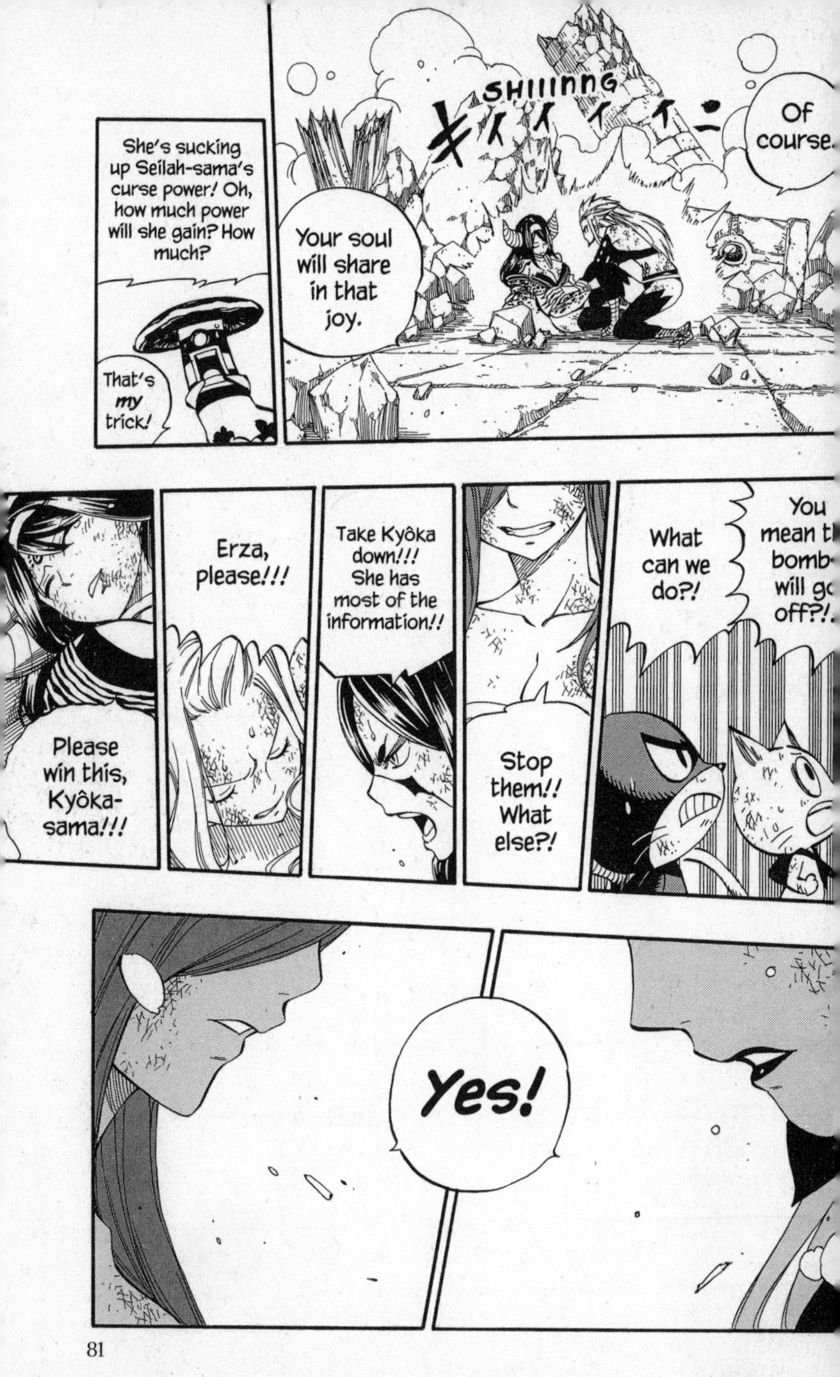
Of course.
SHIIIInnG
Your soul will share in that joy.
She's sucking up Seilah-sama's curse power! Oh, how much power will she gain? How much?
That's *my* trick!
You mean t bomb will g off?!
What can we do?!
Stop them!! What else?!
Take Kyôka down!!! She has most of the information!!
Erza, please!!!
Please win this, Kyôka-sama!!!
Yes!

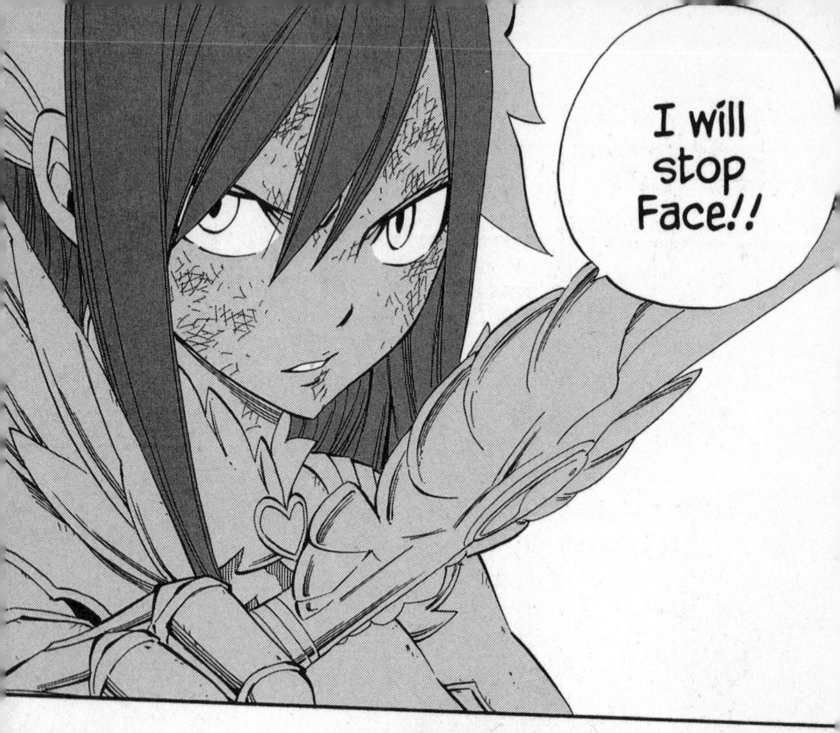
I will stop Face!!
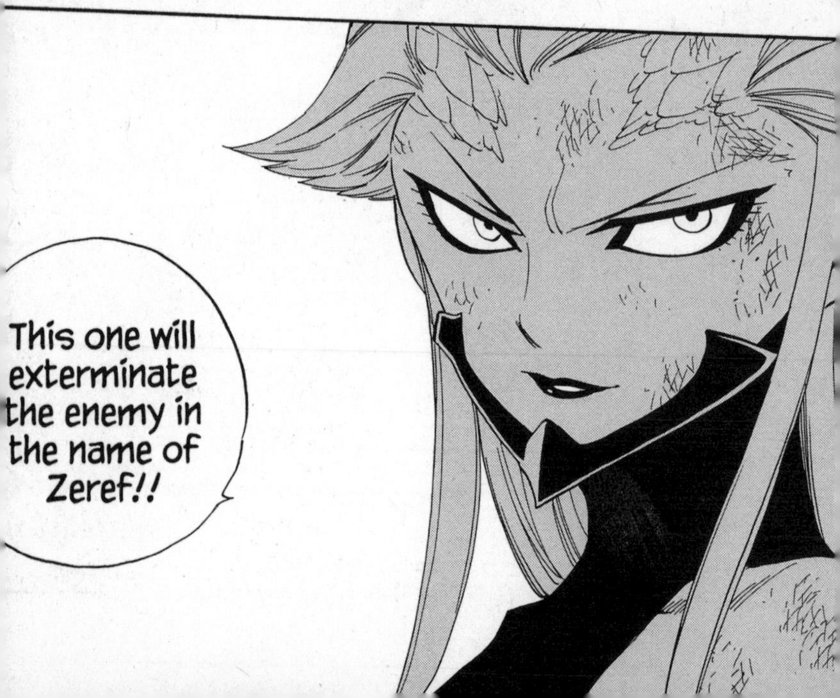
This one will exterminate the enemy in the name of Zeref!!

FAIRY TAIL
フェアリーテイル

Chapter 399: Wings of Despair

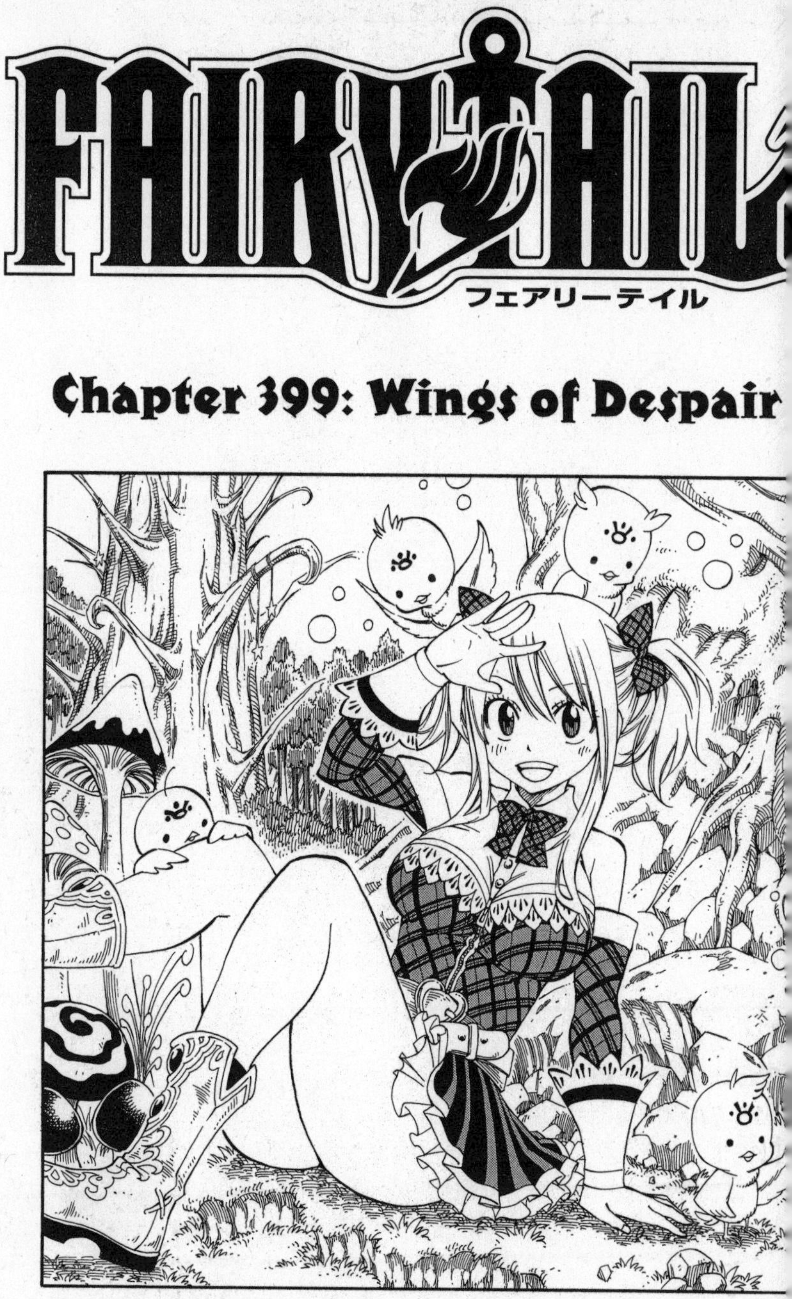

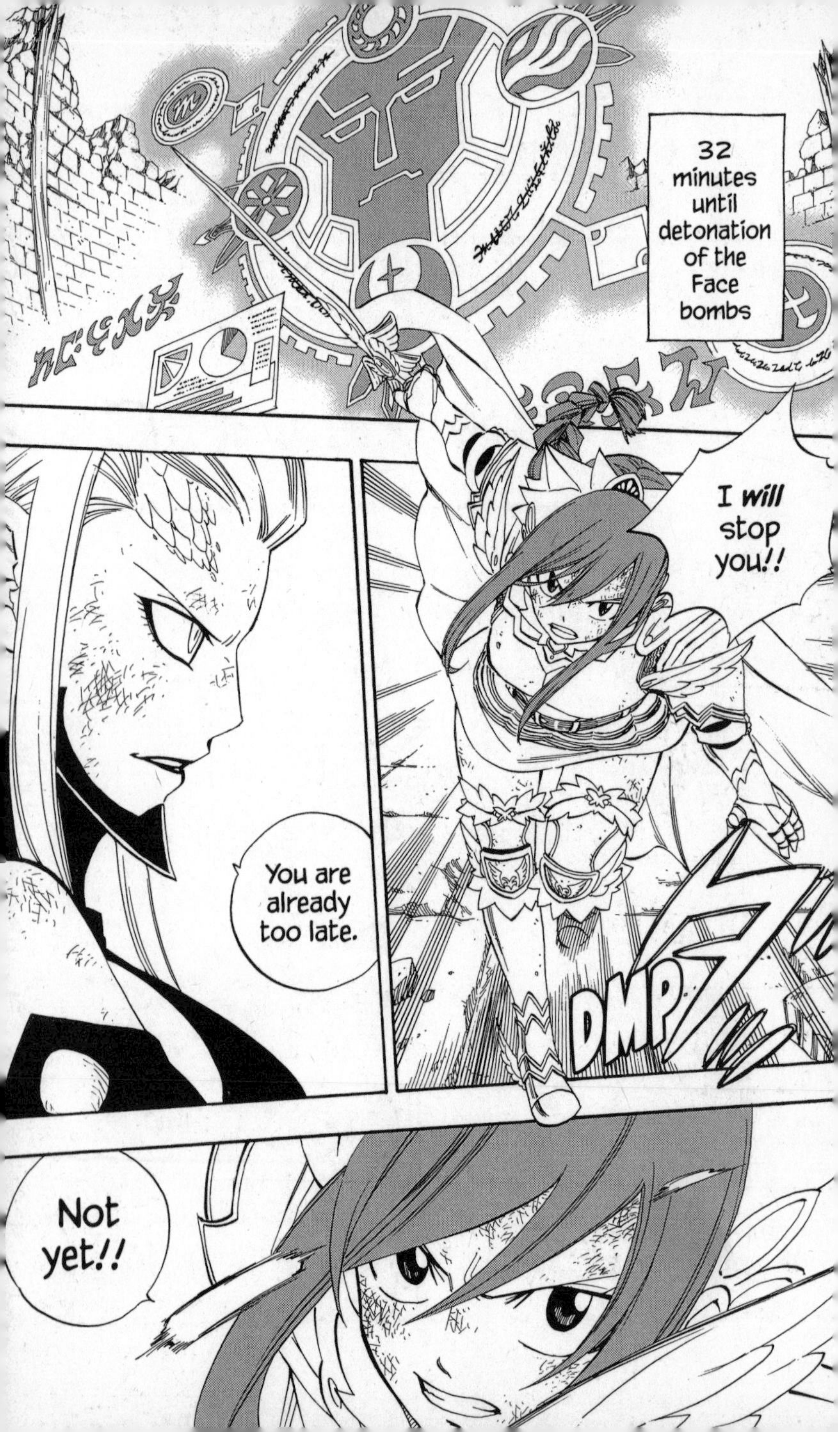
32 minutes until detonation of the Face bombs
I *will* stop you!!
DMP
You are already too late.
Not yet!!

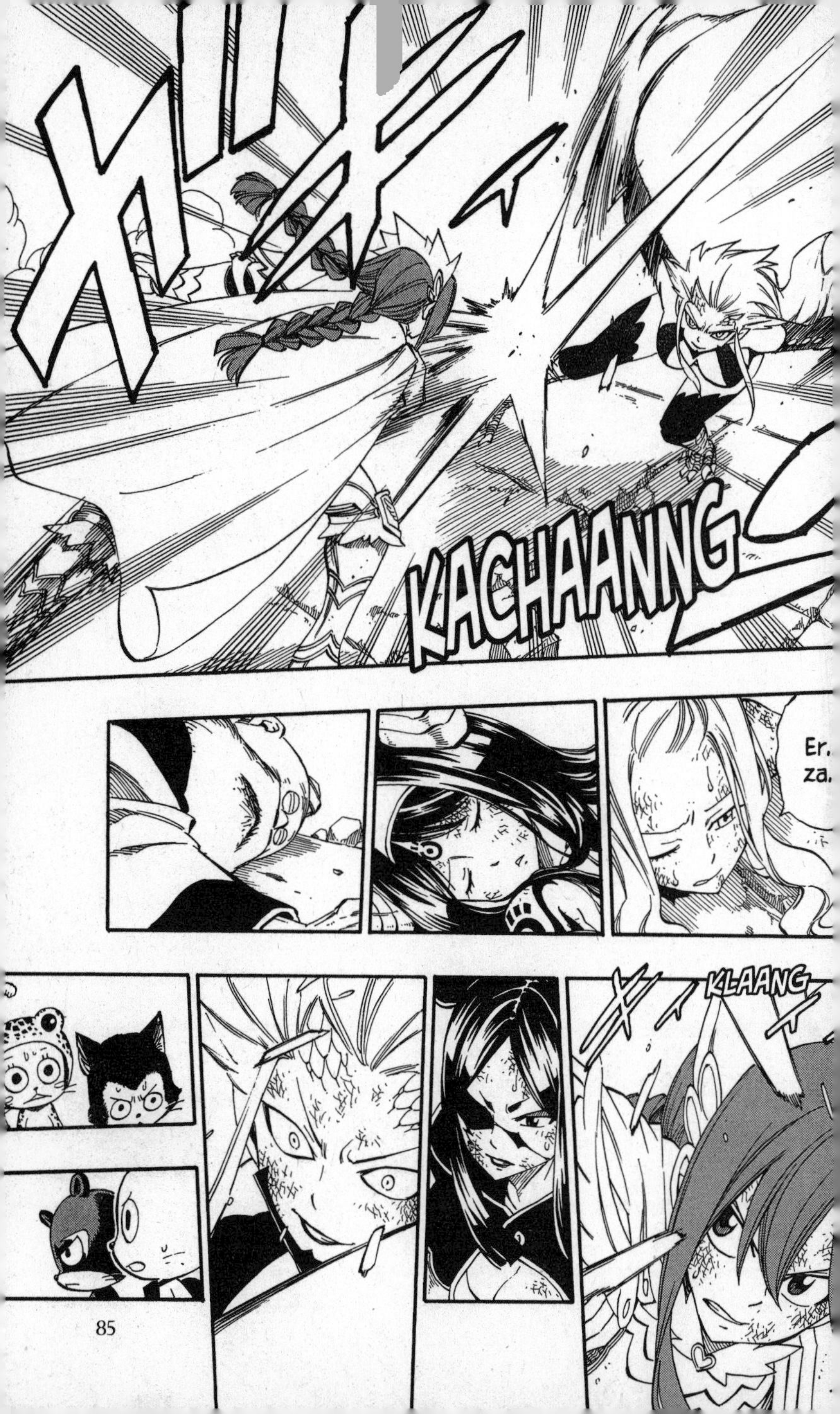

KACHAANNG
Er.
za.
KLAANG

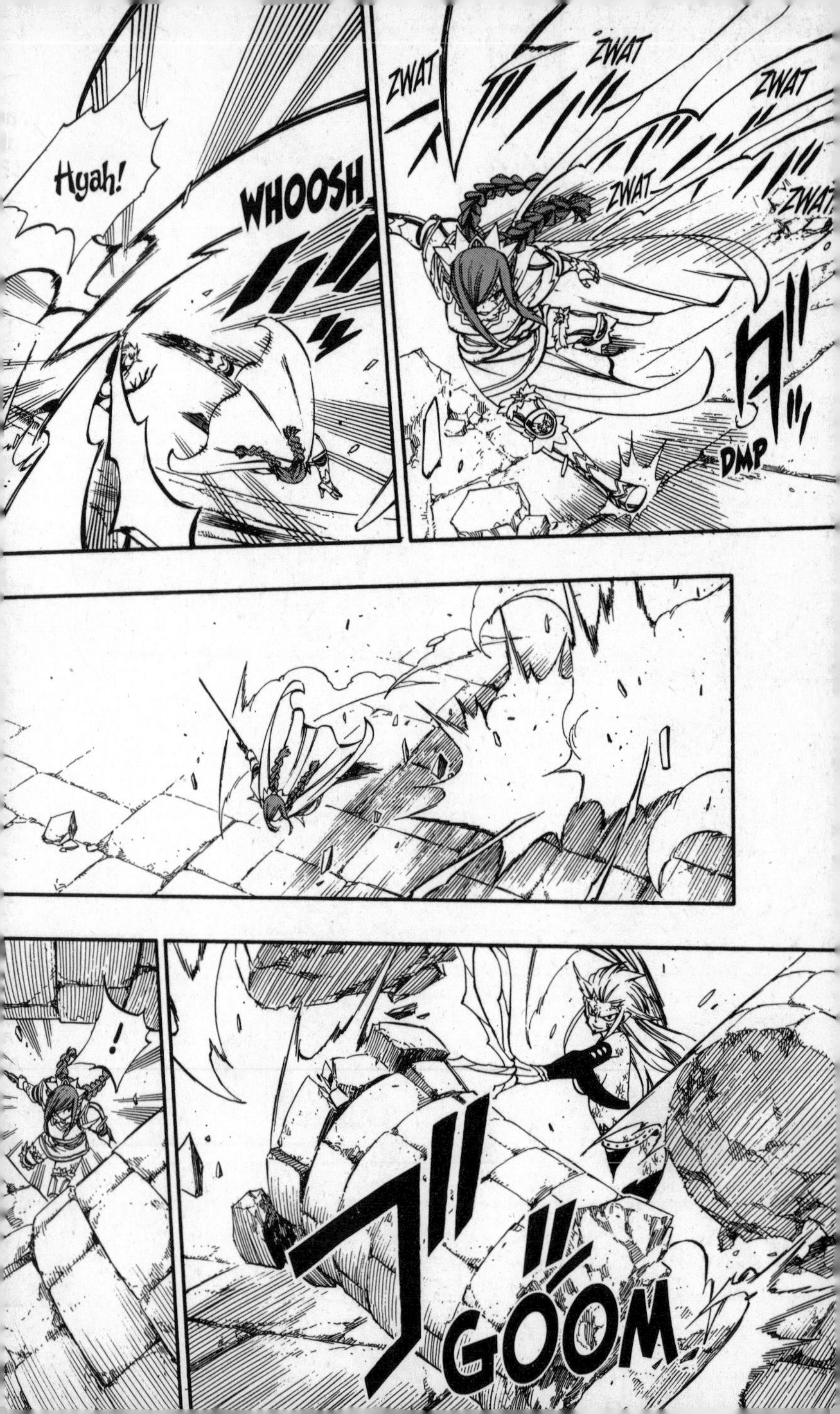
ZWAT
ZWAT
ZWAT
ZWAT
ZWA
DMP
Hyah!
WHOOSH
GOOM
!

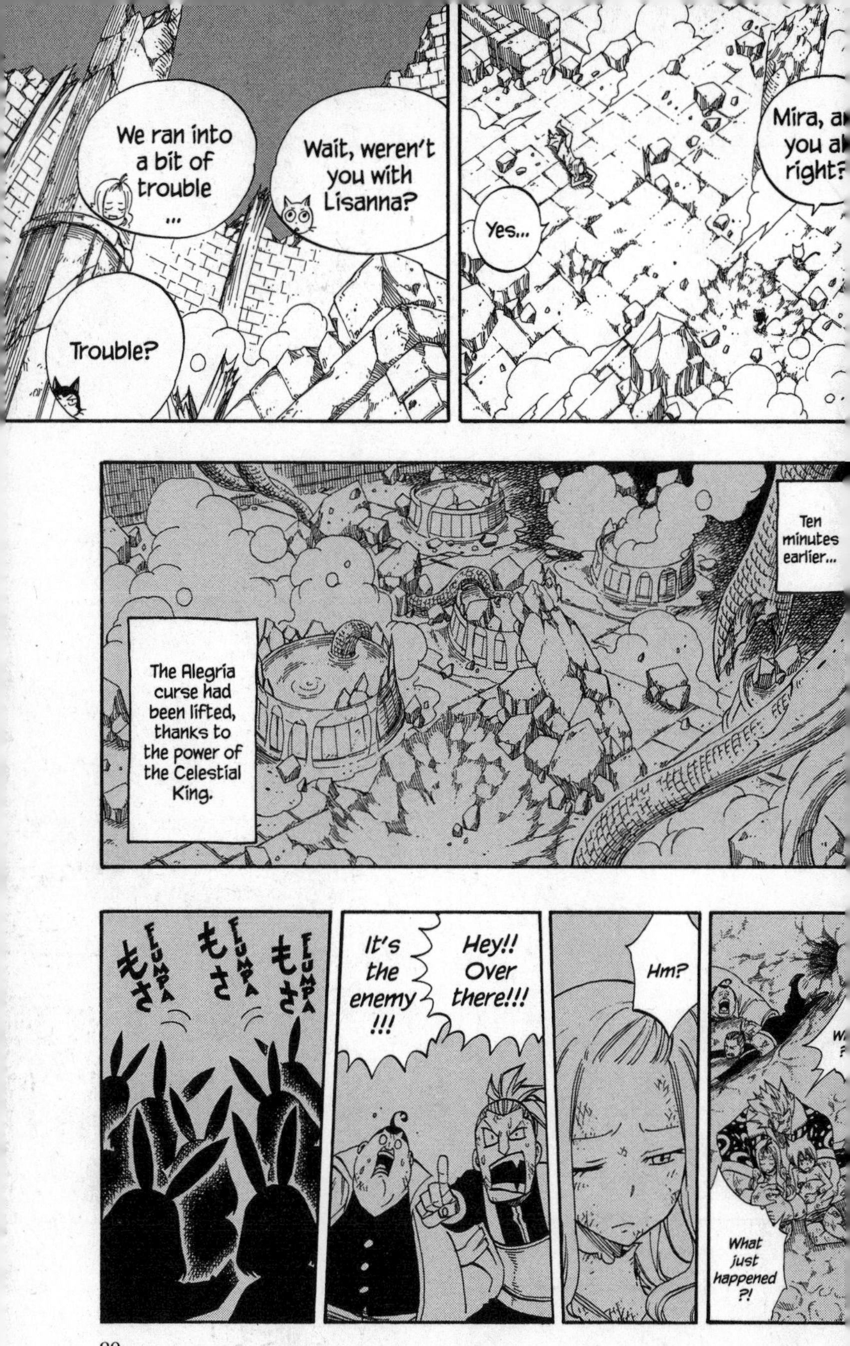
right?
Yes...
Wait, weren't you with Lisanna?
We ran into a bit of trouble ...
Trouble?
Ten minutes earlier...
The Alegria curse had been lifted, thanks to the power of the Celestial King.
What just happened ?!
Hm?
Hey!! Over there!!!
It's the enemy !!!
もさ FLUMPA
もさ FLUMPA
もさ FLUMPA

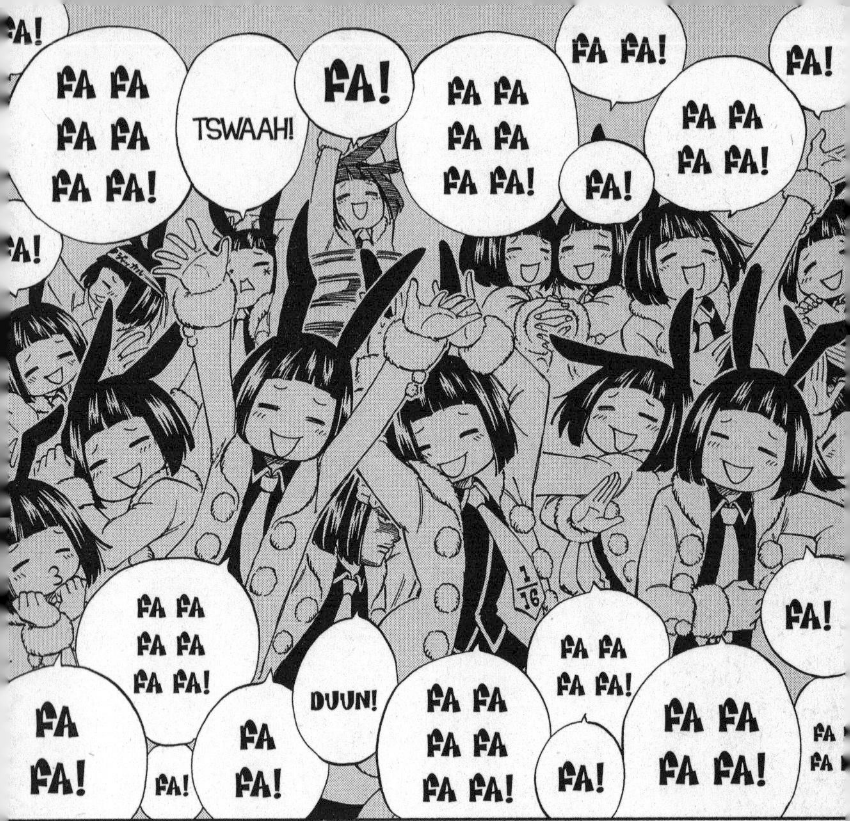
FA!
FA FA!
FA FA FA FA!
FA FA FA FA FA FA!
FA!
FA!
TSWAAH!
FA FA FA FA FA FA!
FA!
FA!
FA!
FA FA FA FA!
FA FA FA FA FA FA!
DUUN!
FA FA FA FA FA FA!
FA FA FA FA FA FA!
FA FA!
FA FA
FA!
FA!
FA FA!
FA!
FA FA!

Headband: "Jackal"

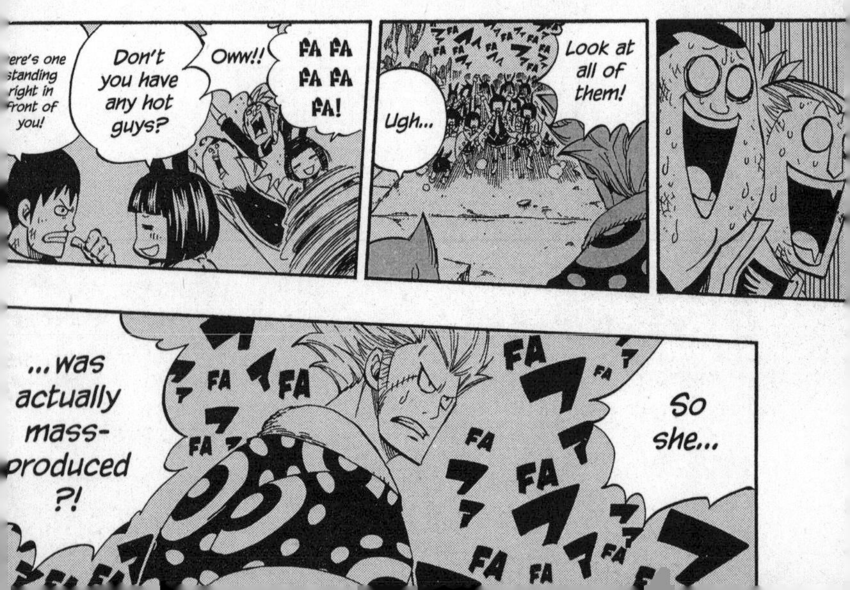
Look at all of them!
Ugh...
FA FA FA FA FA!
Oww!!
Don't you have any hot guys?
ere's one standing right in front of you!
So she...
...was actually mass-produced?!

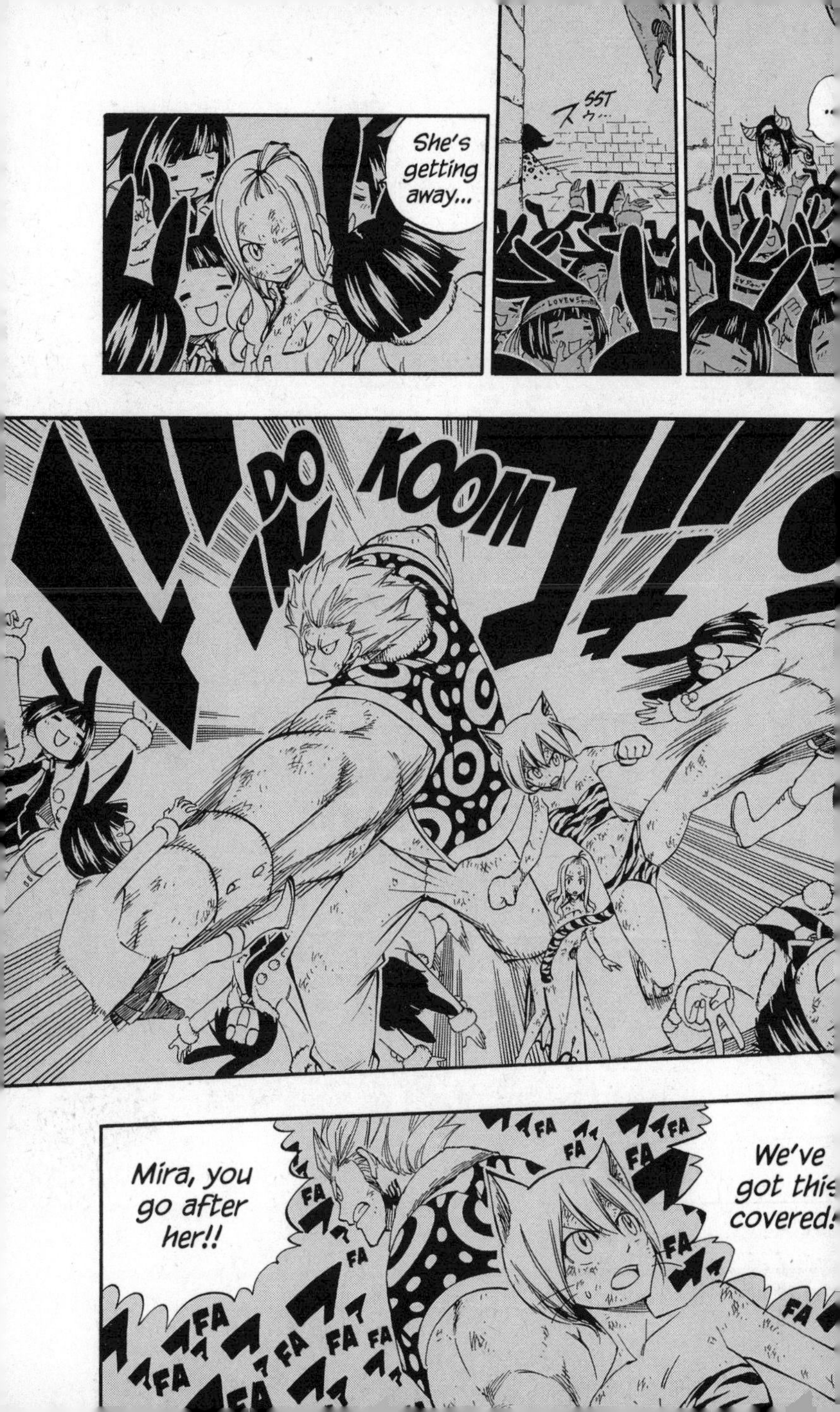
SST
She's getting away...
DO KOOM
We've got this covered!
Mira, you go after her!!
FA FA FA FA FA FA FA FA FA FA FA FA

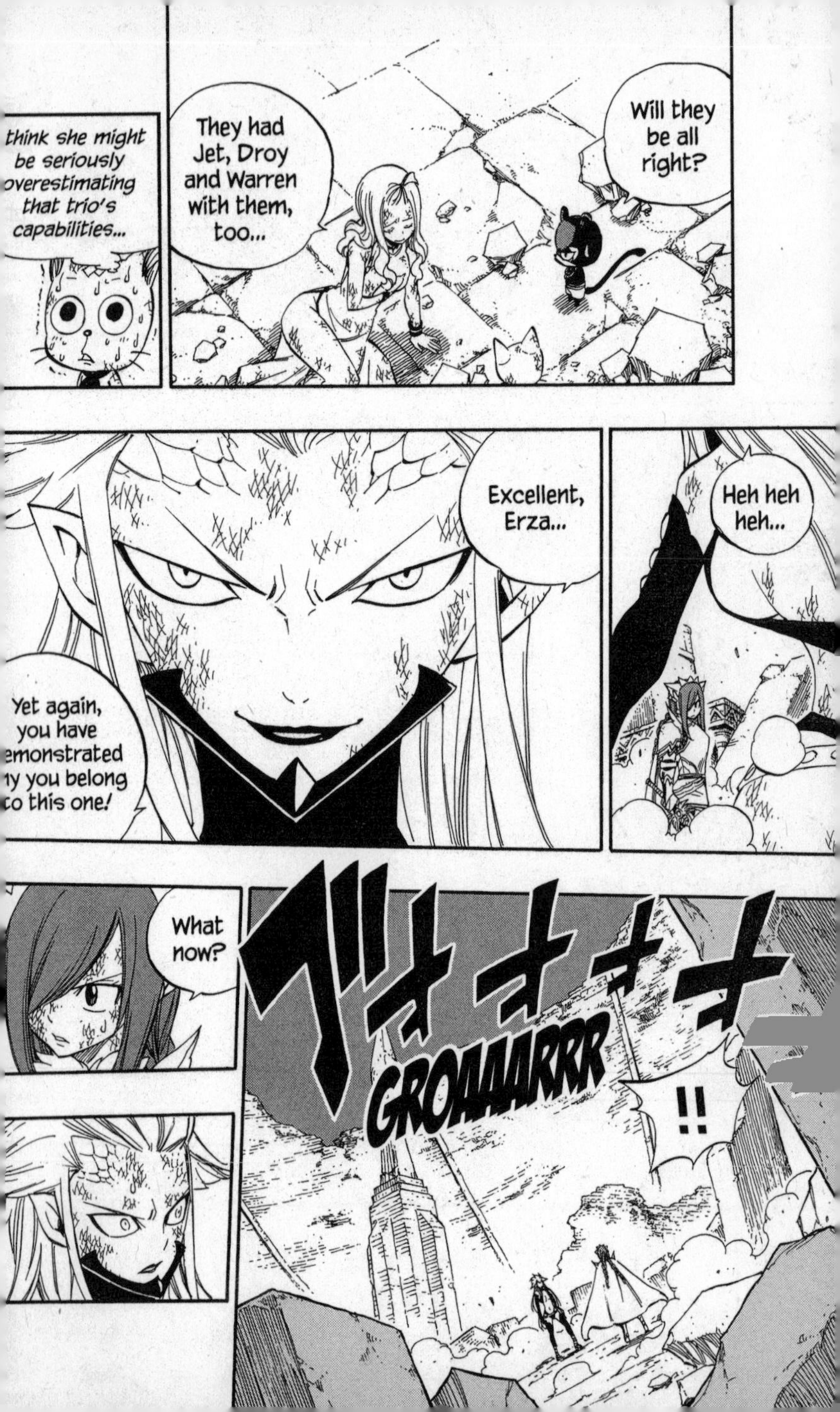

Will they be all right?
They had Jet, Droy and Warren with them, too...
think she might be seriously overestimating that trio's capabilities...
Heh heh heh...
Excellent, Erza...
Yet again, you have emonstrated ny you belong o this one!
GROAAARRR
!!
What now?

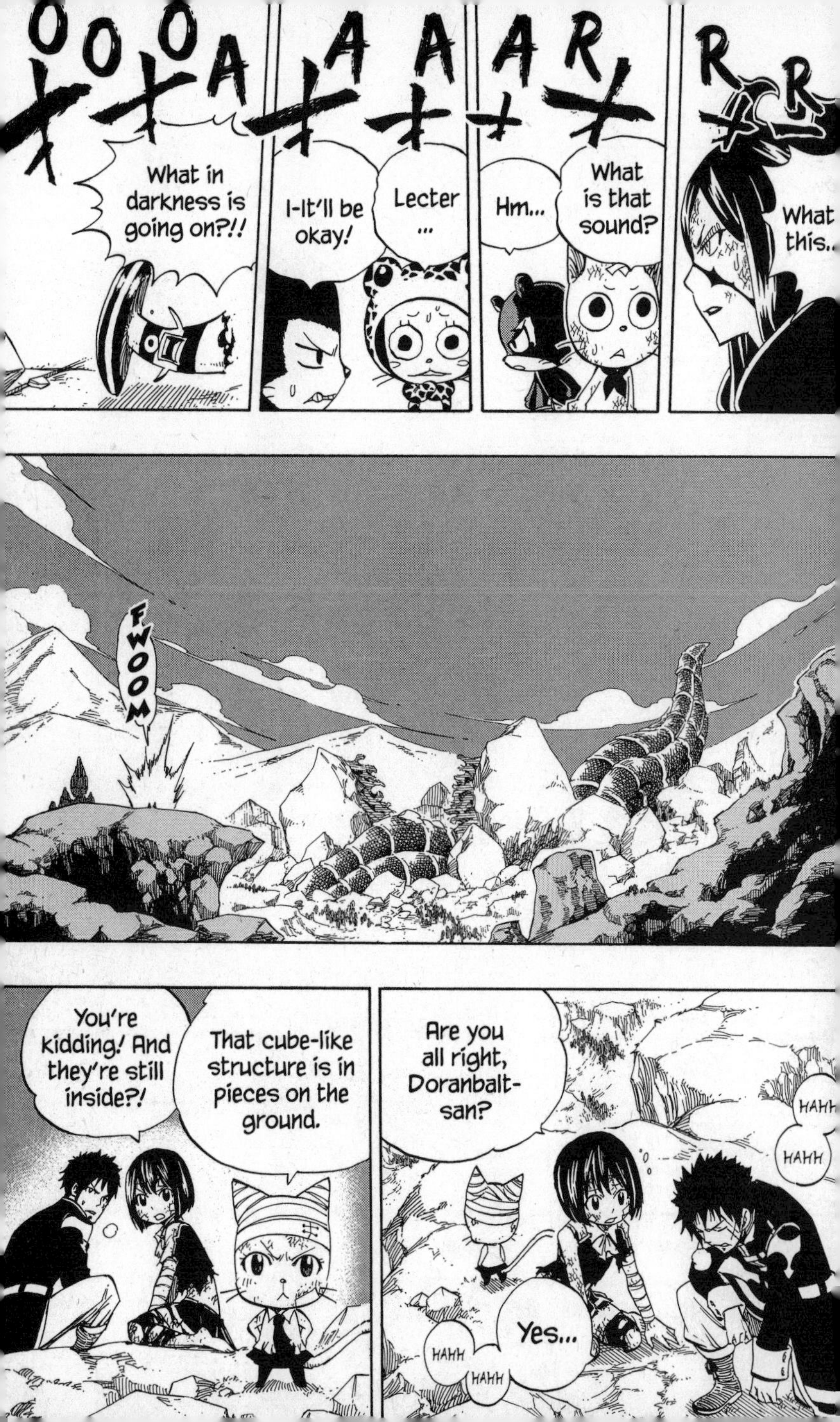
OOOAAAARRR
What this..
What is that sound?
Hm...
Lecter ...
I-It'll be okay!
What in darkness is going on?!!
FWOOM
Are you all right, Doranbalt-san?
HAHH
HAHH
Yes...
HAHH
HAHH
That cube-like structure is in pieces on the ground.
You're kidding! And they're still inside?!

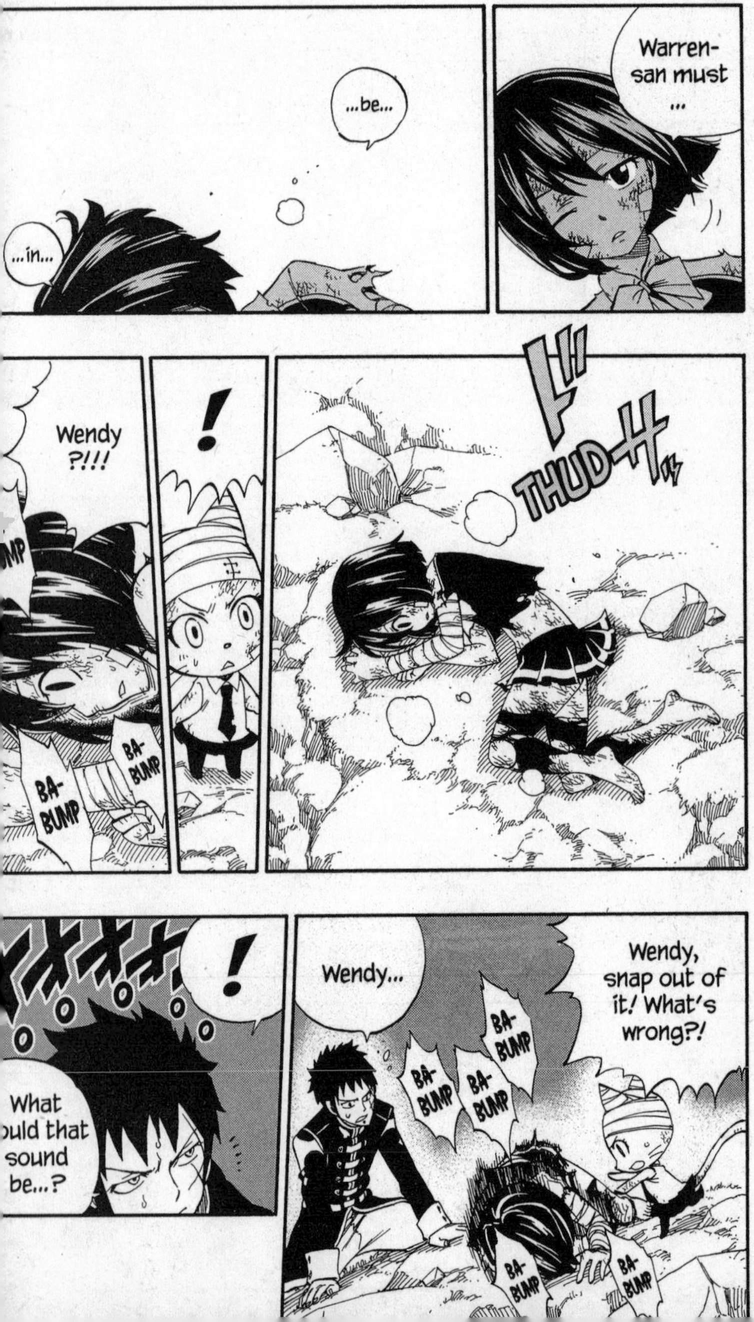

Warren-san must ...
...be...
...in...
THUD
!
Wendy ?!!!
BA-BUMP
BA-BUMP
Wendy, snap out of it! What's wrong?!
Wendy...
BA-BUMP
BA-BUMP
BA-BUMP
BA-BUMP
BA-BUMP
!
What
uld that sound be...?

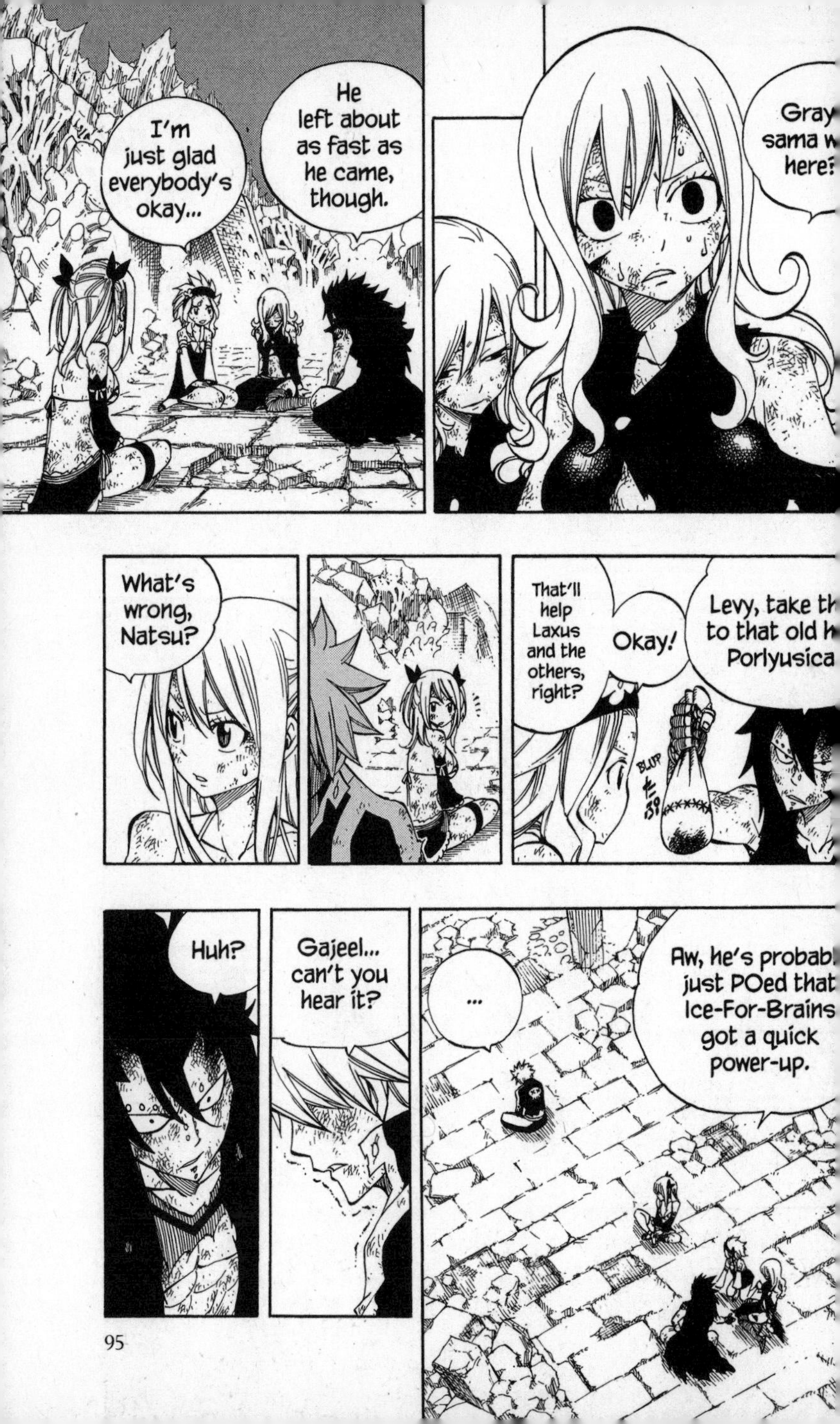
Gray
sama w
here?
He left about as fast as he came, though.
I'm just glad everybody's okay...
Levy, take th
to that old h
Porlyusica
Okay!
That'll help Laxus and the others, right?
BLUP
What's wrong, Natsu?
Aw, he's probab
just POed that
Ice-For-Brains
got a quick power-up.
...
Gajeel... can't you hear it?
Huh?

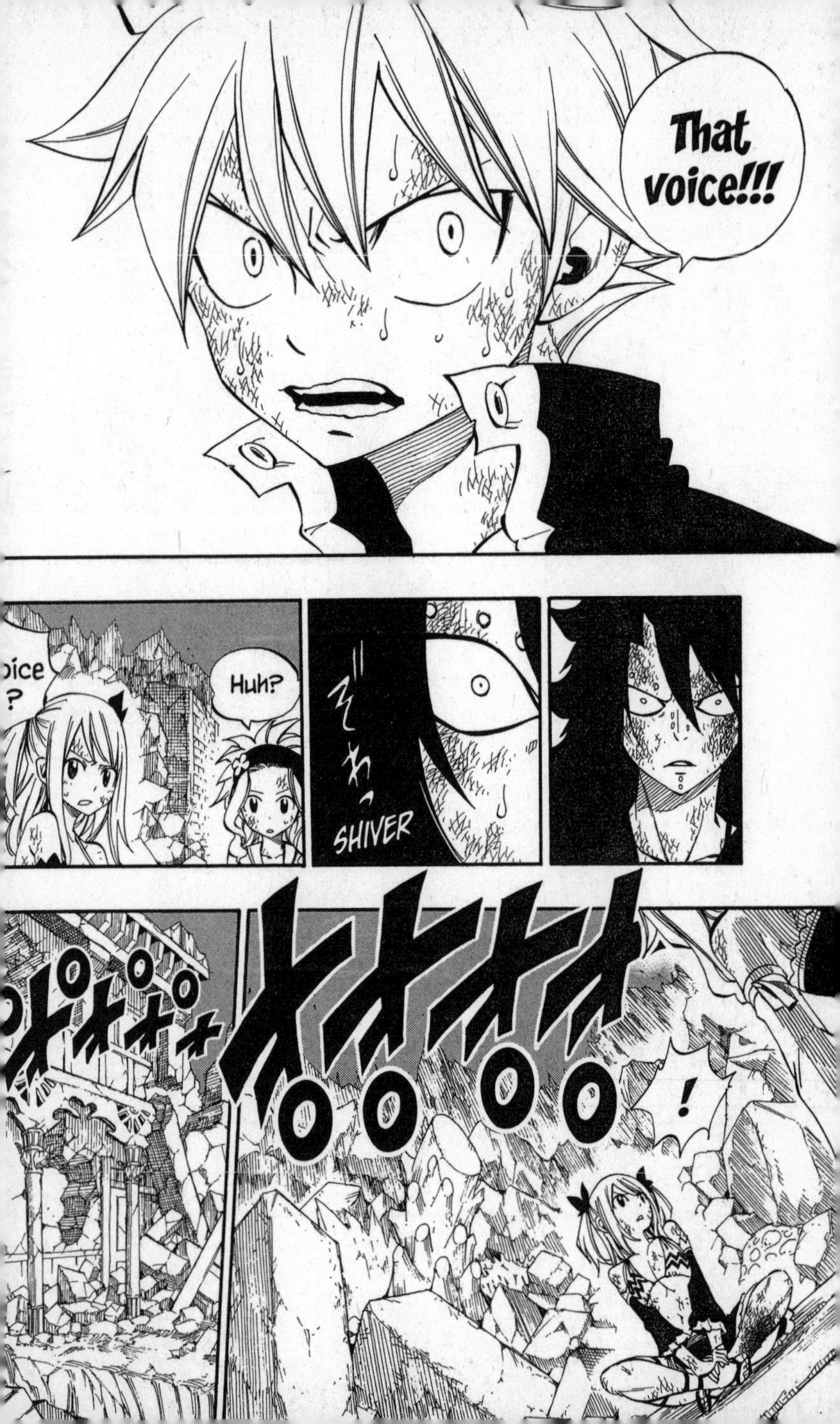

That voice!!!
SHIVER
Huh?
!

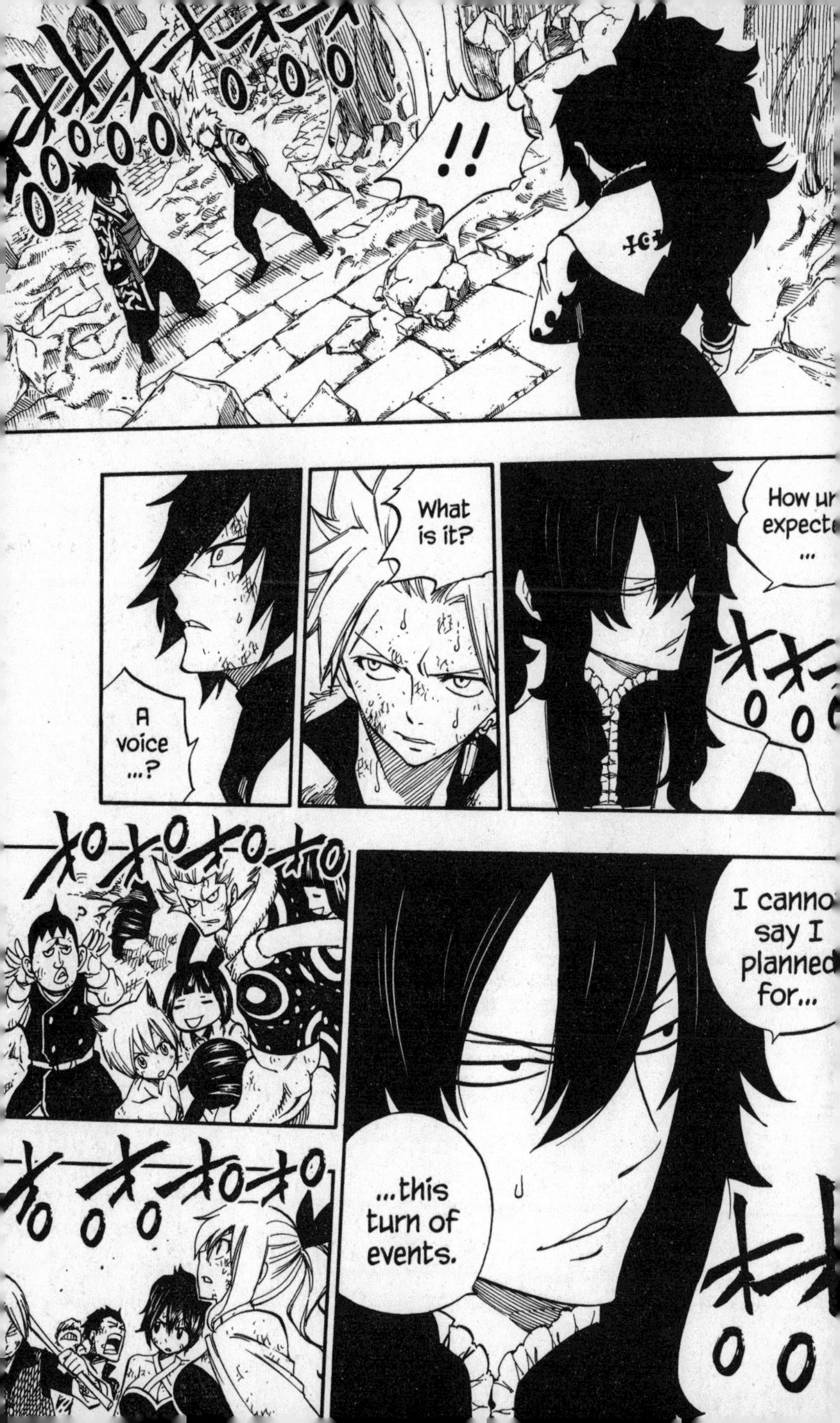
!!
How ur expecte ...
What is it?
A voice ...?
I canno say I planned for...
...this turn of events.

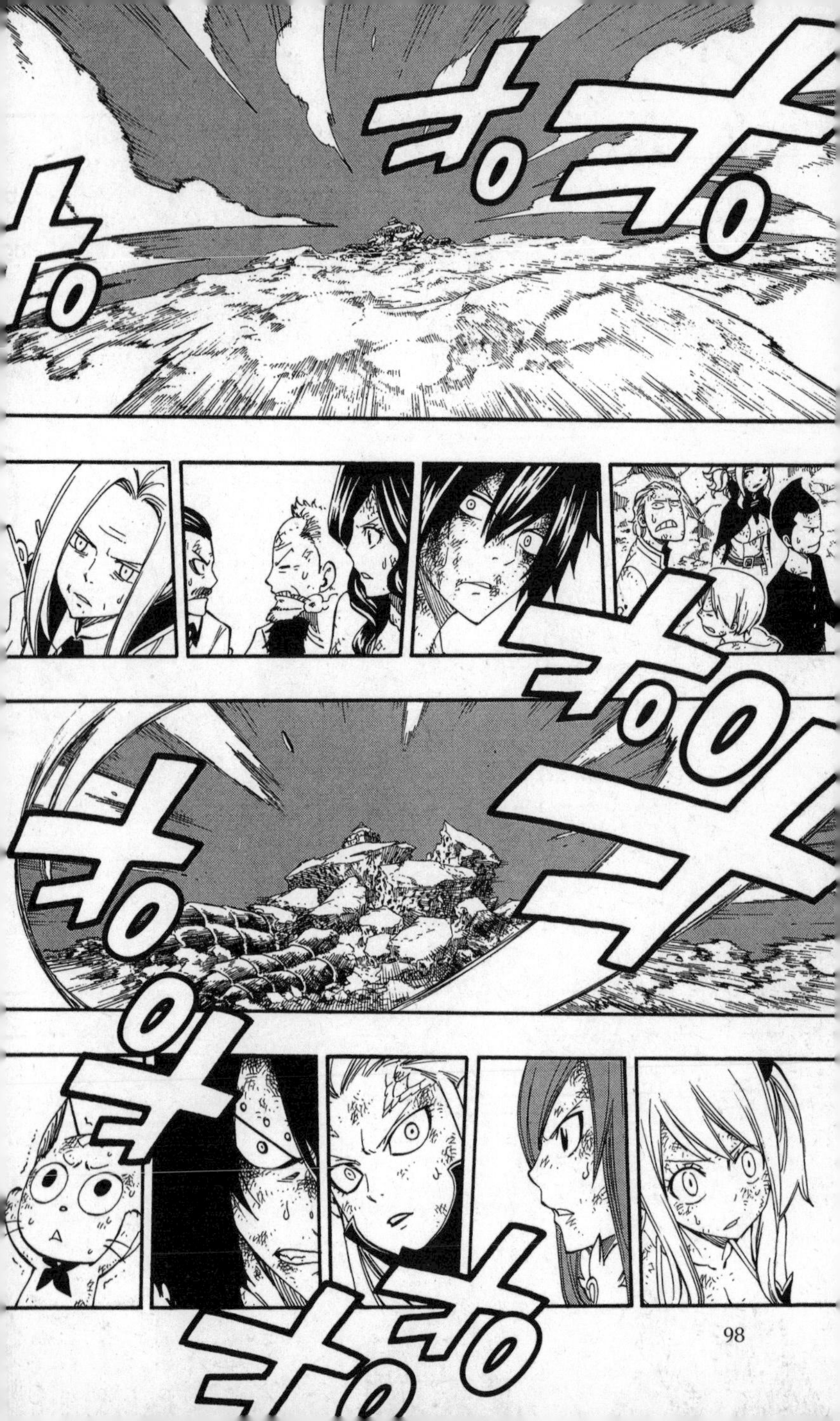

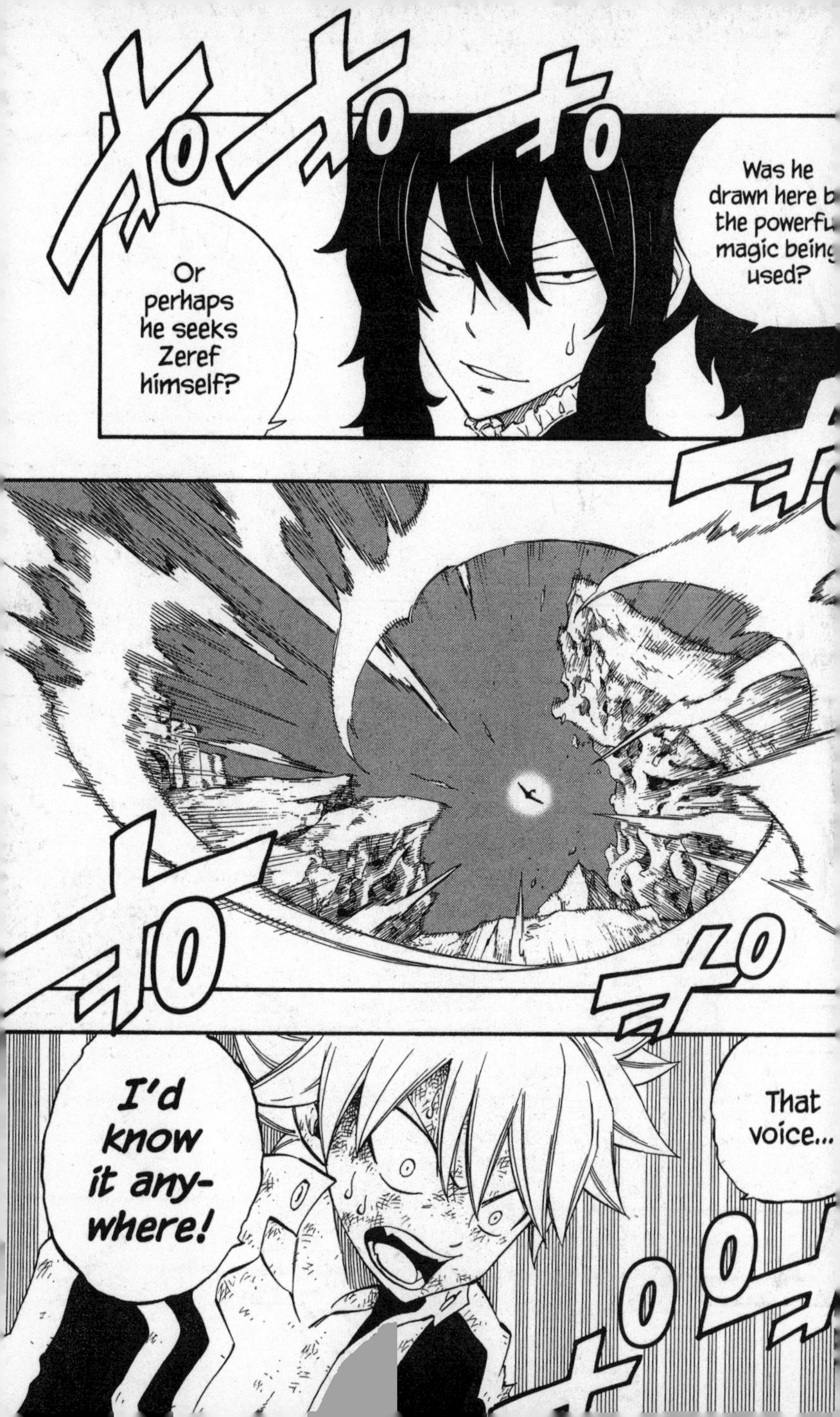
Was he drawn here b the powerfu magic being used?
Or perhaps he seeks Zeref himself?
That voice...
I'd know it any-where!

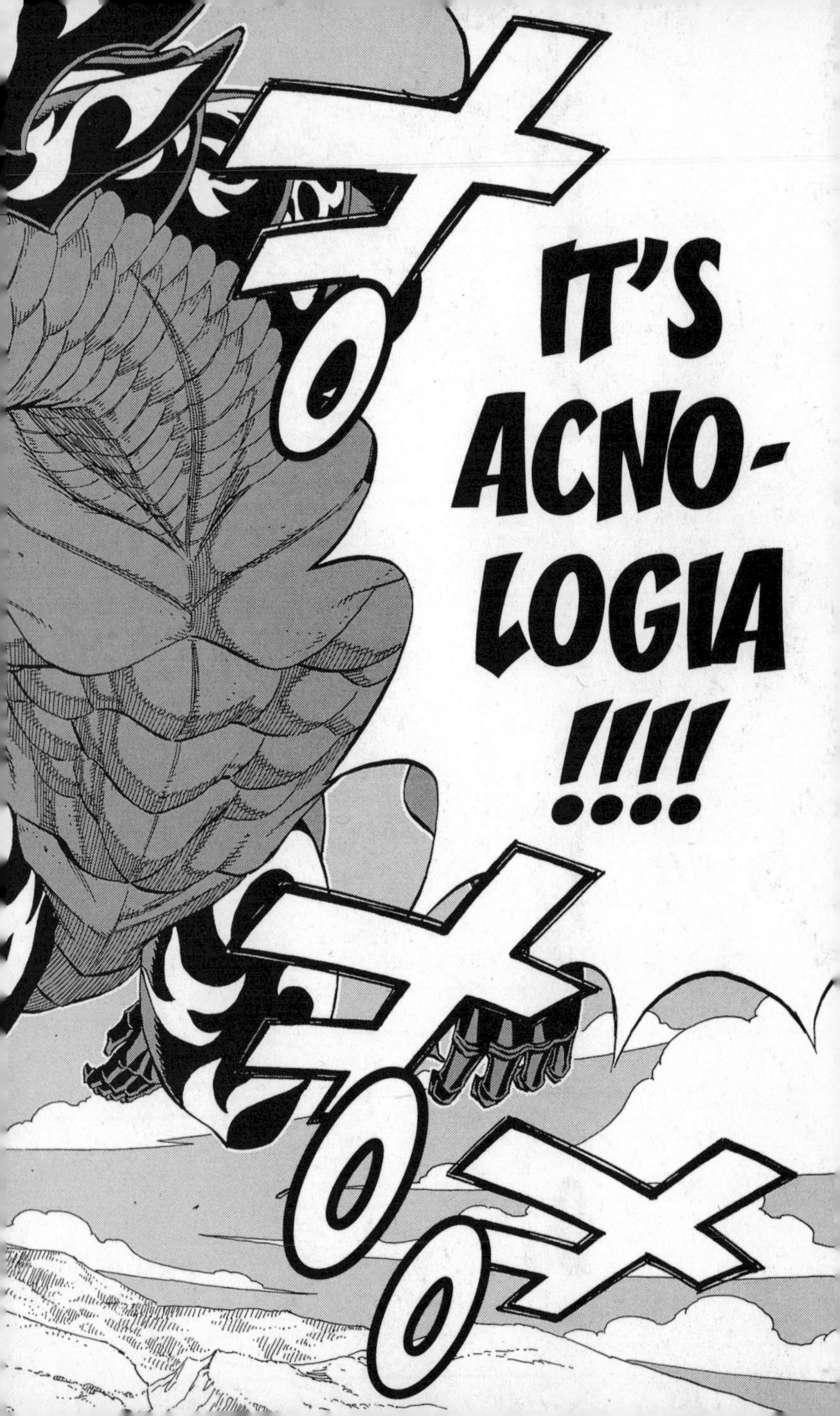
IT'S ACNO-LOGIA!!!!

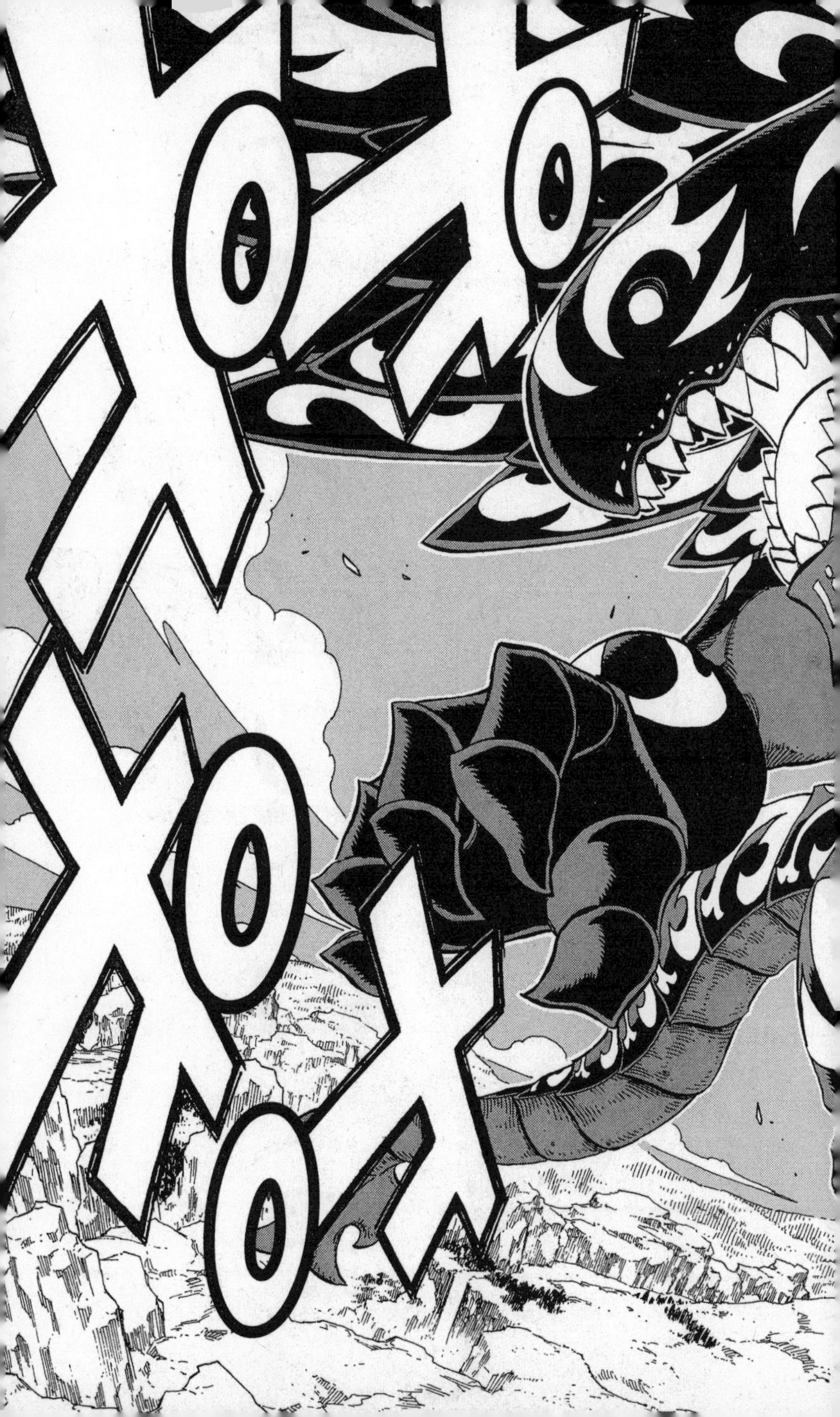

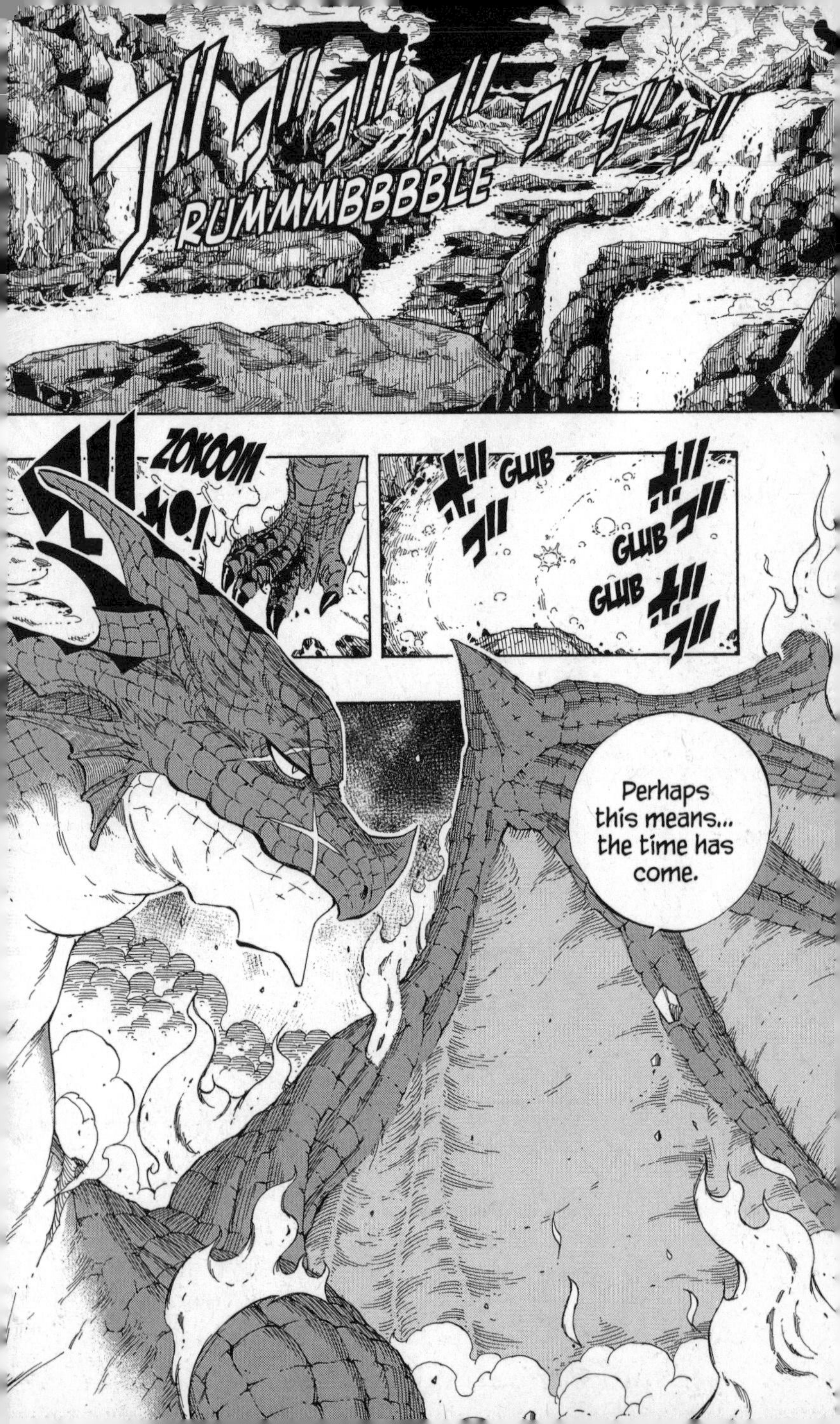
RUMMMBBBBLE
GLUB
GLUB
GLUB
ZOKOOM
Perhaps this means... the time has come.

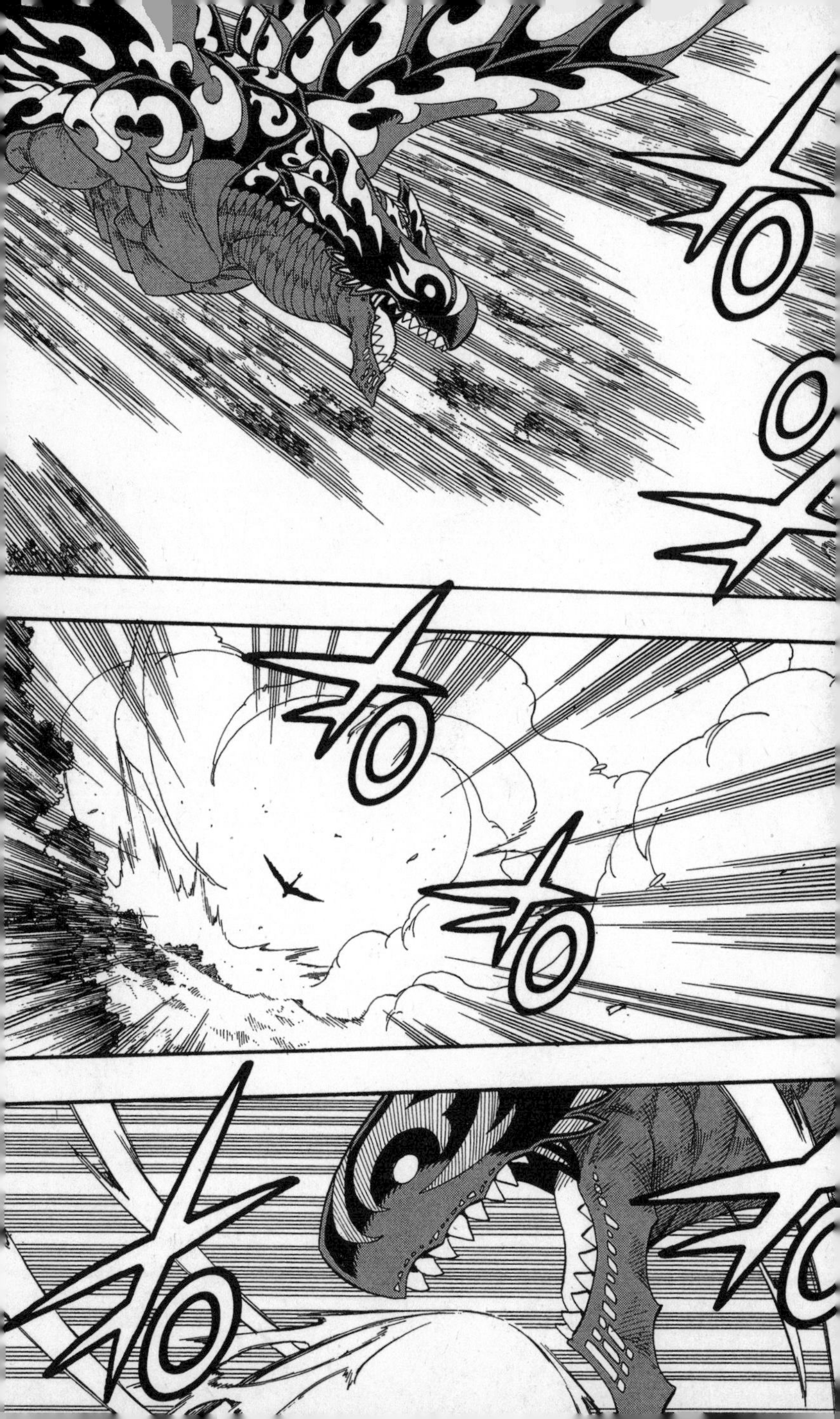

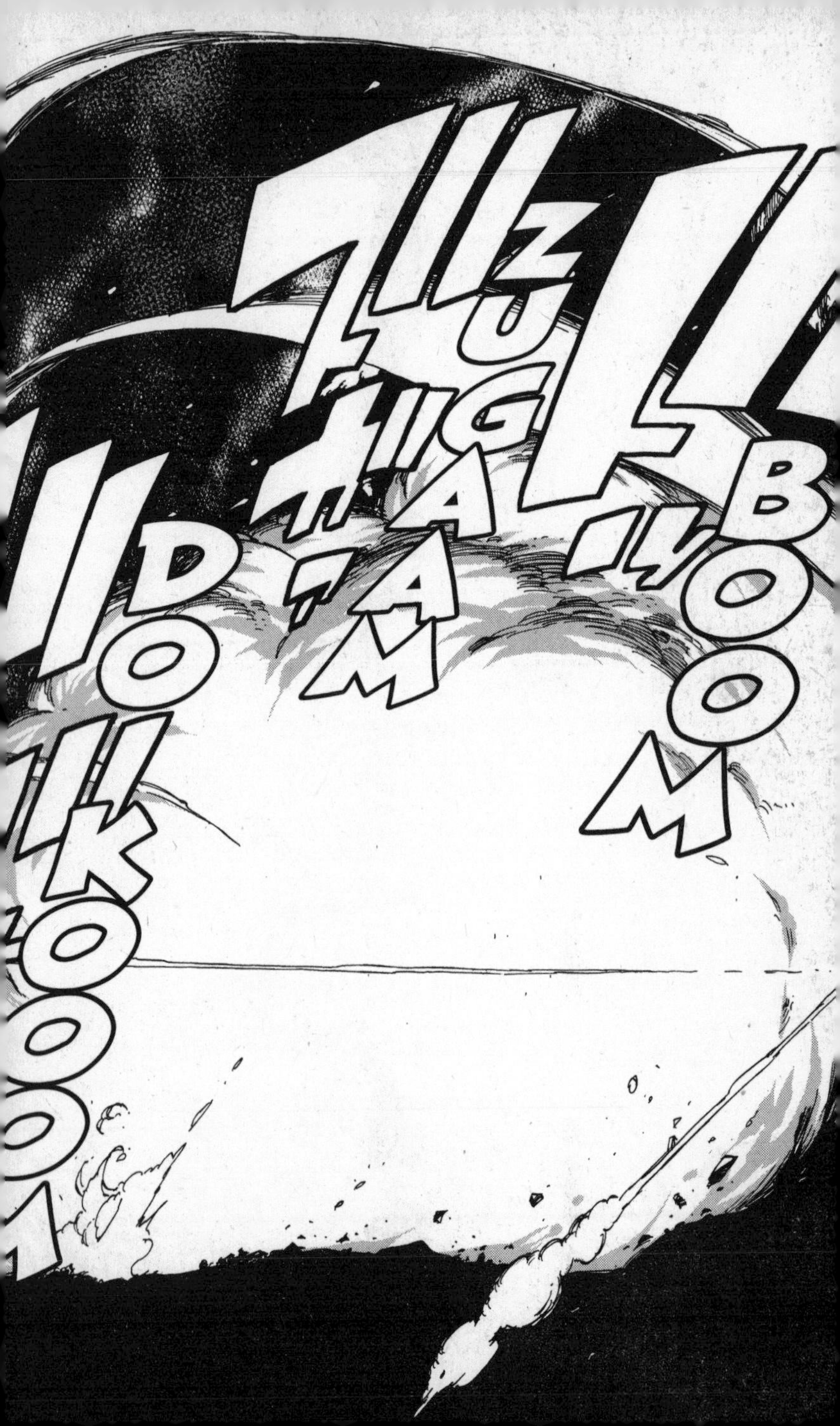
BOOM

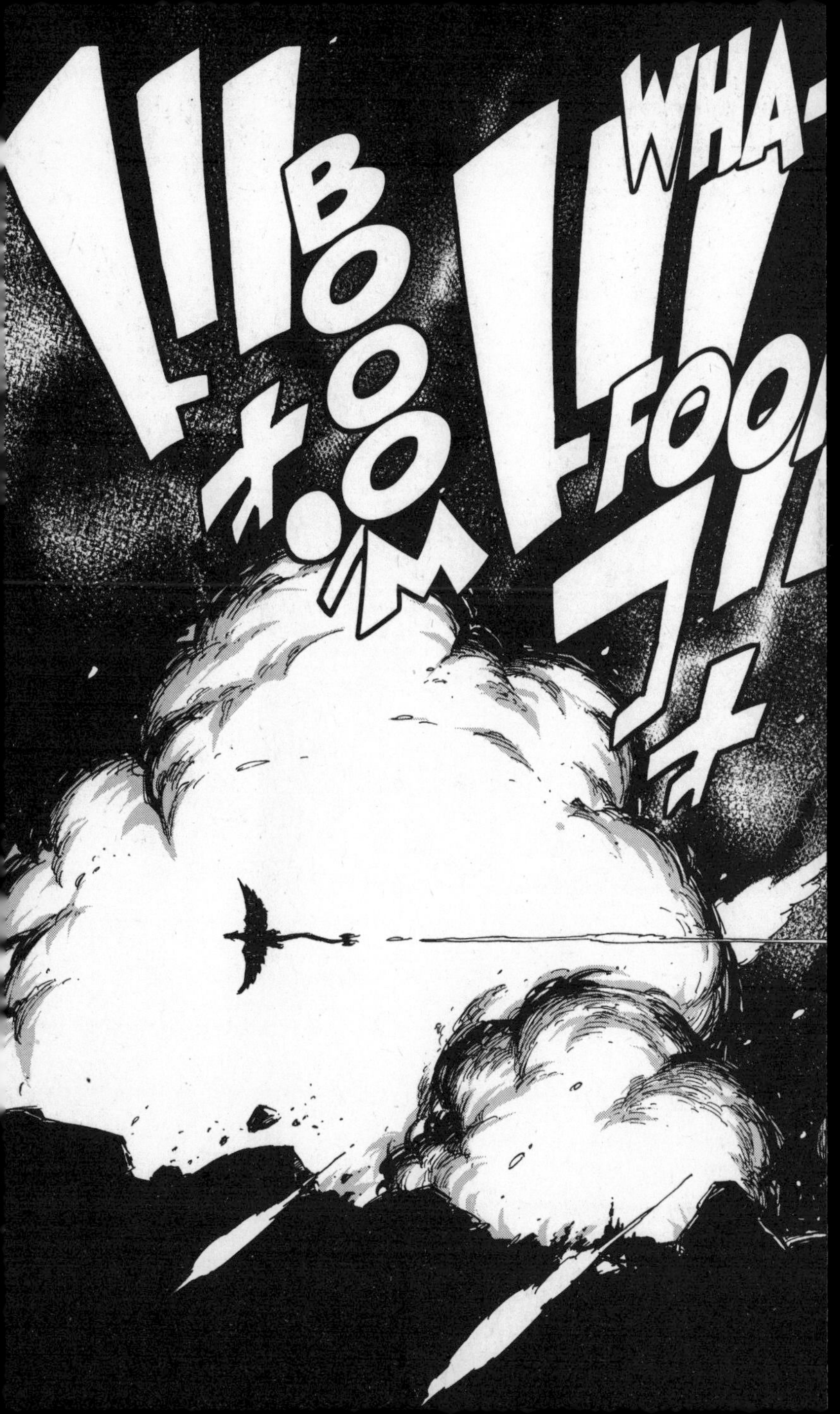
WHA-FOO
BOOOM

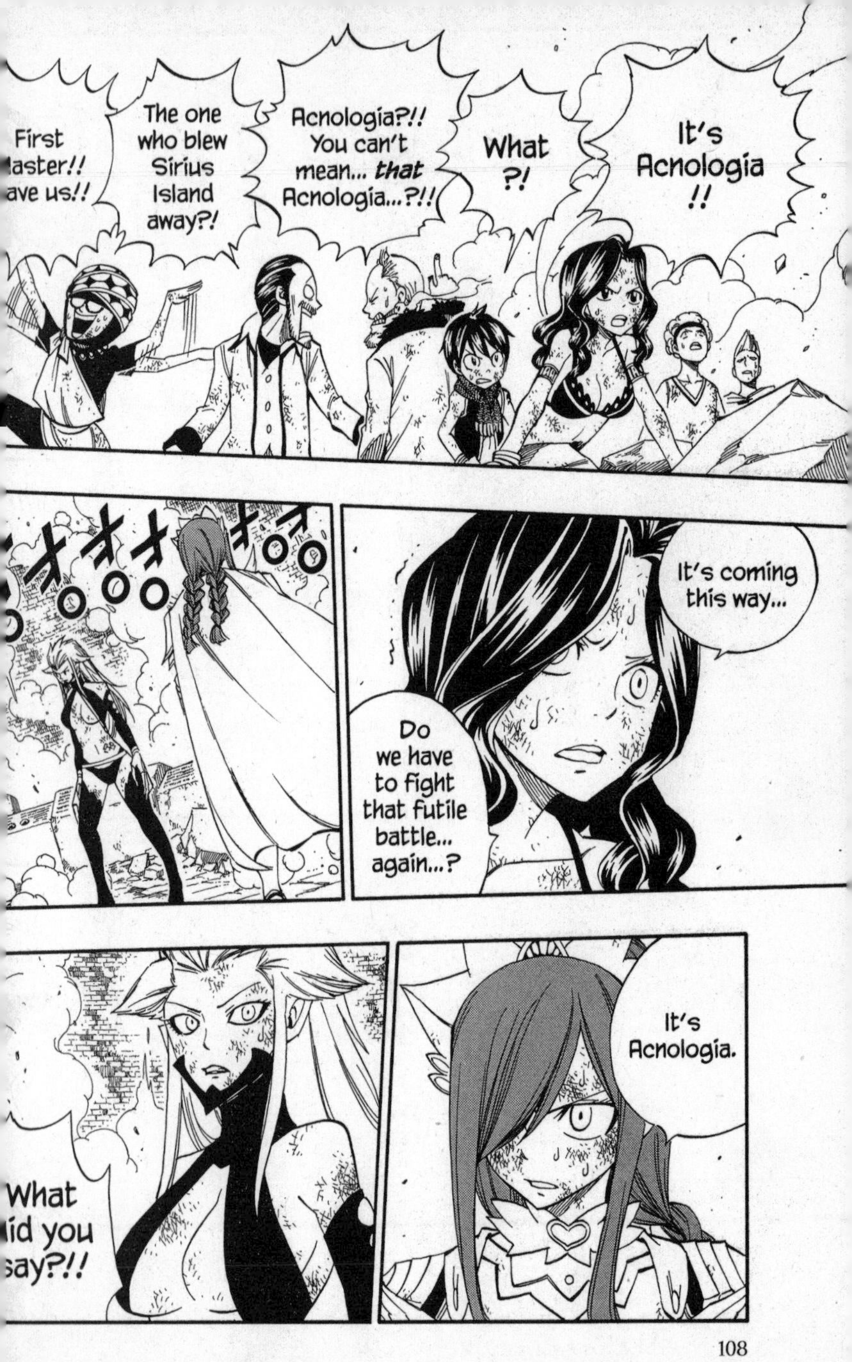
It's Acnologia!!
What?!
Acnologia?!! You can't mean... *that* Acnologia...?!!
The one who blew Sirius Island away?!
First aster!! ave us!!
It's coming this way...
Do we have to fight that futile battle... again...?
It's Acnologia.
What id you say?!!

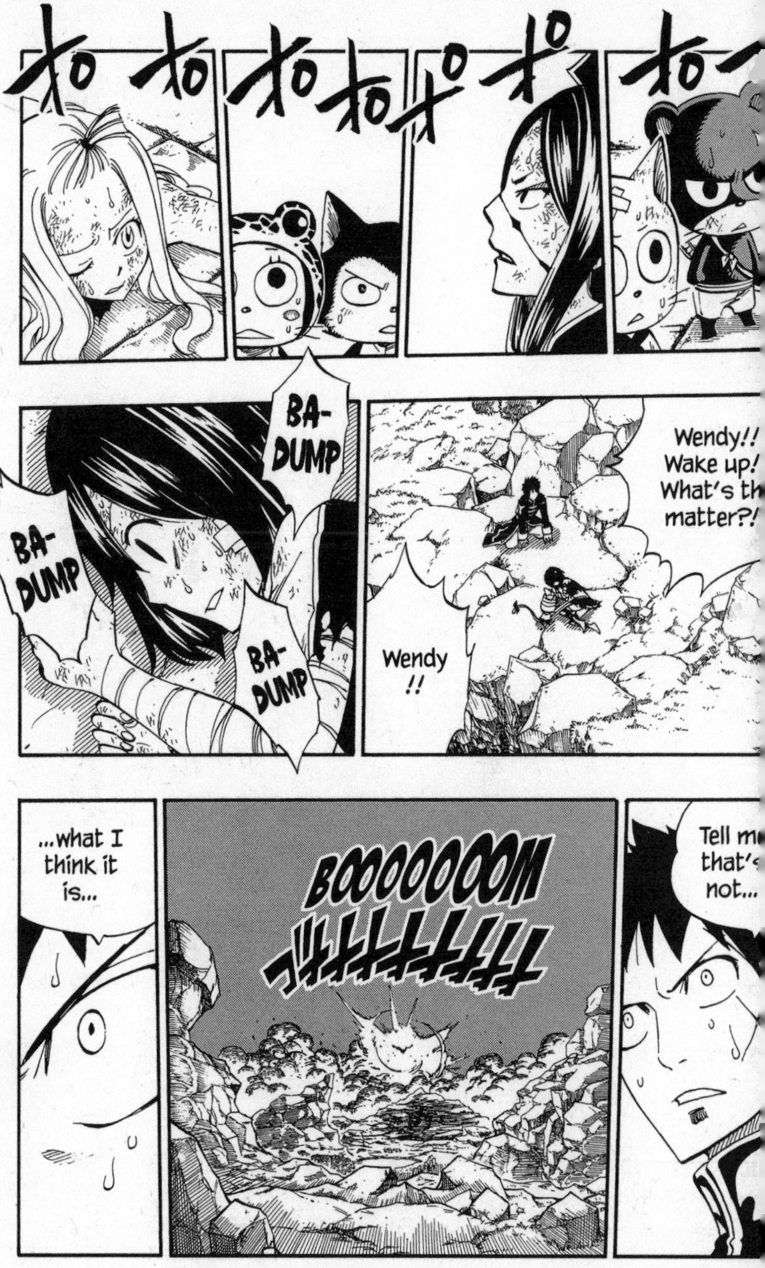
ォォォォォォポポォー
Wendy!! Wake up! What's th matter?!
Wendy !!
BA- DUMP
BA- DUMP
BA- DUMP
Tell m that's not...
BOOOOOOOM
ゴゴゴゴゴゴゴゴっ
...what I think it is...

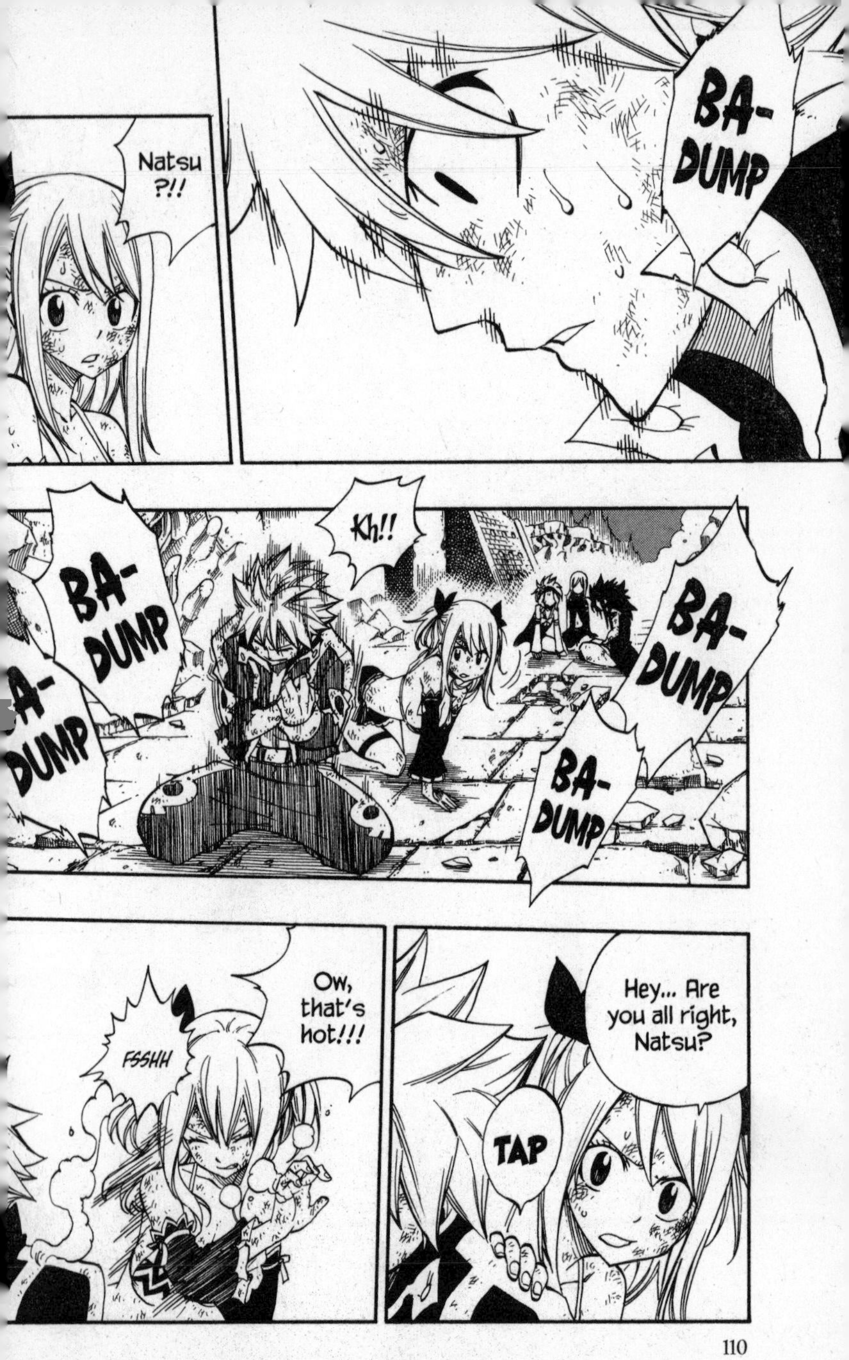
BA-DUMP
Natsu ?!!
BA-DUMP
BA-DUMP
Kh!!
BA-DUMP
BA-DUMP
Hey... Are you all right, Natsu?
TAP
Ow, that's hot!!!
FSSHH

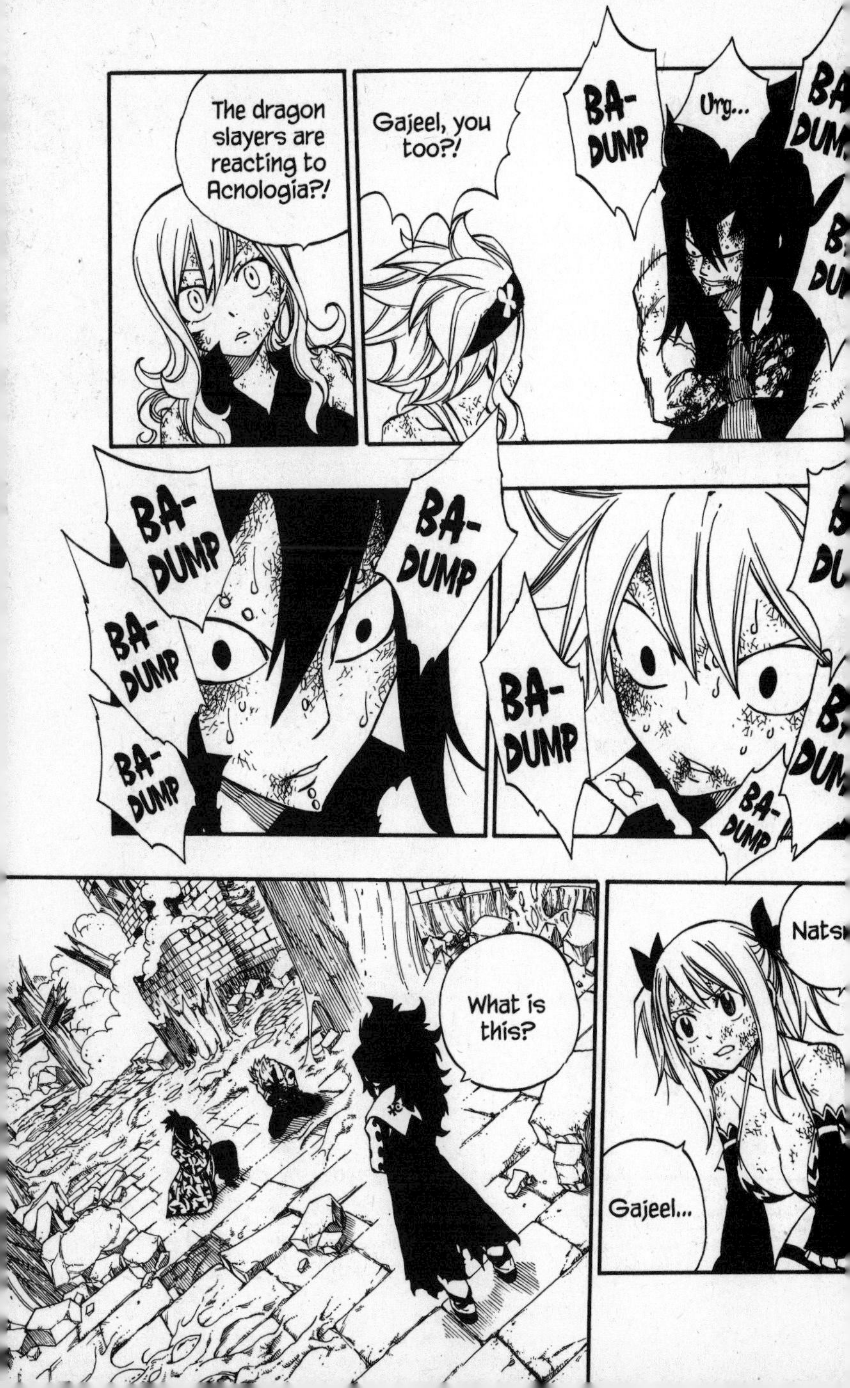
BA-DUMP
Urg...
Gajeel, you too?!
The dragon slayers are reacting to Acnologia?!
BA-DUMP
BA-DUMP
BA-DUMP
BA-DUMP
BA-DUMP
BA-DUMP
Nats
Gajeel...
What is this?

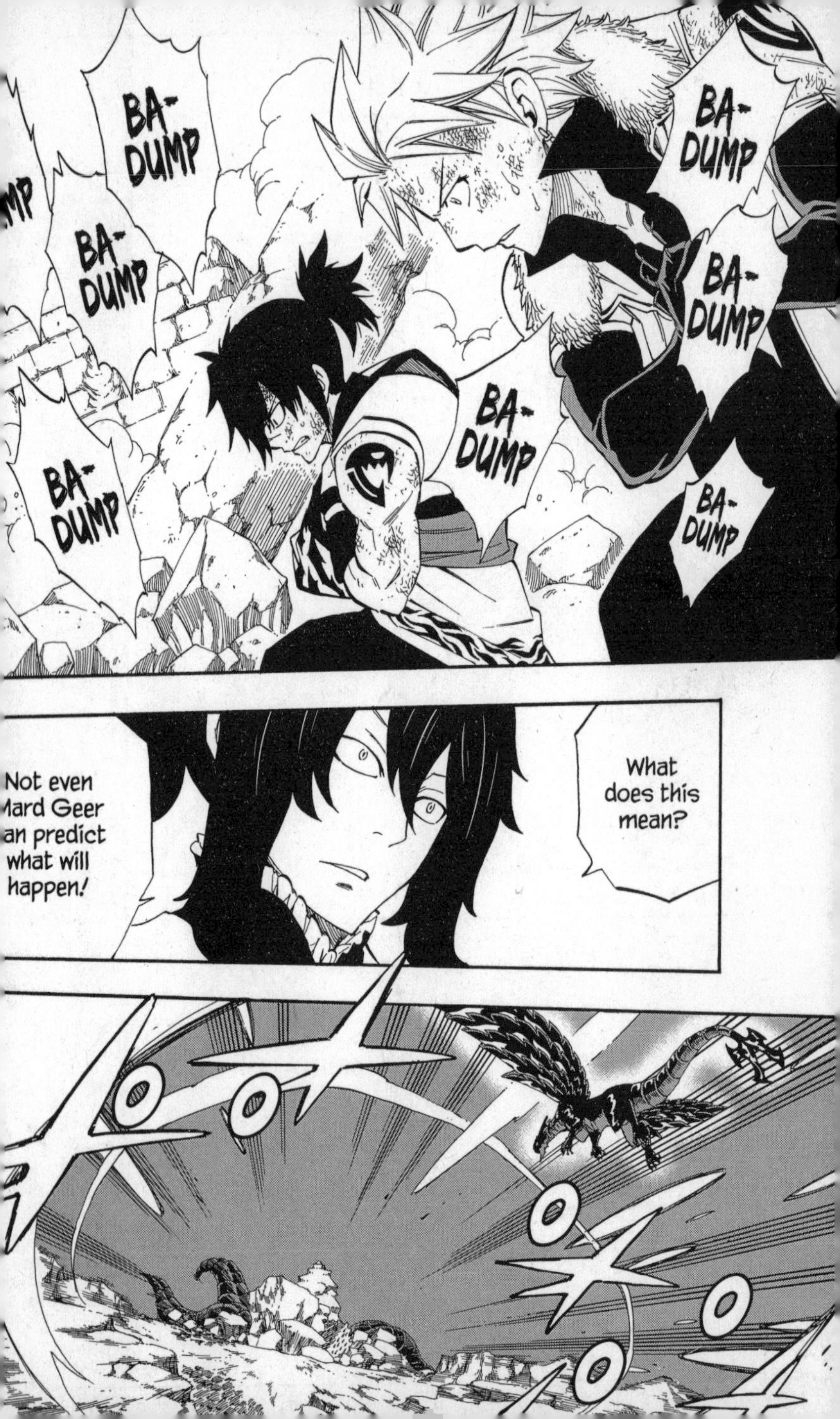
BA-DUMP
BA-DUMP
BA-DUMP
BA-DUMP
BA-DUMP
BA-DUMP
BA-DUMP
What does this mean?
Not even Mard Geer an predict what will happen!

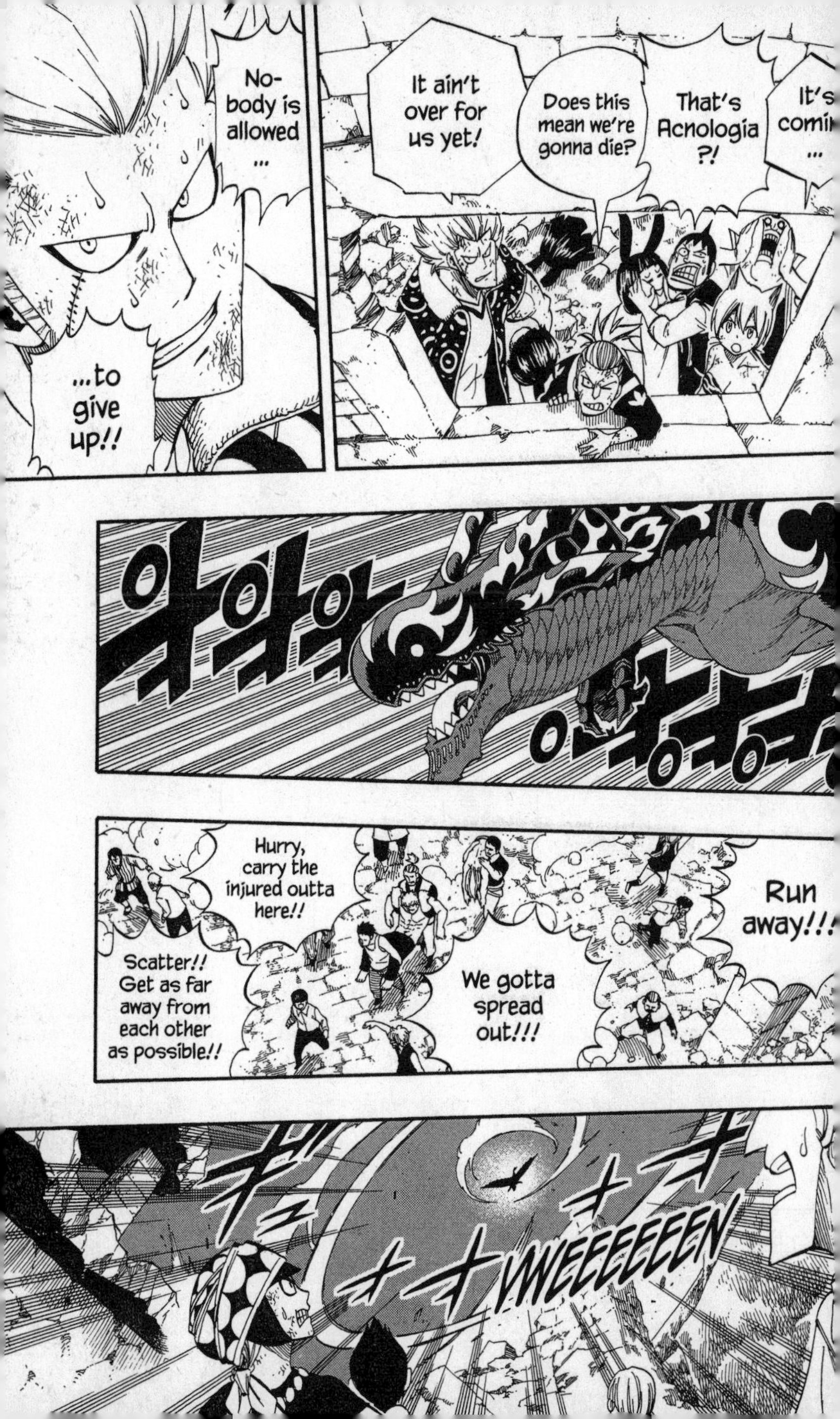
It's comi ...
That's Acnologia ?!
Does this mean we're gonna die?
It ain't over for us yet!
No-body is allowed ...
...to give up!!
Run away!!!
We gotta spread out!!!
Hurry, carry the injured outta here!!
Scatter!! Get as far away from each other as possible!!
WEEEEEEN

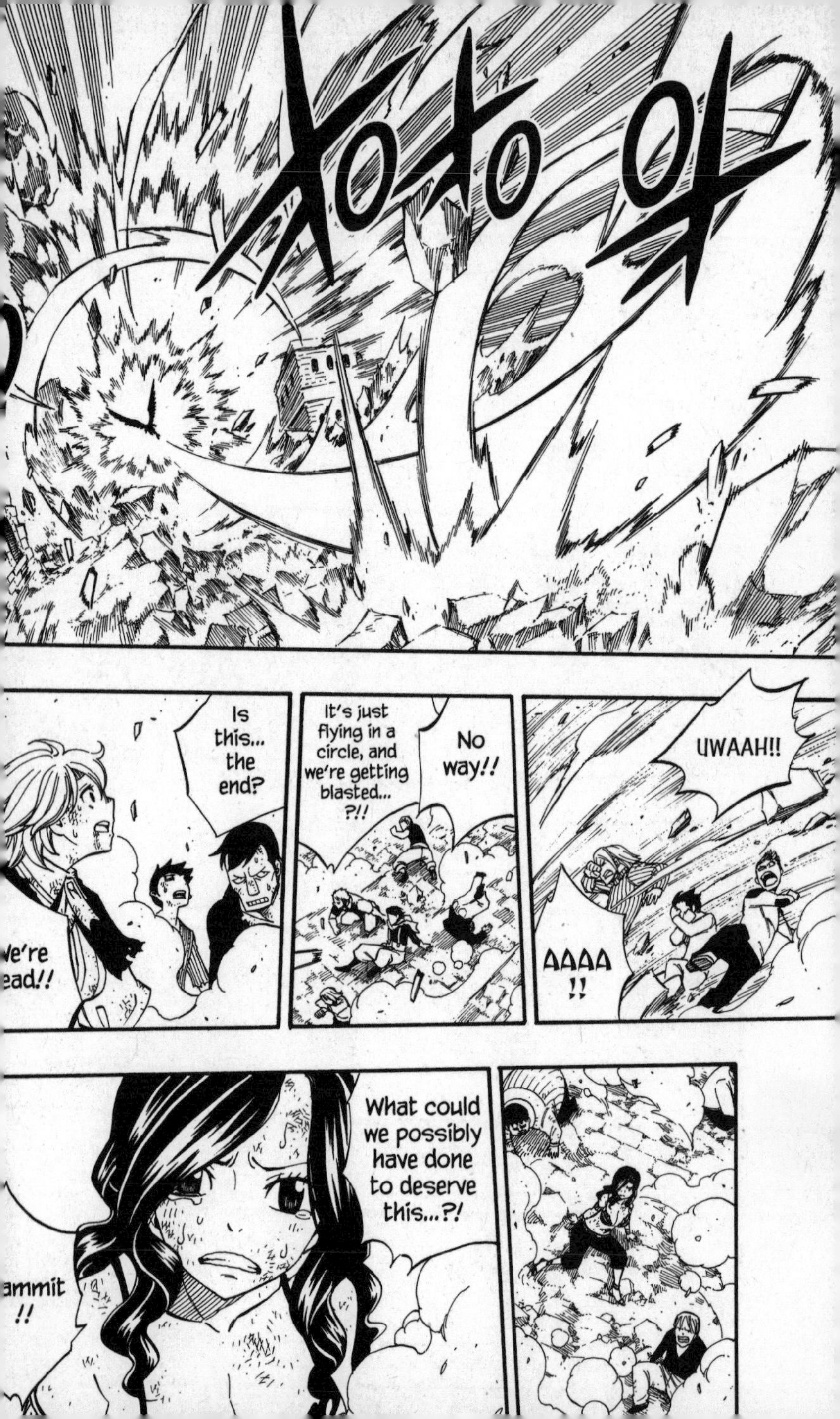
UWAAH!!
AAAA !!
No way!!
It's just flying in a circle, and we're getting blasted... ?!!
Is this... the end?
e're ead!!
What could we possibly have done to deserve this...?!
ammit !!

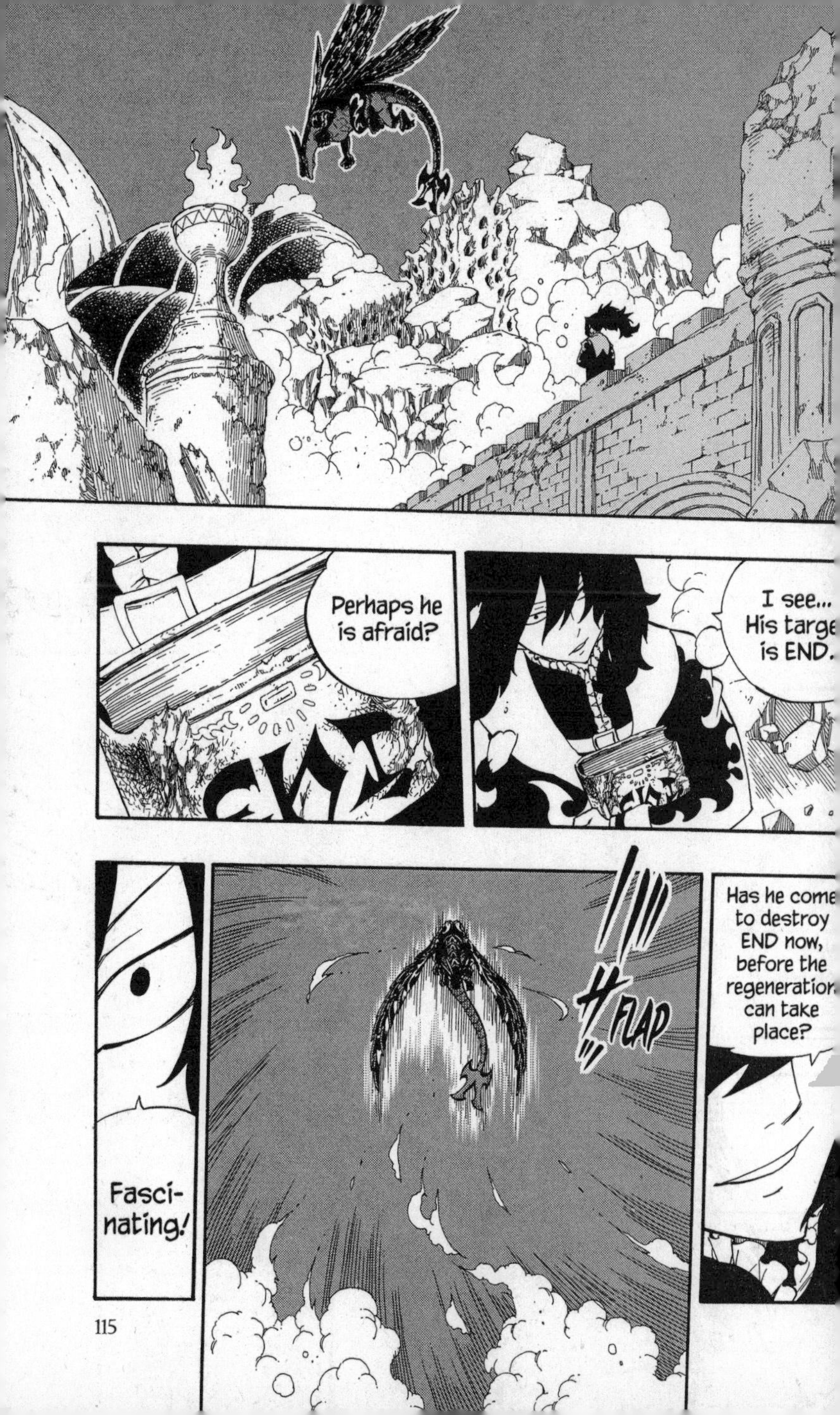
I see... His targe is END.
Perhaps he is afraid?
Has he come to destroy END now, before the regeneratio can take place?
FLAP
Fasci-nating!

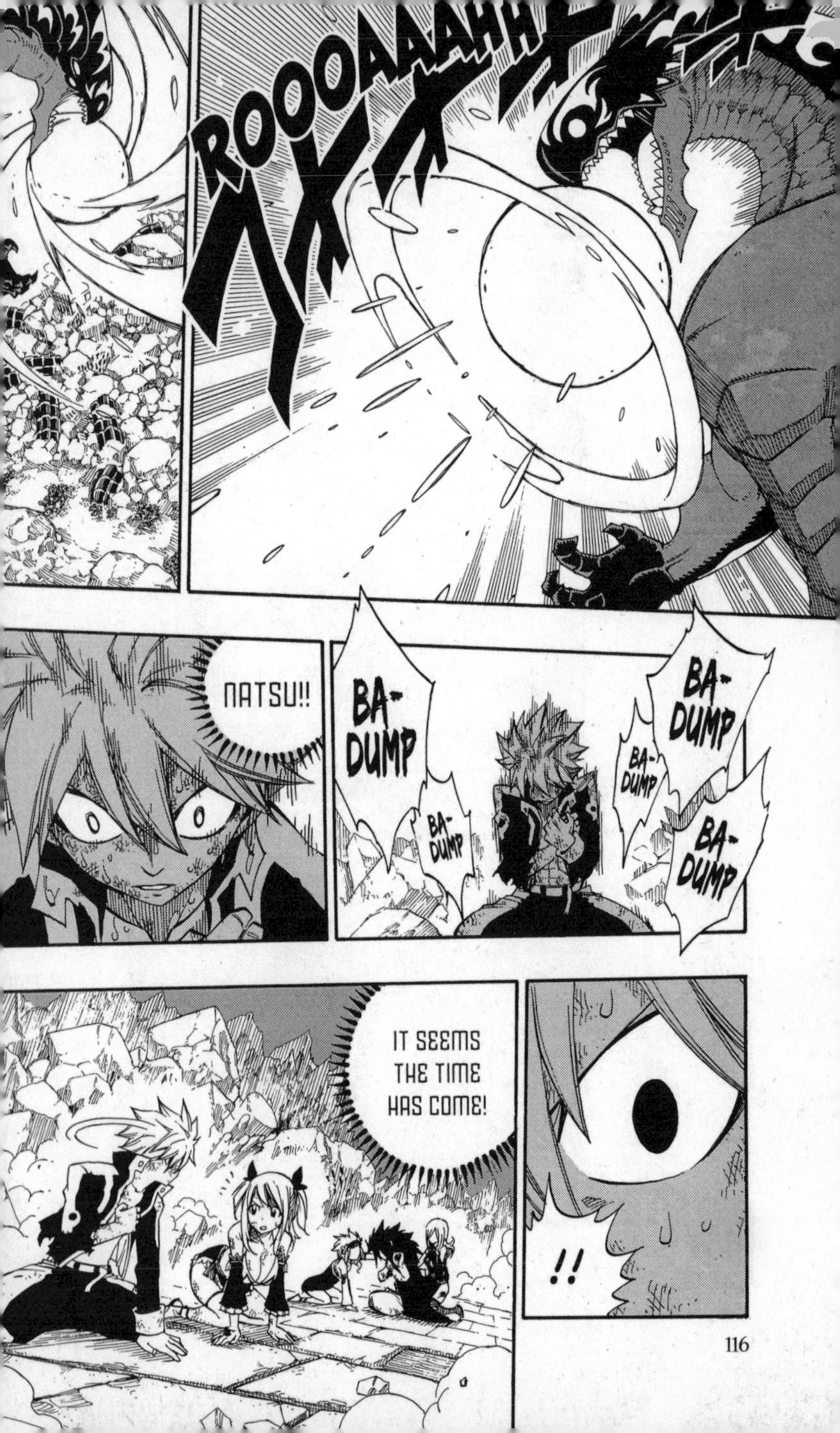
ROOOAAAHH
BA-DUMP
BA-DUMP
BA-DUMP
BA-DUMP
BA-DUMP
NATSU!!
!!
IT SEEMS THE TIME HAS COME!

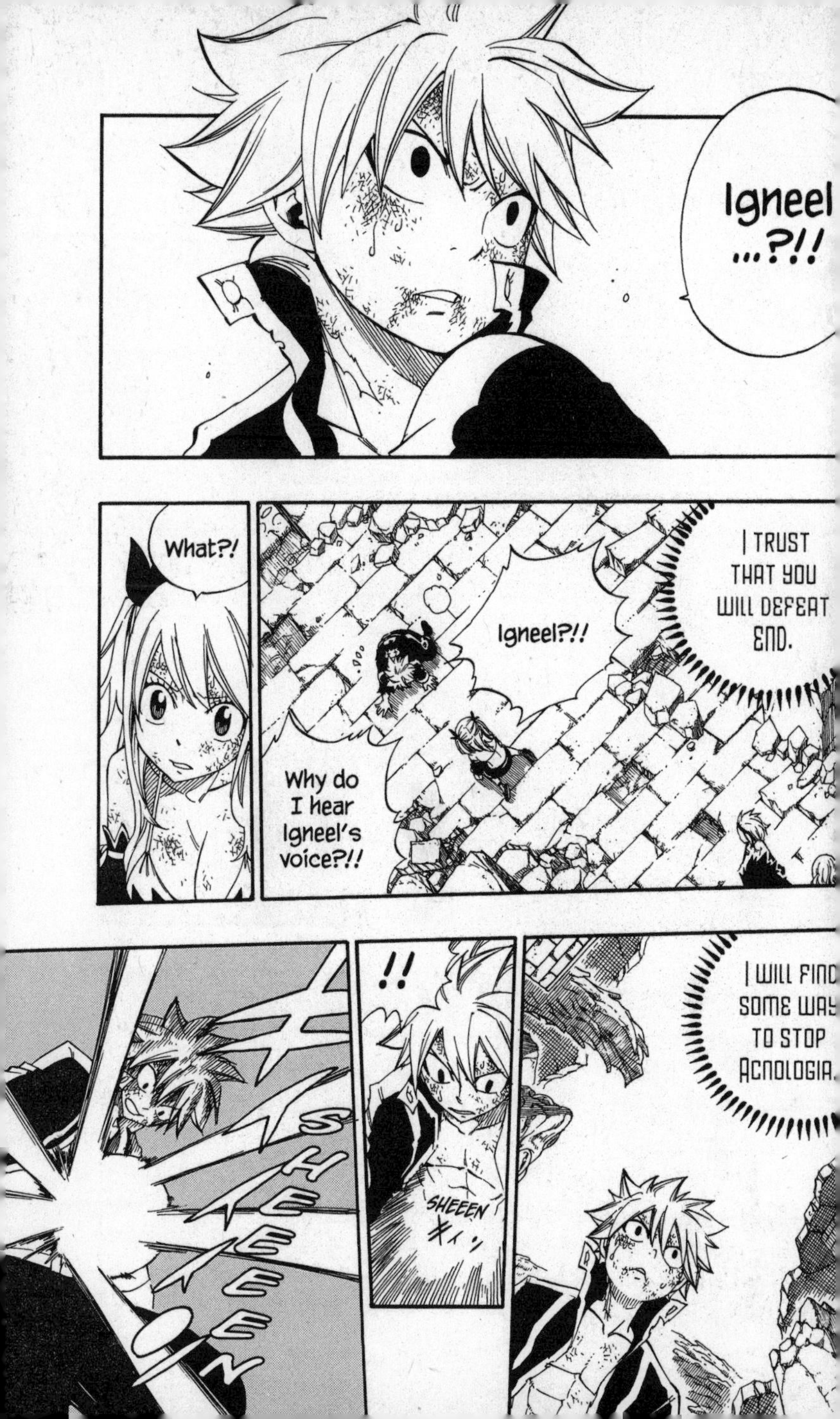

Igneel ...?!!
I TRUST THAT YOU WILL DEFEAT END.
Igneel?!!
Why do I hear Igneel's voice?!!
What?!
I WILL FIND SOME WAY TO STOP ACNOLOGIA.
!!
SHEEEN
キィッ
SHEEEEN

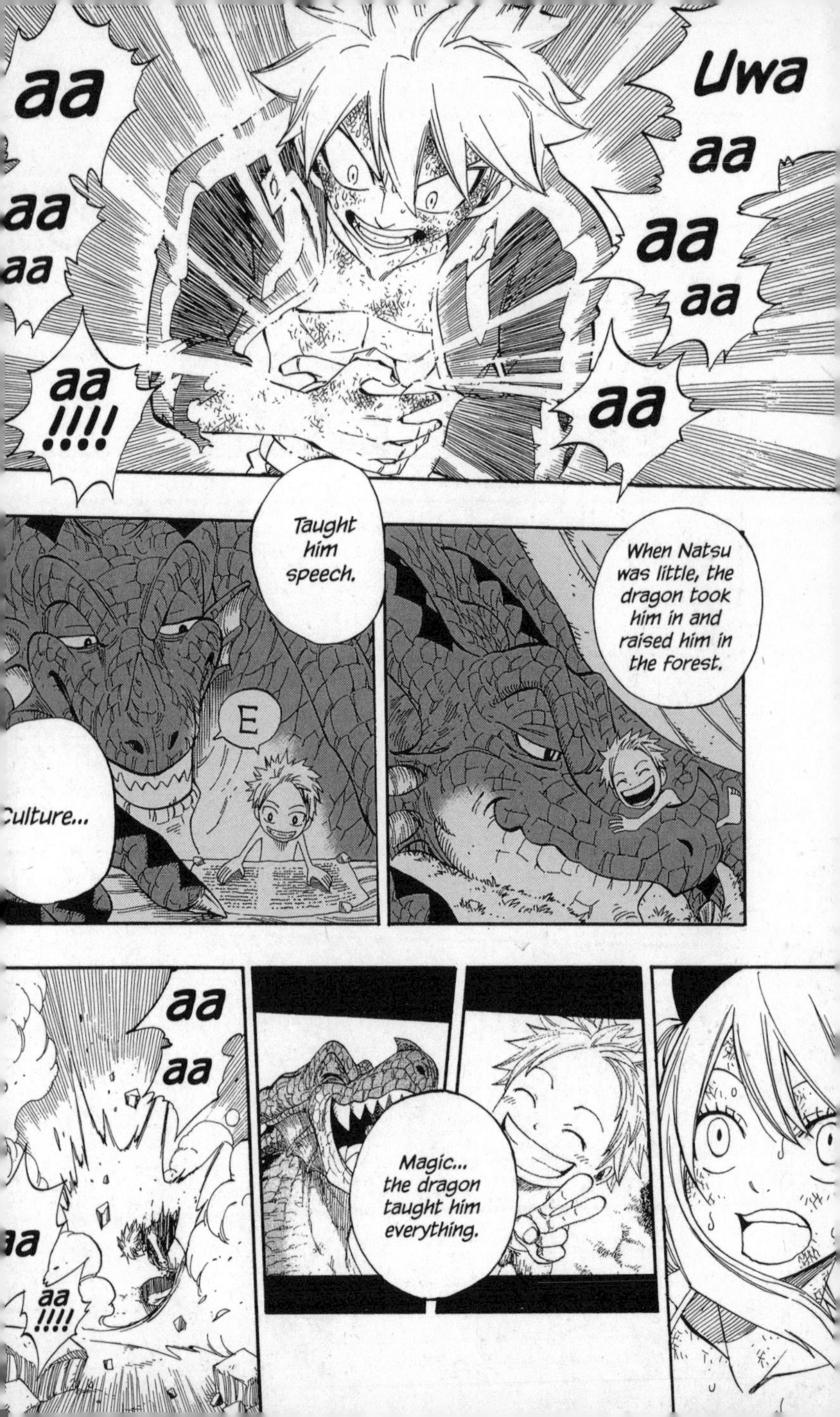
Uwa aa aa aa aa
aa aa aa aa !!!!
When Natsu was little, the dragon took him in and raised him in the forest.
Taught him speech.
E
Culture...
Magic... the dragon taught him everything.
aa aa aa aa !!!!

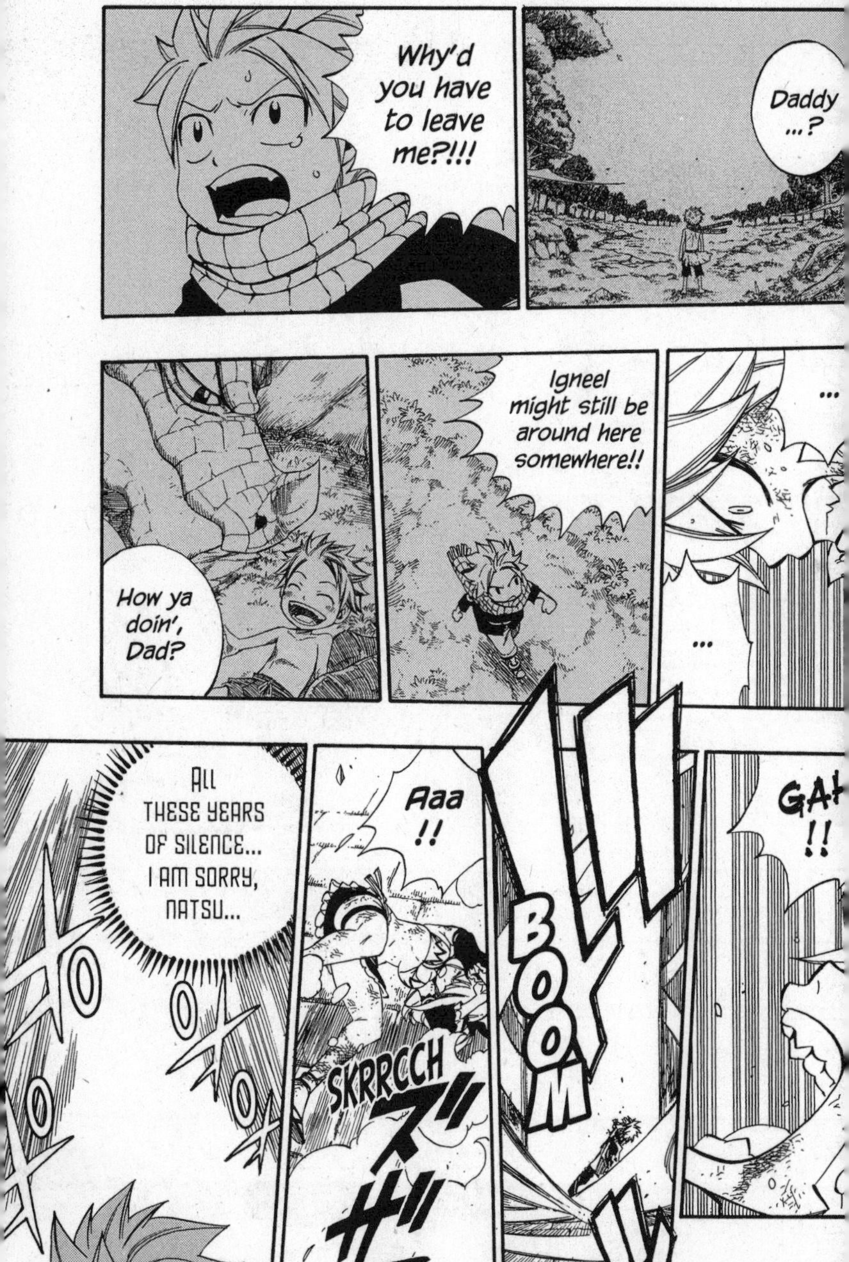
Daddy ...?
Why'd you have to leave me?!!!
...
...
Igneel might still be around here somewhere!!
How ya doin', Dad?
GAH !!
BOOM
Aaa !!
SKRRCCH
ALL THESE YEARS OF SILENCE... I AM SORRY, NATSU...

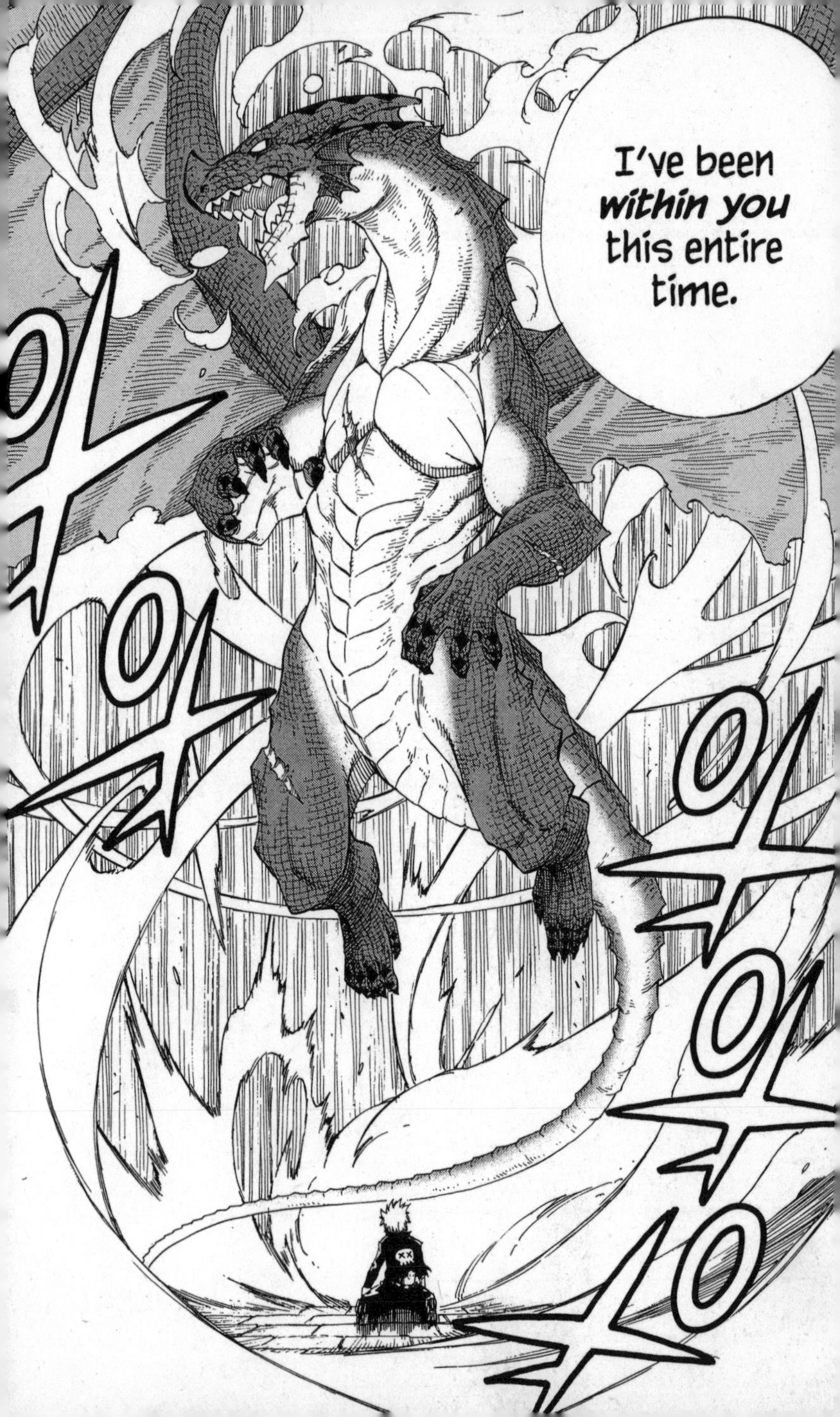
I've been ***within you*** this entire time.

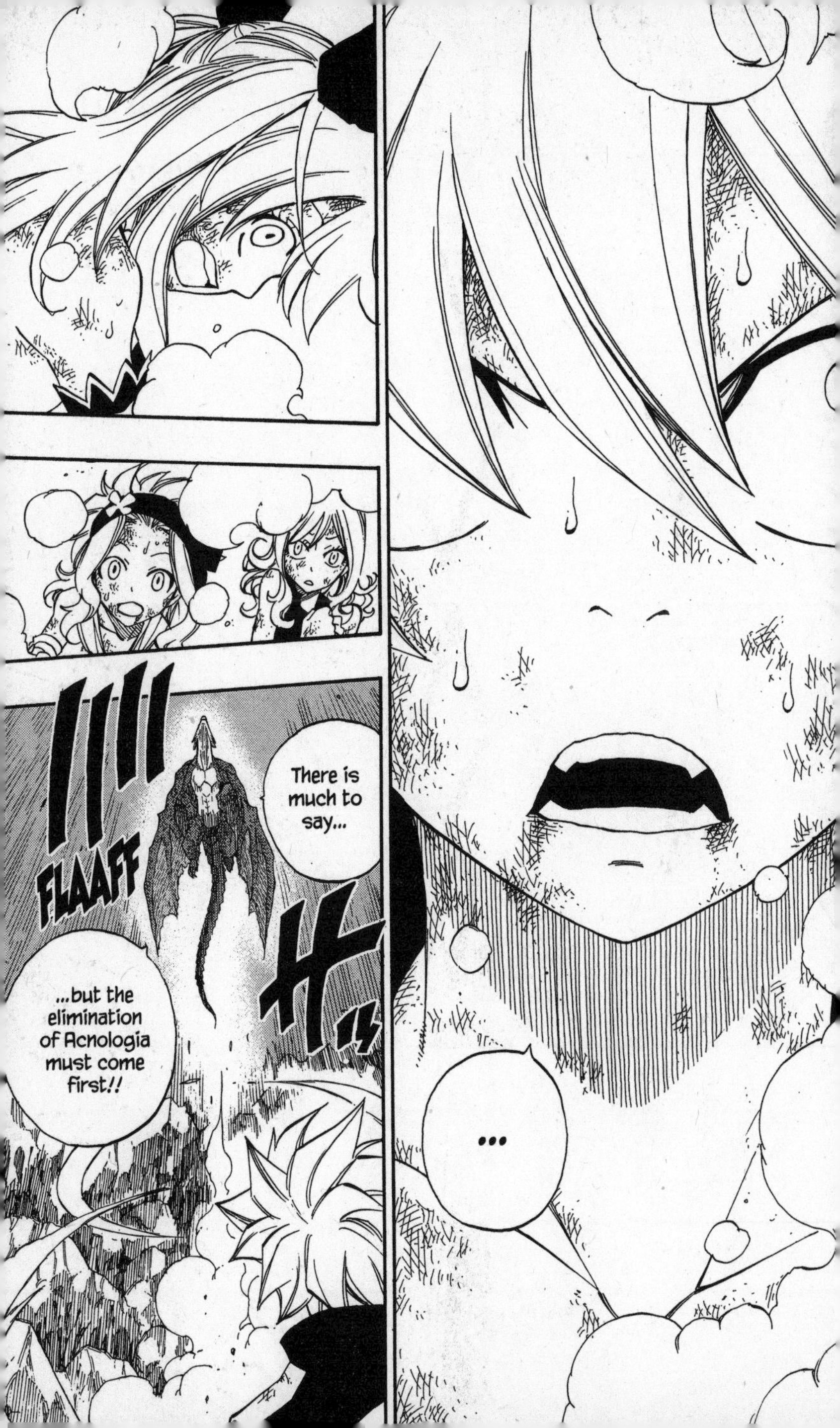
...
There is much to say...
FLAAFF
...but the elimination of Acnologia must come first!!

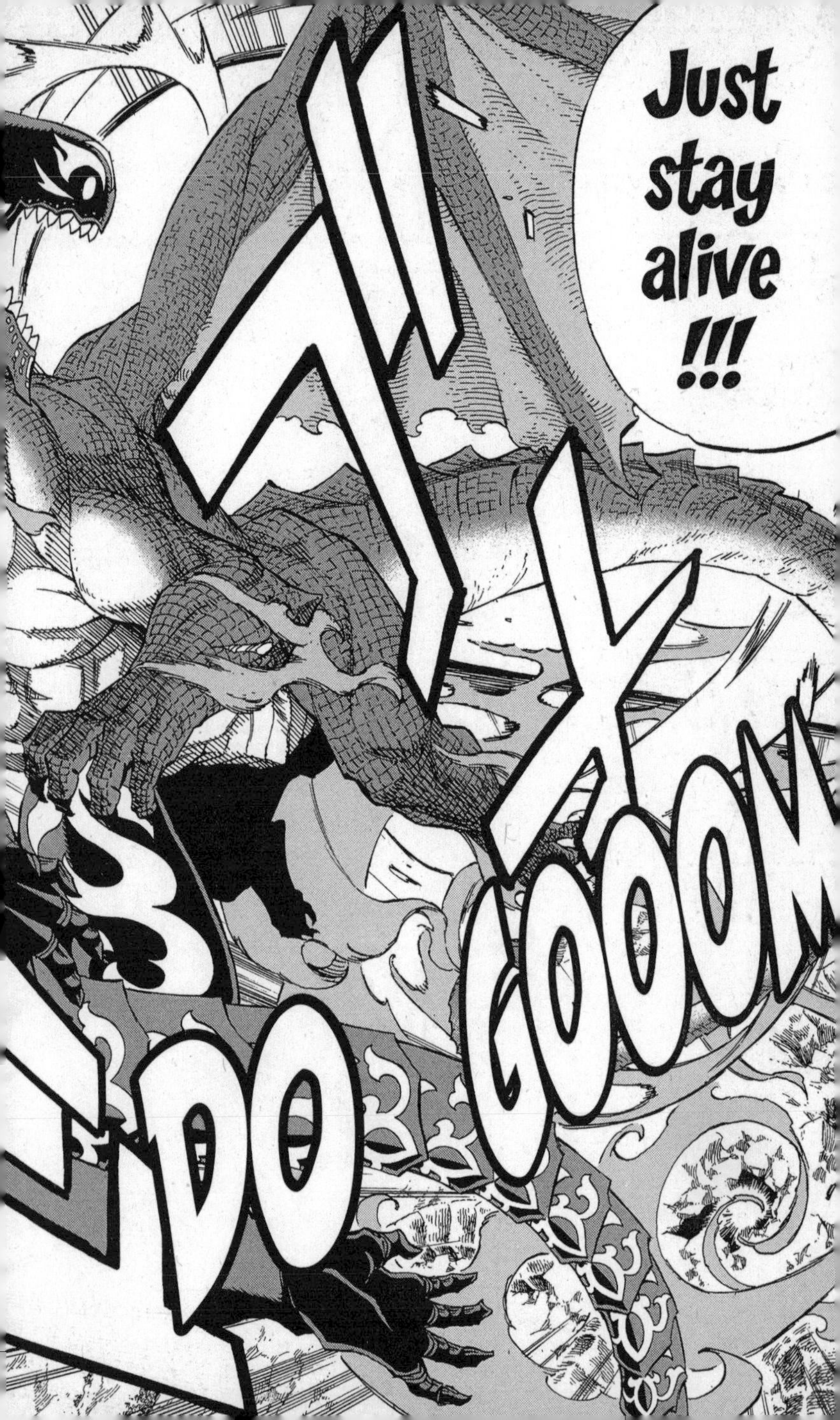
Just stay alive!!!
DOGOOOM

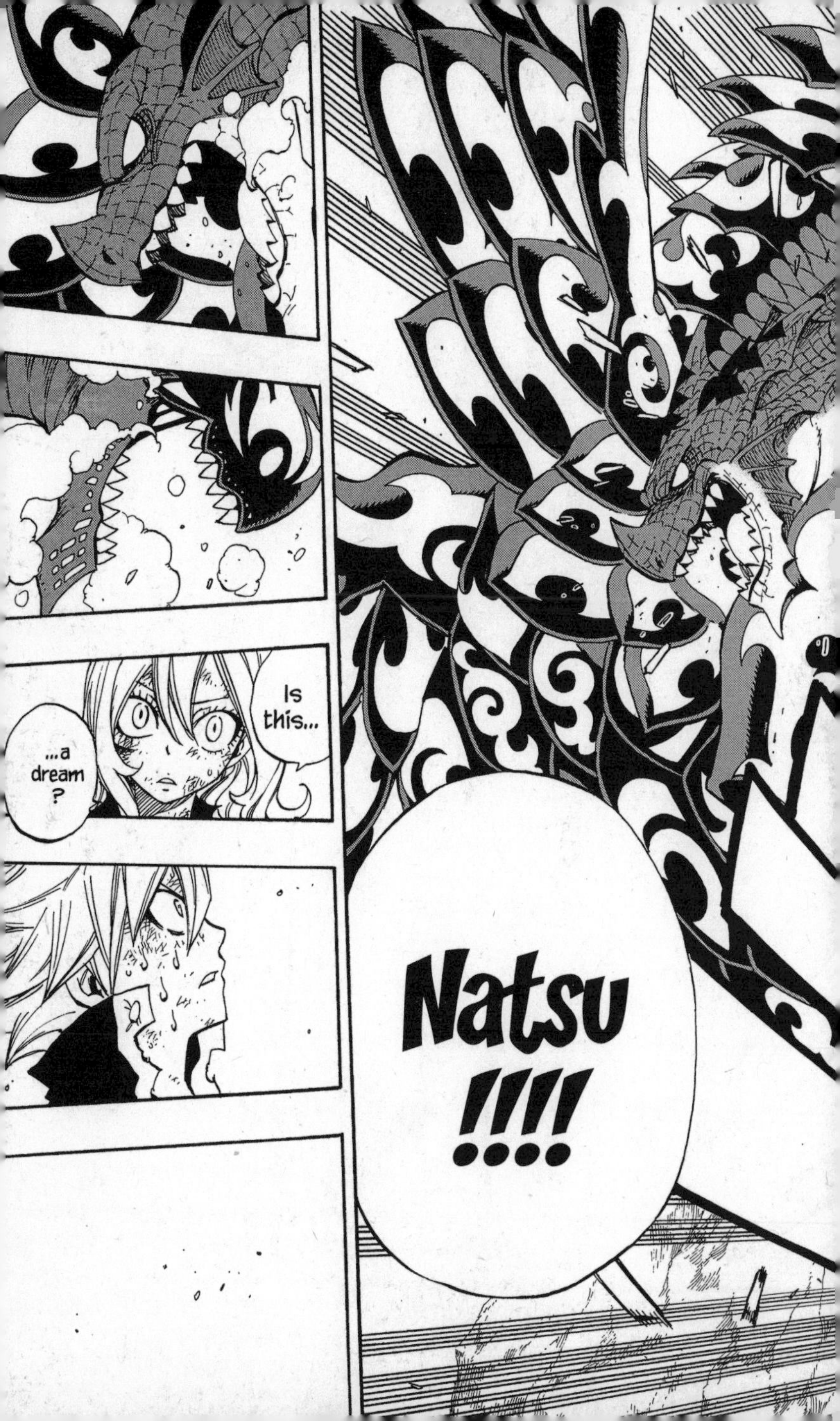
Natsu!!!!
Is this...
...a dream?

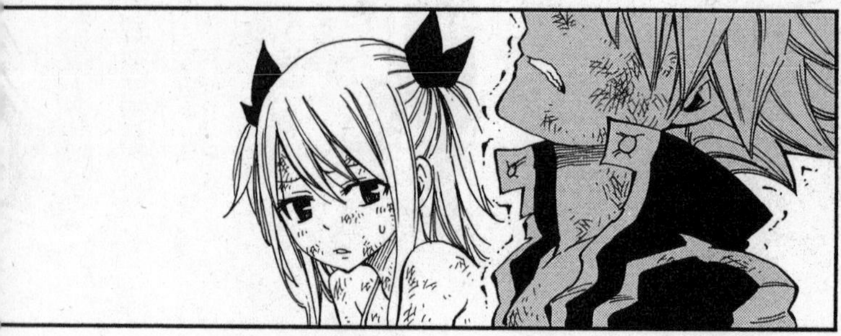
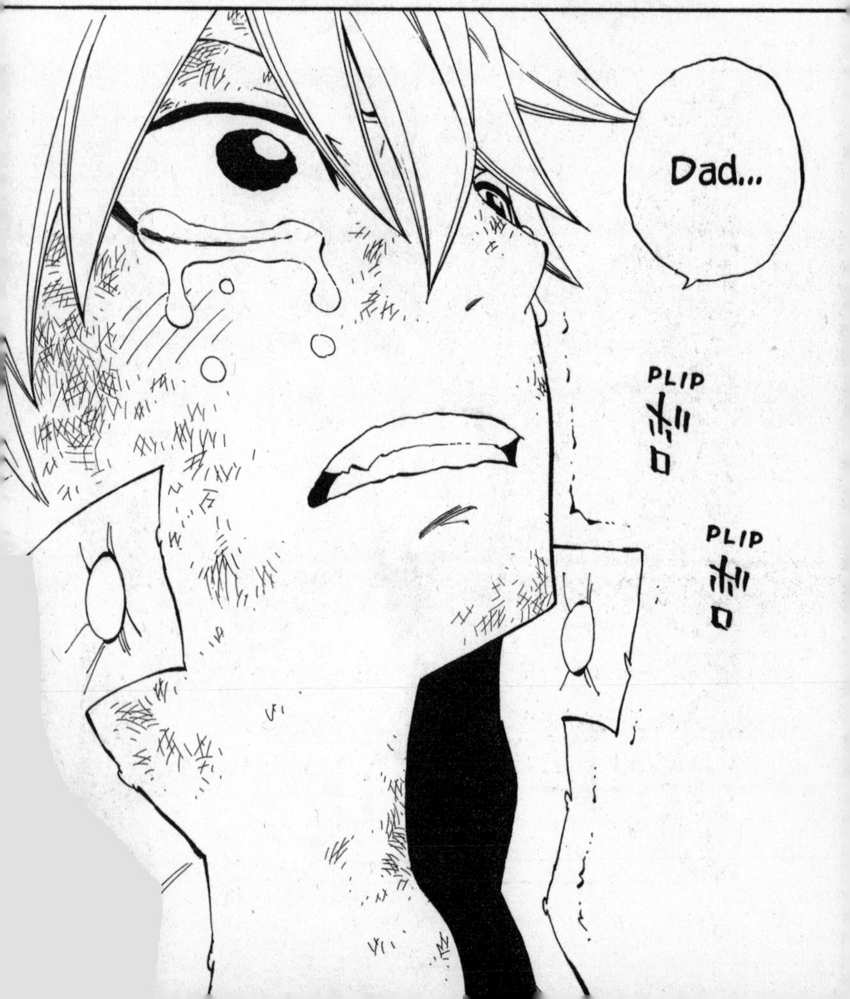
Dad...
PLIP
ボロ
PLIP
ボロ

FAIRY TAIL

フェアリーテイル

Chapter 401: Igneel vs. Acnologi

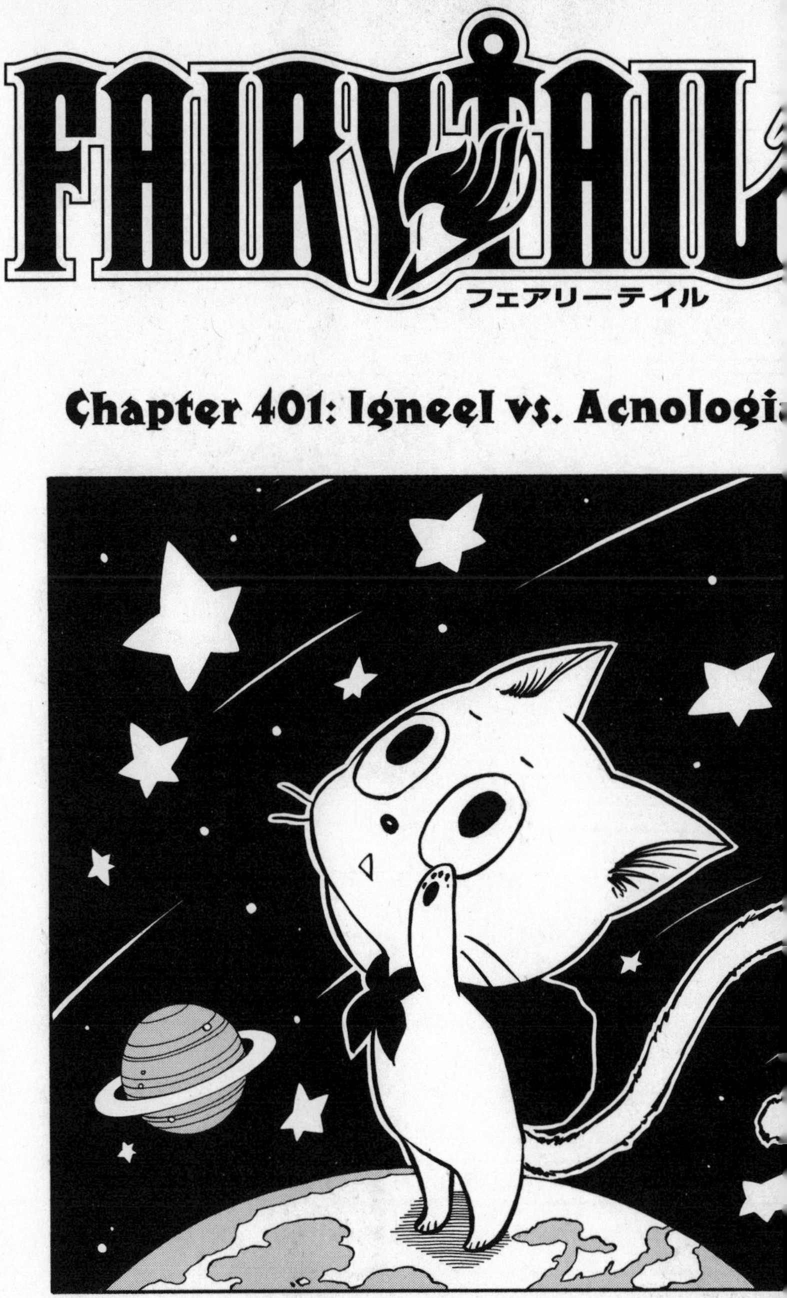

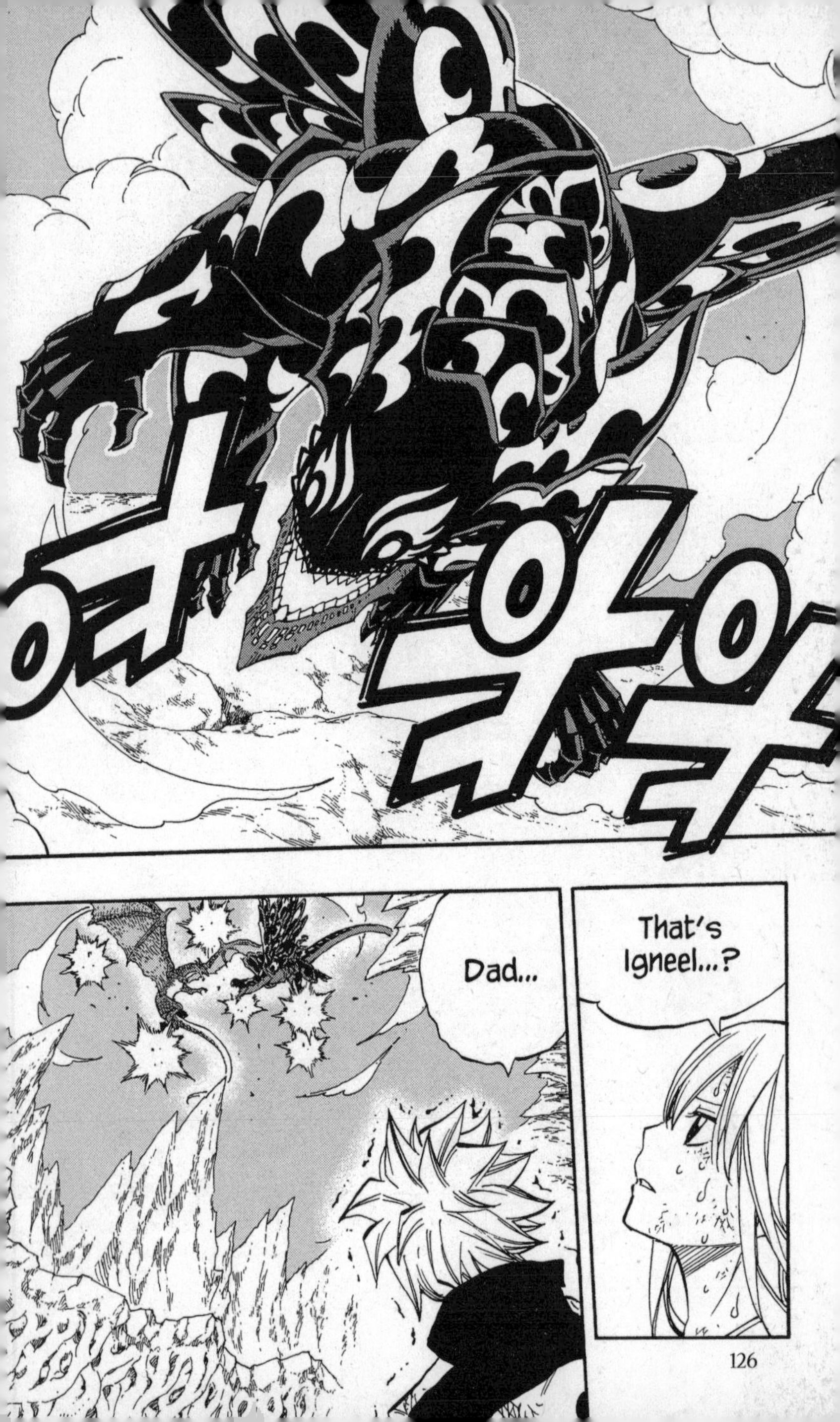
That's Igneel...?
Dad...

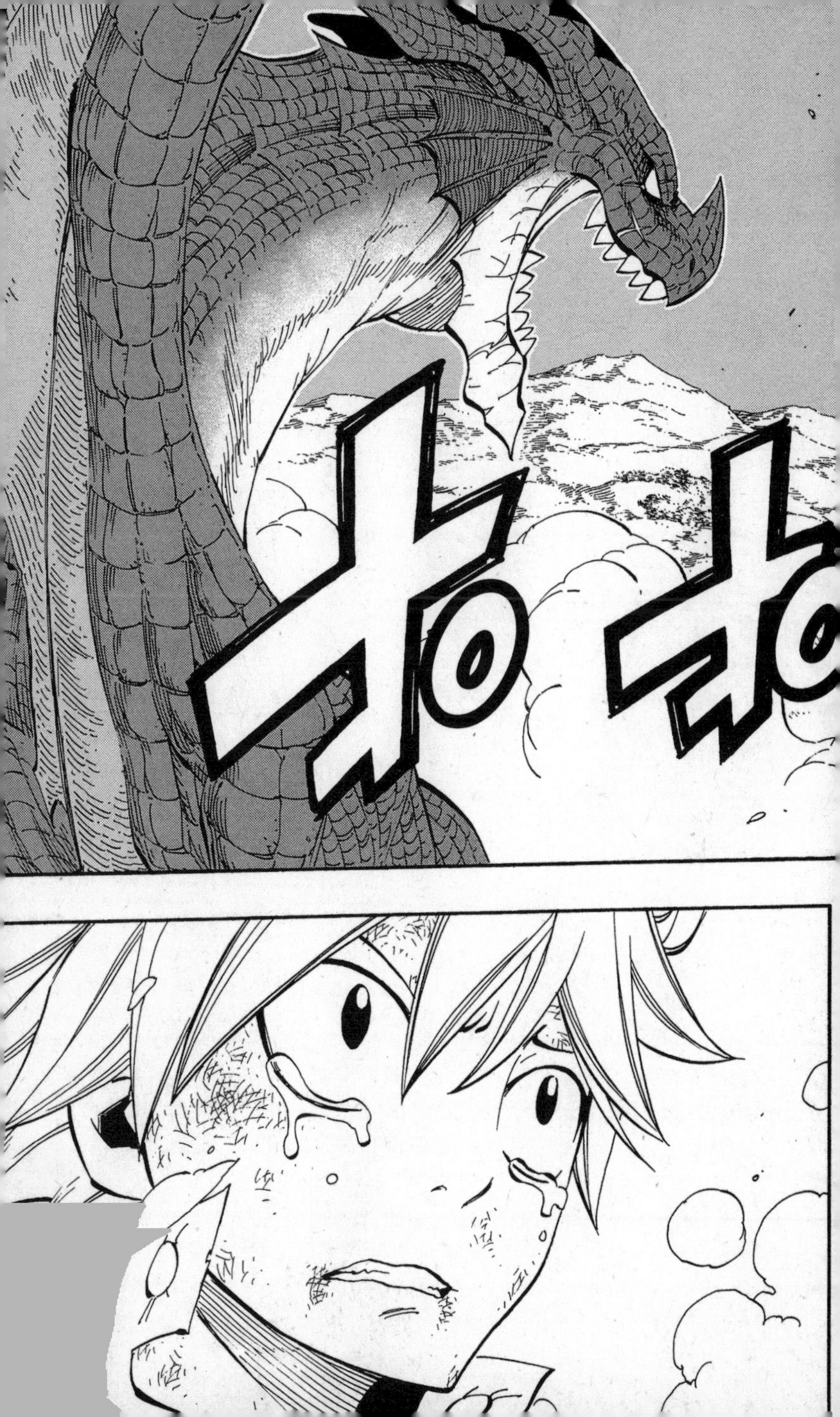

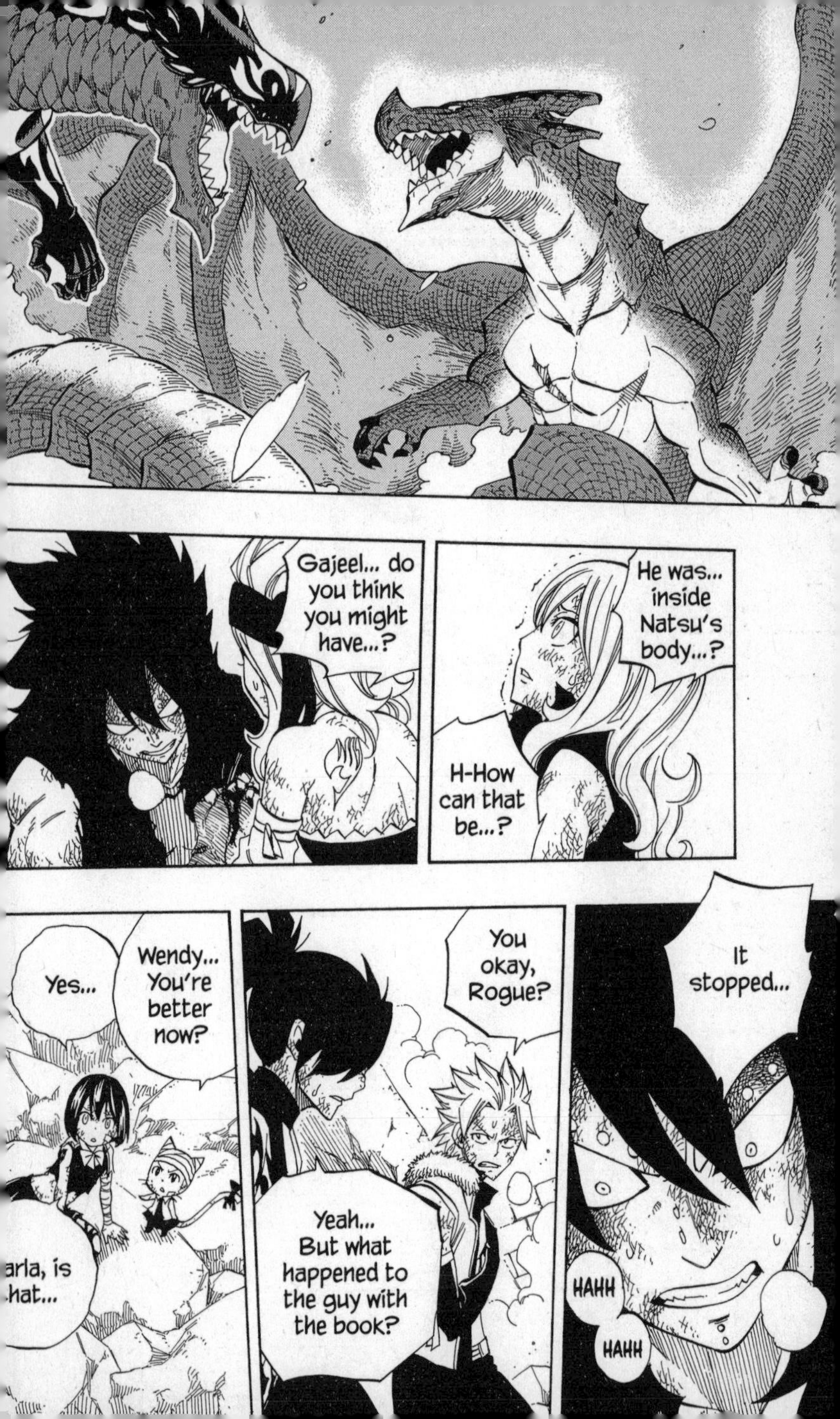
He was... inside Natsu's body...?
H-How can that be...?
Gajeel... do you think you might have...?
It stopped...
HAHH
HAHH
You okay, Rogue?
Yeah... But what happened to the guy with the book?
Wendy... You're better now?
Yes...
arla, is hat...

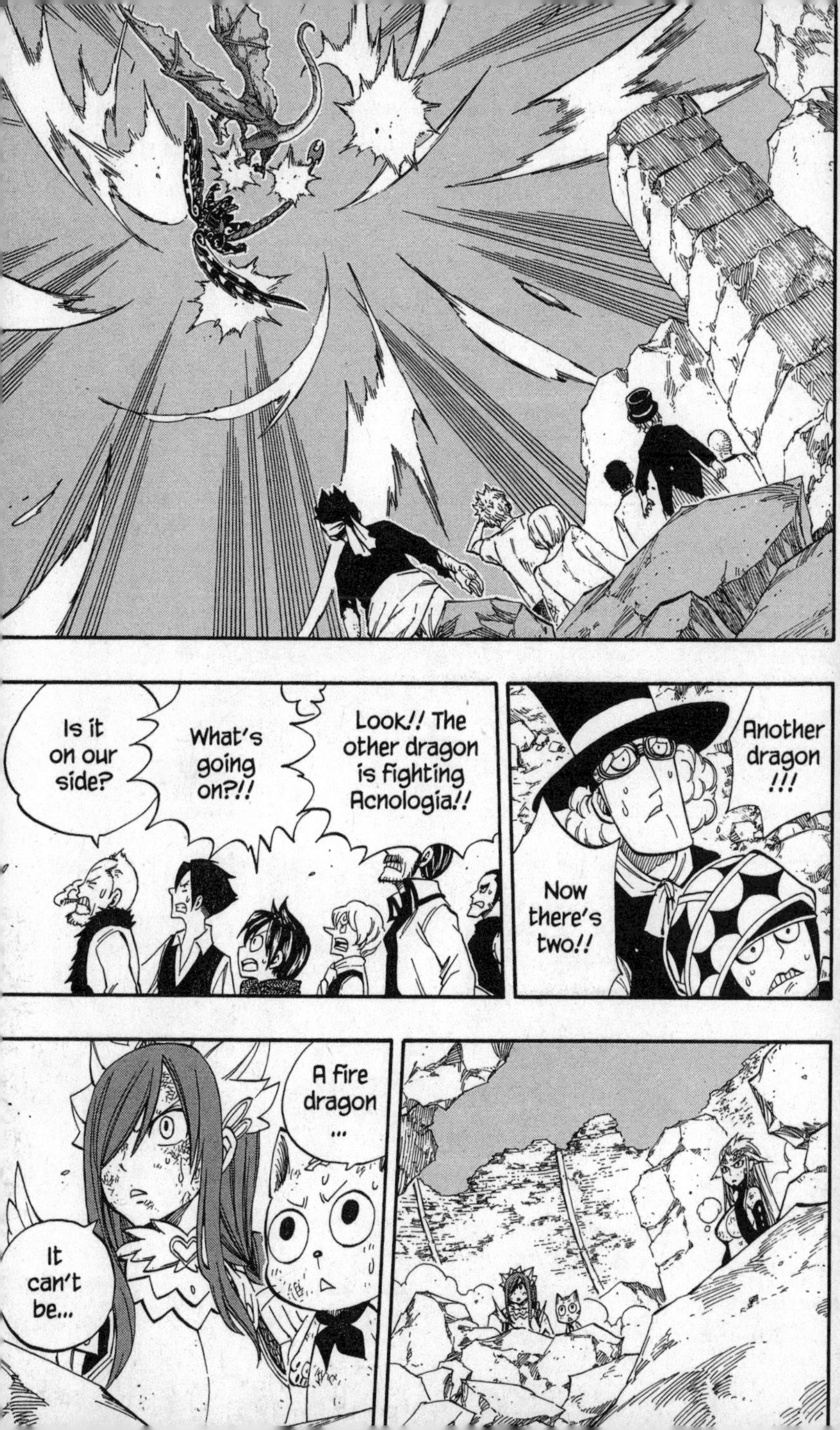
Another dragon!!!
Now there's two!!
Look!! The other dragon is fighting Acnologia!!
What's going on?!!
Is it on our side?
A fire dragon ...
It can't be...

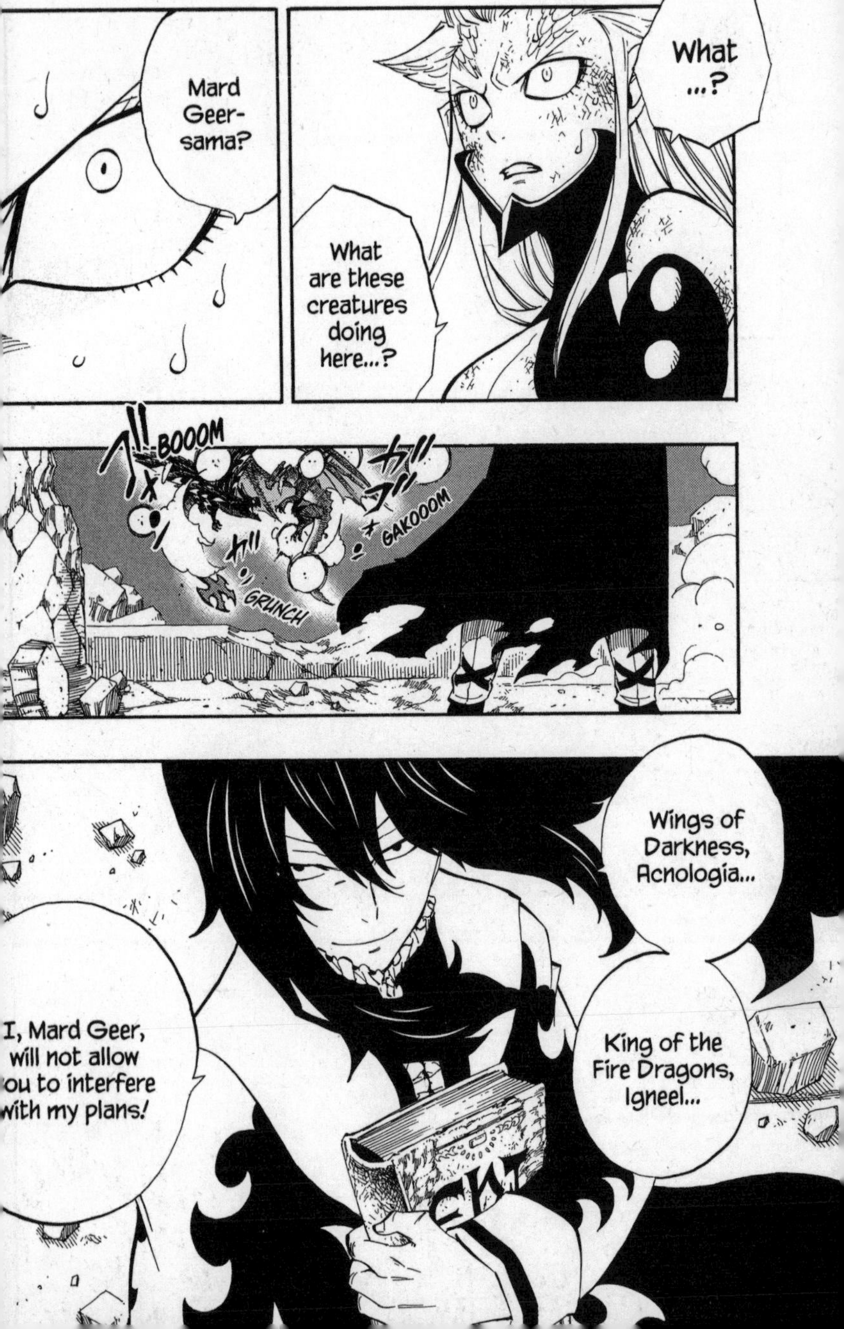
What ...?
What are these creatures doing here...?
Mard Geer-sama?
BOOOM
GAKOOOM
GRUNCH
Wings of Darkness, Acnologia...
King of the Fire Dragons, Igneel...
I, Mard Geer, will not allow ou to interfere with my plans!

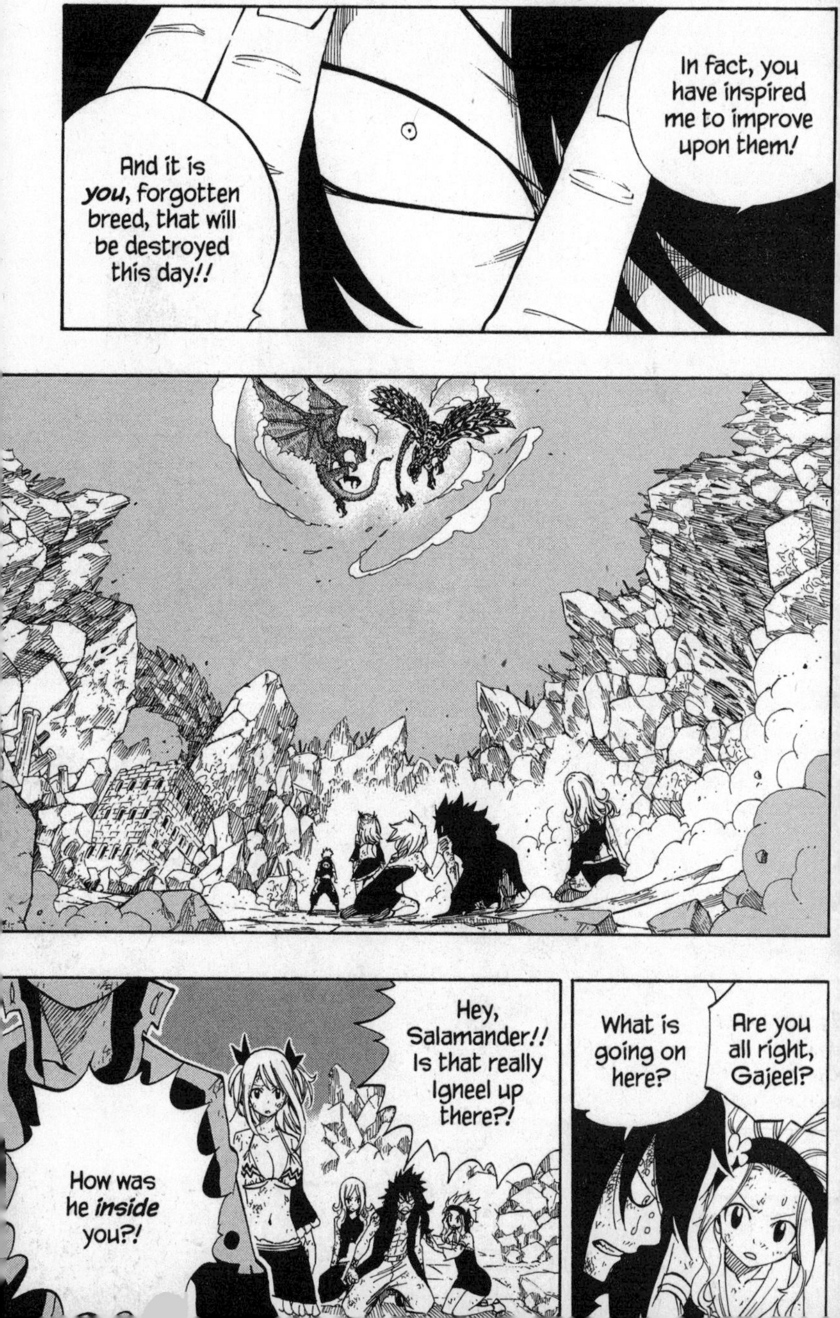
In fact, you have inspired me to improve upon them!
And it is *you*, forgotten breed, that will be destroyed this day!!
Are you all right, Gajeel?
What is going on here?
Hey, Salamander!! Is that really Igneel up there?!
How was he *inside* you?!

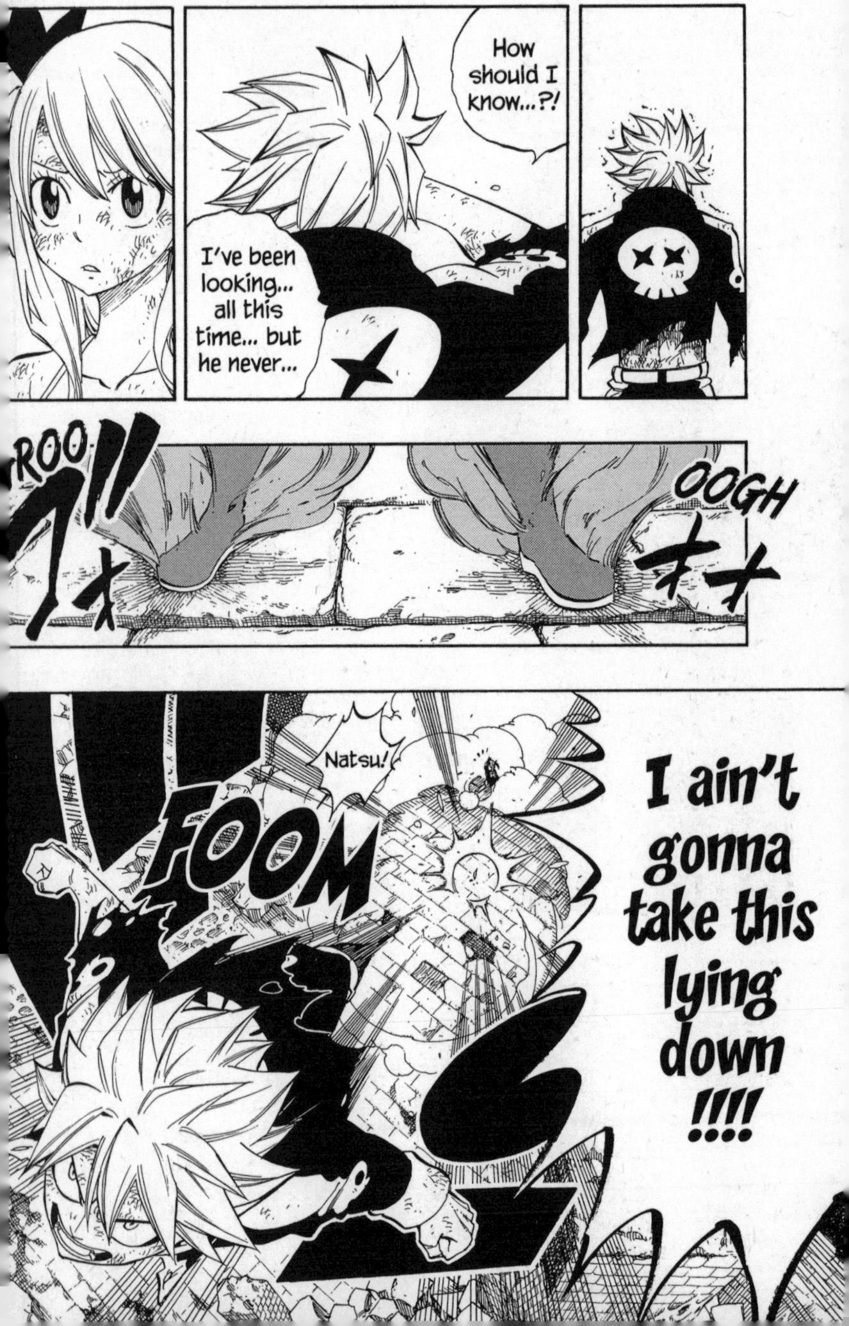
How should I know...?!
I've been looking... all this time... but he never...
OOGH
ROO
Natsu!
I ain't gonna take this lying down!!!!
FOOM

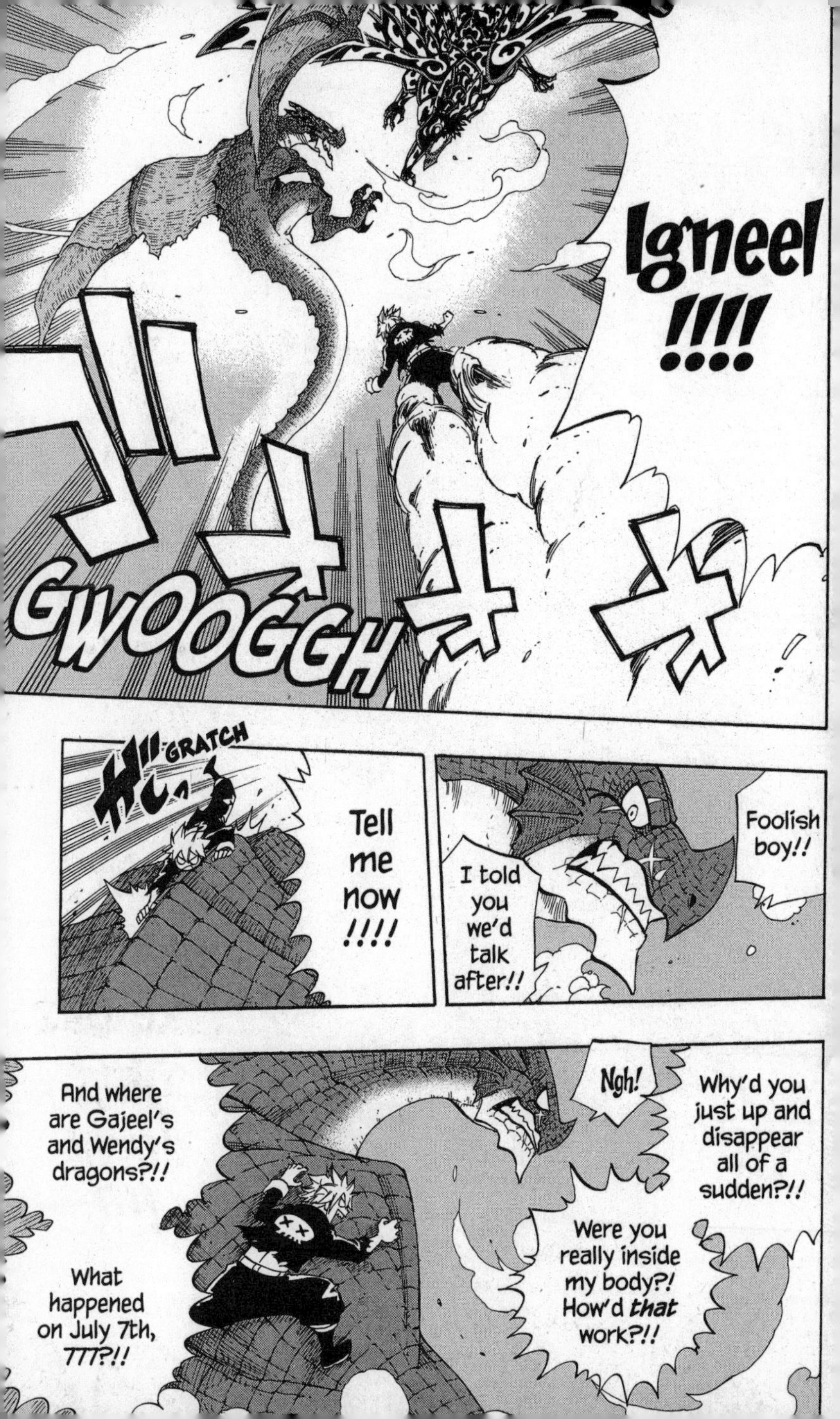

Igneel!!!!
GWOOGGH
Foolish boy!!
I told you we'd talk after!!
GRATCH
Tell me now!!!!
Why'd you just up and disappear all of a sudden?!!
Ngh!
And where are Gajeel's and Wendy's dragons?!!
Were you really inside my body?! How'd *that* work?!!
What happened on July 7th, 777?!!

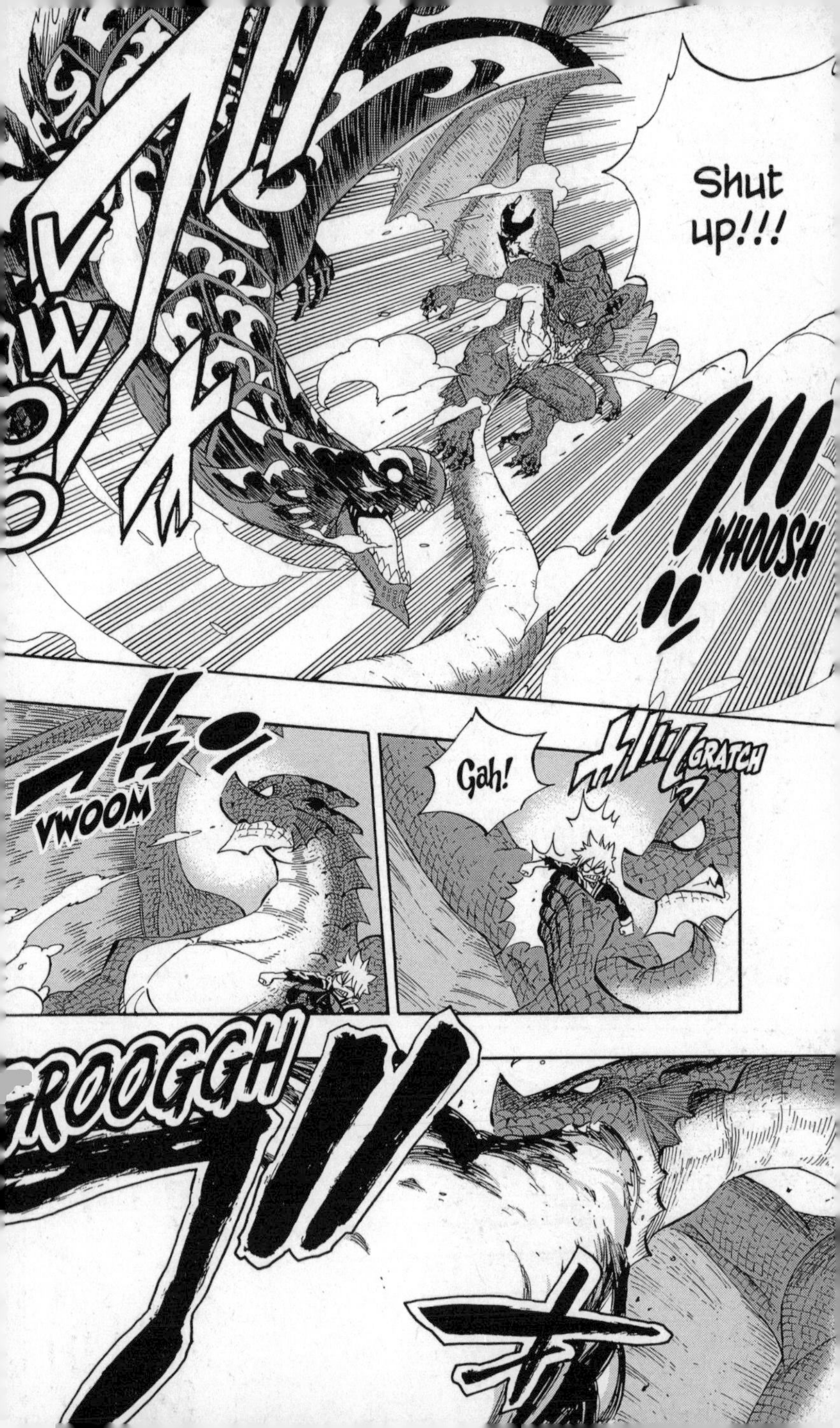
Shut up!!!
WHOOSH
Gah!
GRATCH
VWOOM
ROOGGH

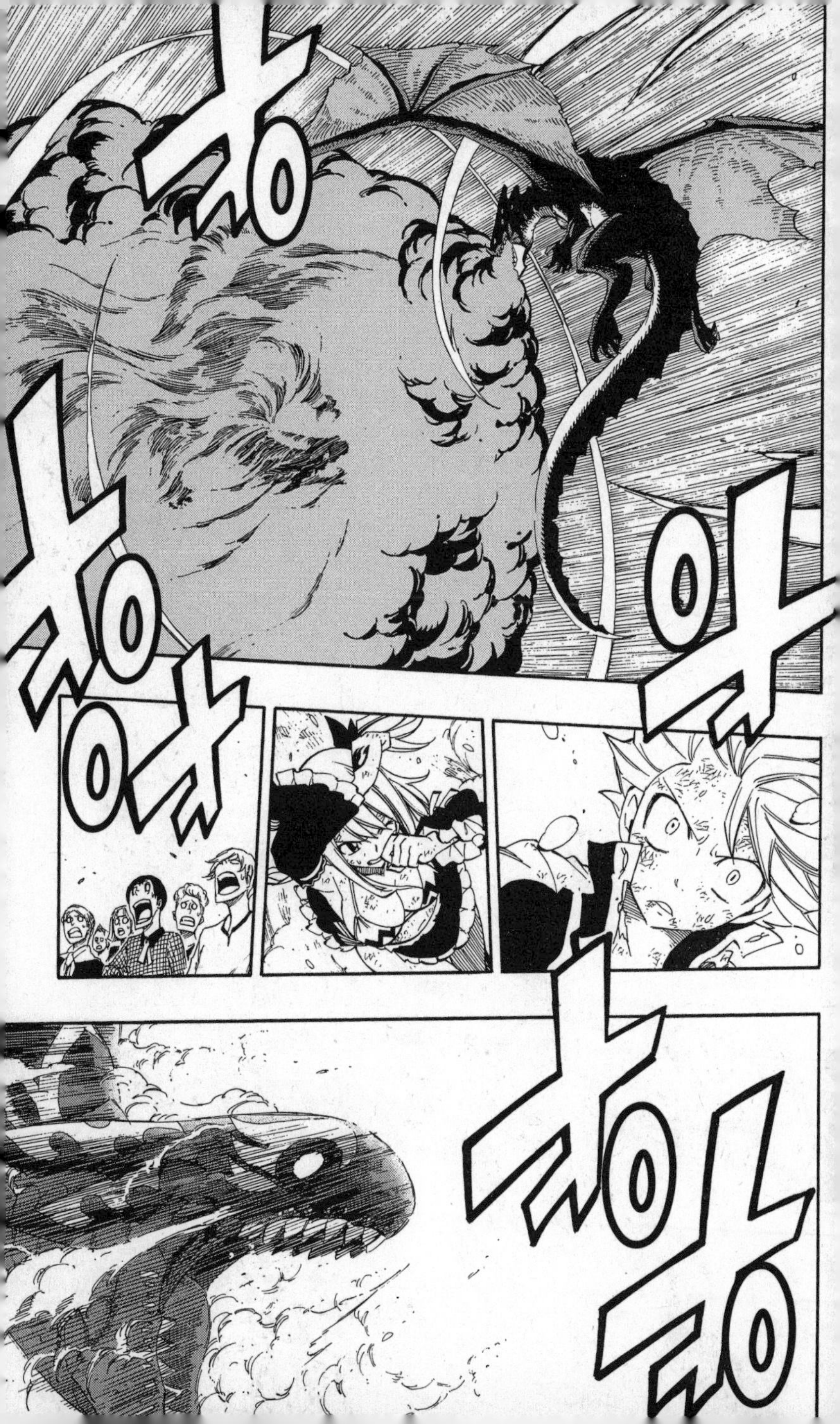

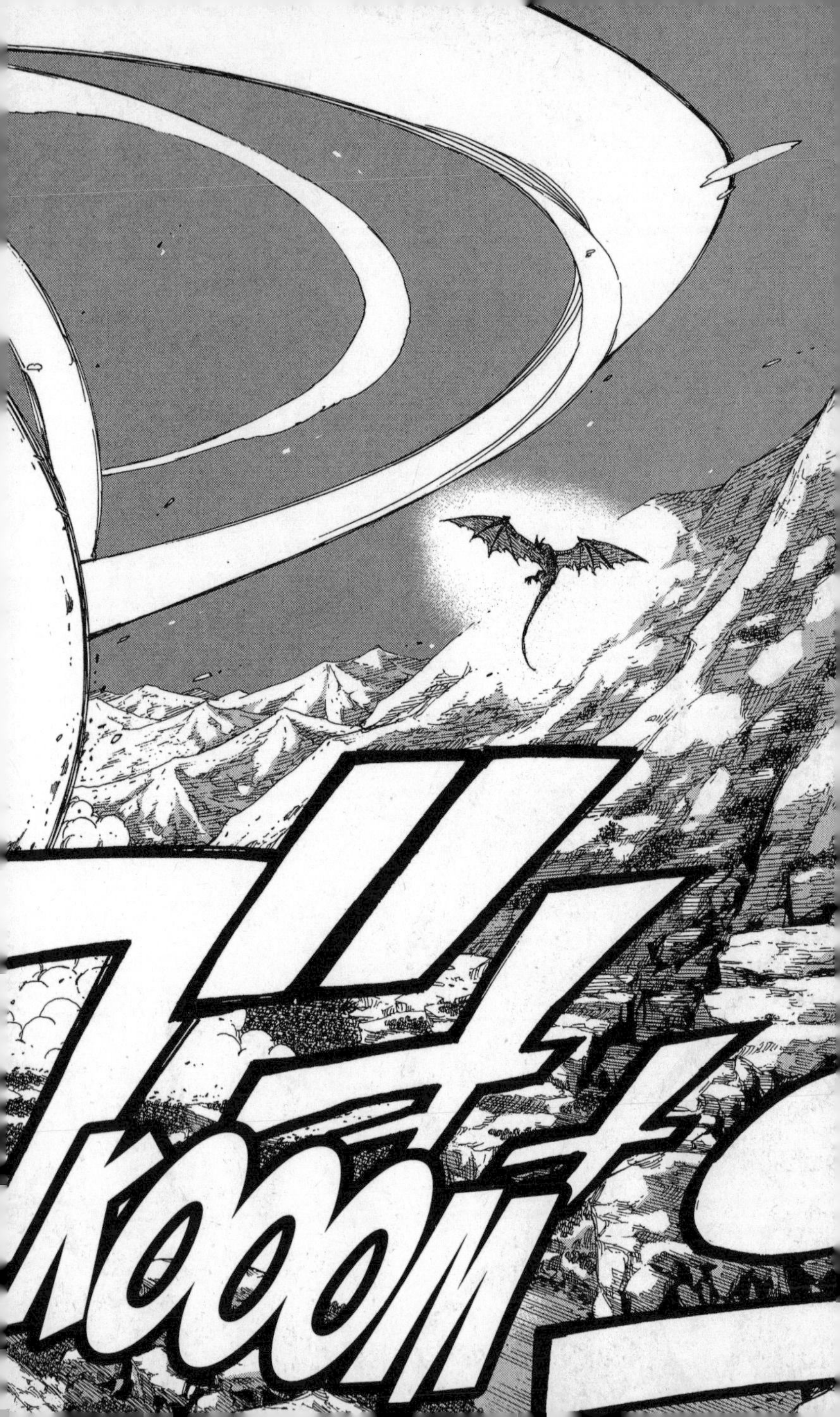

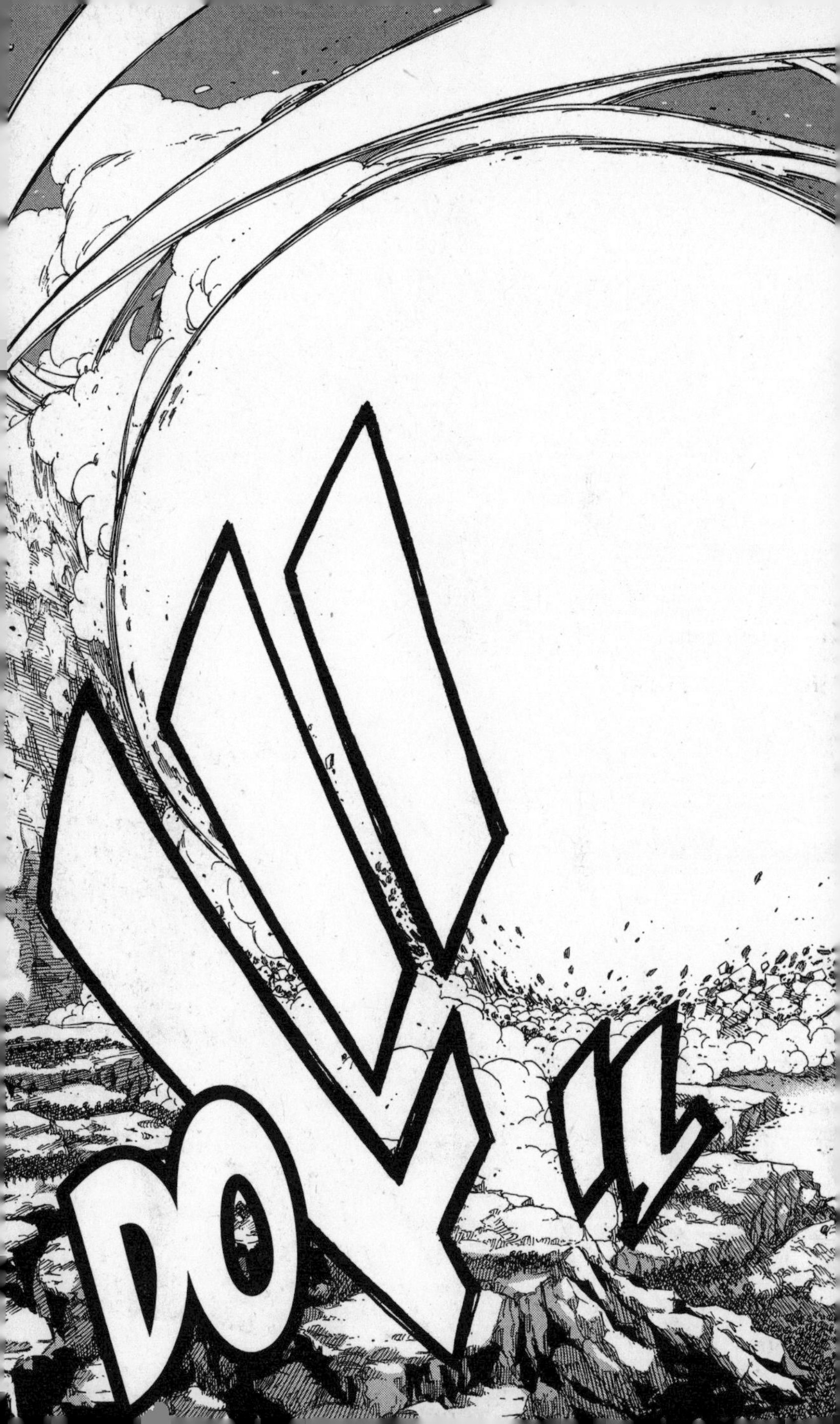
DON!!

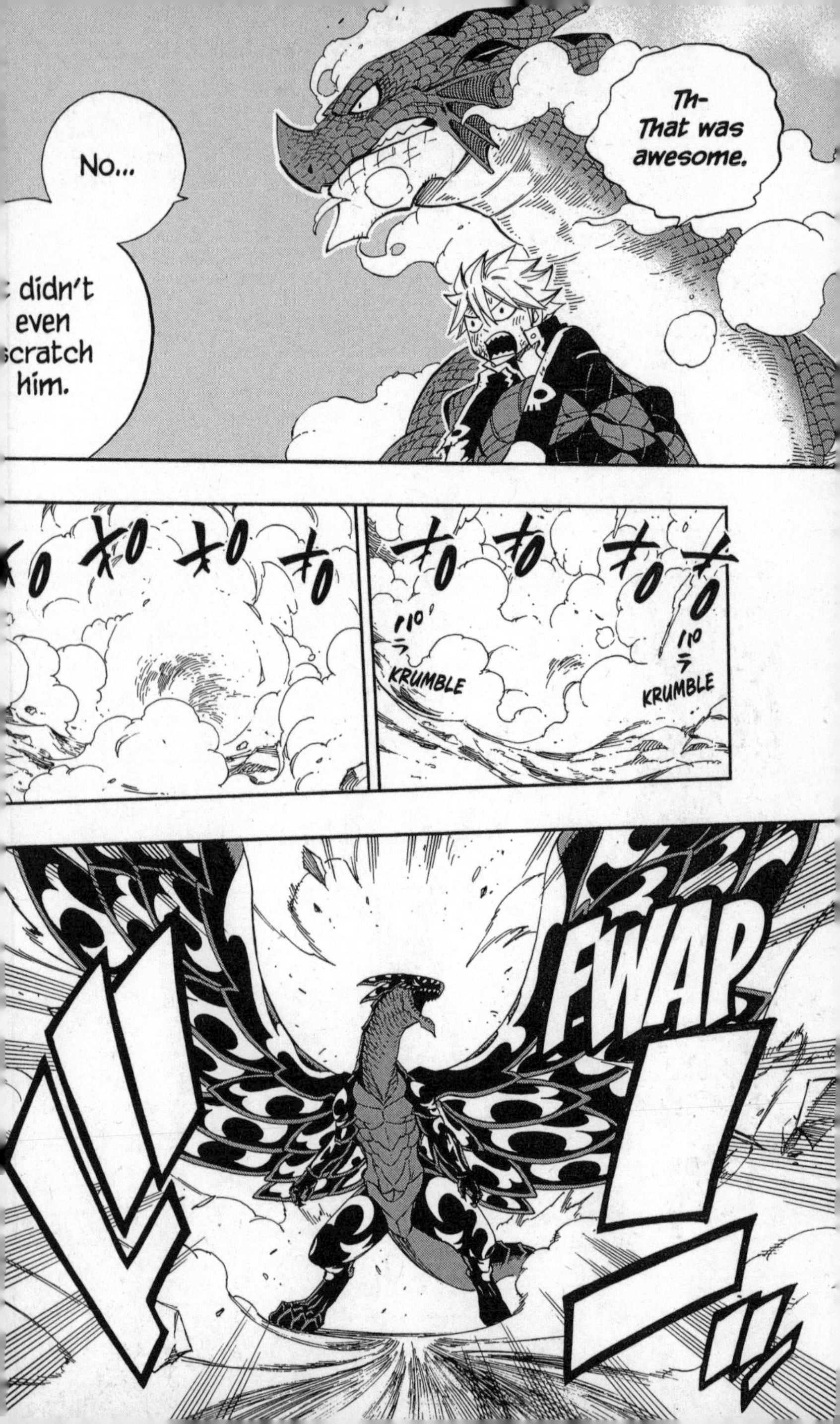

Th- That was awesome.
No...
didn't even scratch him.
KRUMBLE
KRUMBLE
FWAP

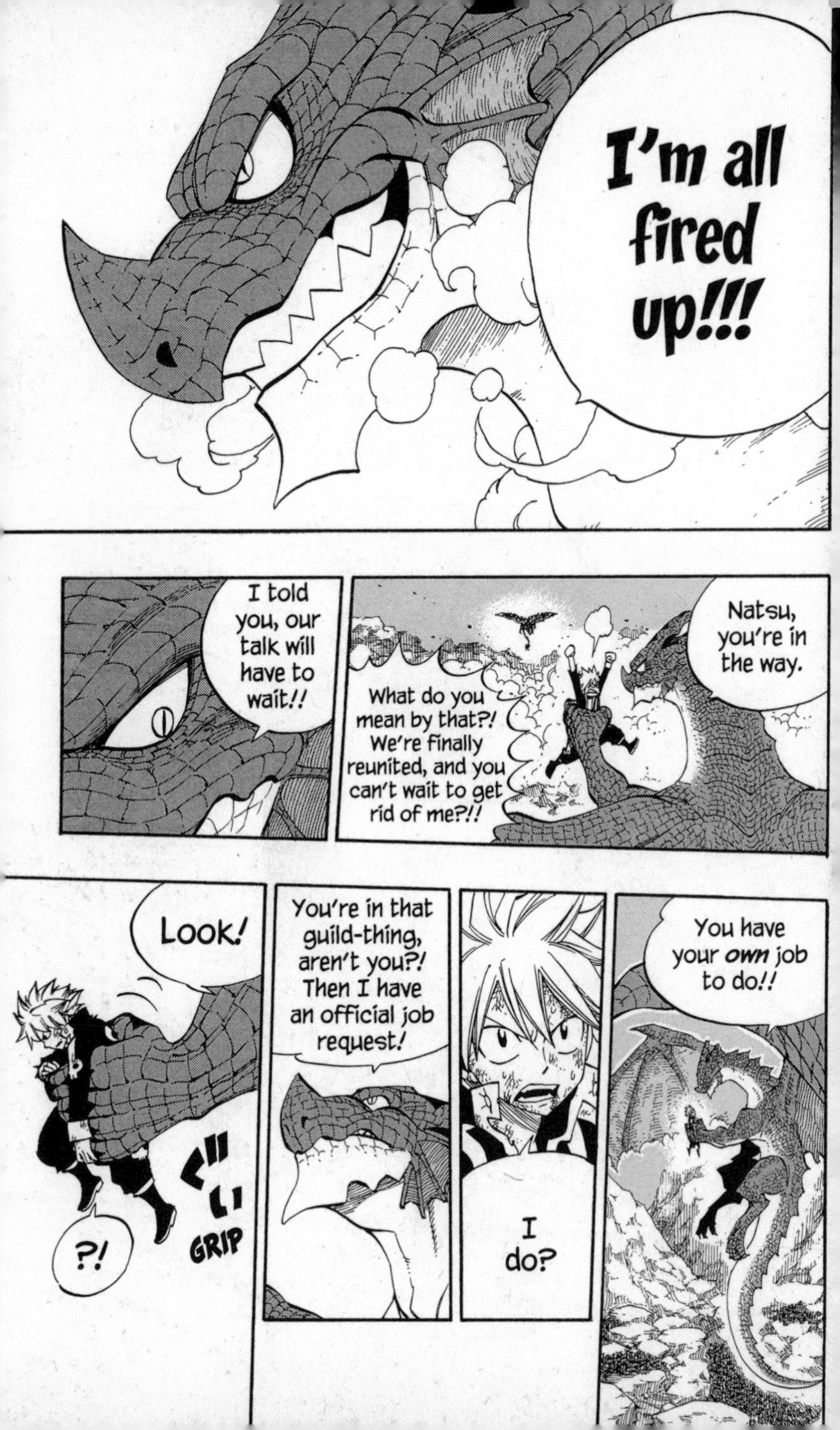
I'm all fired up!!!
Natsu, you're in the way.
What do you mean by that?! We're finally reunited, and you can't wait to get rid of me?!!
I told you, our talk will have to wait!!
You have your *own* job to do!!
I do?
You're in that guild-thing, aren't you?! Then I have an official job request!
Look!
GRIP
?!

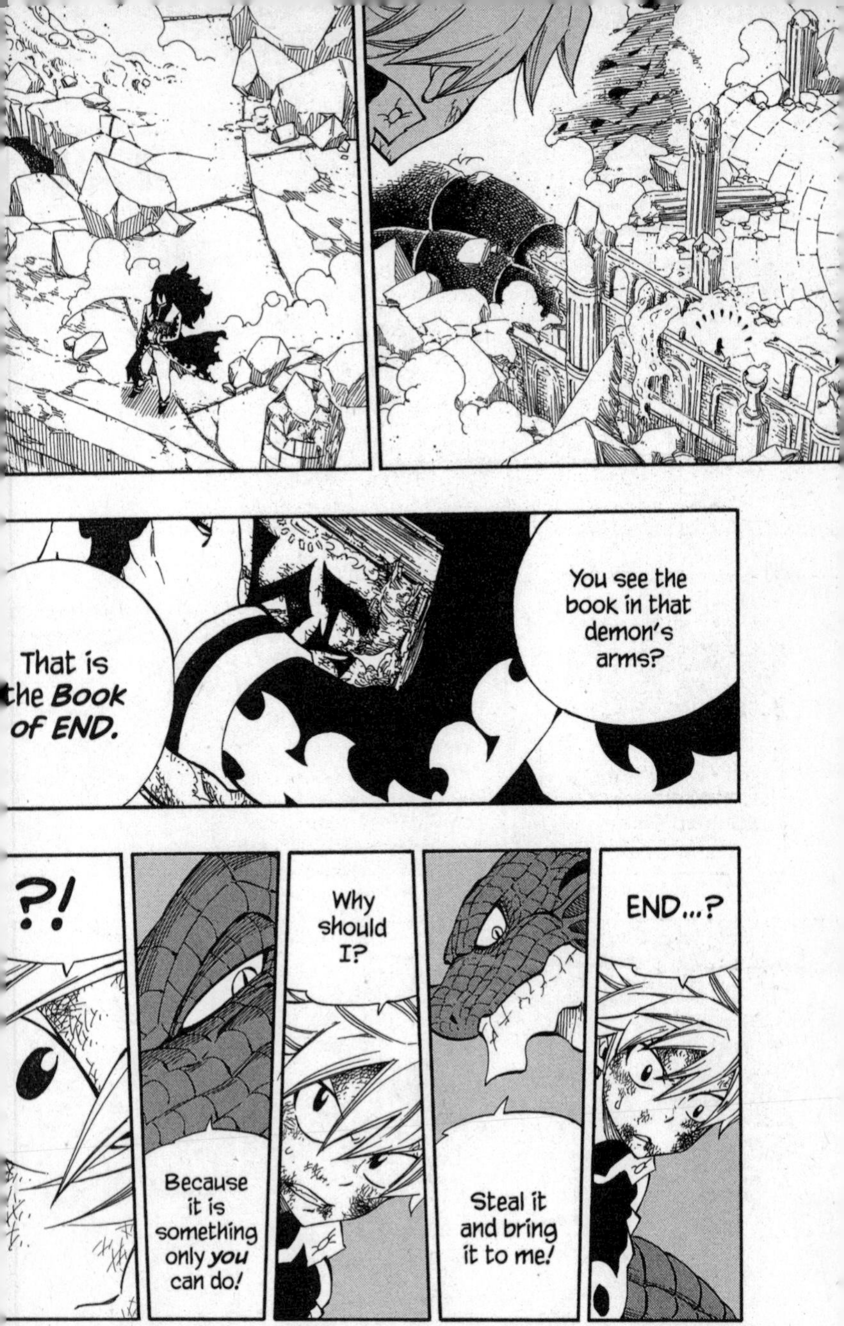
You see the book in that demon's arms?
That is the *Book of END.*
END...?
Steal it and bring it to me!
Why should I?
Because it is something only *you* can do!
?!

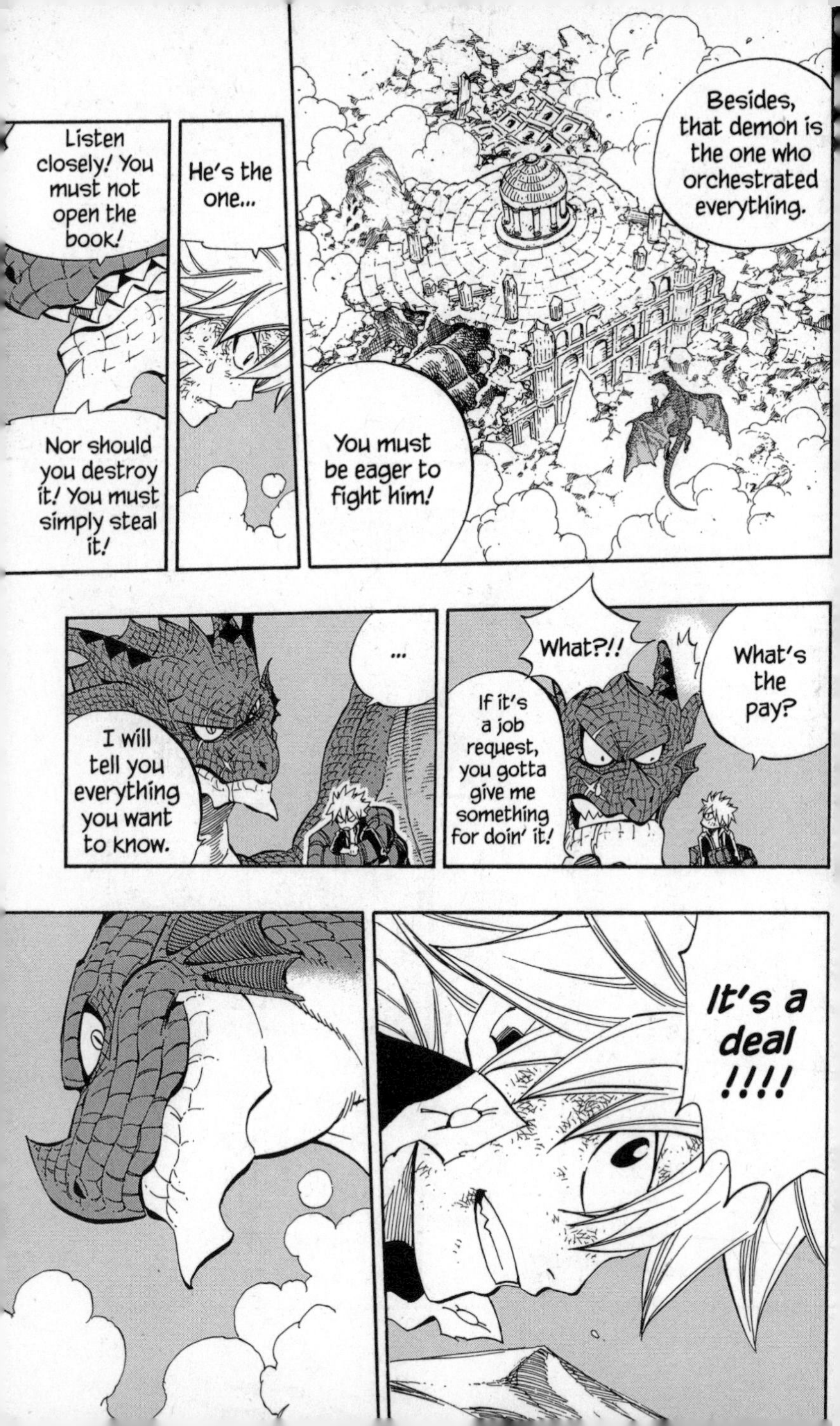

Besides, that demon is the one who orchestrated everything.
You must be eager to fight him!
He's the one...
Listen closely! You must not open the book!
Nor should you destroy it! You must simply steal it!
What?!!
What's the pay?
If it's a job request, you gotta give me something for doin' it!
...
I will tell you everything you want to know.
It's a deal !!!!

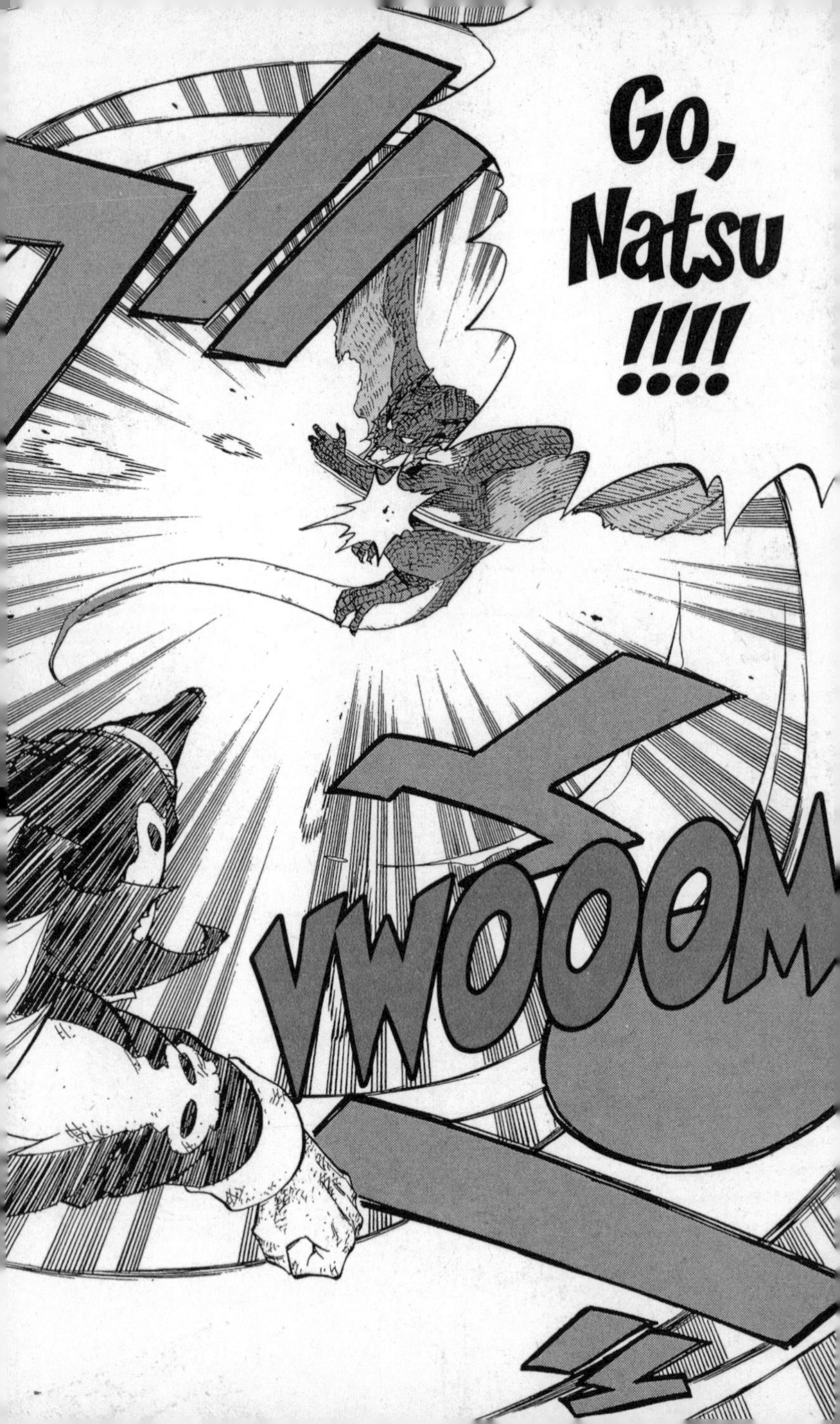

Go, Natsu!!!!
VWOOOM

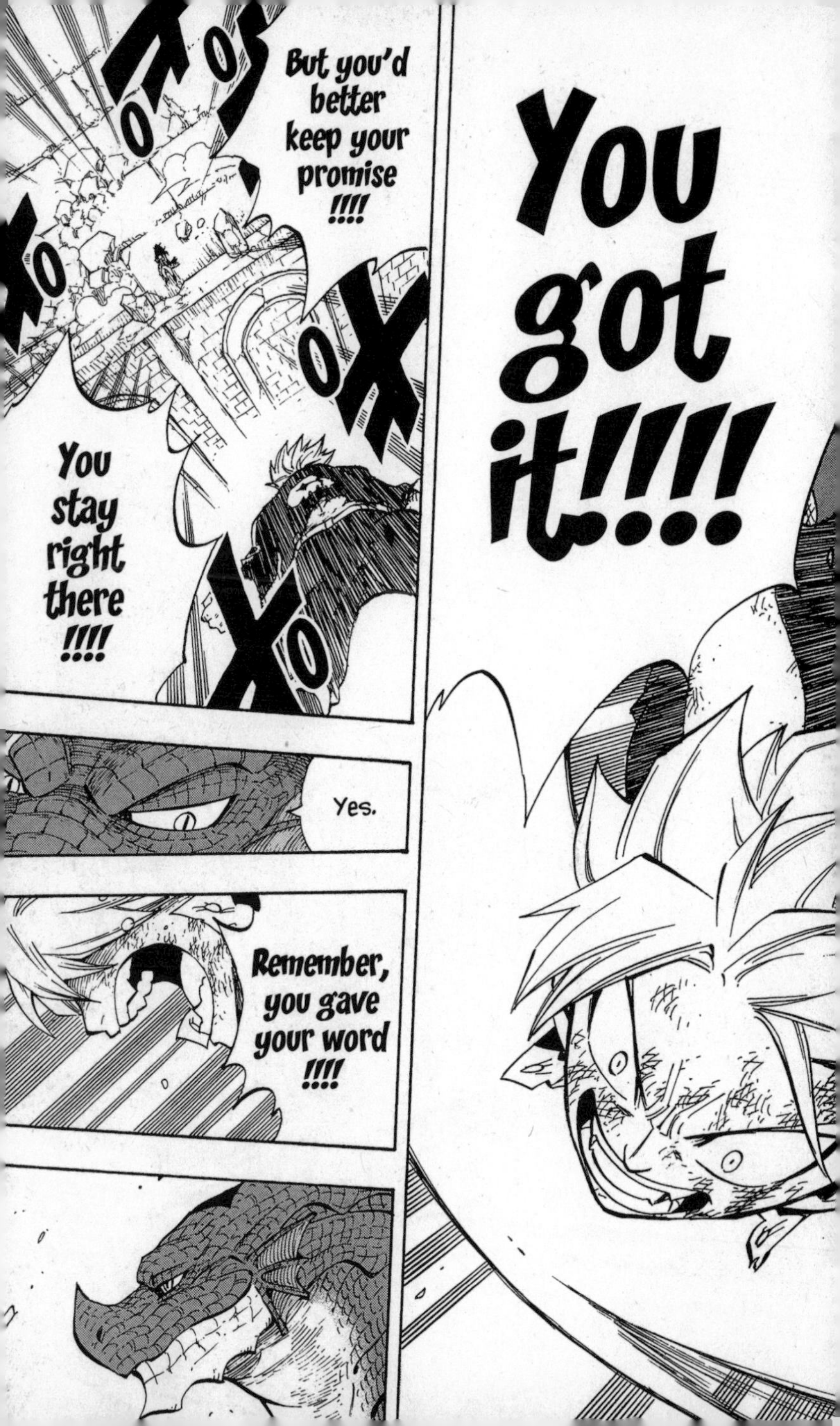
You got it!!!!
But you'd better keep your promise!!!!
You stay right there!!!!
Yes.
Remember, you gave your word!!!!

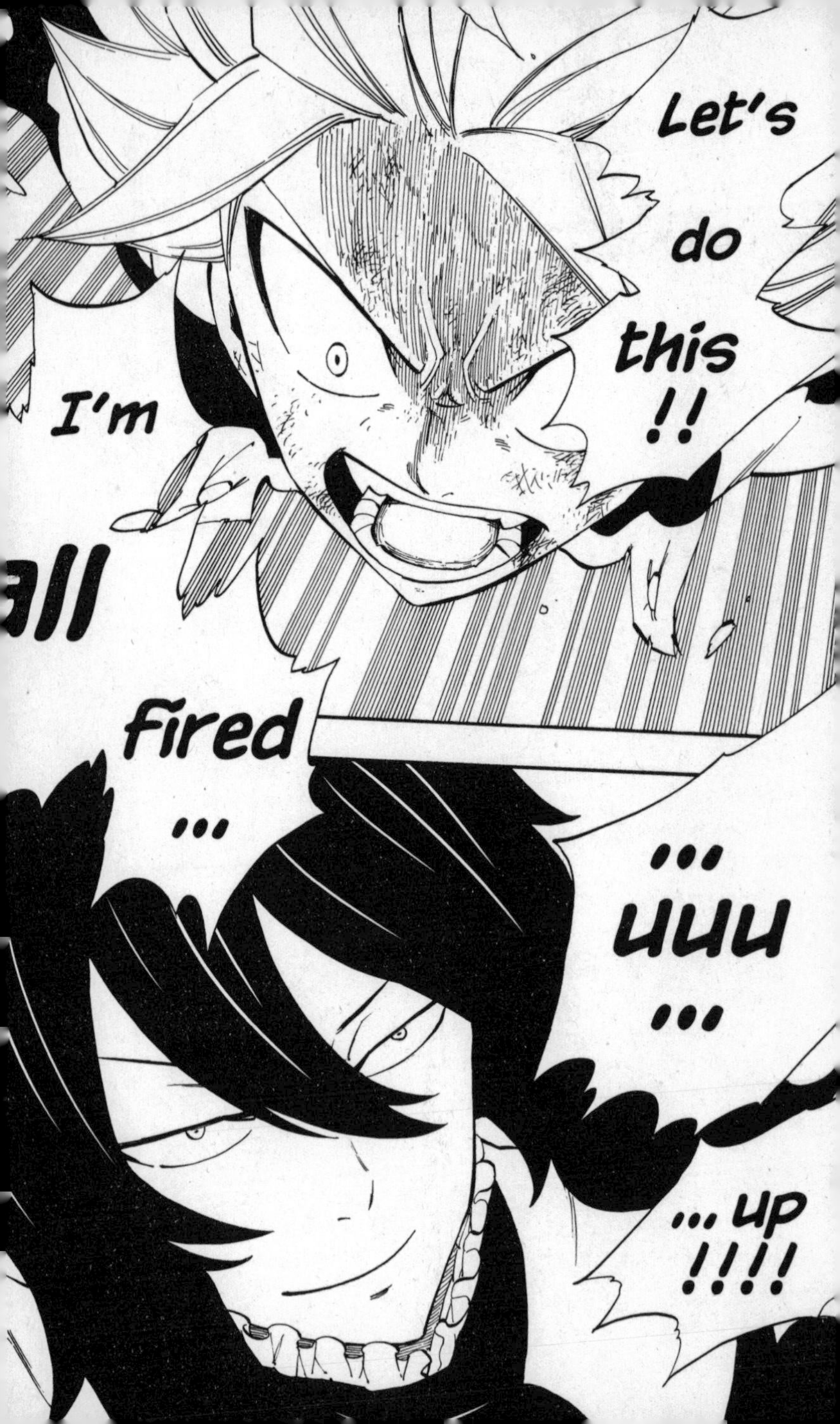
Let's do this!!
I'm all fired ...
...uuu...
...up!!!!

Chapter 402: The Fire Dragon's Iron Fis

Bridge Marker: Mashima Gardens

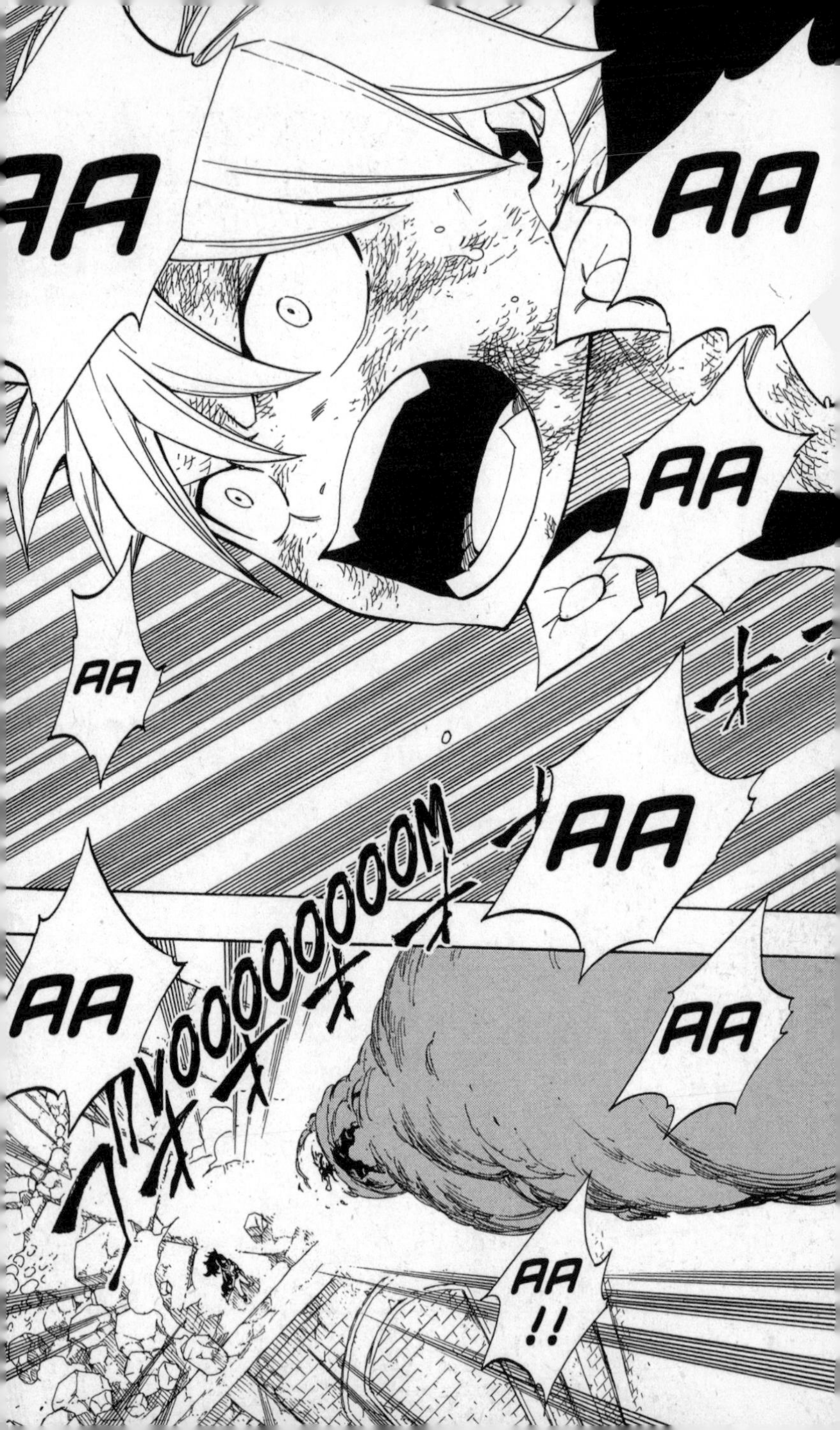

AA
AA
AA
AA
AA
VOOOOOOOOM
AA
AA
AA !!

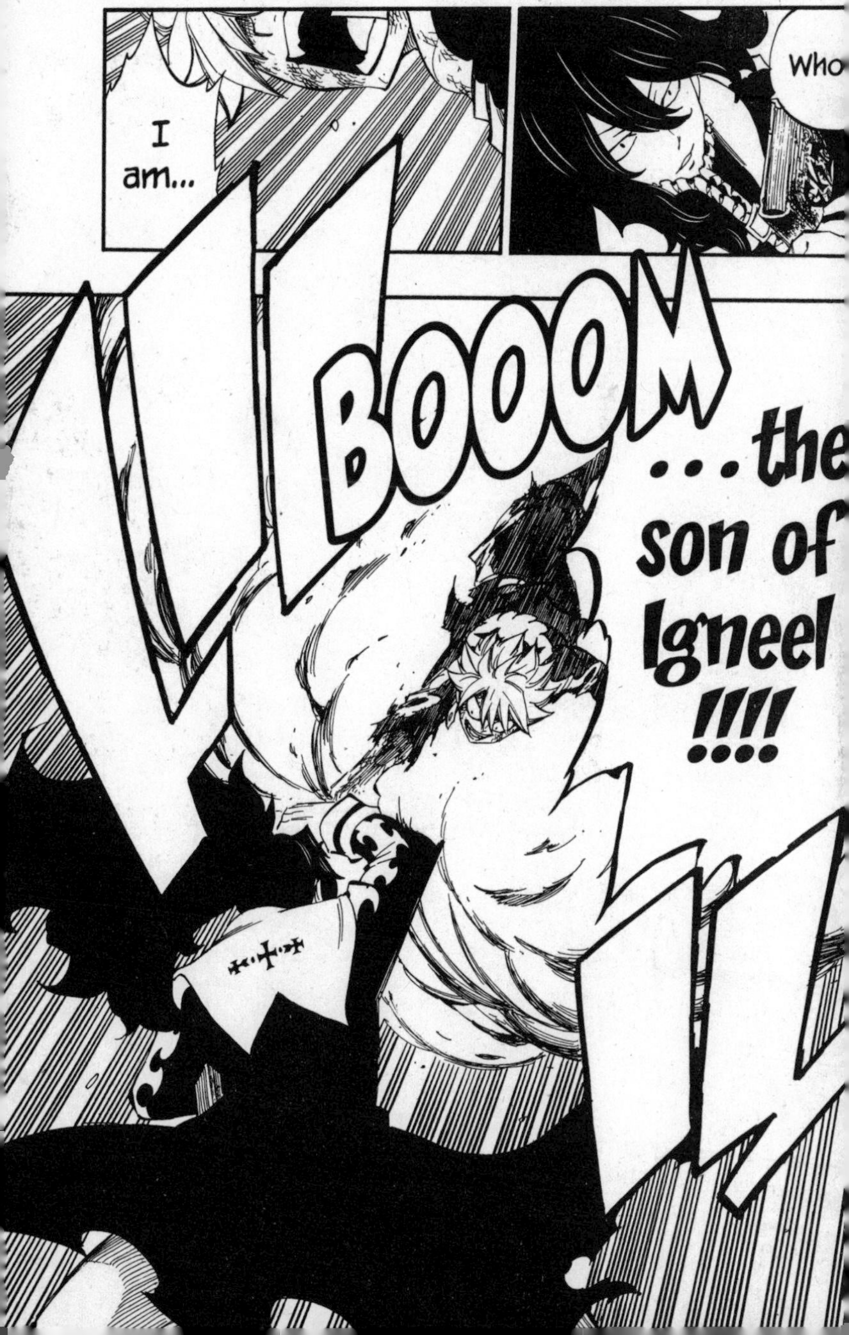
Who
I am...
BOOOM
...the son of Igneel!!!!

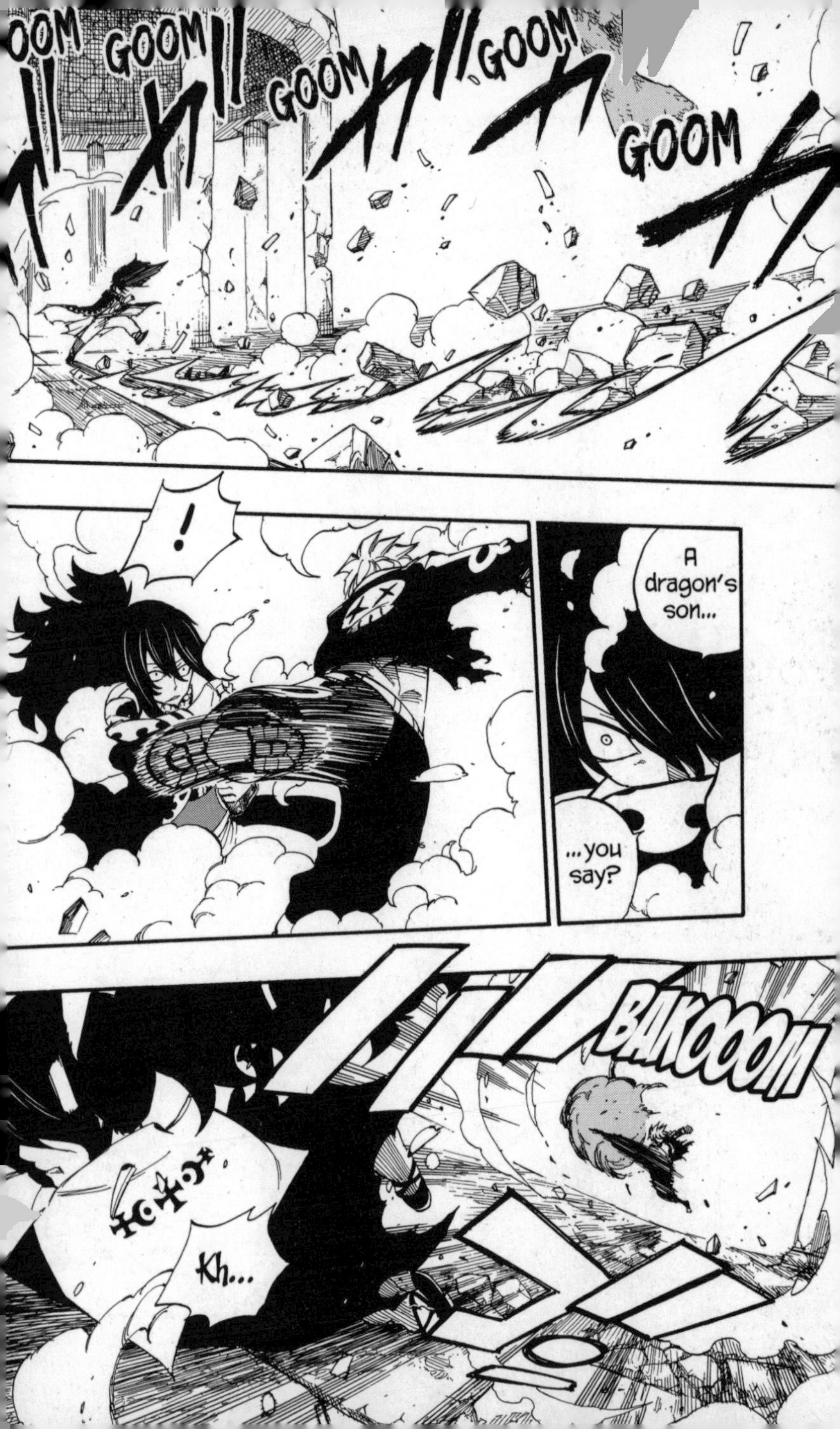
GOOM
GOOM
GOOM
GOOM
GOOM
A dragon's son...
...you say?
!
BAKOOOM
Kh...

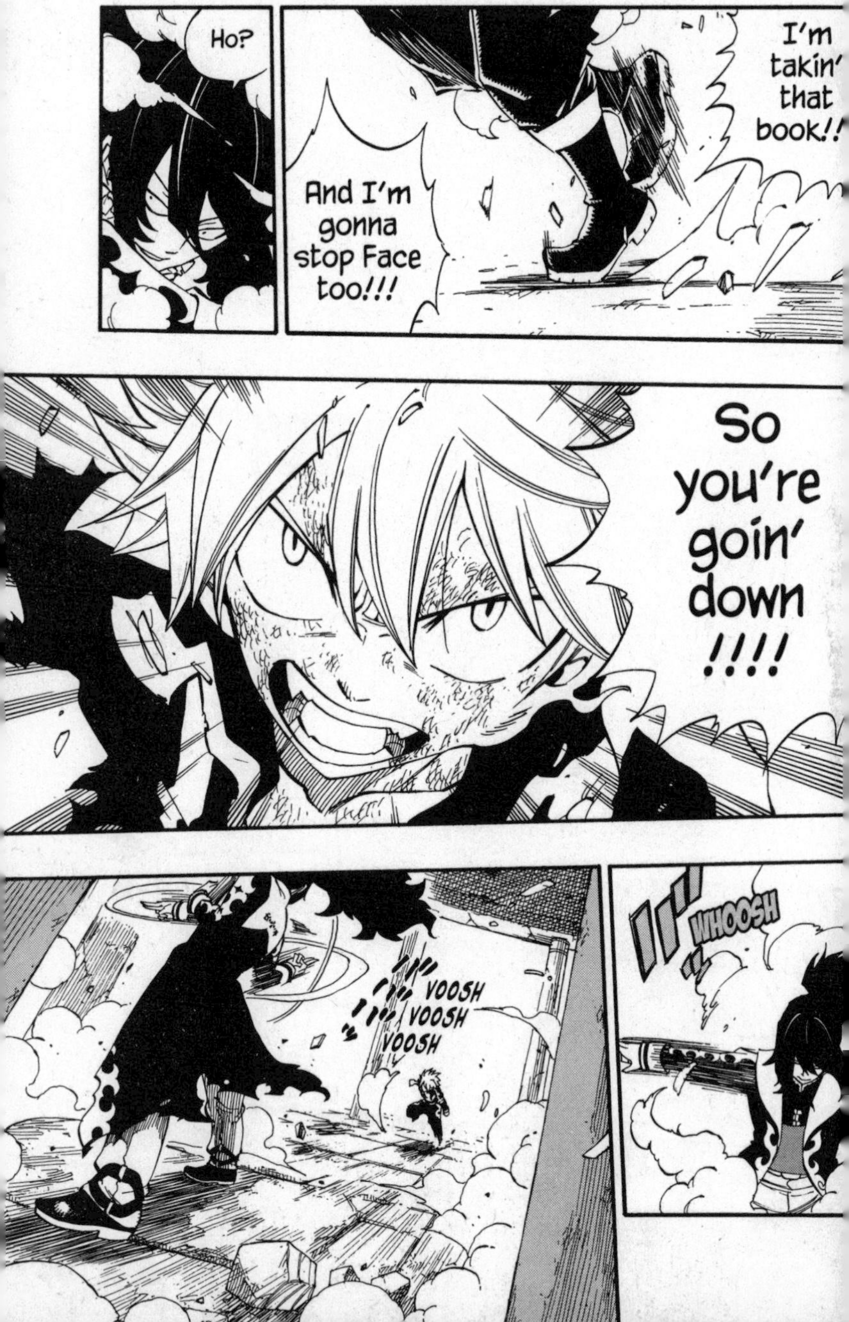
I'm takin' that book!!
And I'm gonna stop Face too!!!
Ho?
So you're goin' down!!!!
WHOOSH
VOOSH
VOOSH
VOOSH

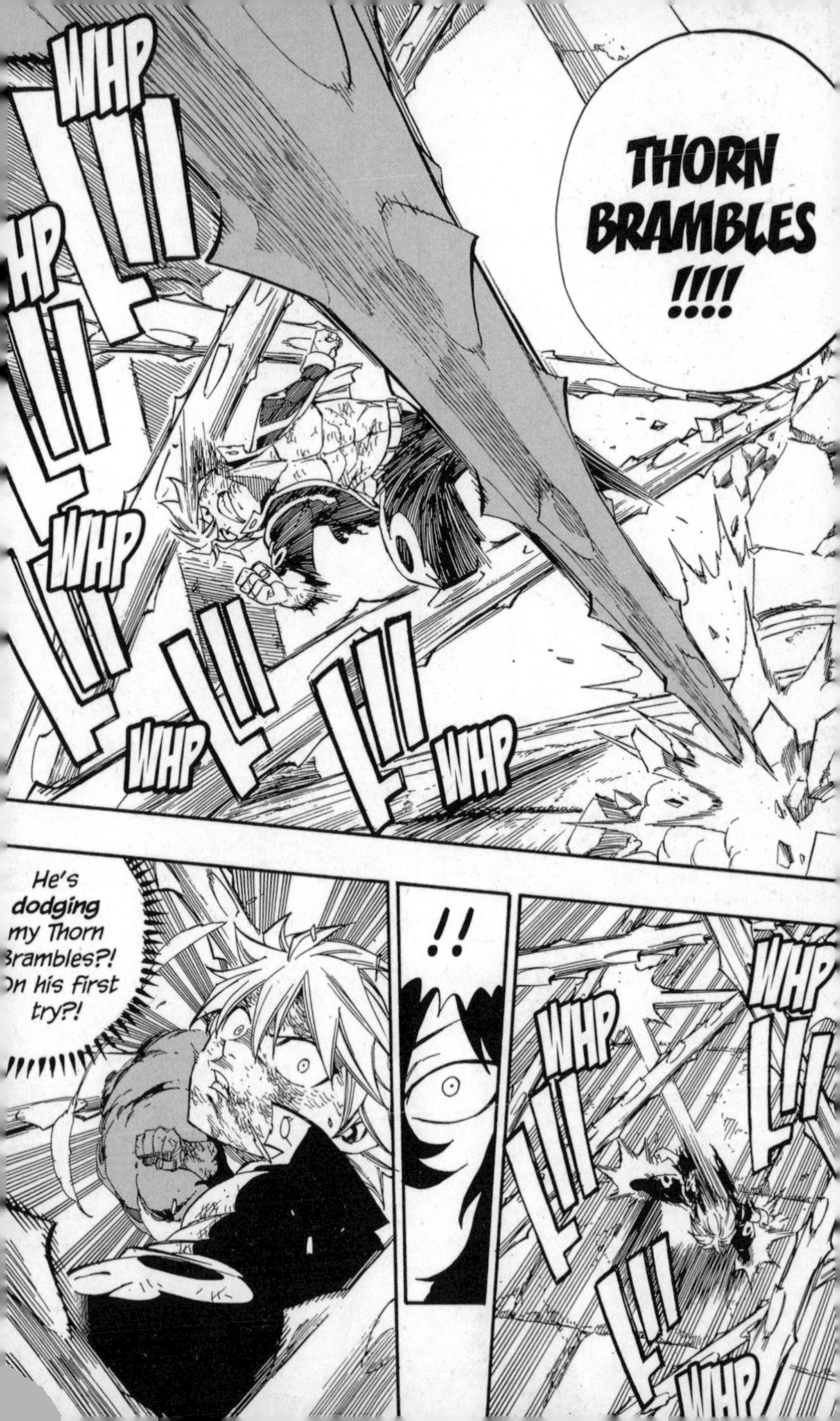
THORN BRAMBLES !!!!
WHP
HP
WHP
WHP
WHP
WHP
WHP
WHP
!!
He's dodging my Thorn Brambles?! On his first try?!

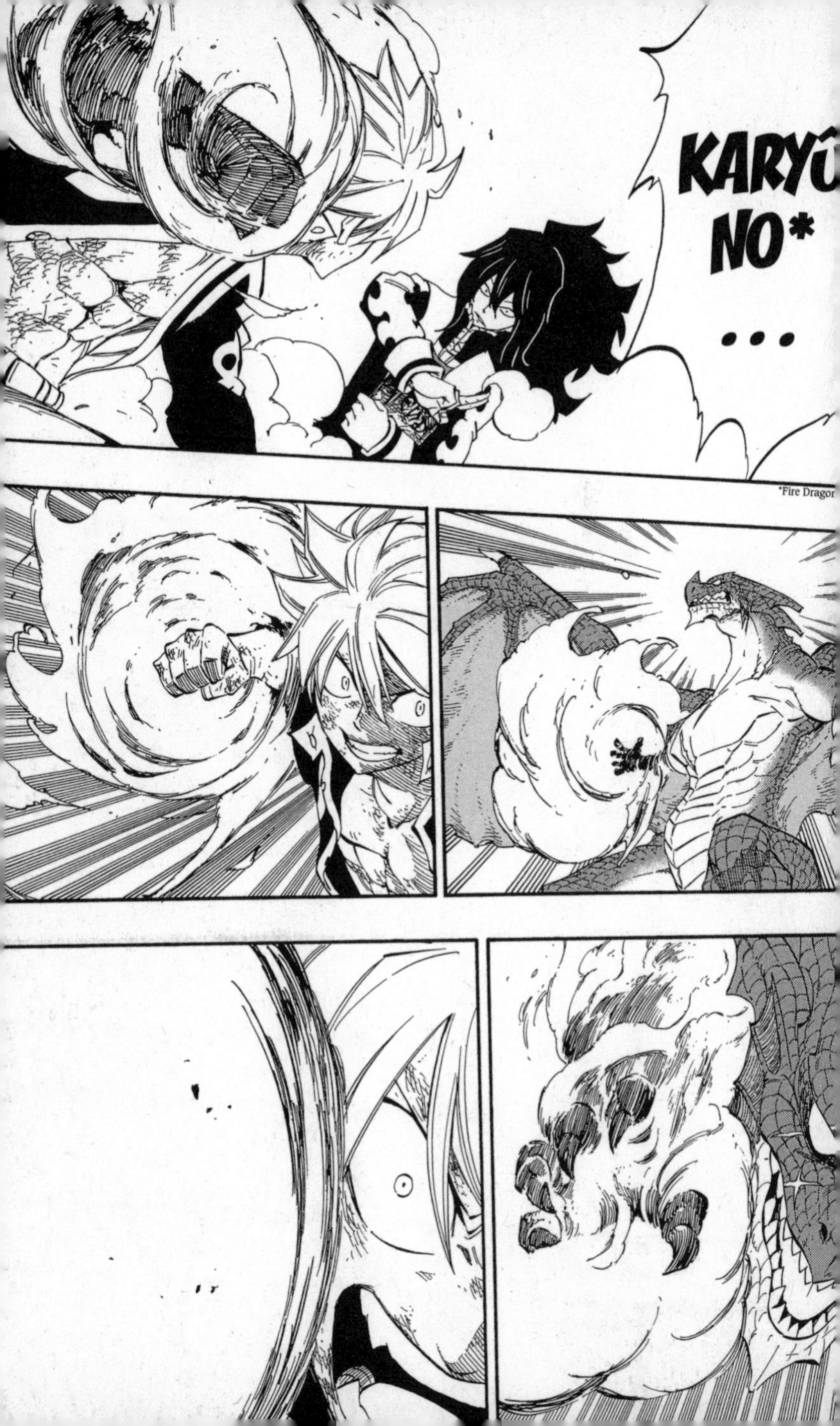
KARYÛ NO* . . .
*Fire Dragon

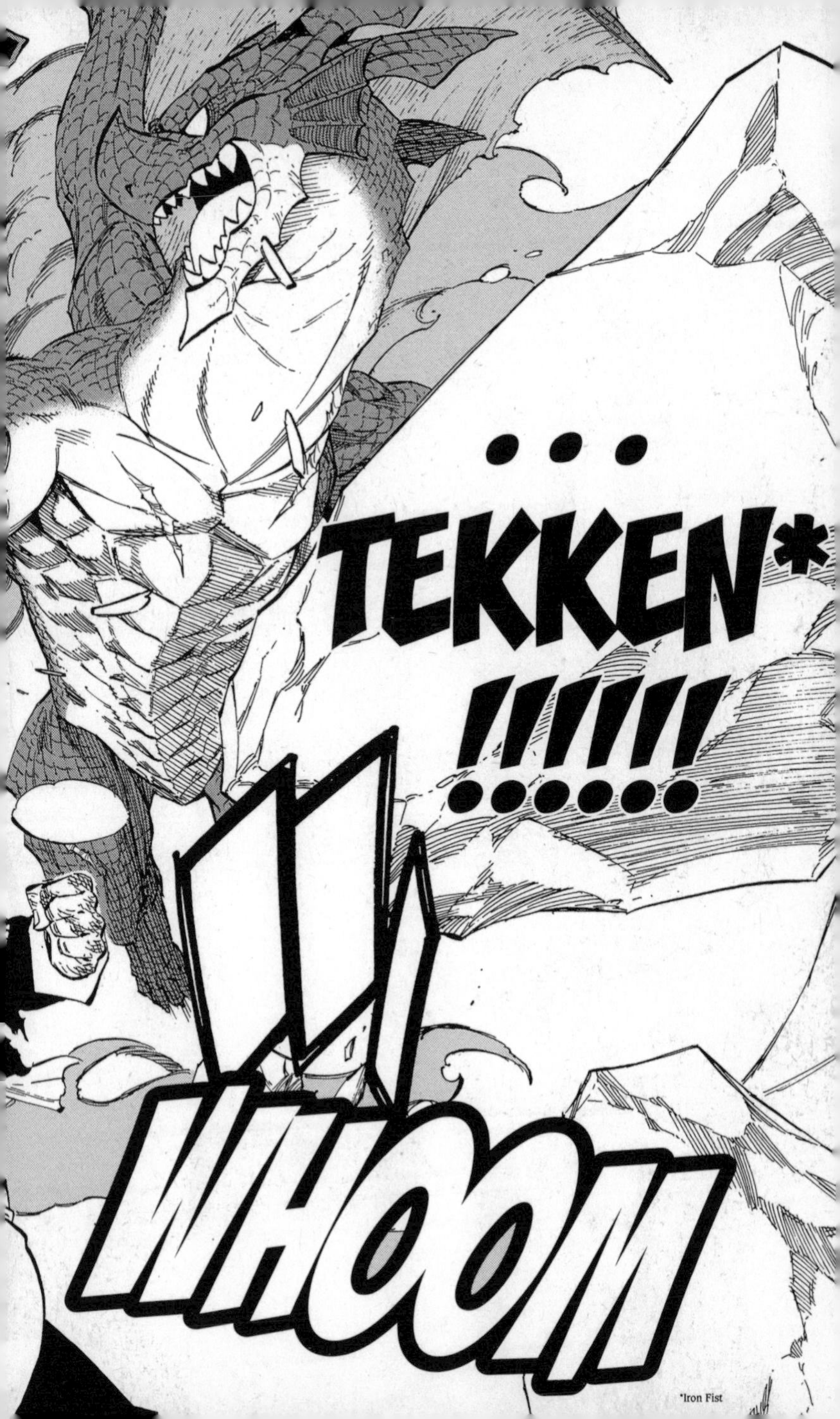
...
TEKKEN*!!!!!!
WHOOM

*Iron Fist

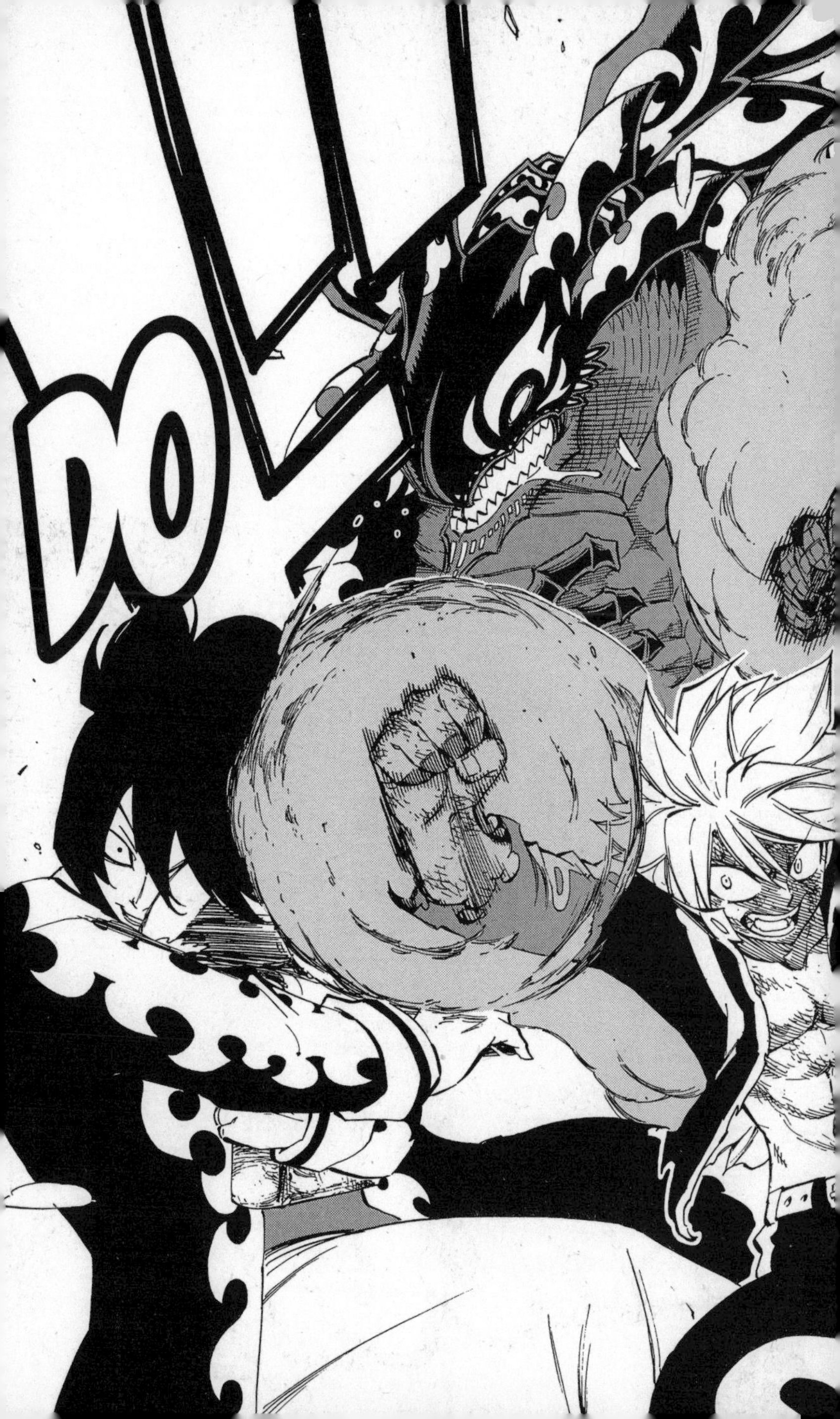
DO

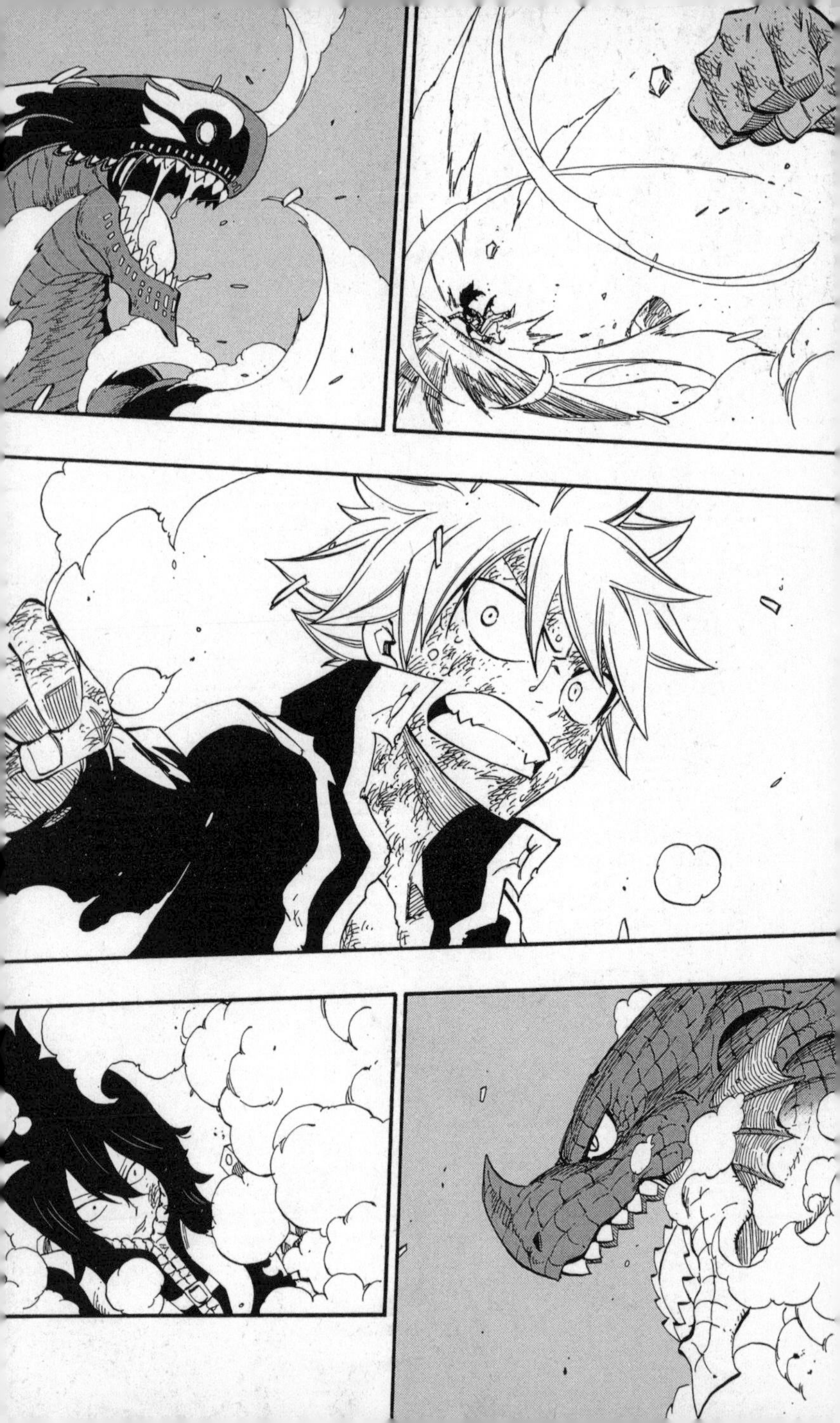

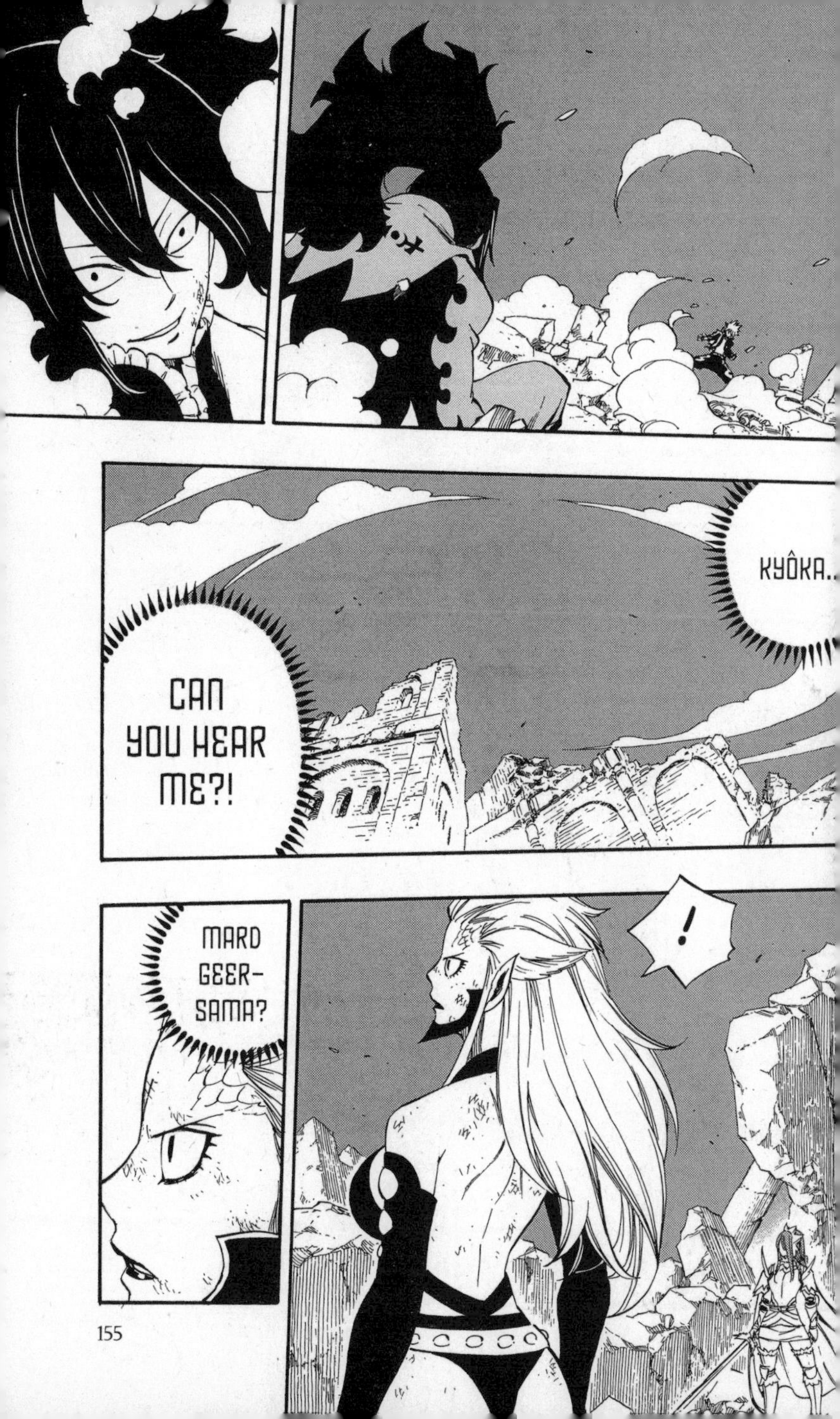
KYÔKA...
CAN YOU HEAR ME?!
!
MARD GEER-SAMA?

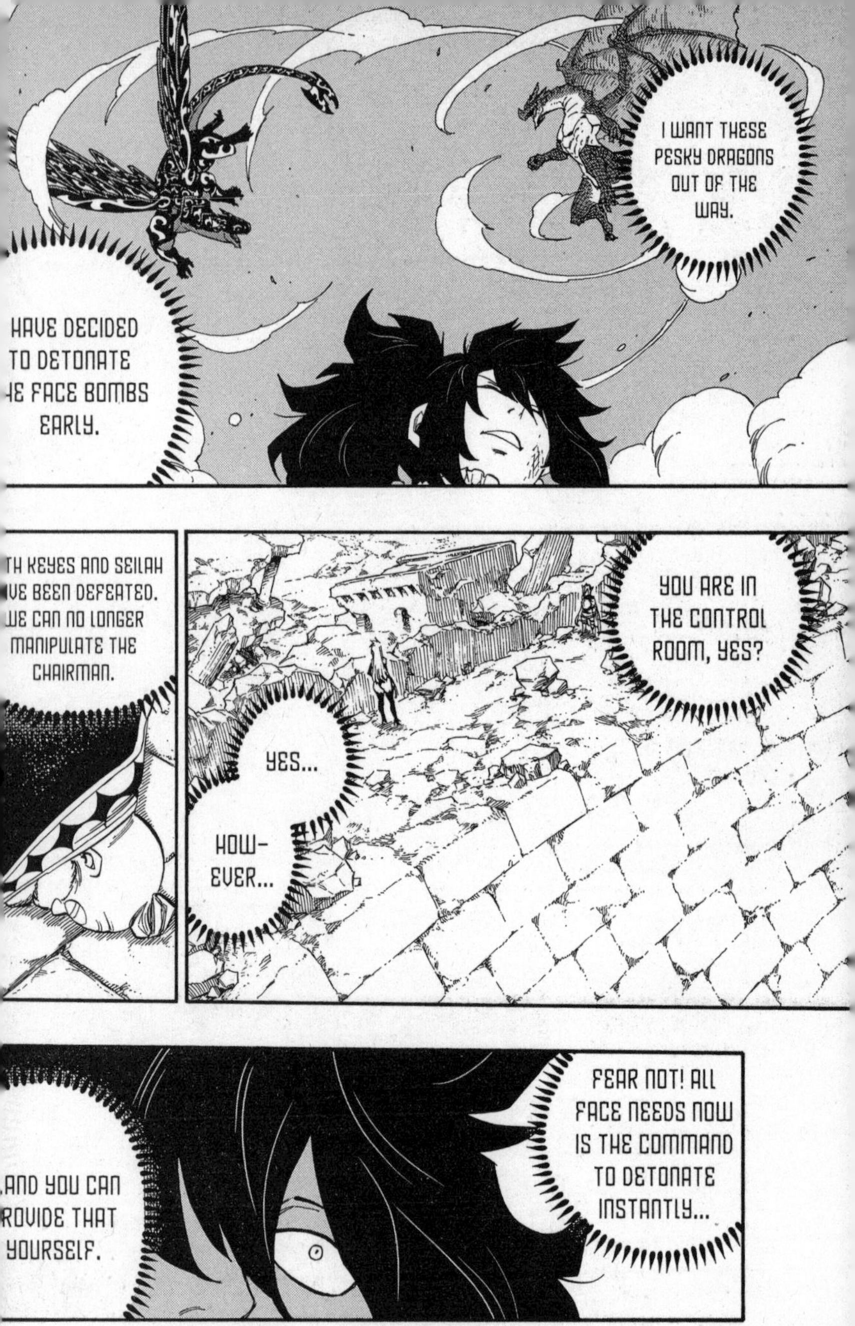
I WANT THESE PESKY DRAGONS OUT OF THE WAY.
HAVE DECIDED TO DETONATE HE FACE BOMBS EARLY.
YOU ARE IN THE CONTROL ROOM, YES?
YES...
HOW-EVER...
TH KEYES AND SEILAH VE BEEN DEFEATED. WE CAN NO LONGER MANIPULATE THE CHAIRMAN.
FEAR NOT! ALL FACE NEEDS NOW IS THE COMMAND TO DETONATE INSTANTLY...
.AND YOU CAN ROVIDE THAT YOURSELF.

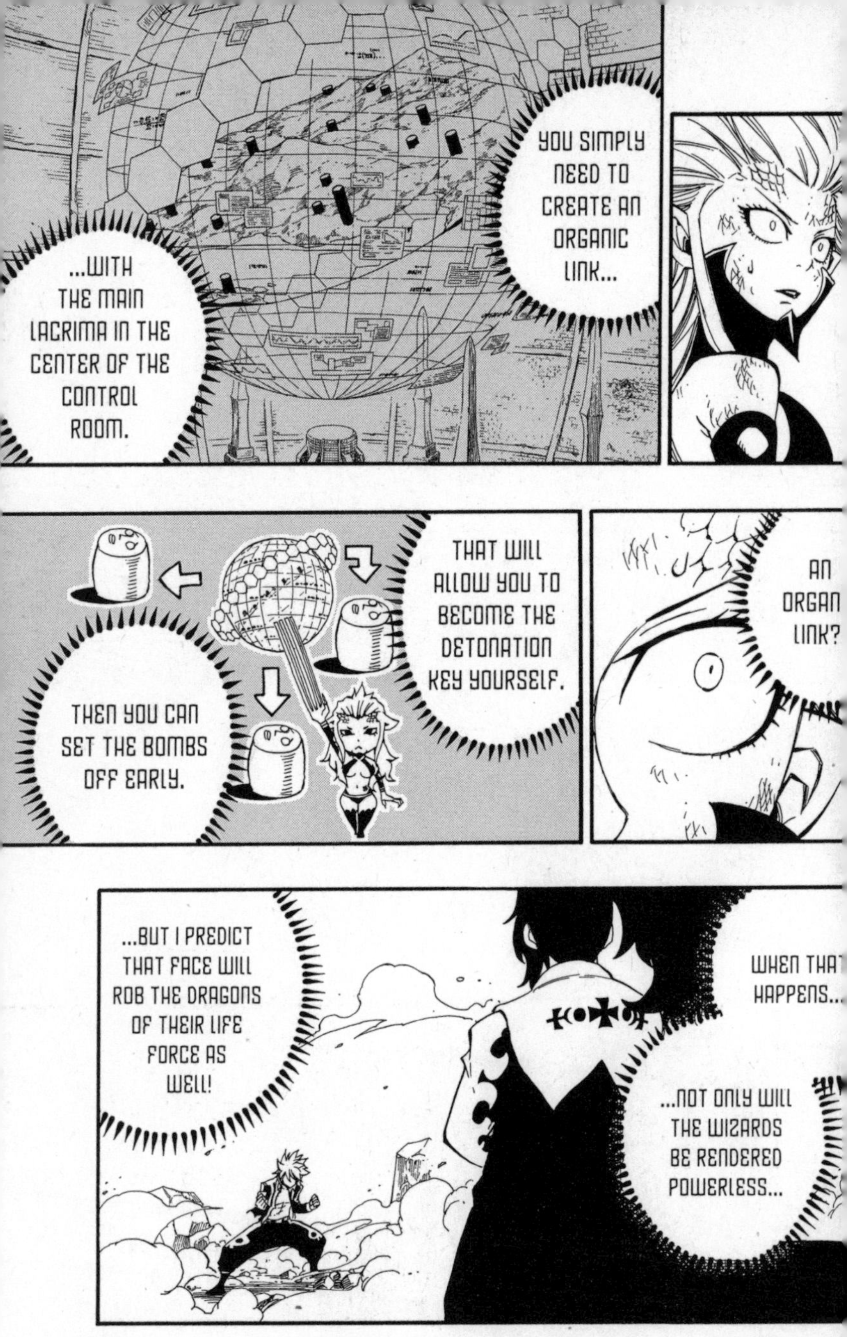
YOU SIMPLY NEED TO CREATE AN ORGANIC LINK...
...WITH THE MAIN LACRIMA IN THE CENTER OF THE CONTROL ROOM.
AN ORGAN LINK?
THAT WILL ALLOW YOU TO BECOME THE DETONATION KEY YOURSELF.
THEN YOU CAN SET THE BOMBS OFF EARLY.
WHEN THA HAPPENS...
...NOT ONLY WILL THE WIZARDS BE RENDERED POWERLESS...
...BUT I PREDICT THAT FACE WILL ROB THE DRAGONS OF THEIR LIFE FORCE AS WELL!

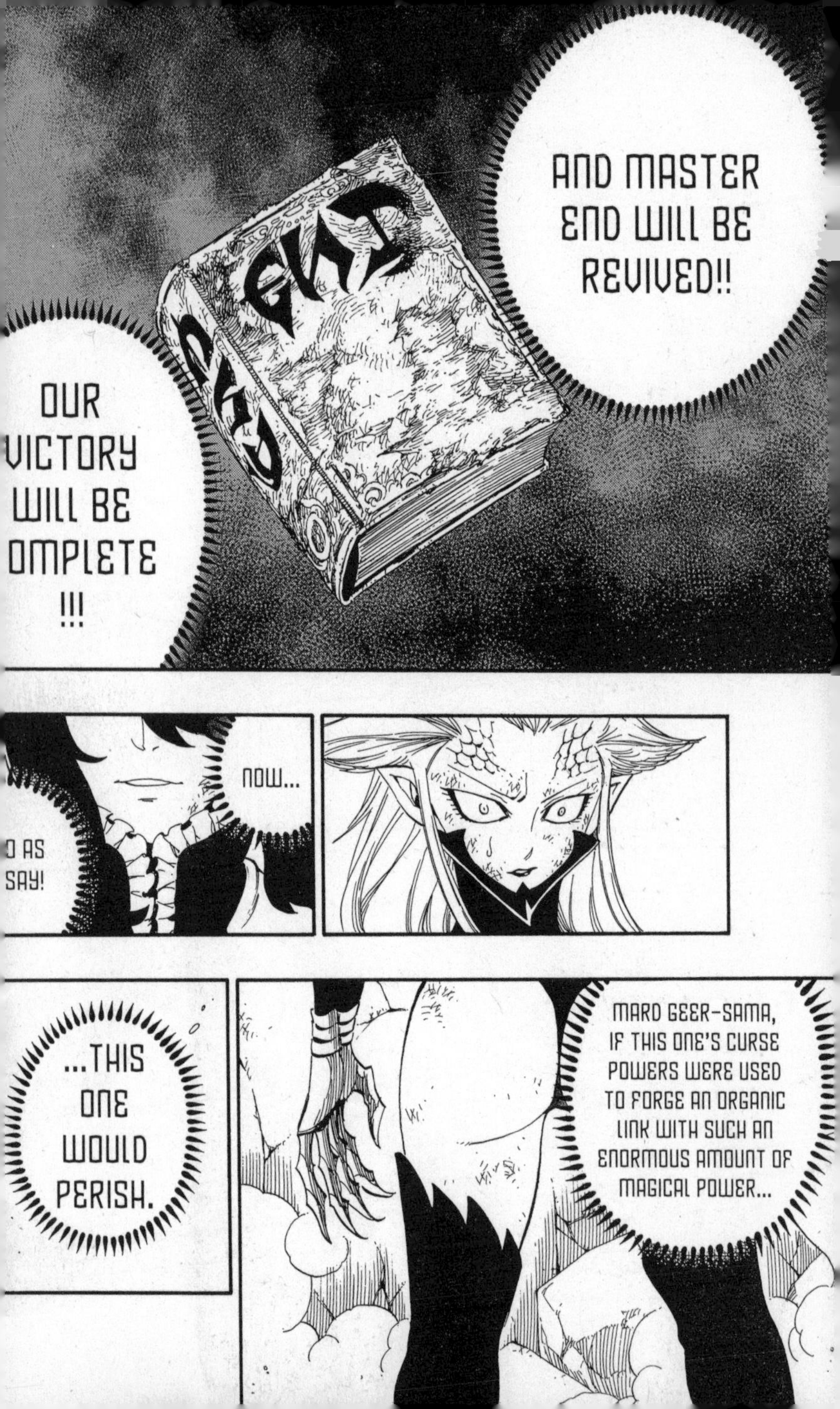
AND MASTER END WILL BE REVIVED!!
OUR VICTORY WILL BE OMPLETE !!!
NOW...
D AS SAY!
MARD GEER-SAMA, IF THIS ONE'S CURSE POWERS WERE USED TO FORGE AN ORGANIC LINK WITH SUCH AN ENORMOUS AMOUNT OF MAGICAL POWER...
...THIS ONE WOULD PERISH.

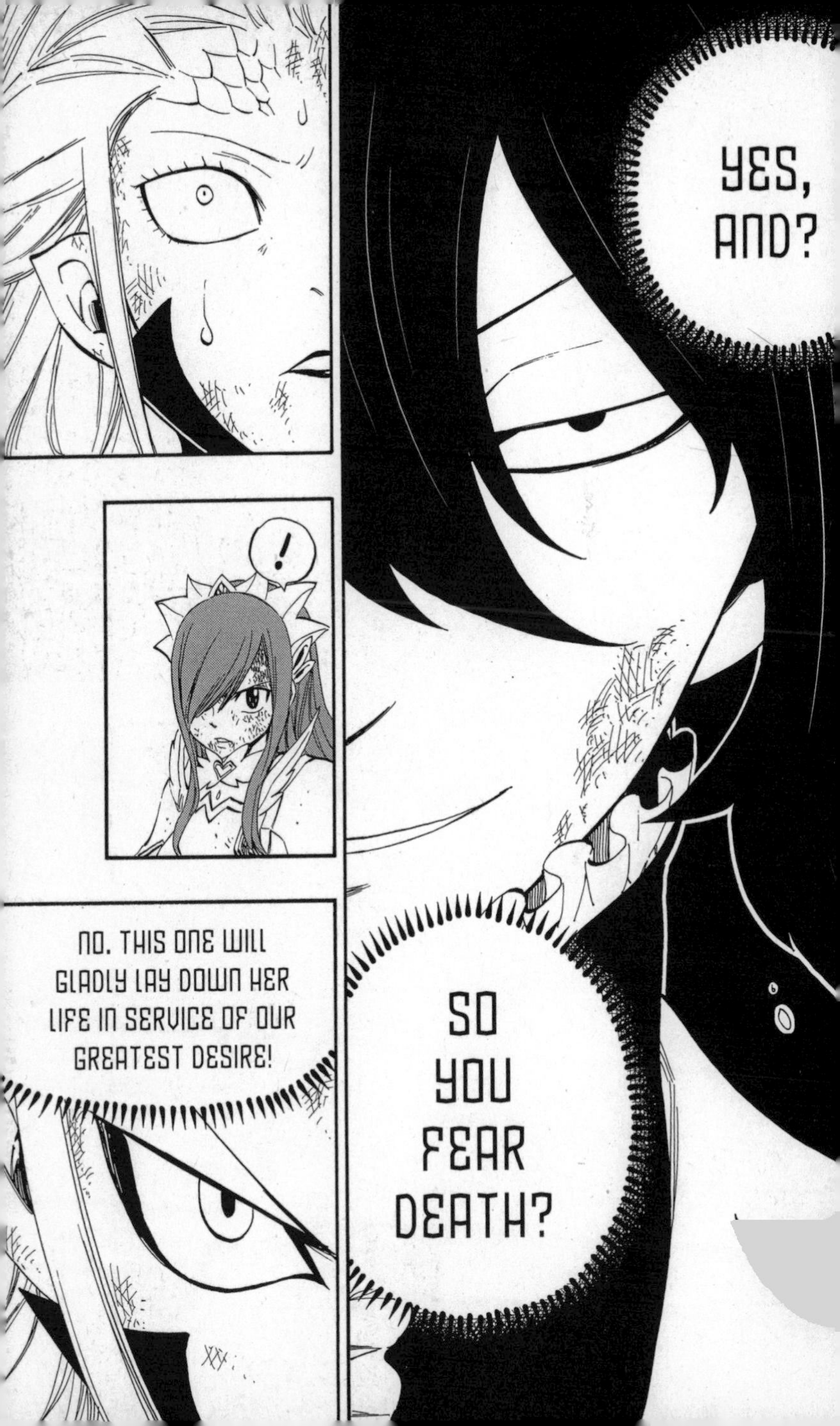
YES, AND?
SO YOU FEAR DEATH?
!
NO. THIS ONE WILL GLADLY LAY DOWN HER LIFE IN SERVICE OF OUR GREATEST DESIRE!

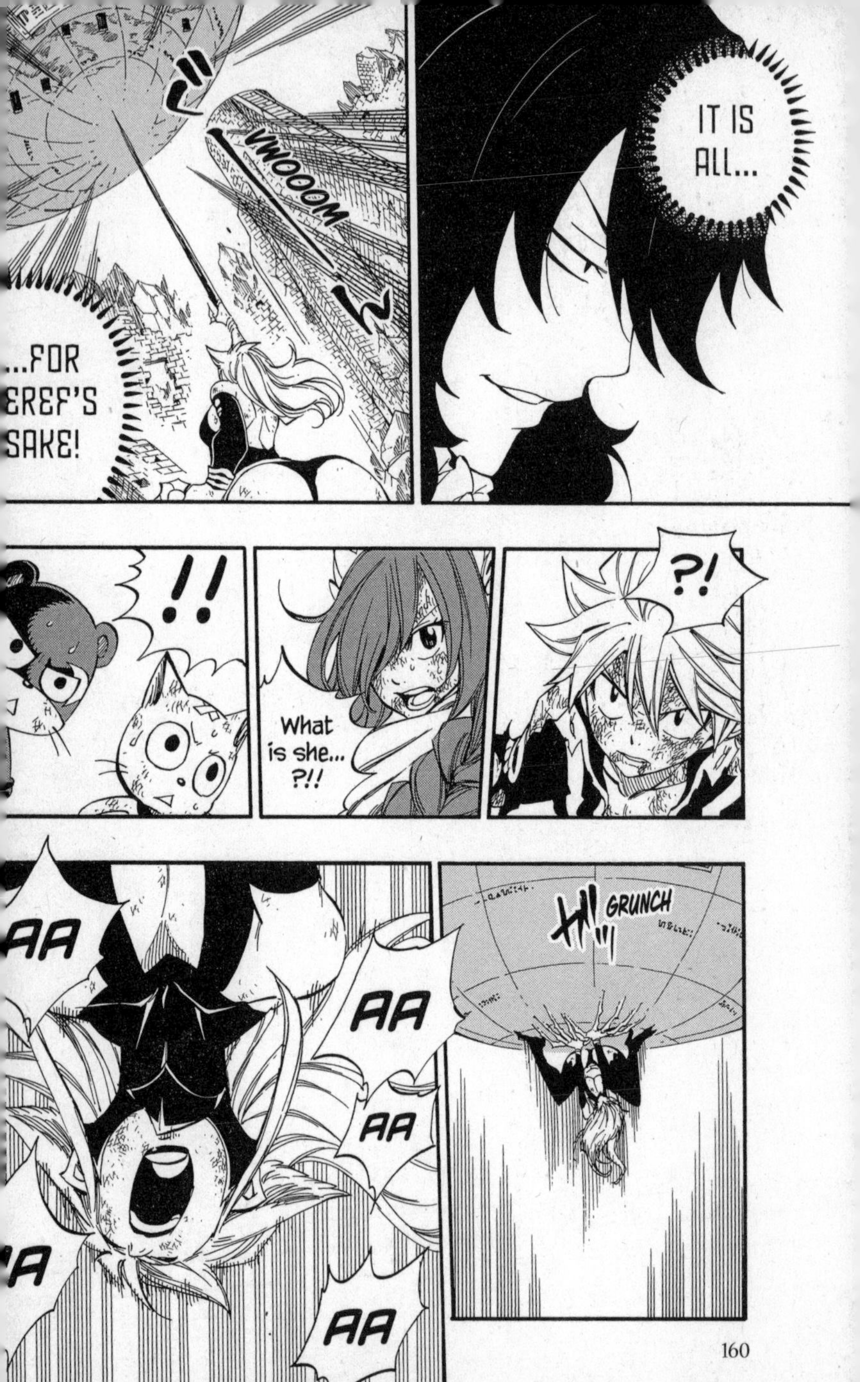
IT IS ALL...
VWOOOM
...FOR EREF'S SAKE!
?!
What is she... ?!!
!!
GRUNCH
AA
AA
AA
AA
AA
AA

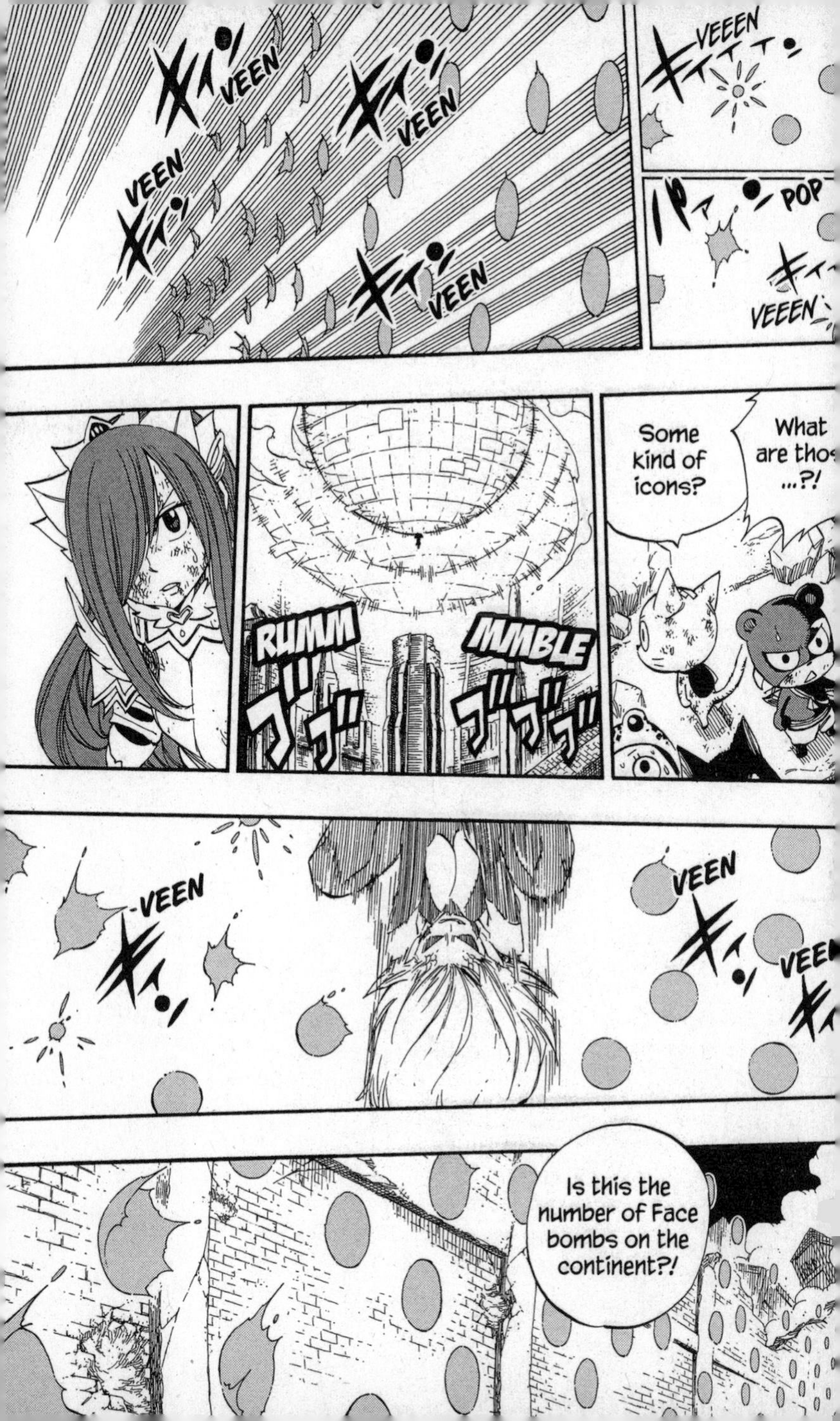
VEEEN
POP
VEEEN
VEEN
VEEN
VEEN
VEEN
What are thos ...?!
Some kind of icons?
RUMM
MMBLE
VEEN
VEE
-VEEN
Is this the number of Face bombs on the continent?!

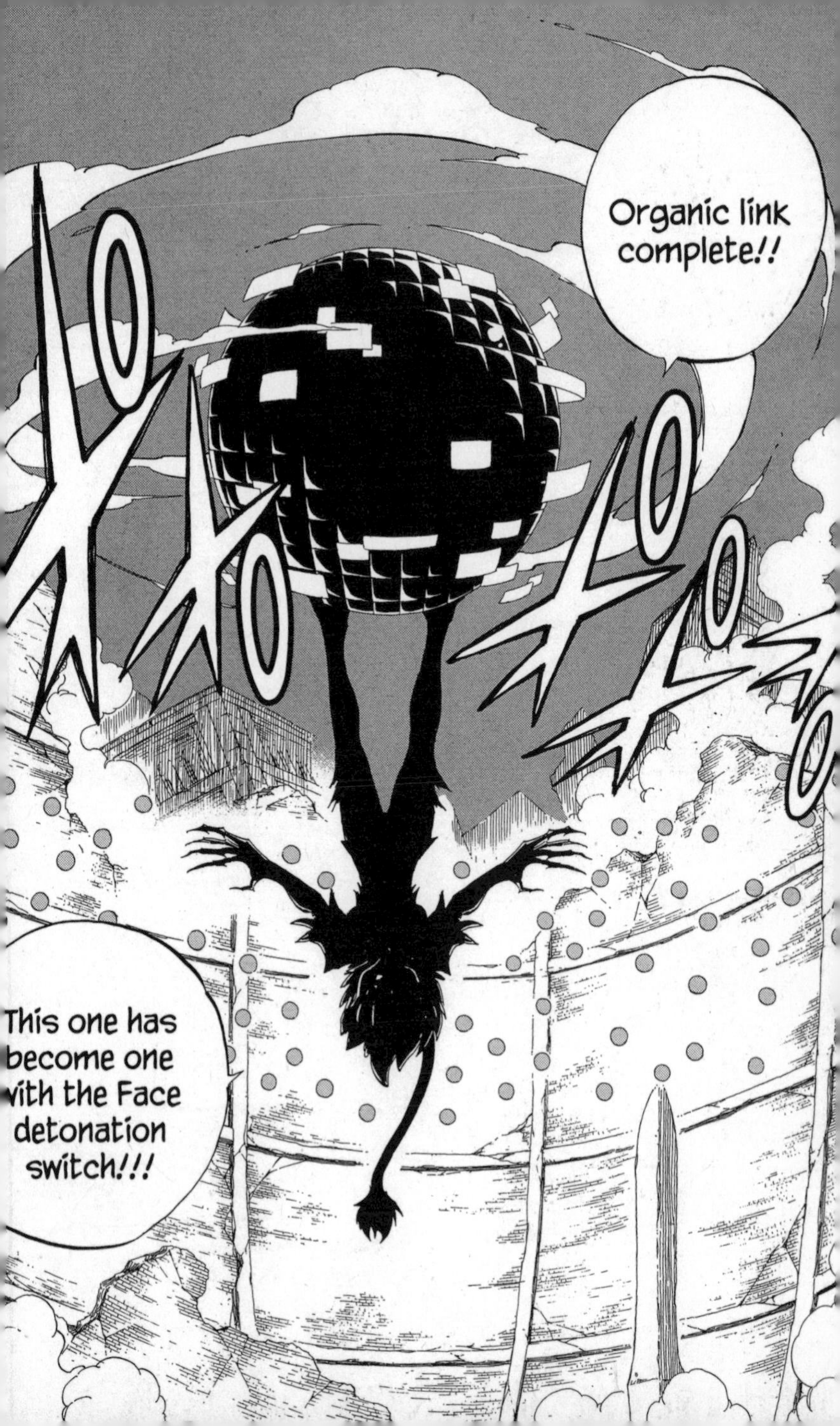
Organic link complete!!
This one has become one with the Face detonation switch!!!

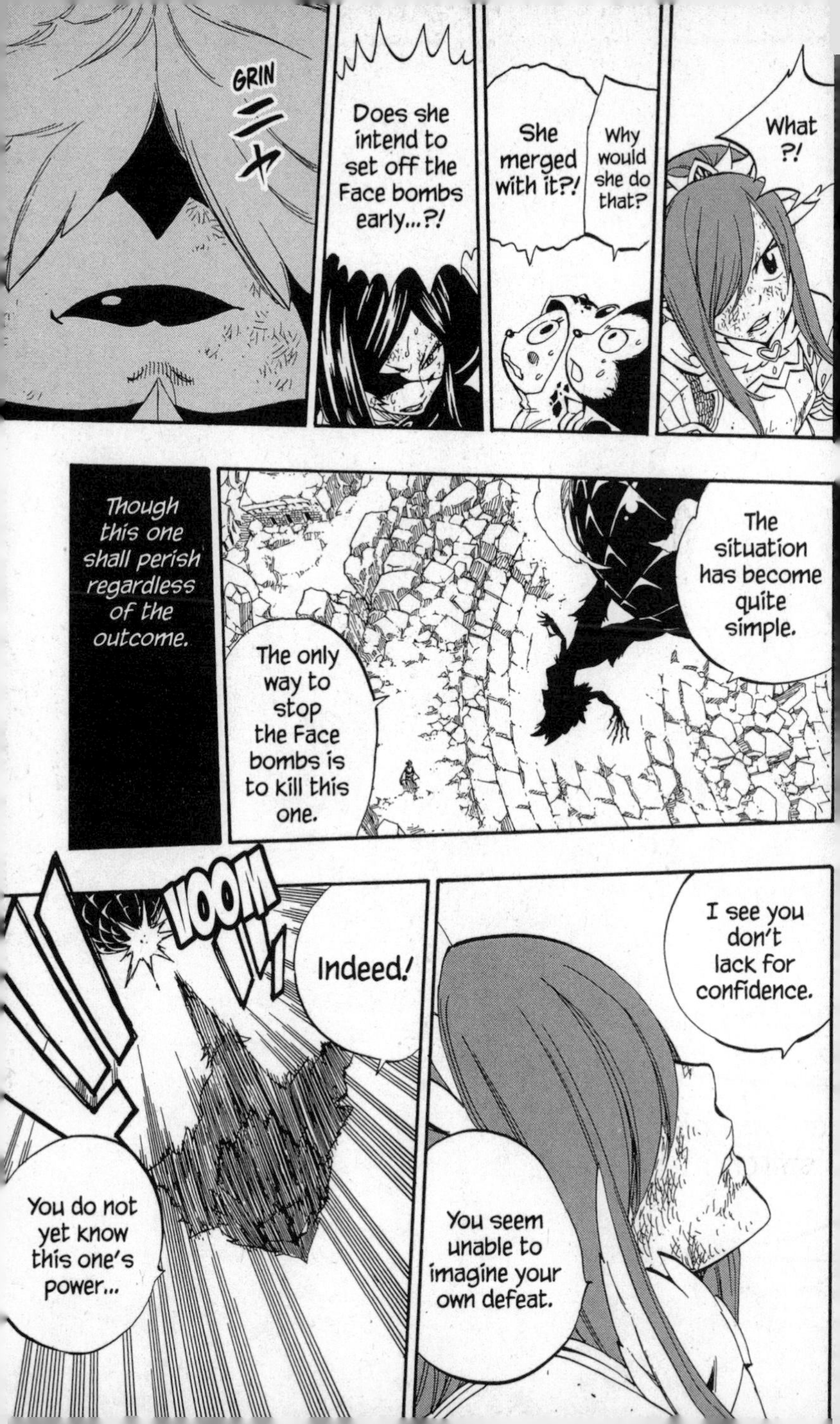
What ?!
Why would she do that?
She merged with it?!
Does she intend to set off the Face bombs early...?!
GRIN
ニヤ
The situation has become quite simple.
The only way to stop the Face bombs is to kill this one.
Though this one shall perish regardless of the outcome.
I see you don't lack for confidence.
You seem unable to imagine your own defeat.
Indeed!
VOOM
You do not yet know this one's power...

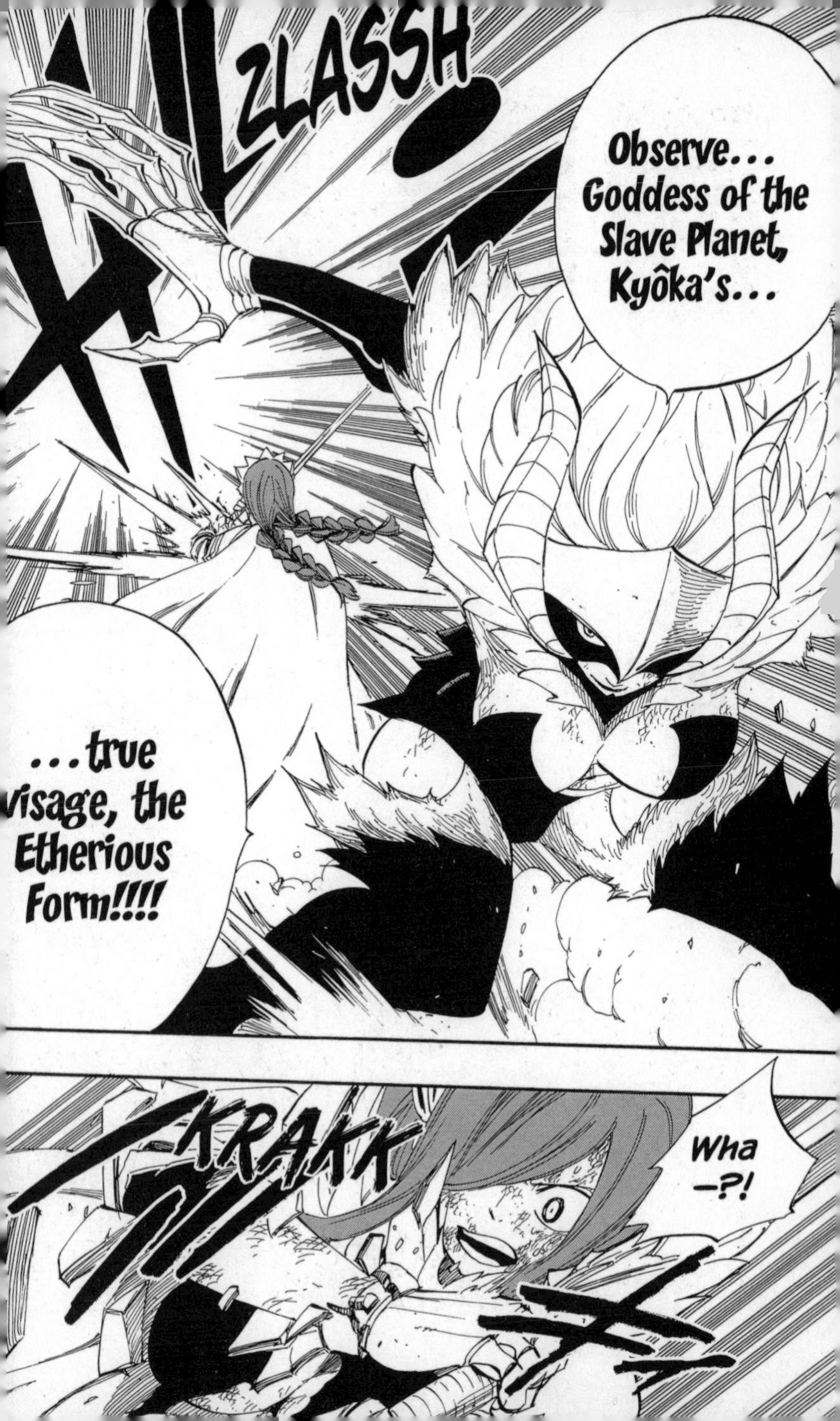
ZLASSH
Observe... Goddess of the Slave Planet, Kyôka's...
...true visage, the Etherious Form!!!!
Wha—?!
KRAKK

FAIRY TAIL
フェアリーテイル

Chapter 403: Erza vs. Kyôka

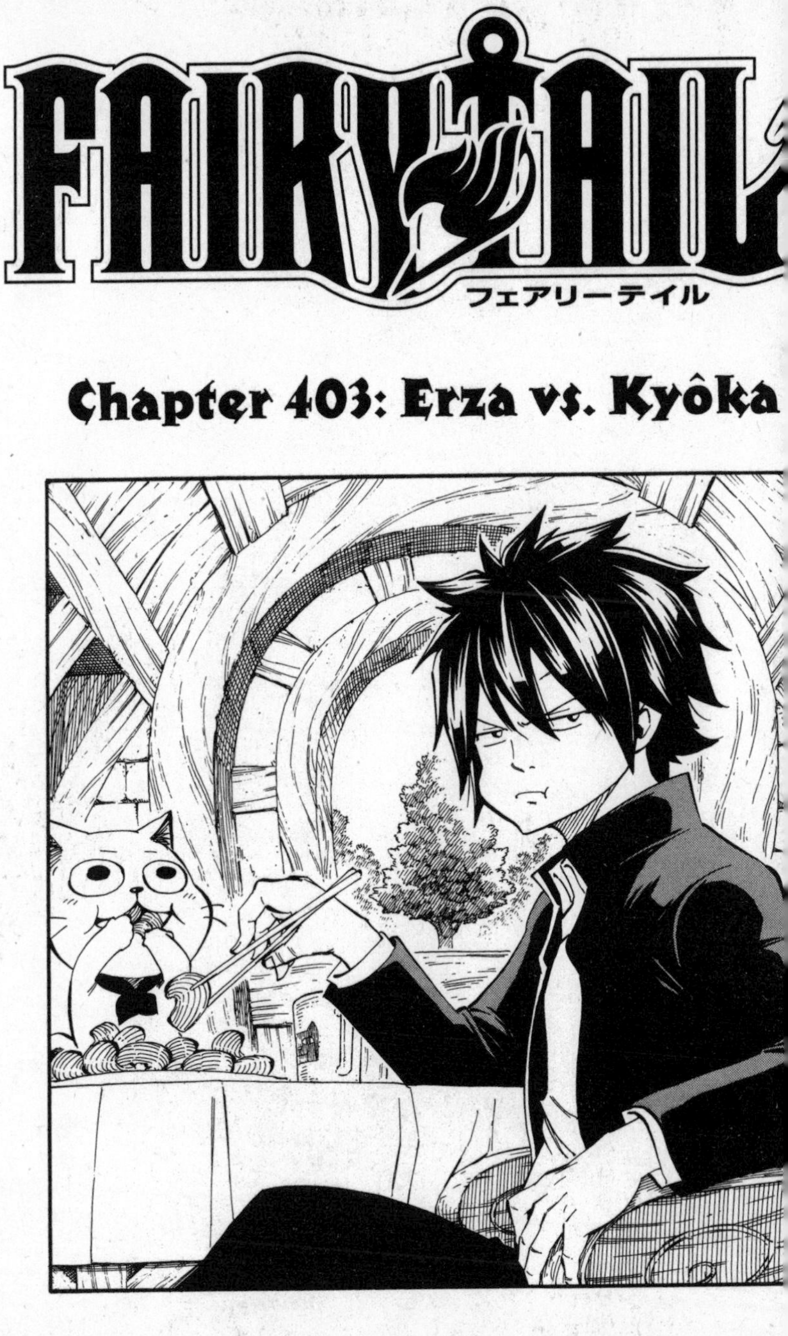

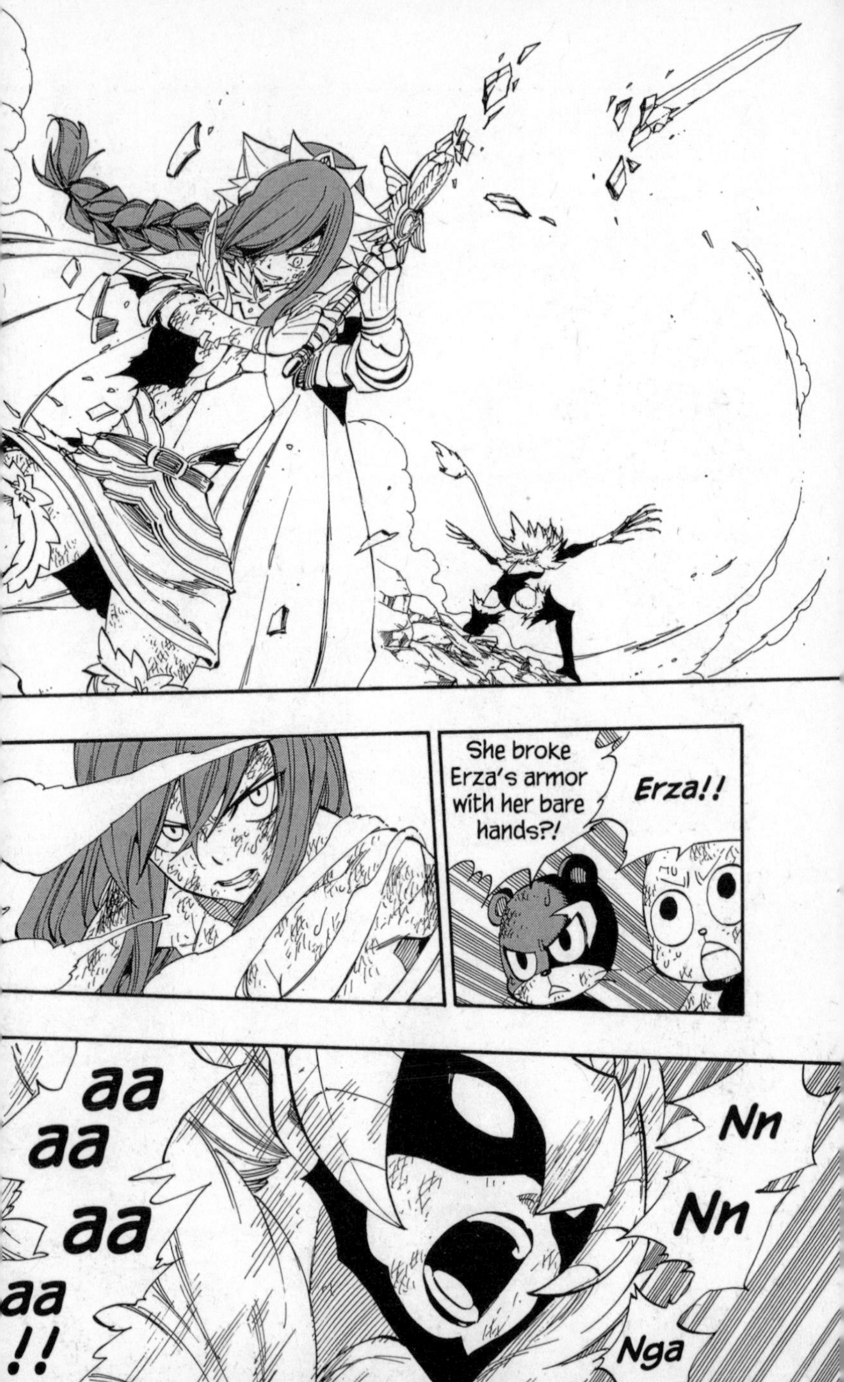
Erza!!
She broke Erza's armor with her bare hands?!
Nn Nn Nga
aa aa aa aa!!

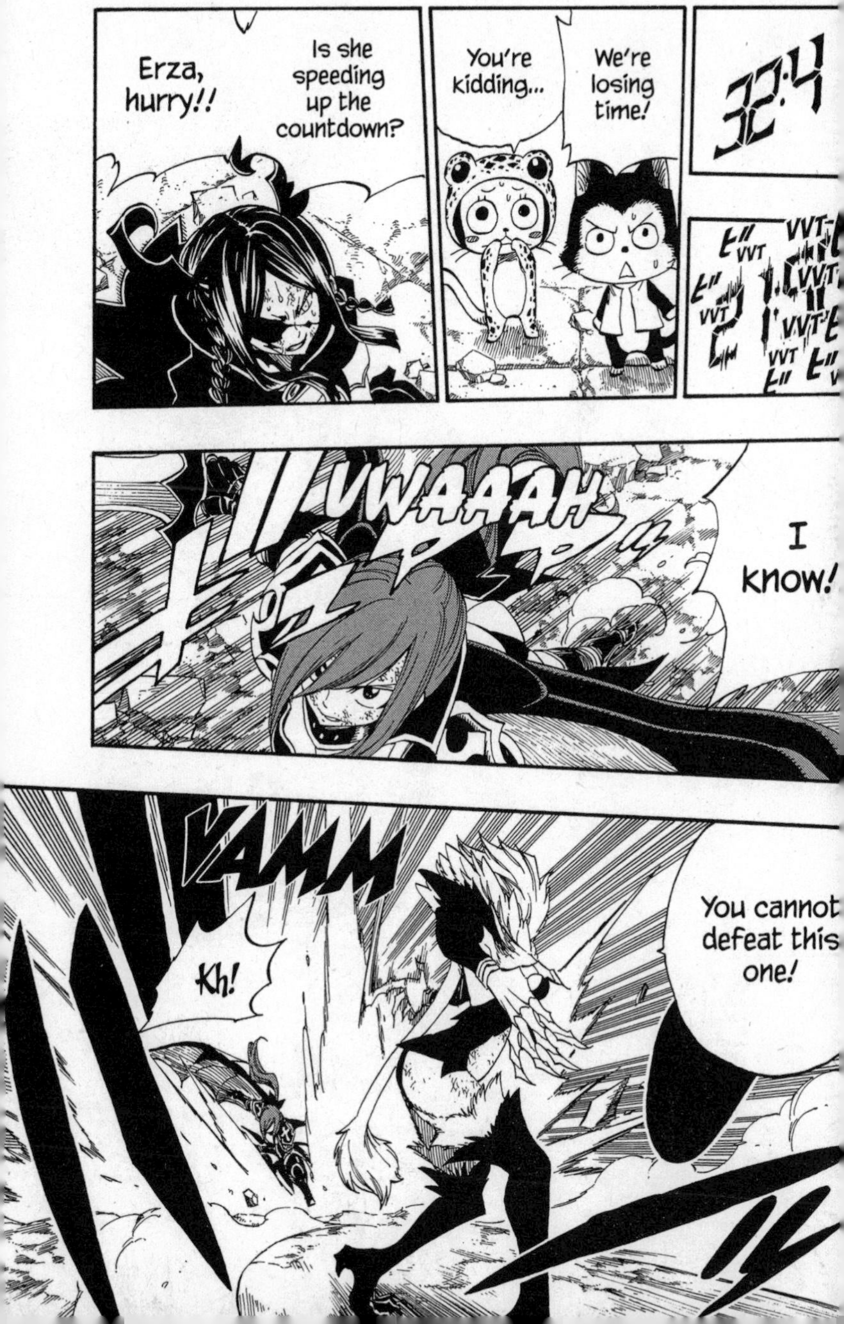

32:4
VVT
We're losing time!
You're kidding...
Is she speeding up the countdown?
Erza, hurry!!
I know!
VWAAAH
You cannot defeat this one!
VAMM
Kh!

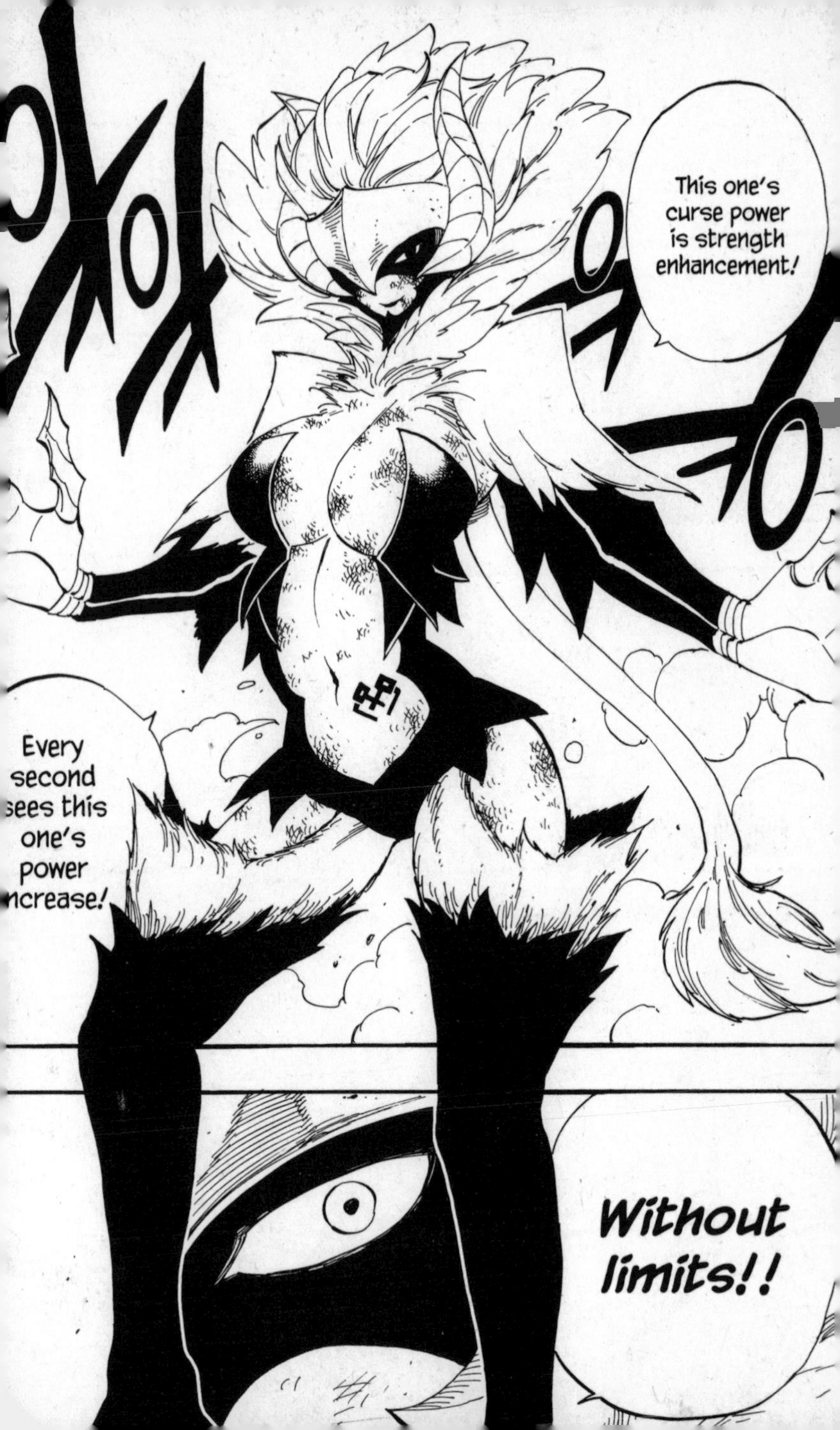
This one's curse power is strength enhancement!
Every second sees this one's power ncrease!
Without limits!!

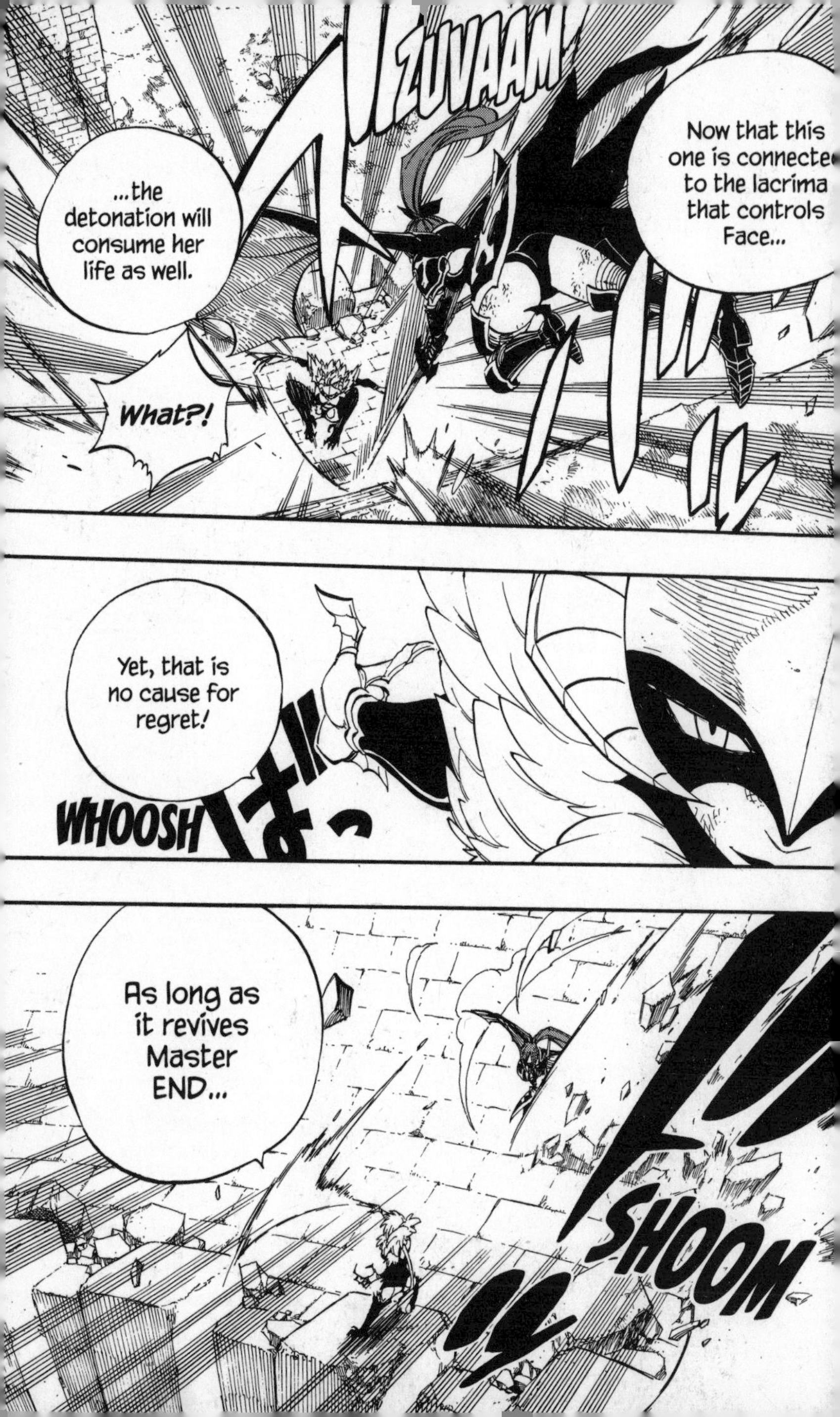

Now that this one is connecte to the lacrima that controls Face...
ZUVAAM
...the detonation will consume her life as well.
What?!
Yet, that is no cause for regret!
WHOOSH
As long as it revives Master END...
SHOOM

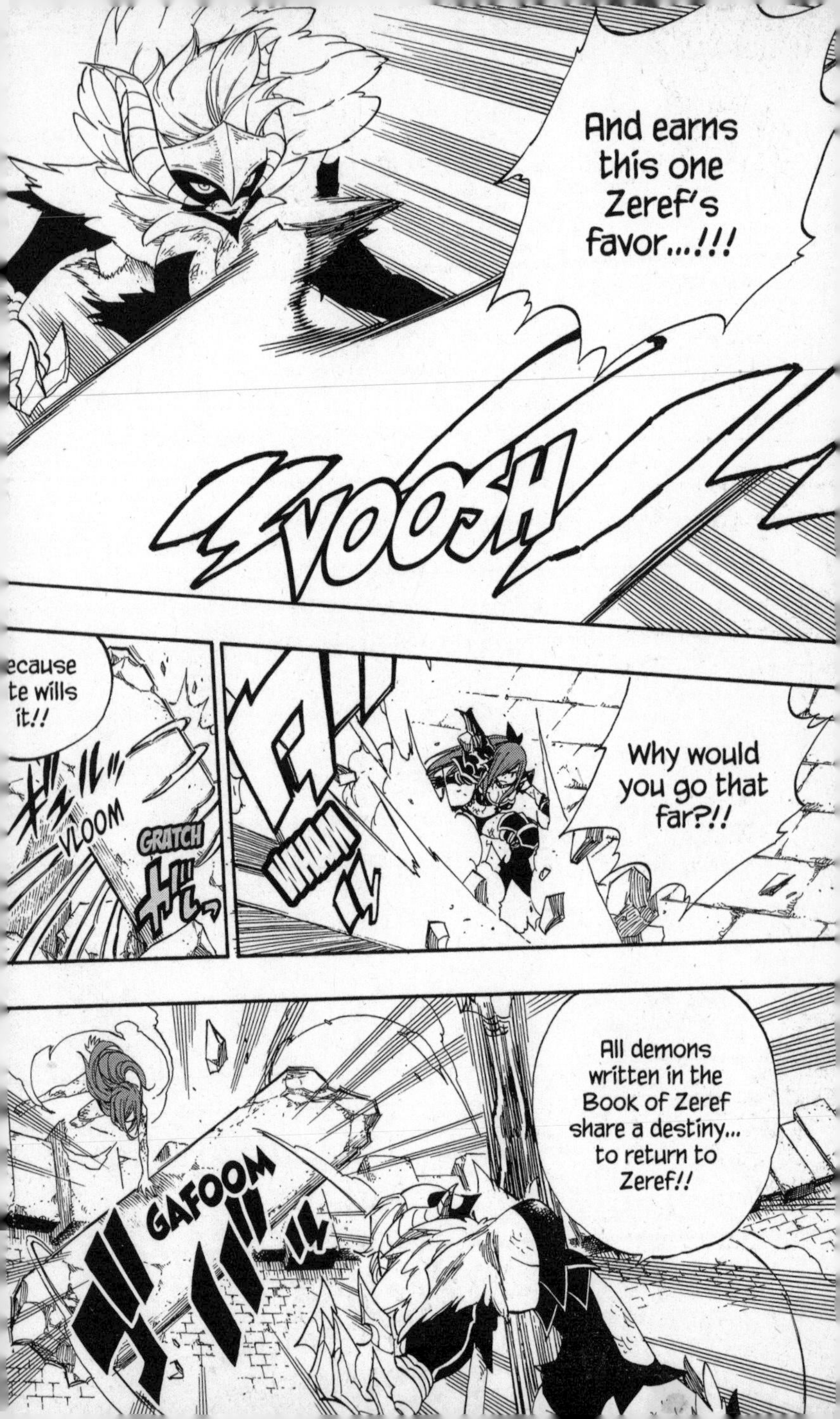

And earns this one Zeref's favor...!!!
VOOSH
Why would you go that far?!!
WHAM
ecause
te wills it!!
VLOOM
GRATCH
All demons written in the Book of Zeref share a destiny... to return to Zeref!!
GAFOOM

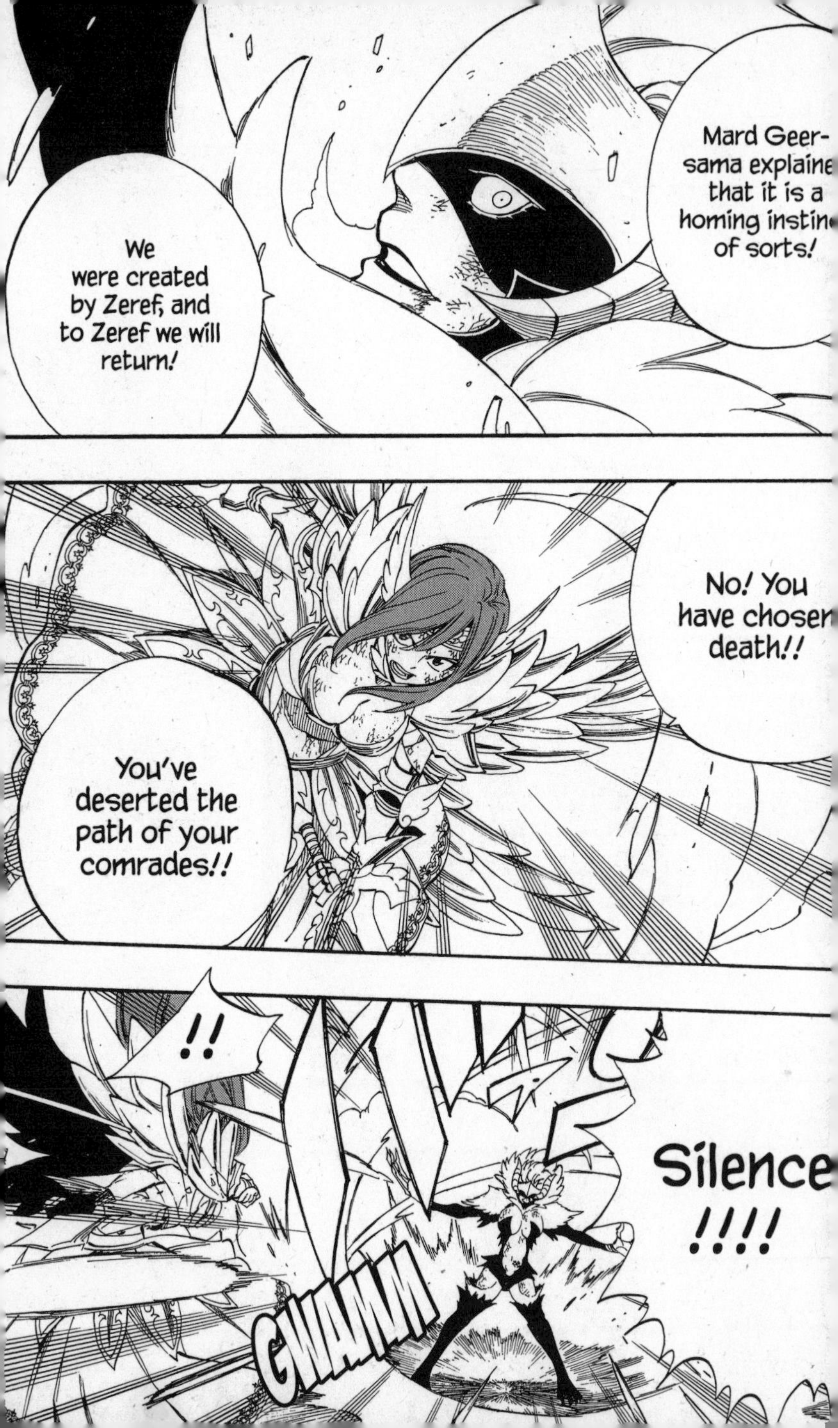
Mard Geer-sama explaine that it is a homing instin of sorts!
We were created by Zeref, and to Zeref we will return!
No! You have chosen death!!
You've deserted the path of your comrades!!
Silence !!!!
!!
GWANM

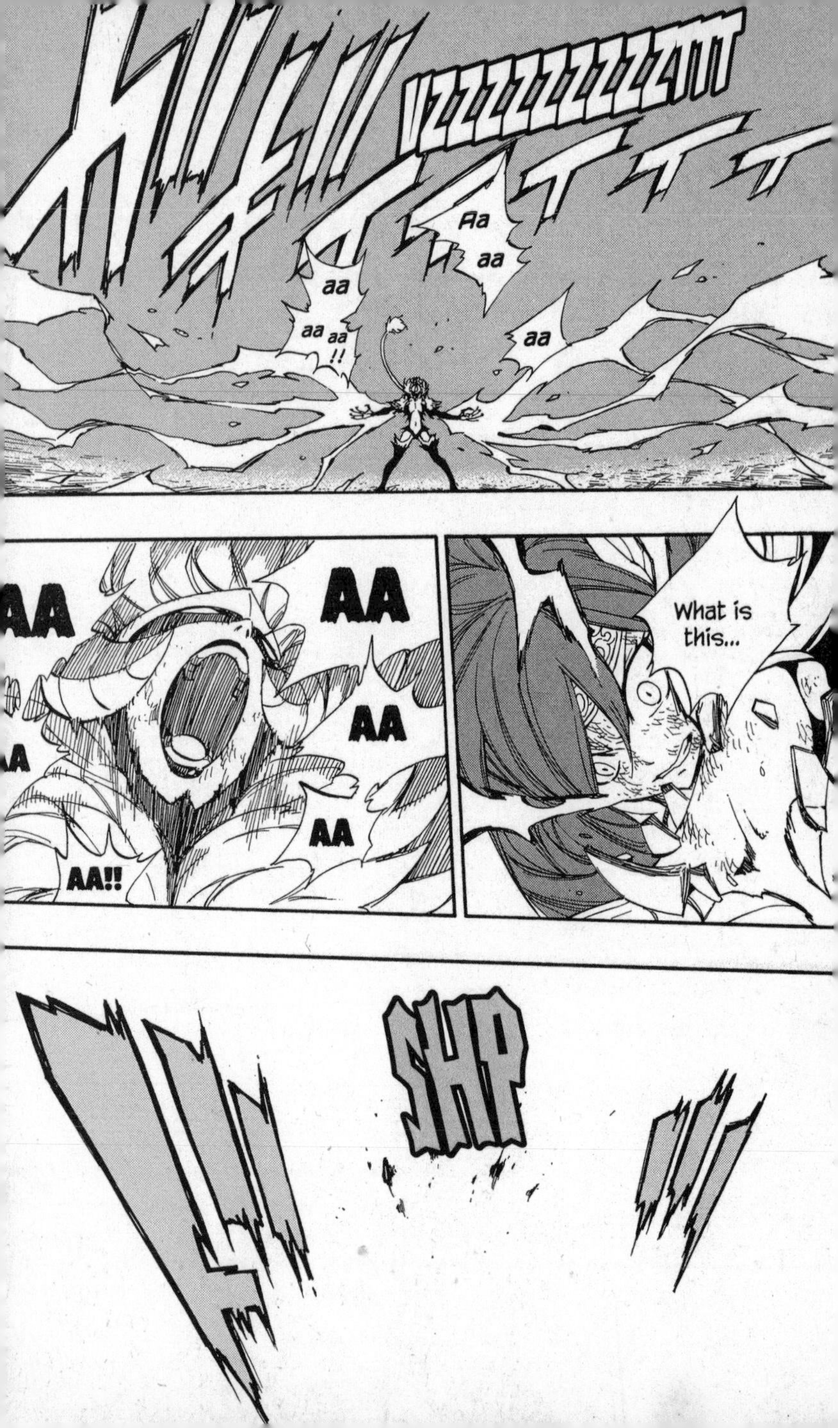
VZZZZZZZZZTTT
Aa aa
aa
aa aa aa !!
What is this...
AA
AA
AA
AA
AA
AA!!
SHP

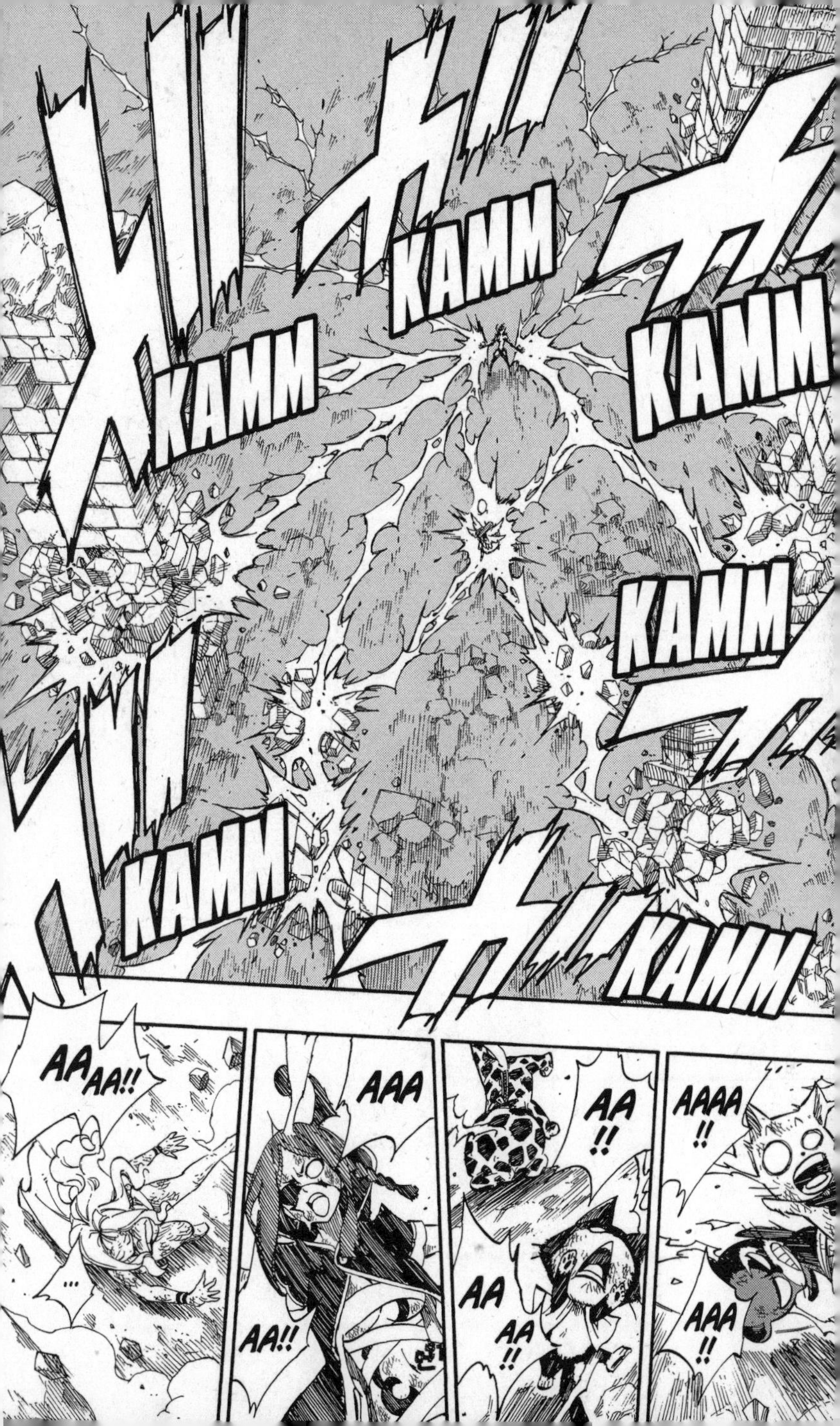
KAMM
KAMM
KAMM
KAMM
KAMM
KAMM
AAAA !!
AAA !!
AA !!
AA
AA !!
AAA
AA!!
AAAA!!
...

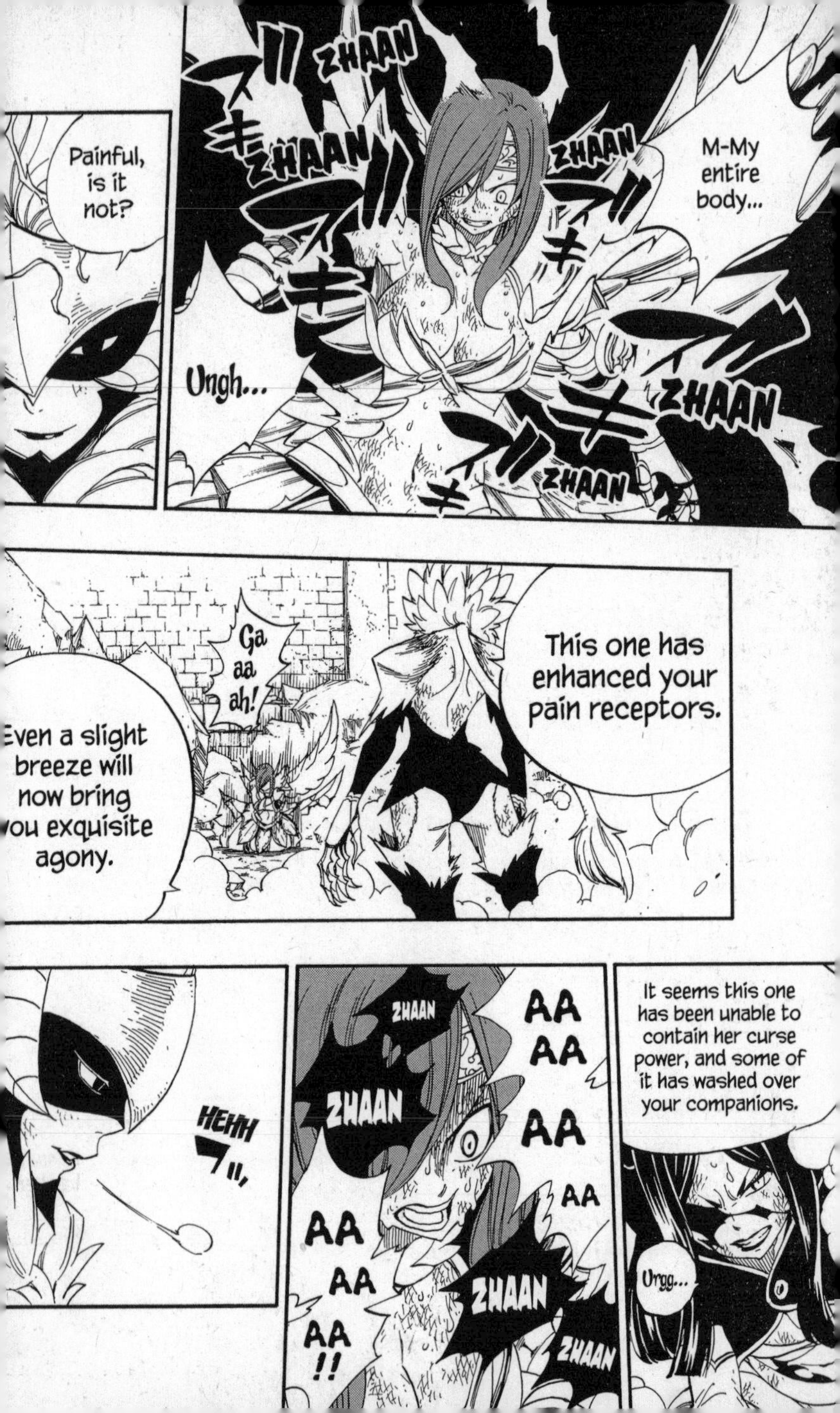
ZHAAN
ZHAAN
M-My entire body...
ZHAAN
ZHAAN
ZHAAN
Ungh...
ZHAAN
Painful, is it not?
This one has enhanced your pain receptors.
Ga aa ah!
Even a slight breeze will now bring you exquisite agony.
It seems this one has been unable to contain her curse power, and some of it has washed over your companions.
Urgg...
AA AA AA AA AA AA AA!!
ZHAAN
ZHAAN
ZHAAN
ZHAAN
HEHH

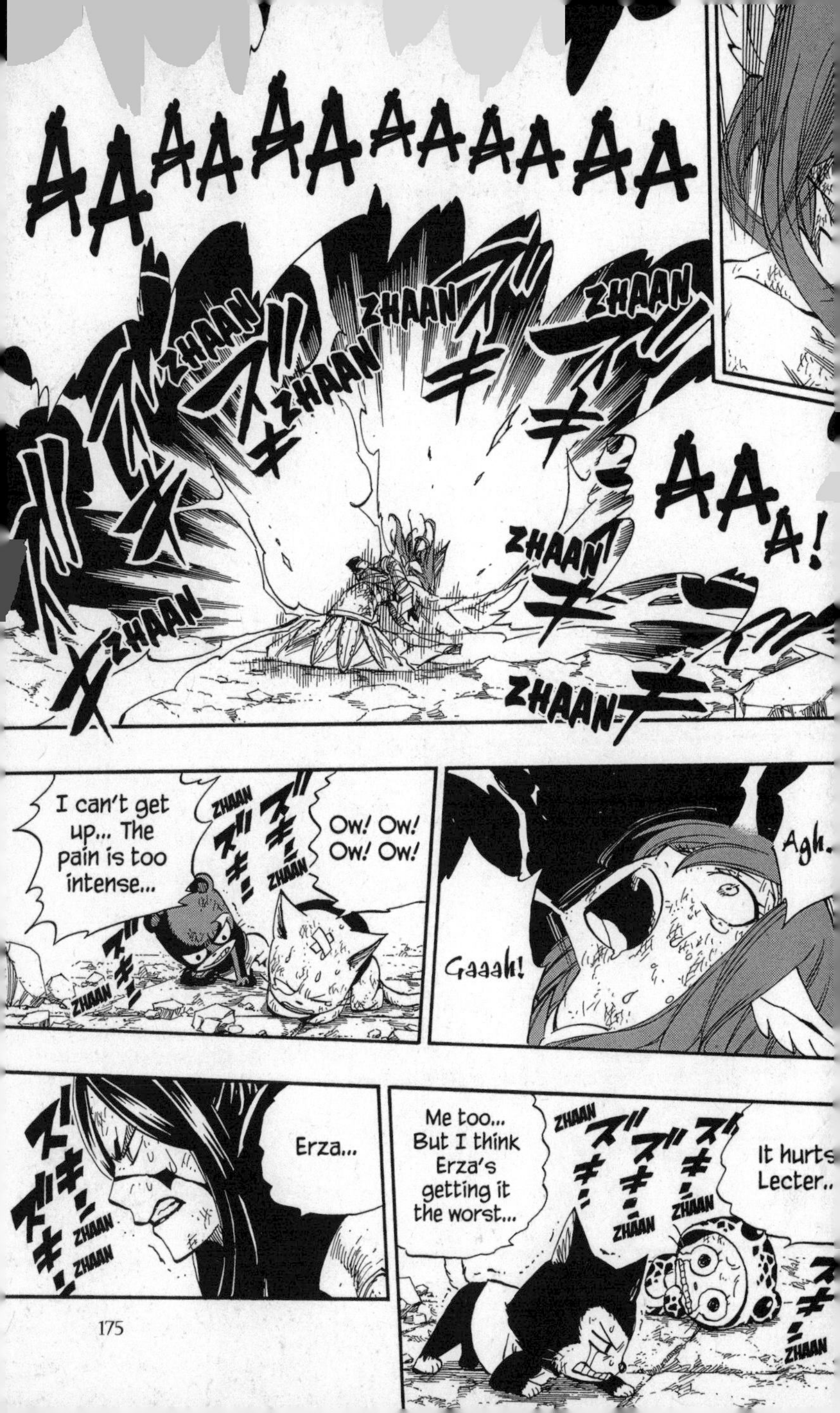
AAAAAAAAAAAAA
ZHAAN
ZHAAN
ZHAAN
ZHAAN
ZHAAN
AAAA!
ZHAAN
ZHAAN
ZHAAN
Agh...
Gaaah!
Ow! Ow! Ow! Ow!
ZHAAN
ZHAAN
I can't get up... The pain is too intense...
ZHAAN
It hurts Lecter...
ZHAAN
ZHAAN
ZHAAN
ZHAAN
ZHAAN
Me too... But I think Erza's getting it the worst...
Erza...
ZHAAN
ZHAAN

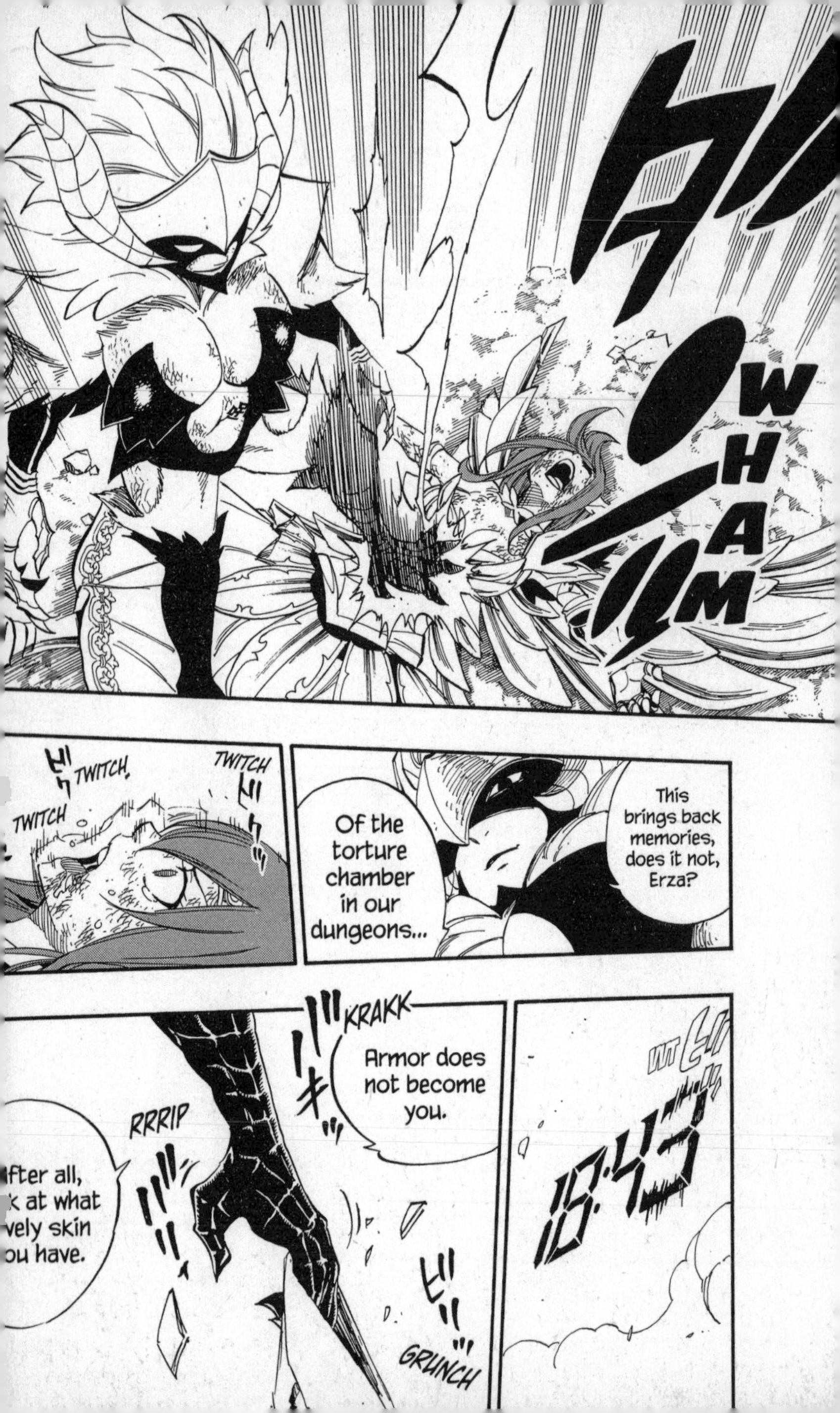
WHAM
This brings back memories, does it not, Erza?
Of the torture chamber in our dungeons...
TWITCH
TWITCH
TWITCH
KRAKK
Armor does not become you.
RRRIP
fter all, k at what vely skin ou have.
GRUNCH

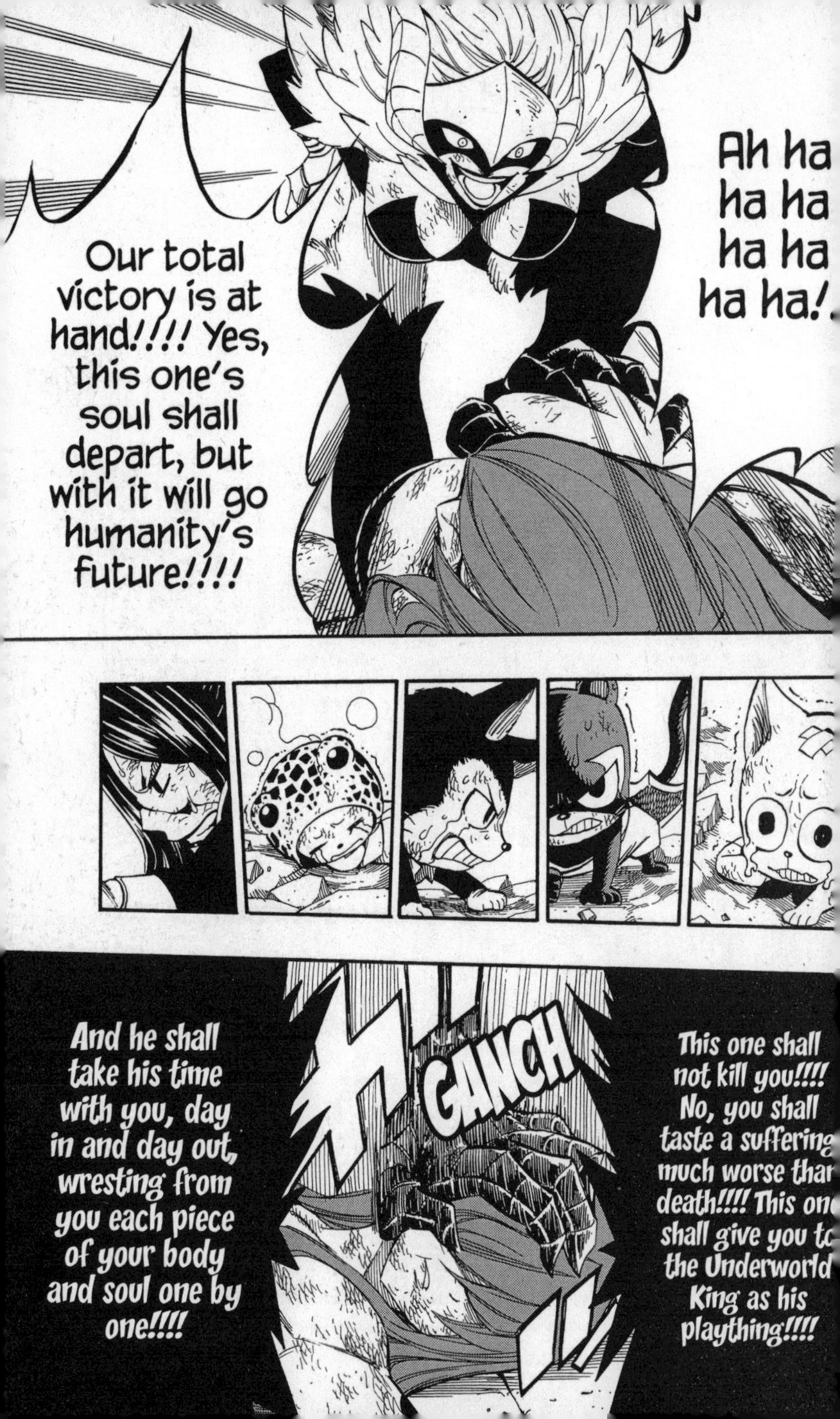
Ah ha ha ha ha ha ha ha!
Our total victory is at hand!!!! Yes, this one's soul shall depart, but with it will go humanity's future!!!!
This one shall not kill you!!!! No, you shall taste a suffering much worse than death!!!! This one shall give you to the Underworld King as his plaything!!!!
GANCH
And he shall take his time with you, day in and day out, wresting from you each piece of your body and soul one by one!!!!

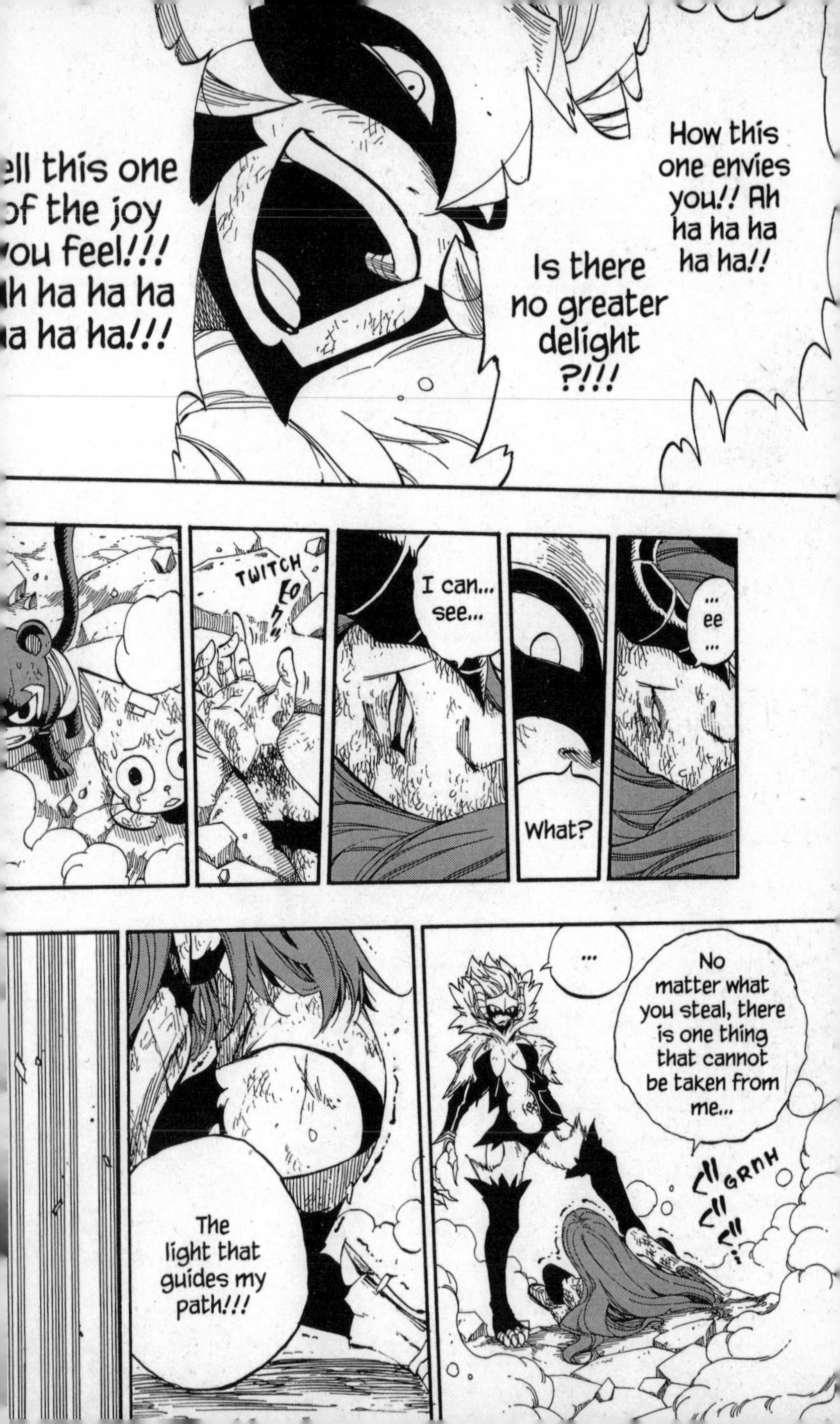
How this one envies you!! Ah ha ha ha ha ha!!
Is there no greater delight ?!!!
ell this one of the joy ou feel!!! h ha ha ha a ha ha!!!
... ee ...
What?
I can... see...
TWITCH
...
No matter what you steal, there is one thing that cannot be taken from me...
GRNH
The light that guides my path!!!

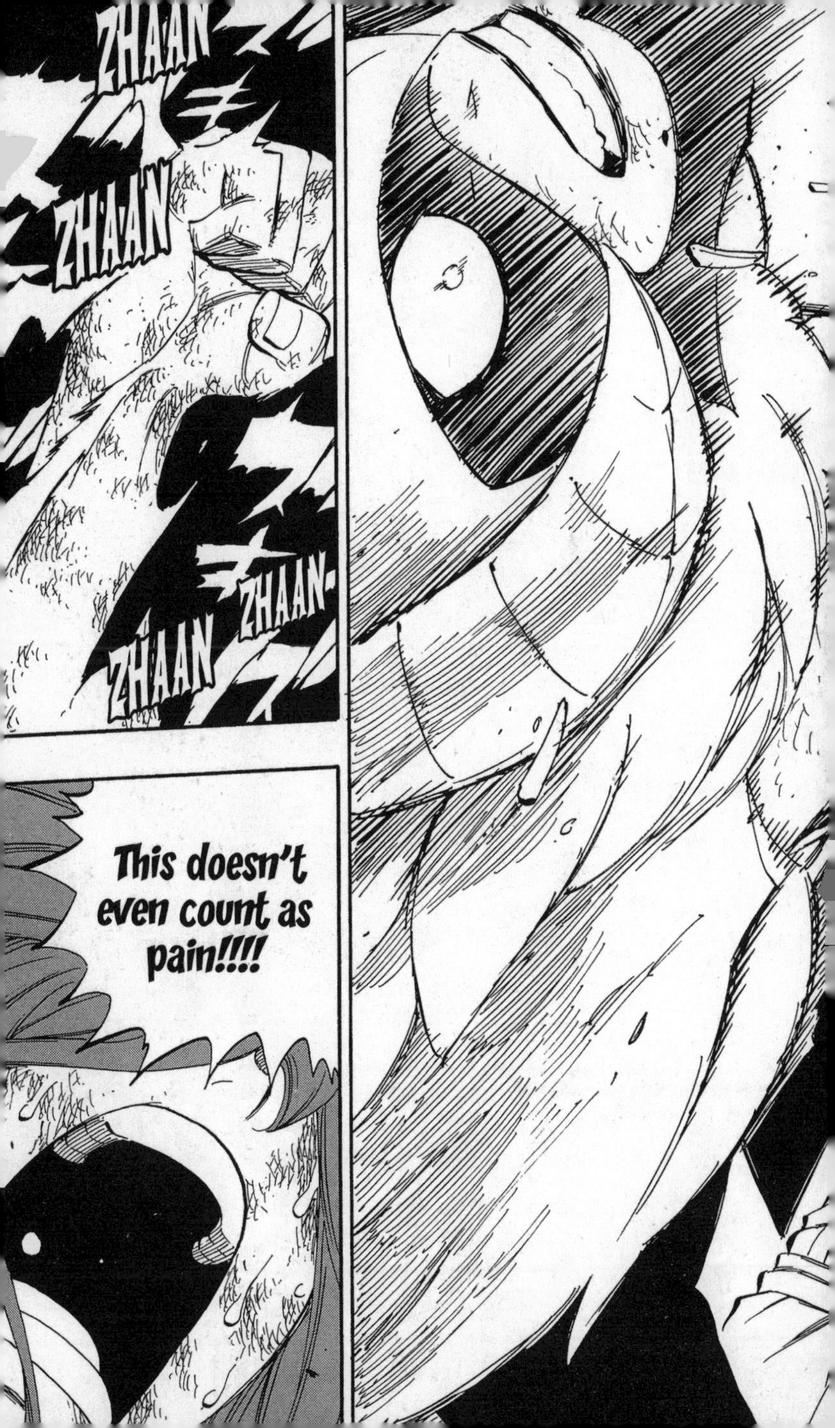
ZHAAN
ZHAAN
ZHAAN-
ZHAAN
This doesn't even count as pain!!!!

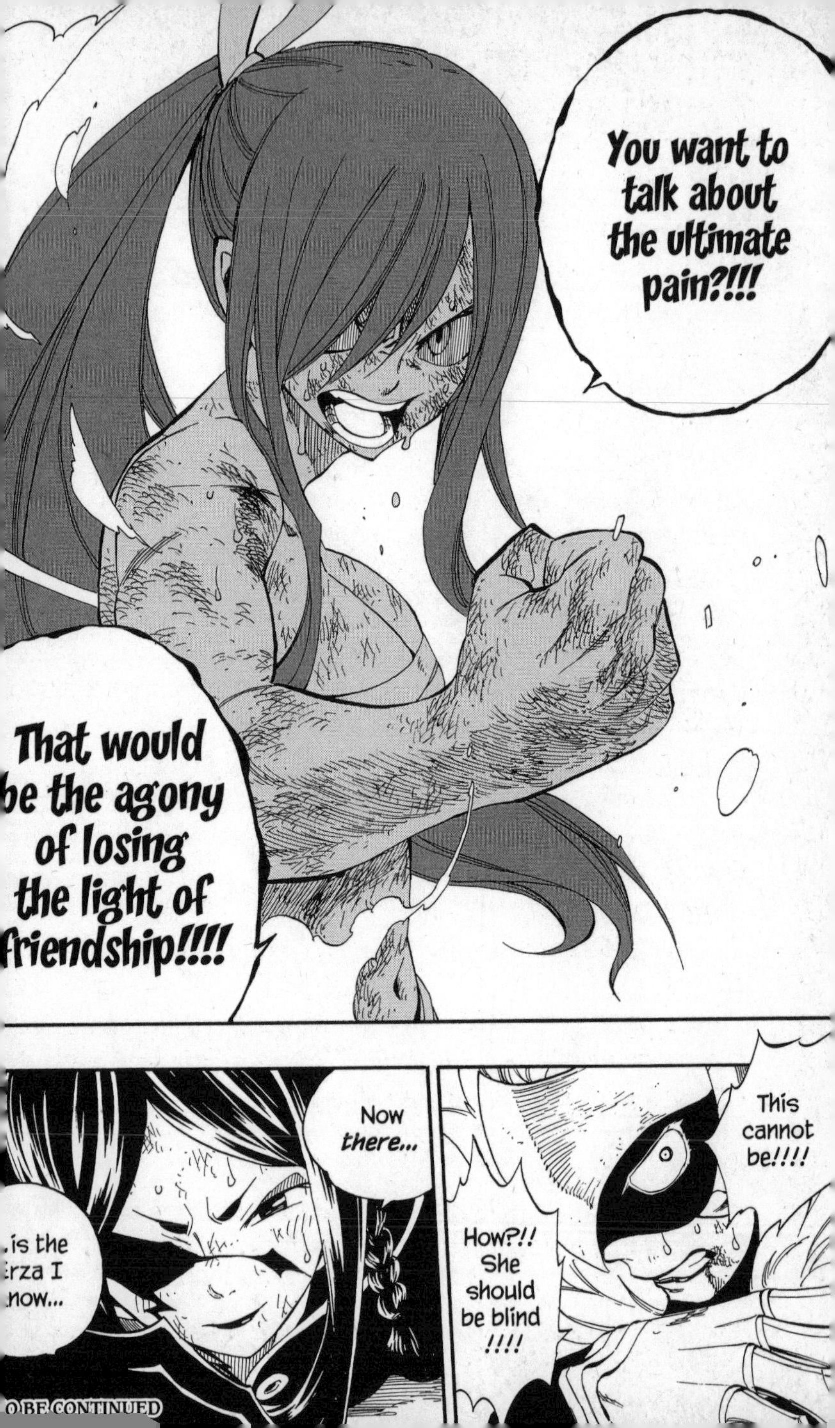
You want to talk about the ultimate pain?!!!
That would be the agony of losing the light of friendship!!!!
This cannot be!!!!
How?!! She should be blind !!!!
Now there...
.is the rza I now...
O BE CONTINUED

あとがき
Afterword

This volume contains Gajeel's backstory with Elder Belno. Actually I've had this bit of plot for a long time. The truth is I had this chapter where Elder Belno was the trigger that got Gajeel to join Fairy Tail, but since that changed to Makarov getting him to join, his story with Elder Belno was shelved, forever, I thought. Here, where all of the members and former members of the Council were involved, I thought that just possibly I could sneak that backstory in, but there was also the possibility that I couldn't follow up on it, so the chapter had to be simplified.

Now I wish I had done proper foreshadowing on it.

Personally, I love to drop little foreshadowing clues, but there are so many characters in this manga! Add to it the fact that I'm doing not only this weekly manga but a monthly too, and my mind is getting pretty messed up by it all (heh)! Plus, I'm getting these impossible requests to do one-shots on top of all that!

And so, I've dropped a bunch of foreshadowing hints that I won't be able to include (stories I'm no longer scheduled to do), and from here on, there will be a bunch more (including red herrings), so you'll probably see a whole lot of plots I'm trying to hint at.

In any case, I'm still looking forward to clearing up a whole bunch more mysteries, so please look forward to that!

nued from the
-hand page. ⬇

ucy: I hear there are all sorts of explanations. Like there are sixteen Lummys or that she can only use 1/16th of her power...

ira: But the real answer is so stupid, I don't even want to write it here.

ucy: But we can't just ignore it, can we...?

ira: Fine, but it will take a while to explain. Lummy is modeled after a member of Mashima-sensei's staff.

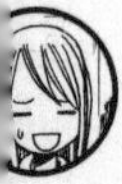
: Sigh...

ira: And one day, she suddenly made a rather pointless announcement.

ucy: Sigh...

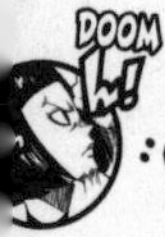
DOOM
: *"I AM 1/16TH RUSSIAN! (WHADDYA THINK OF THAT?)"*

ucy: Um... If 1/2 is half, and 1/4th is quarter, what is 1/16th
...???
Might as well just say she's fully Japanese.

Mira: Normally the story would just end with someone saying, "Really?" or, "Wow." But it was so sudden, and she put on such a, "What do you say to that?!" face! Still, it just slipped right on past the rest of the staff.

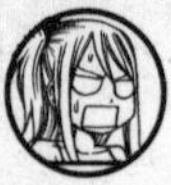
: You mean that Lummy's "slip-all" curse power was from that?

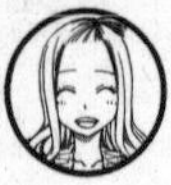
: Exactly! It came because the staff members let it slip by.

Lucy: The part about how she has a thing for hot guys too?

Mira: Of course!

Lucy: And that creepy "fa fa fa" laughter too?

Mira: All from that staff member.

Lucy: Come to think of it, she was a pretty impressive character!

Mira: And so, the real reason for the 1/16 tie was because she was 1/16th Russian.

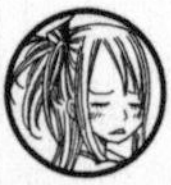
: I kind of wish nobody had ever asked.

Mira: It wasn't just her. Kain Hikaru and Kinana were both modeled after staff members. And in a strange way, so was Gemini.

Lucy: Huh?!!

Mira: Their weird "piiri piiri" sound was taken from a member of the staff who, way back in grade school, remembered his whole school saying it at the time.

Lucy: I kind of wish nobody had ever asked.

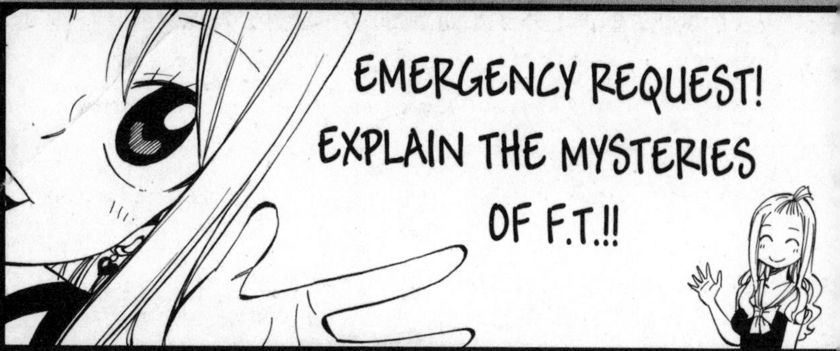

EMERGENCY REQUEST! EXPLAIN THE MYSTERIES OF F.T.!!

At a Magnolia ramen joint...

Lucy: Hi Everybody!

Mira: Okay, let's get straight to the questions!

Why did Mard Geer allow Silver in the Nine Demon Gates?

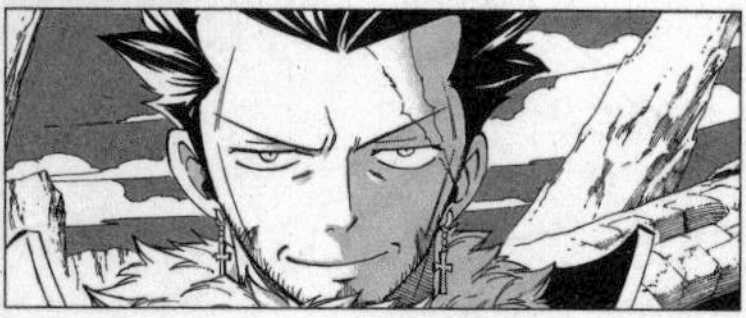

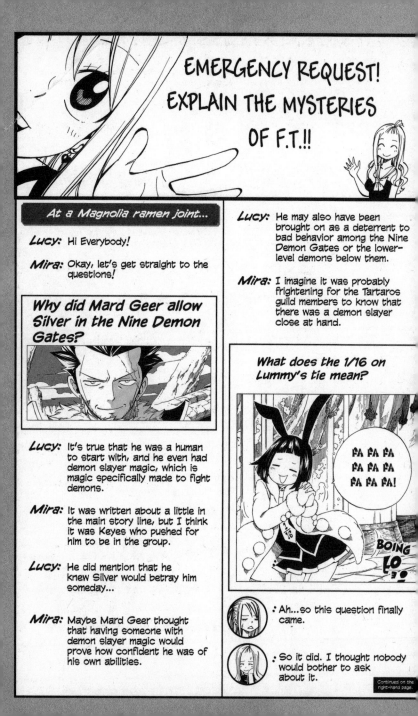

Lucy: It's true that he was a human to start with, and he even had demon slayer magic, which is magic specifically made to fight demons.

Mira: It was written about a little in the main story line, but I think it was Keyes who pushed for him to be in the group.

Lucy: He did mention that he knew Silver would betray him someday...

Mira: Maybe Mard Geer thought that having someone with demon slayer magic would prove how confident he was of his own abilities.

Lucy: He may also have been brought on as a deterrent to bad behavior among the Nine Demon Gates or the lower-level demons below them.

Mira: I imagine it was probably frightening for the Tartaros guild members to know that there was a demon slayer close at hand.

What does the 1/16 on Lummy's tie mean?

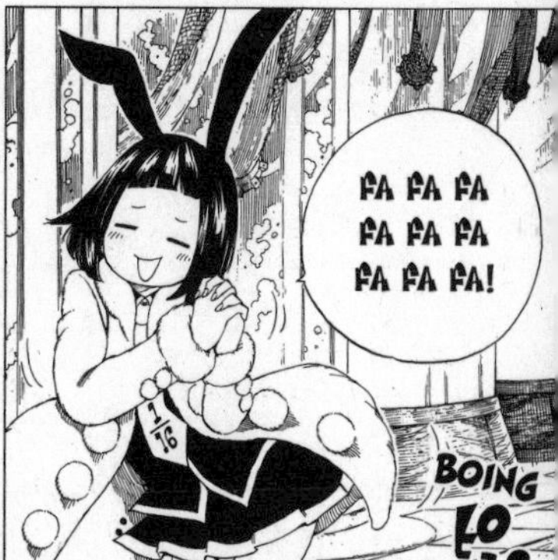
FA FA FA
FA FA FA
FA FA FA!
1/16
BOING

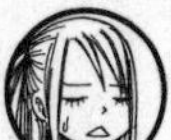
: Ah...so this question finally came.

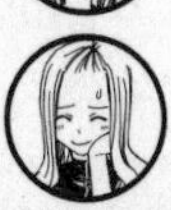
: So it did. I thought nobody would bother to ask about it.

Continued on the right-hand page.

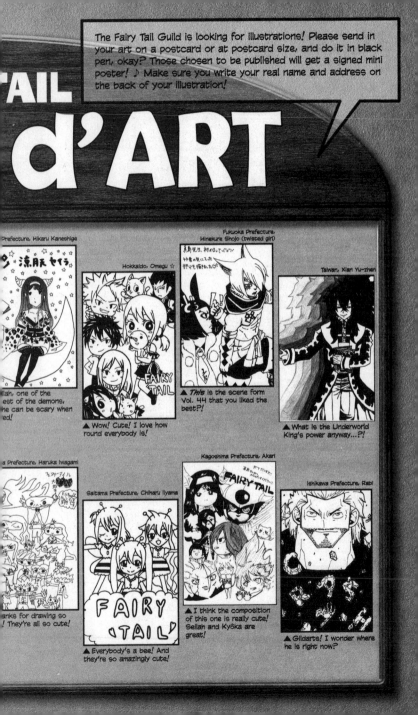

The Fairy Tail Guild is looking for illustrations! Please send in your art on a postcard or at postcard size, and do it in black pen, okay? Those chosen to be published will get a signed mini poster! ♪ Make sure you write your real name and address on the back of your illustration!

TAIL
d'ART

Prefecture, Hikaru Kaneshige

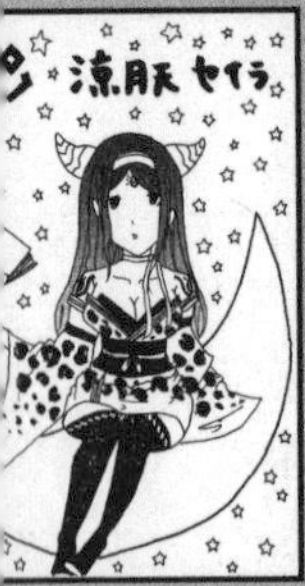

ilah, one of the
est of the demons,
he can be scary when
ed!

Hokkaido, Omegu ☆

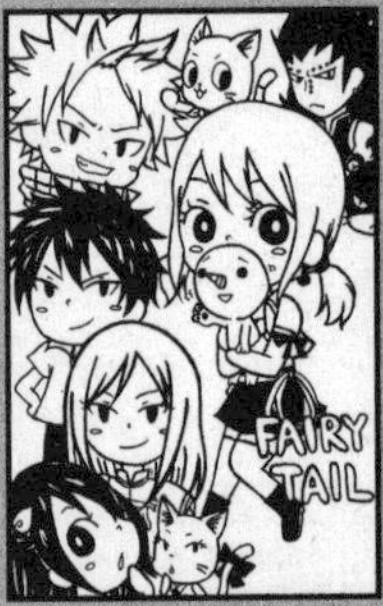
FAIRY TAIL

▲Wow! Cute! I love how round everybody is!

Fukuoka Prefecture, Hinekure Shojo (twisted girl)

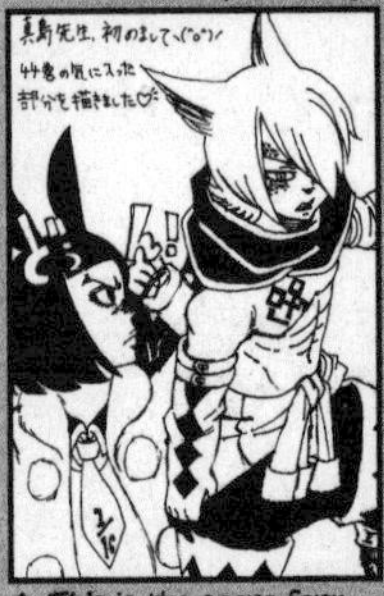

▲*This* is the scene form Vol. 44 that you liked the best?!

Taiwan, Xian Yu-zhen

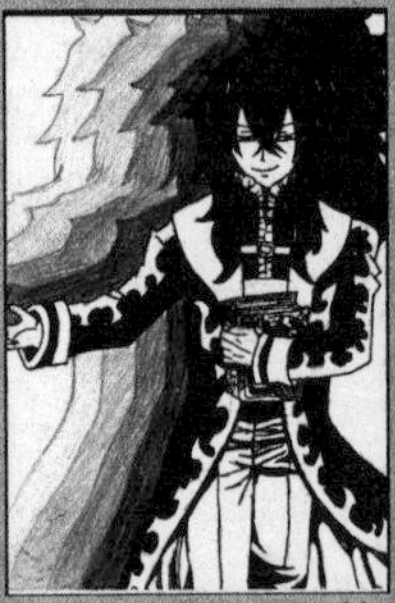

▲What is the Underworld King's power anyway...?!

a Prefecture, Haruka Iwagami

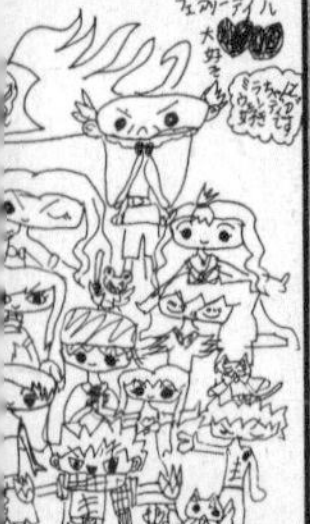

anks for drawing so
! They're all so cute!

Saitama Prefecture, Chiharu Iiyama

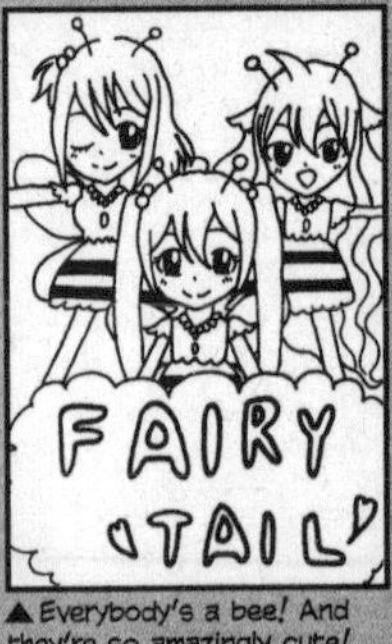
FAIRY TAIL

▲Everybody's a bee! And they're so amazingly cute!

Kagoshima Prefecture, Akari

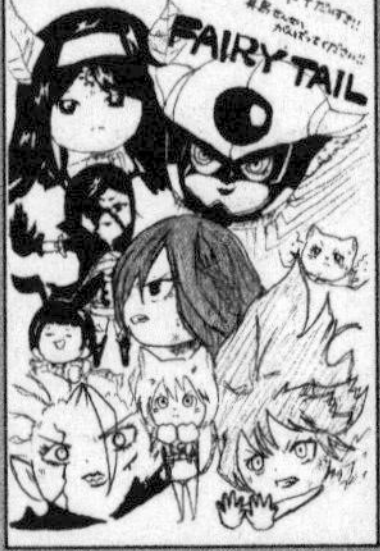
FAIRY TAIL

▲I think the composition of this one is really cute! Seilah and Kyôka are great!

Ishikawa Prefecture, Rabi

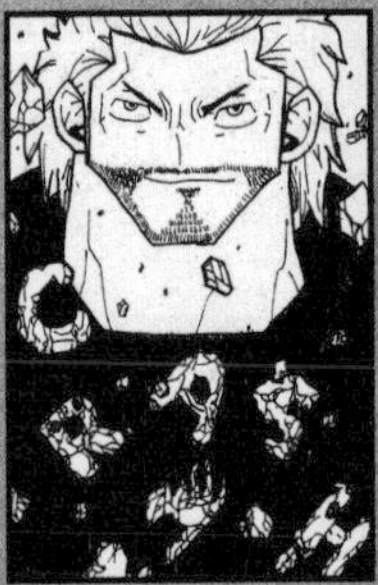

▲Gildarts! I wonder where he is right now?

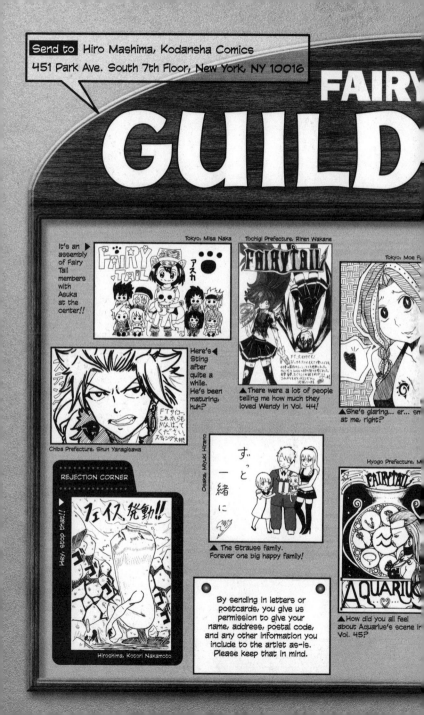

Send to Hiro Mashima, Kodansha Comics
451 Park Ave. South 7th Floor, New York, NY 10016

FAIRY [TAIL] GUILD

Tokyo, Misa Naka

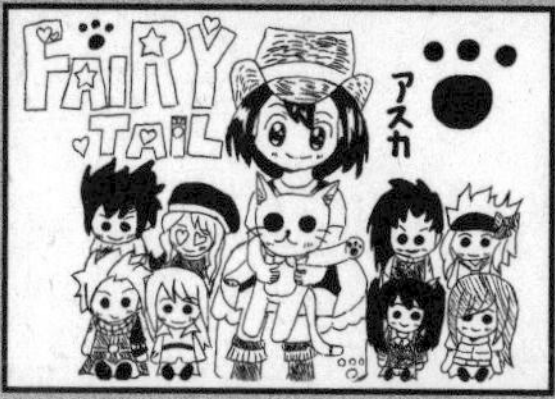
FAIRY TAIL
アスカ

It's an assembly of Fairy Tail members with Asuka at the center!!

Tochigi Prefecture, Riren Wakane

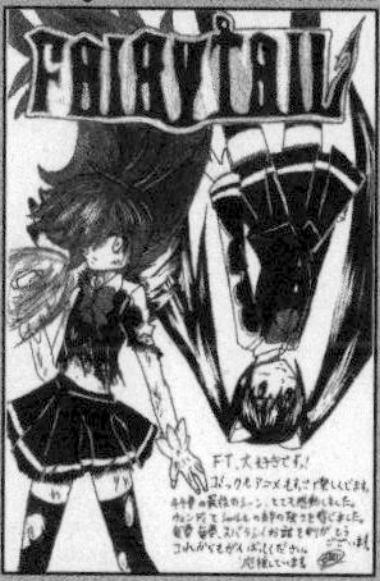
FAIRY TAIL

▲There were a lot of people telling me how much they loved Wendy in Vol. 44!

Tokyo, Moe F

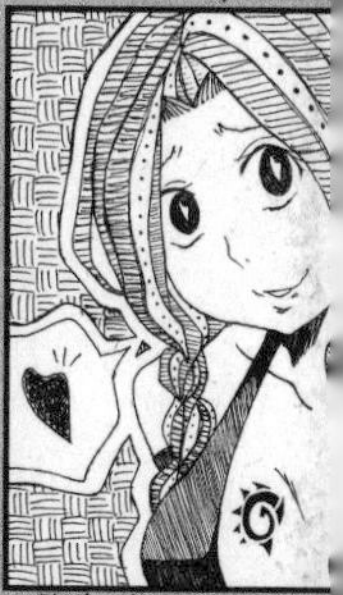

▲She's glaring... er... sm
at me, right?

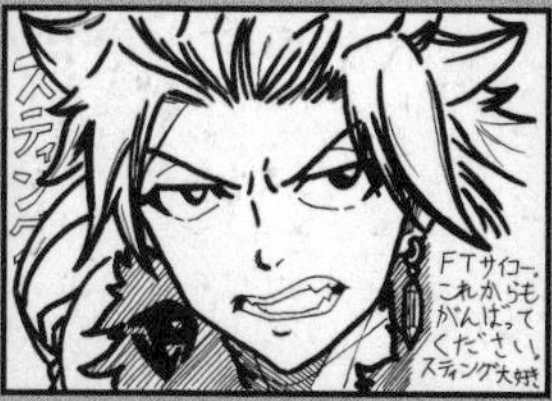
FTサイコー。
これからも
がんばって
ください。
スティング大好き

Here's Sting after quite a while. He's been maturing, huh?

Chiba Prefecture, Shun Yanagisawa

Osaka, Miyuki Hirano

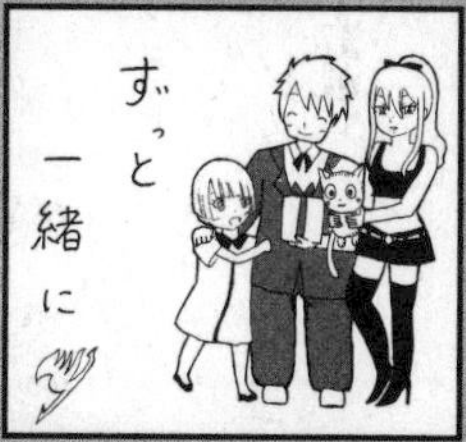
ずっと一緒に

▲ The Strauss family. Forever one big happy family!

REJECTION CORNER

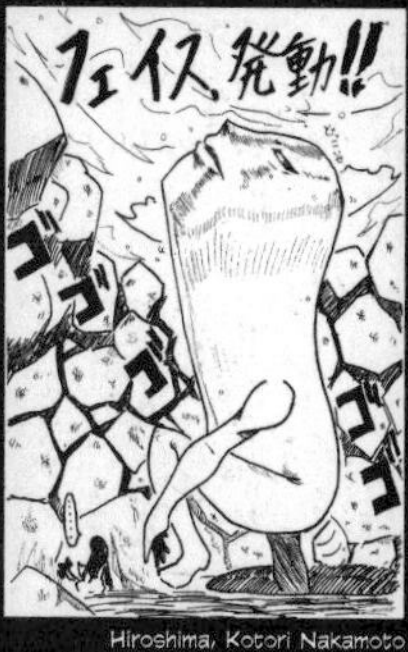
フェイス発動!!

Hey, stop that!!

Hiroshima, Kotori Nakamoto

By sending in letters or postcards, you give us permission to give your name, address, postal code, and any other information you include to the artist as-is. Please keep that in mind.

Hyogo Prefecture, M

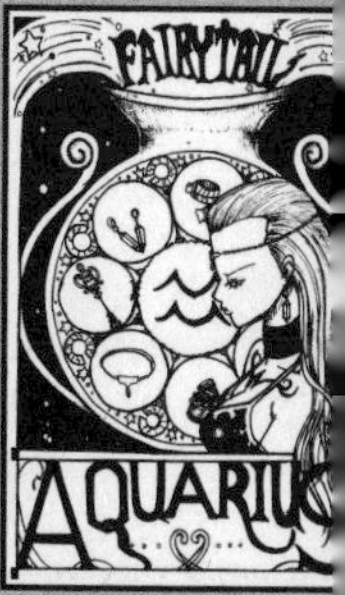
FAIRY TAIL

▲How did you all feel about Aquarius's scene i
Vol. 45?

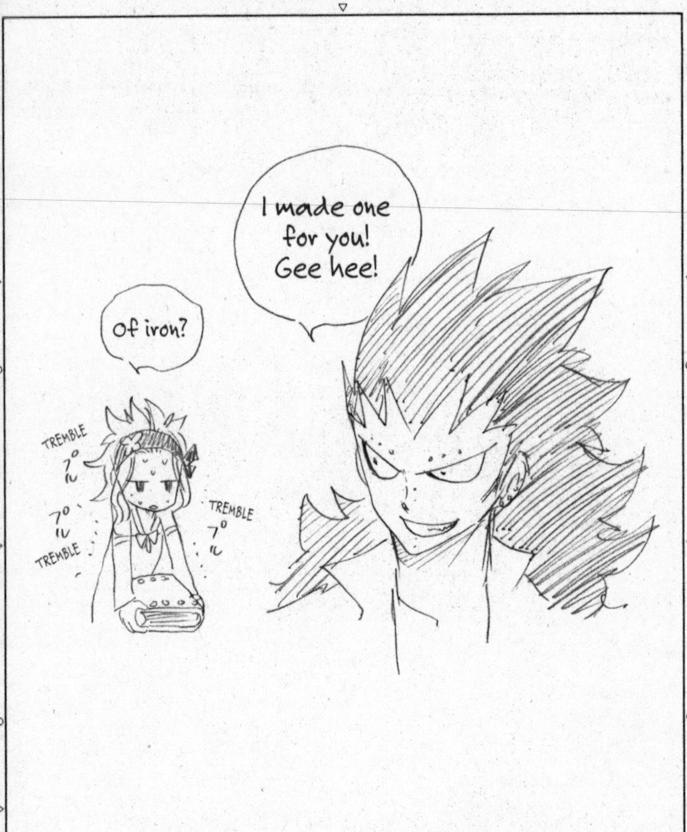
I made one for you! Gee hee!
Of iron?
TREMBLE
TREMBLE
TREMBLE

FAIRY TAIL
フェアリーテイル

47

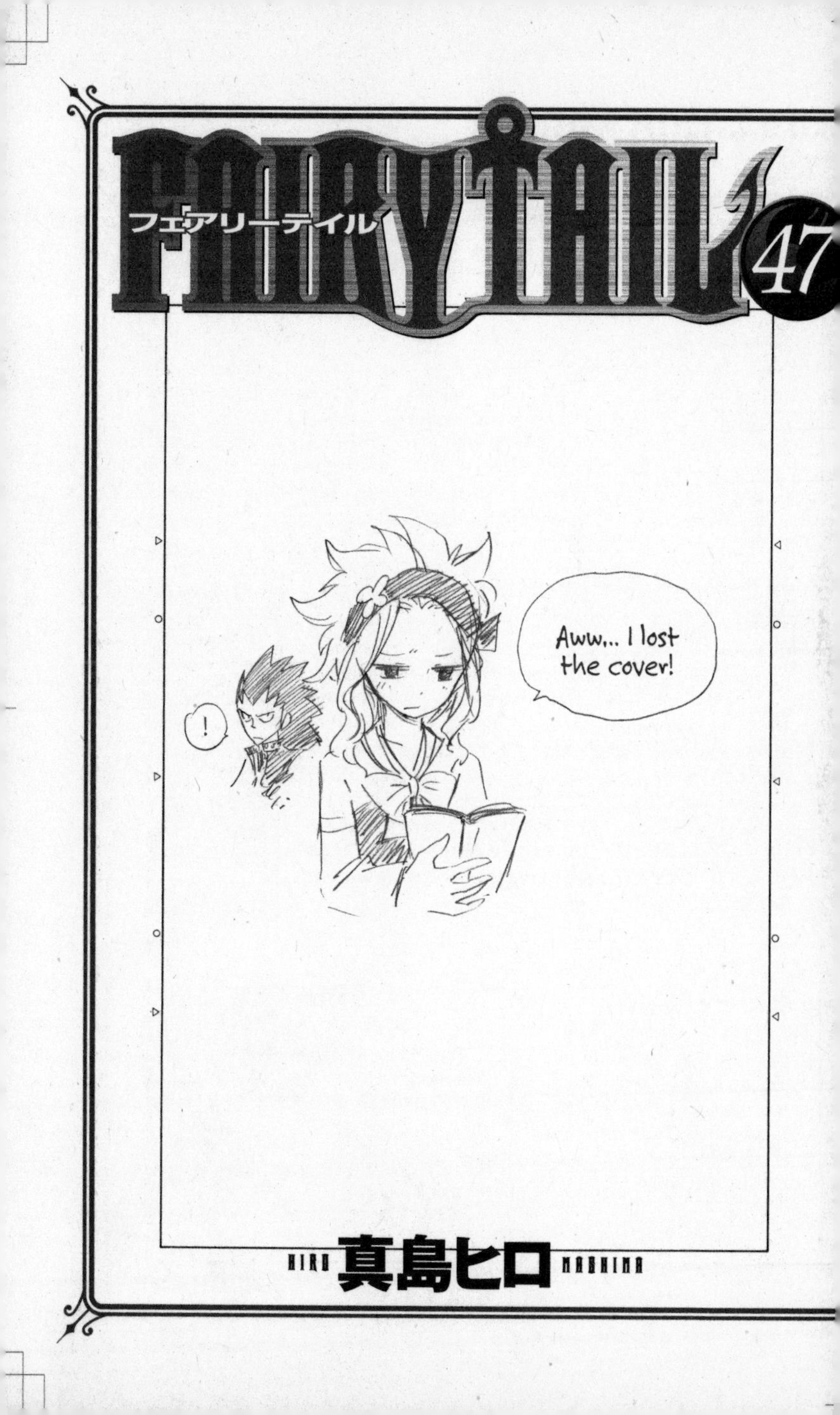
Aww... I lost the cover!
!

HIRO 真島ヒロ MASHIMA

ranslation Notes:

anese is a tricky language for most Westerners, and translation is often more than science. For your edification and reading pleasure, here are notes on some he places where we could have gone in a different direction with our transla- 1 of the work, or where a Japanese cultural reference is used.

ge 13, Etherious

ose of you who bought early printings or e-books of Volume 45, or followed the ry when as it is published weekly online, might have noticed that the spelling for erious used to be spelled Aetherious. The spelling with an "A" was a mistake on (the translator's) part. In a later chapter, it became obvious that Etherious is the re accurate spelling. We haven't come to that chapter yet in the graphic novels, don't want to spoil it for anyone, but the spelling was changed for a very good son. I offer my apologies for the previous misspellings.

ge 59, Steel

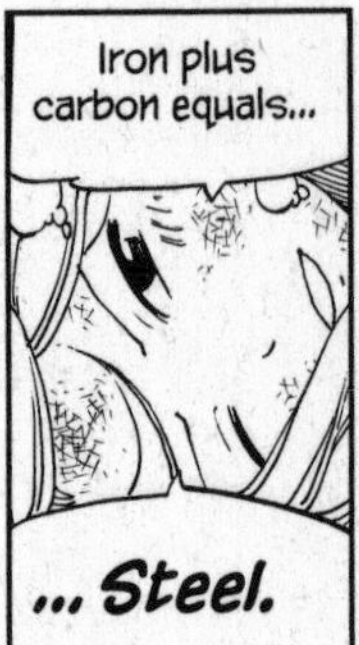
Iron plus carbon equals...
... Steel.

ating steel from iron isn't quite as easy as just adding some bon. In reality, steel needs to be made by removing impuri- s through a number of different processes (open hearth nace, the Bessemer process, or the basic oxygen furnace are ee popular methods) and creating a consistent concentra- n of carbon (0.5% - 1.5%). Still, considering that Gajeel's iron is gic iron (and dragon magic at that) then we can probably ume there are few-to-no impurities. And considering the ngs Gajeel can do with the iron in his body, it's easy to imag- that he can manage to create a consistent carbon content oughout his own body.

ge 80, Zeref-kyô

mentioned in the notes of Vol- e 26, there are a number of hon- fics that are known to modern panese, but are not in common ge. One of the more uncommon, re polite honorifics is *-kyô*, which ght be translated as "my lord."

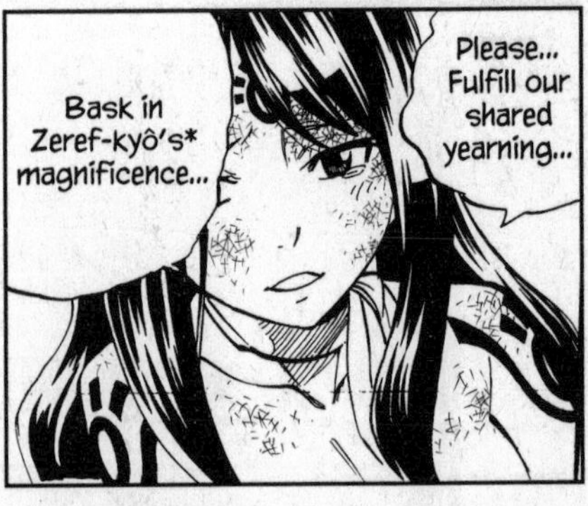
Please... Fulfill our shared yearning...
Bask in Zeref-kyô's* magnificence...

FROM HIRO MASHIMA

I am completely hooked on the social game Fairy Tail Brave Saga. The modeling of the characters is so cute, and it's all so well done! I'm pretty sure that there will be more and more characters added, so I hope you all will be able to give it a try!!

Fairy Tail Brave Saga
Official Home Page
https://www.taito.co.jp/fairytailbs

Original Jacket Design: Hisao Ogawa

Preview of Next Volume

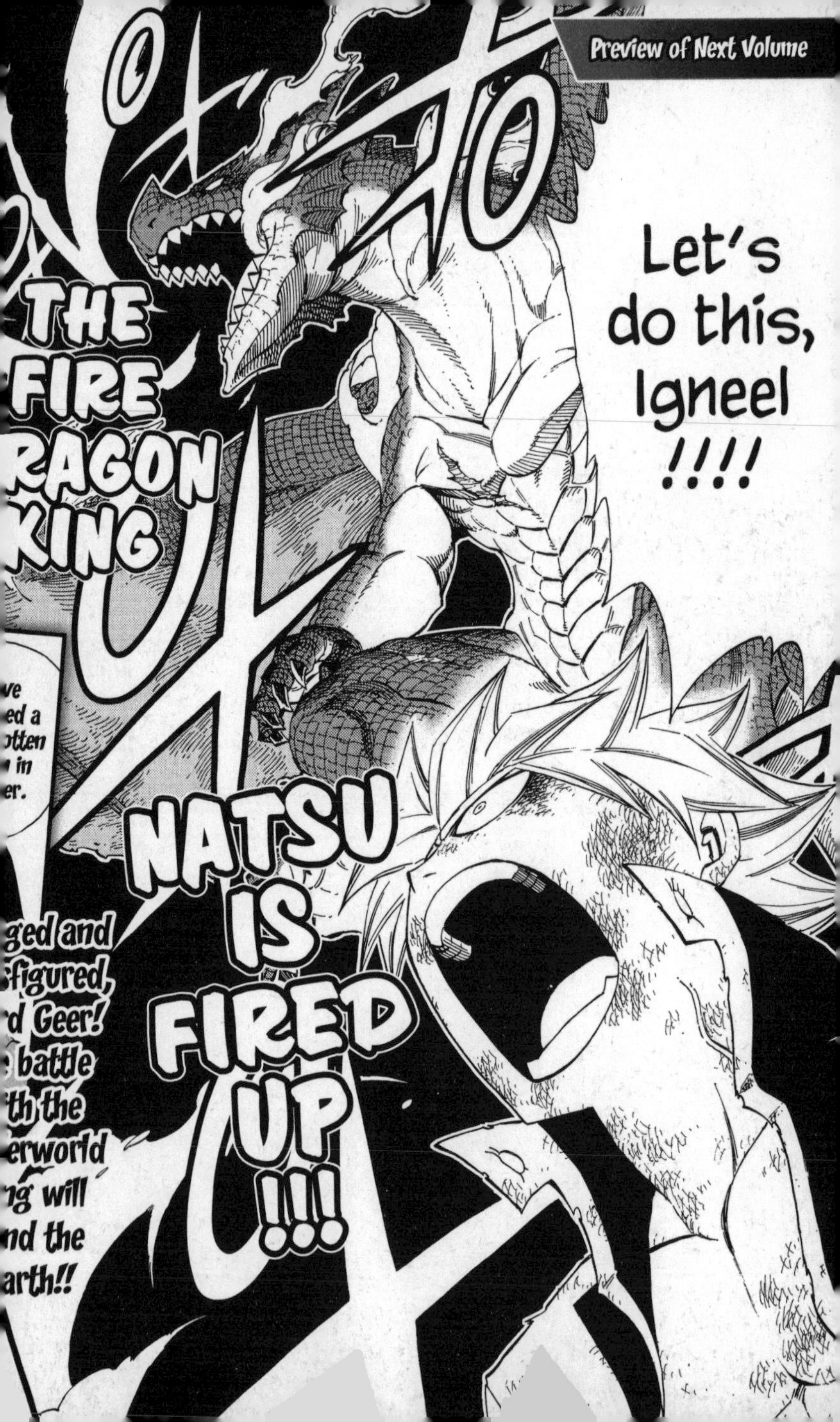
Let's do this, Igneel!!!!
THE FIRE RAGON KING
NATSU IS FIRED UP!!!
ve
ed a
otten
in
er.
ged and
sfigured,
d Geer!
battle
th the
erworld
ng will
nd the
arth!!

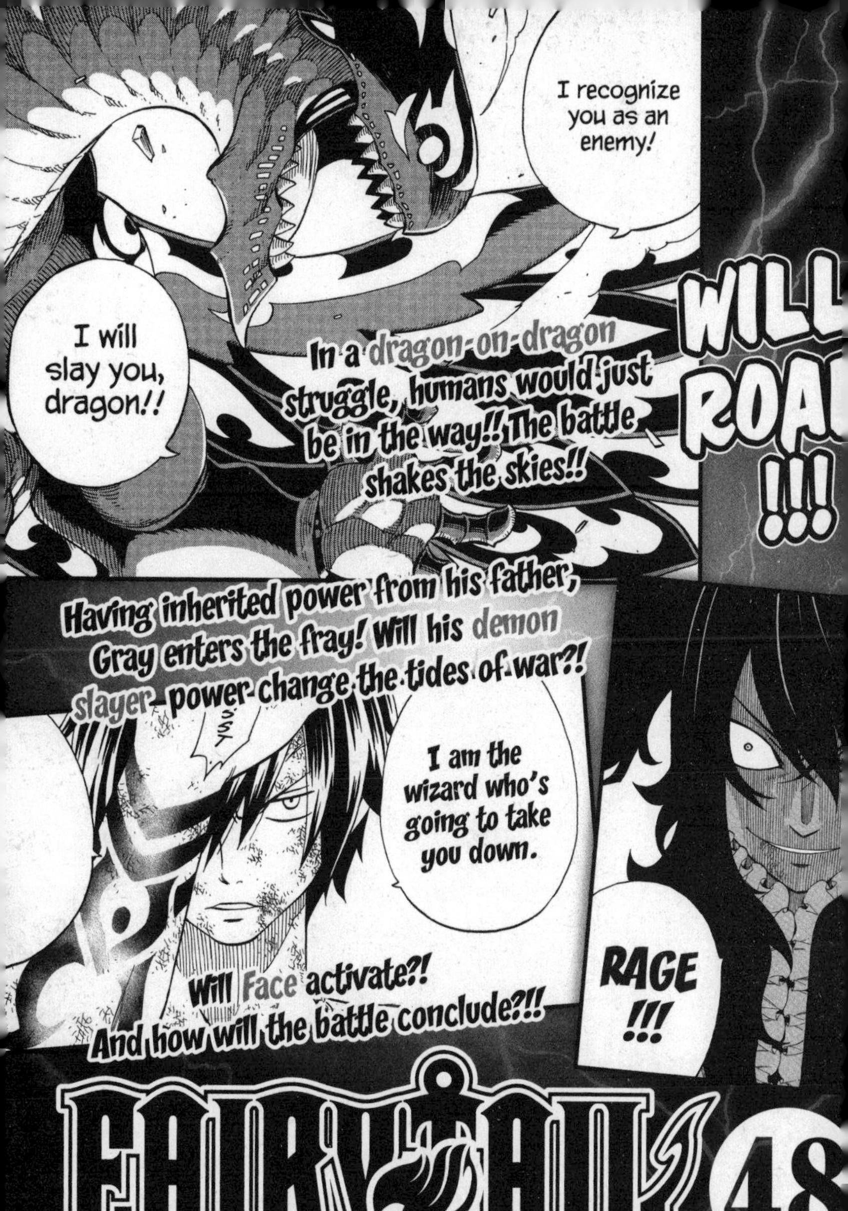
WILL ROA
!!!
I recognize you as an enemy!
I will slay you, dragon!!
In a dragon-on-dragon struggle, humans would just be in the way!! The battle shakes the skies!!
RAGE !!!
Having inherited power from his father, Gray enters the fray! Will his demon slayer power change the tides of war?!
I am the wizard who's going to take you down.
Will Face activate?! And how will the battle conclude?!!
FAIRY TAIL
48

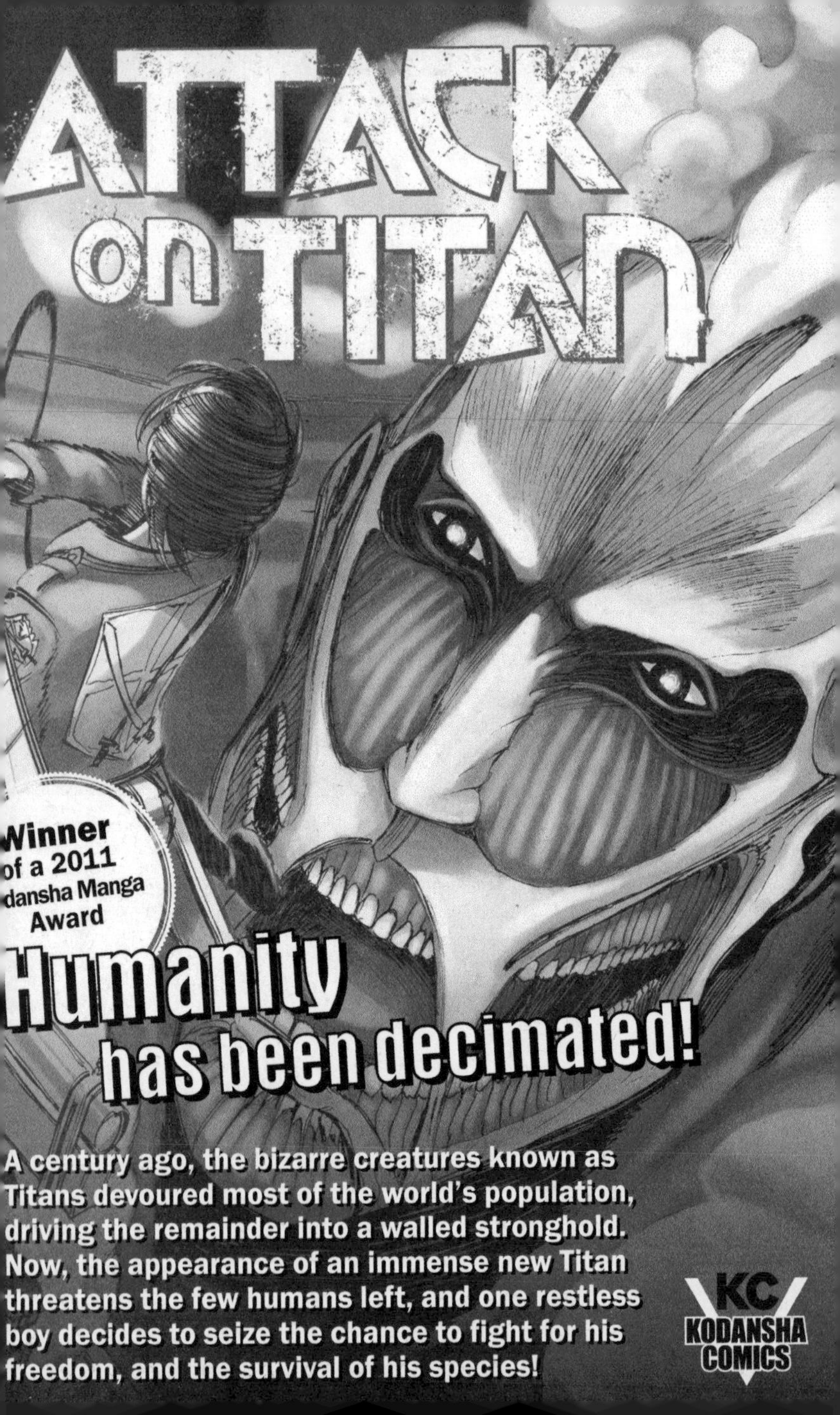
ATTACK on TITAN
Winner
of a 2011
dansha Manga
Award
Humanity
has been decimated!
A century ago, the bizarre creatures known as Titans devoured most of the world's population, driving the remainder into a walled stronghold. Now, the appearance of an immense new Titan threatens the few humans left, and one restless boy decides to seize the chance to fight for his freedom, and the survival of his species!
KC
KODANSHA COMICS

Say I Love You.

ei Tachibana has no friends — and says she doesn't need them!

t everything changes when she accidentally roundhouse kicks the most pular boy in school! However, Yamato Kurosawa isn't angry in the slightest— fact, he thinks his ordinary life could use an unusual girl like Mei. But winning ei's trust will be a tough task. How long will she refuse to say, "I love you"?

NO.6

A PERFECT LIFE
IN A PERFECT CITY

For Shion, an elite student in the technologically sophisticated city No. 6, life is carefully choreographed. One fateful day, he takes a misstep, sheltering a fugitive his age from a typhoon. Helping this boy throws Shion's life down a path to discovering the appalling secrets behind the "perfection" of No. 6.

KODANSHA
COMICS

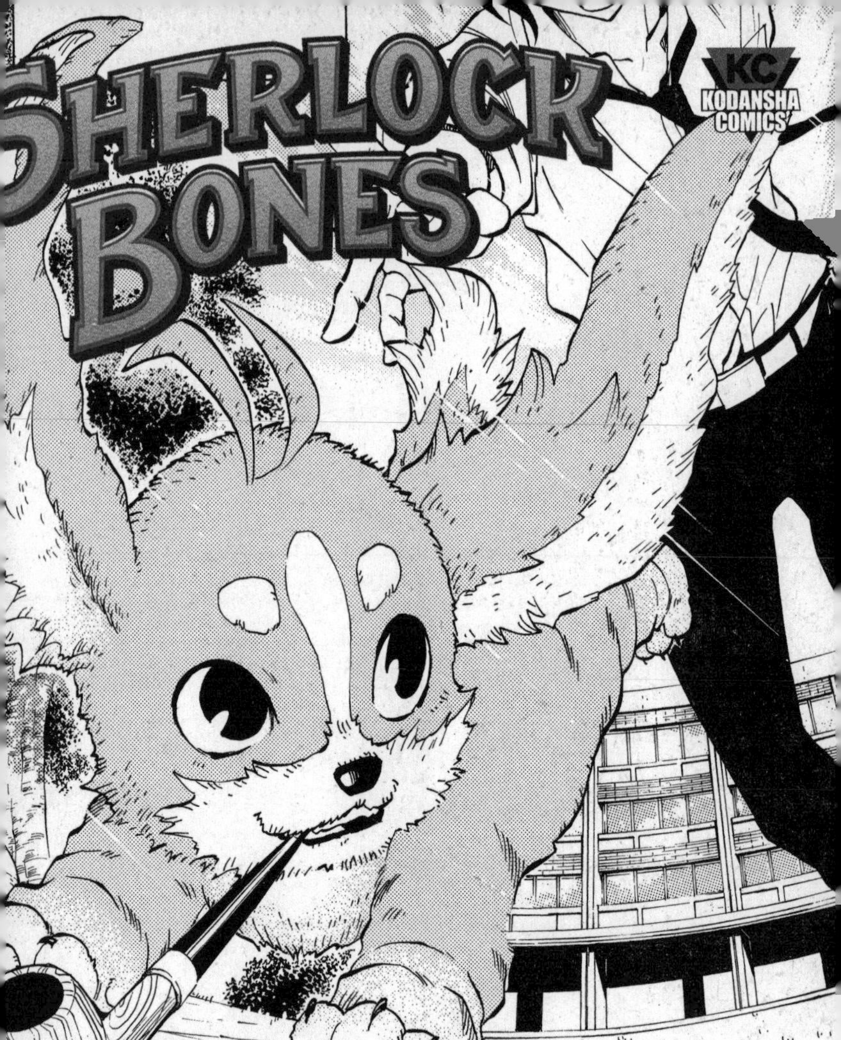
KC
KODANSHA COMICS

SHERLOCK BONES

DEDUCTIVE DOG DETECTIVE

When Takeru adopts a new pet, he's in for a surprise—the dog is none other than the reincarnation of Sherlock Holmes. With no one else able to communicate with Holmes, Takeru is roped into becoming Sherdog's assistant, John Watson. Using his sleuthing skills, Holmes uncovers clues to solve the trickiest crimes.

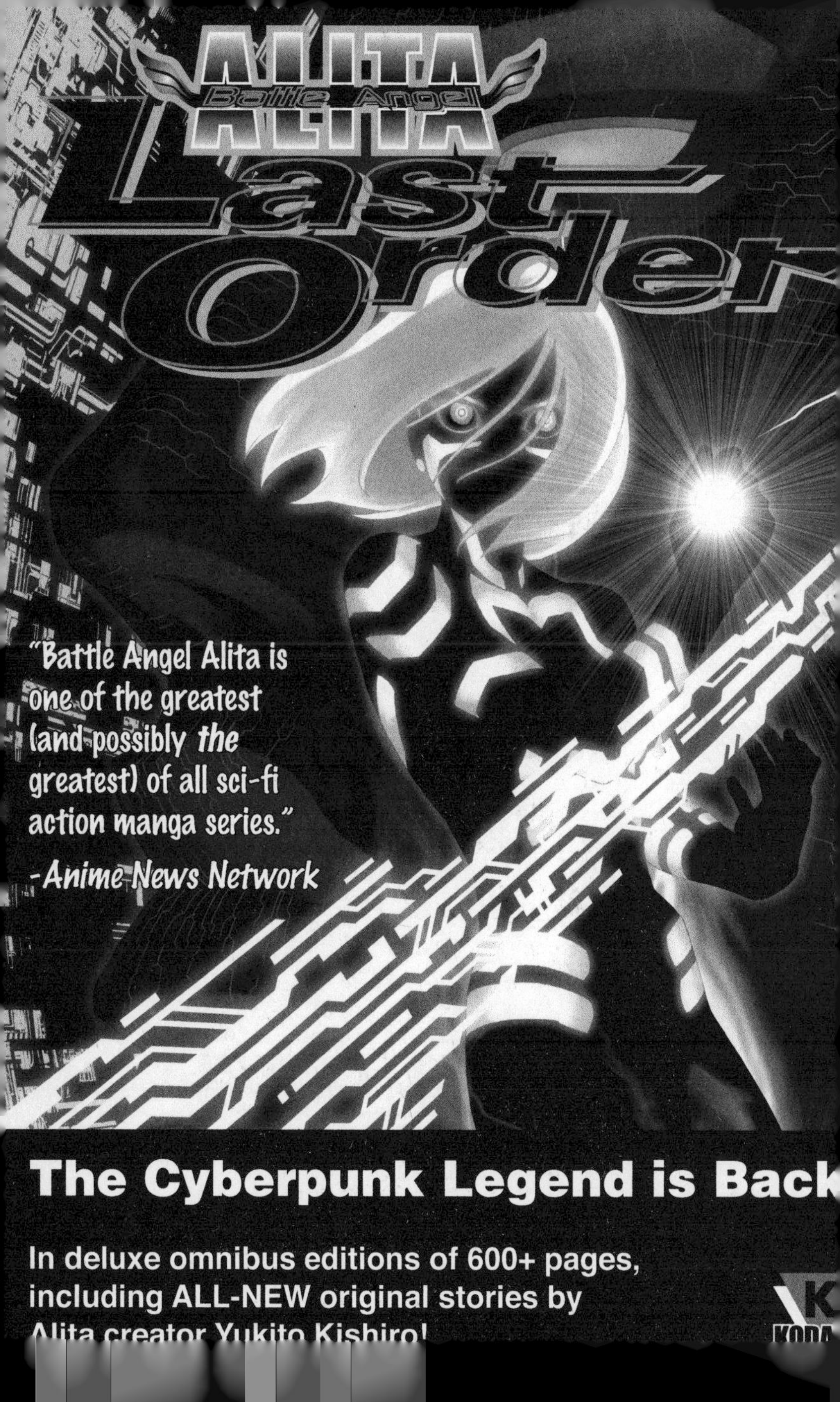
ALITA
Battle Angel
ALITA
Last Order
"Battle Angel Alita is one of the greatest (and possibly *the* greatest) of all sci-fi action manga series."
-Anime News Network

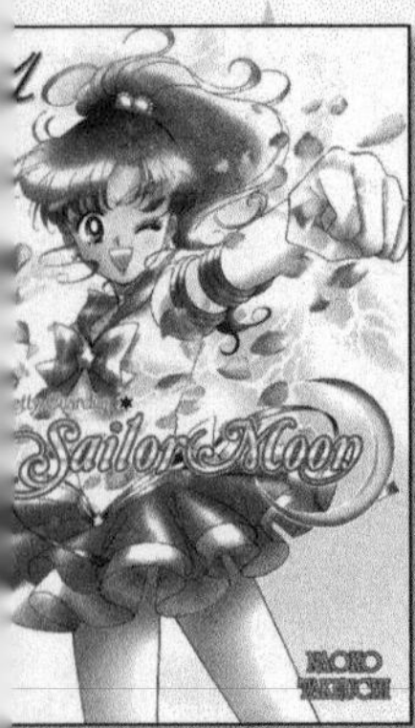
Sailor Moon
NAOKO TAKEUCHI
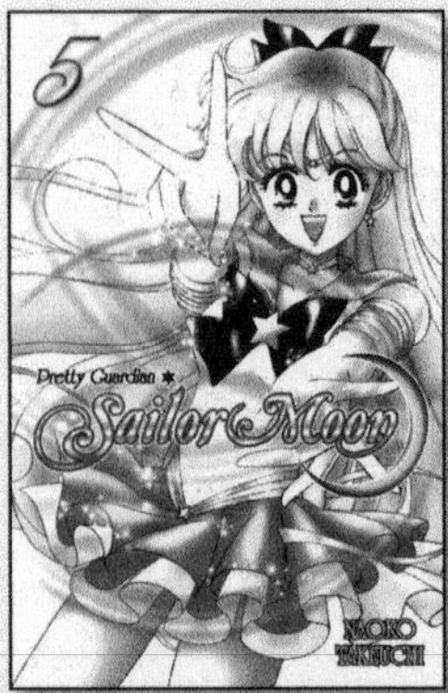
5
Pretty Guardian
Sailor Moon
NAOKO TAKEUCHI
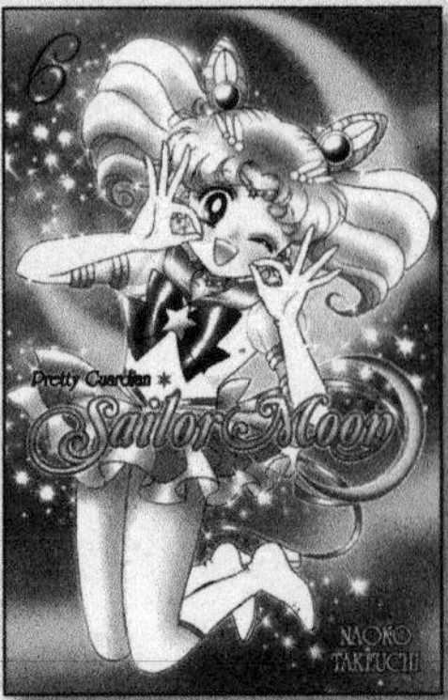
6
Pretty Guardian
Sailor Moon
NAOKO TAKEUCHI
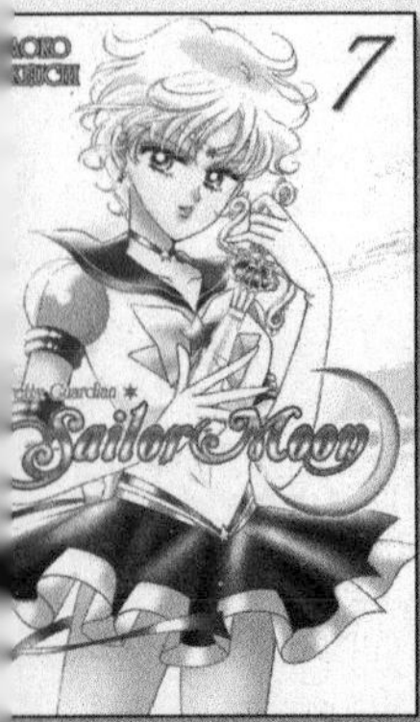
7
Sailor Moon
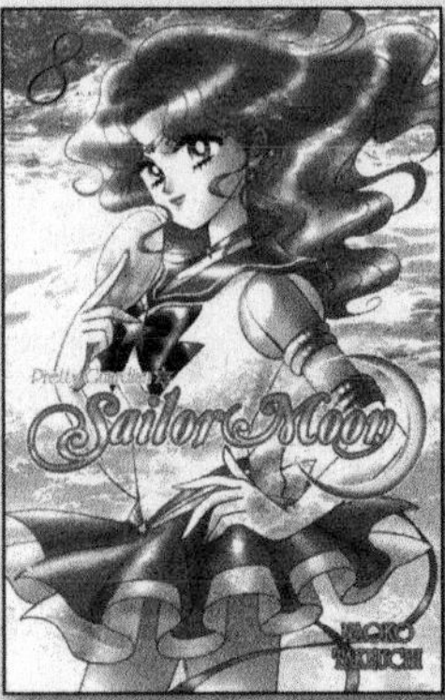
8
Sailor Moon
NAOKO TAKEUCHI
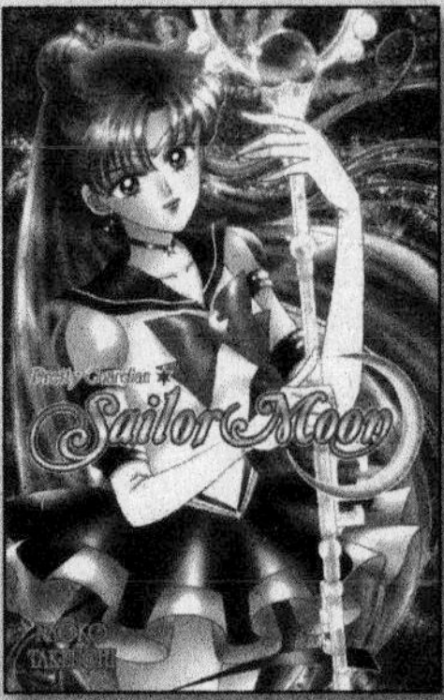
Sailor Moon
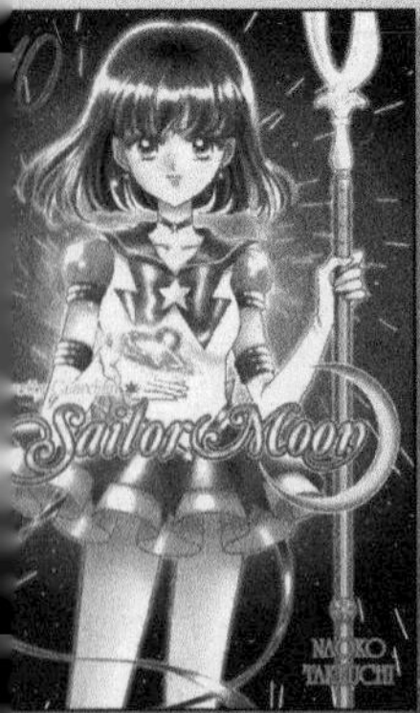
Sailor Moon
NAOKO TAKEUCHI
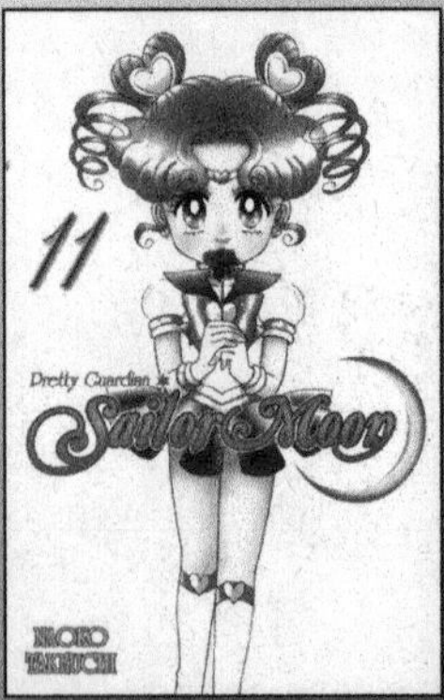
11
Pretty Guardian
Sailor Moon
NAOKO TAKEUCHI
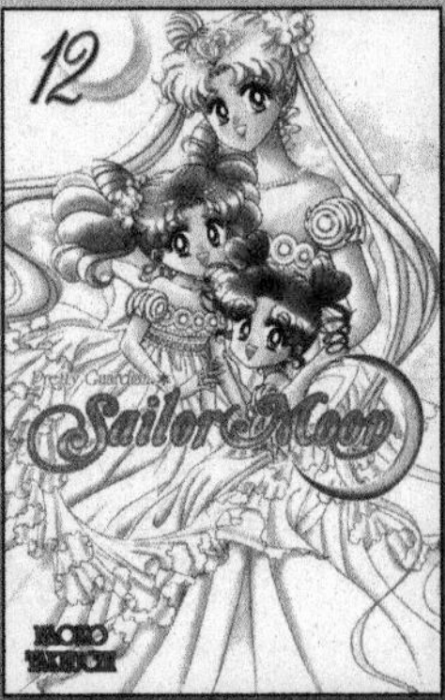
12
Sailor Moon
NAOKO TAKEUCHI

The Pretty Guardians are back!

★

Kodansha Comics is proud to present *Sailor Moon* with all new translations.

MARDOCK SCRAMBLE

マルドゥック・スクランブル

Created by
Tow Ubukata

Manga by
Yoshitoki Oima

'd rather be dead."

MARDOCK
マルドゥック・スクランブル
SCRAMBLE
1
created by
TOW UBUKATA
manga by
YOSHITOKI OIMA

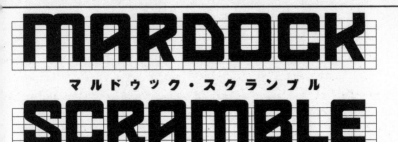

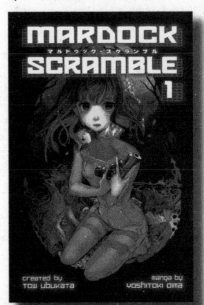

Rune Balot was a lost girl with
iothing to live for. A man
iamed Shell took her in and
:ared for her...until he tried
o murder her. Standing at
he precipice of death Rune is
aved by Dr. Easter, a private
nvestigator, who uses an
experimental procedure known
is "Mardock Scramble 09."
The procedure grants Balot
extraordinary abilities. Now,
Rune must decide whether to
ise her new powers to help Dr.
Easter bring Shell to justice, or if she even has the will to keep
iving a life that's been broken so badly.

Ages: 16+

KC KODANSHA COMICS

VISIT KODANSHACOMICS.COM TO:

- View release date calendars for upcoming volumes
- Find out the latest about upcoming Kodansha Comics series

Fairy Tail volume 47 is a work of fiction. Names, characters, places, and incider
are the products of the author's imagination or are used fictitiously. Any resemblance to actual events, locales, or persons, living or dead, is entirely coincidental.

A Kodansha Comics Trade Paperback Original.

Published in the United States by Kodansha Comics, an imprint of Kodansha USA Publishing, LLC, New York.

Publication rights for this English edition arranged through Kodansha Ltd., Tokyo.

First published in Japan in 2015 by Kodansha Ltd., Tokyo
ISBN 978-1-61262-798-4

Printed in the United States of America.

www.kodanshacomics.com

9 8 7 6 5 4 3 2 1

Translation: William Flanagan
Lettering: AndWorld Design
Editing: Ben Applegate
Kodansha Comics edition cover design by Phil Balsman

TOMARE!

止まれ

[STOP!]

You're going the wrong way!

Manga is a completely different type of reading experience.

To start at the *beginning,* go to the *end!*

t's right! Authentic manga is read the traditional Japanese way—
n right to left, exactly the *opposite* of how American books are
d. It's easy to follow: Just go to the other end of the book and read
h page—and each panel—from right side to left side, starting at
top right. Now you're experiencing manga as it was meant to be!